Current EC Legal Developments

Regulation of Food Products by the European Community

Current EC Legal Developments

Regulation of Food Products by the European Community

Charles Lister
Covington & Burling, London

Butterworths
London, Dublin, Edinburgh, Brussels
1992

United Kingdom	Butterworth & Co (Publishers) Ltd, 88 Kingsway, LONDON WC2B 6AB 4 Hill Street, EDINBURGH EH2 3JZ
Australia	Butterworths Pty Ltd, SYDNEY, MELBOURNE, BRISBANE, ADELAIDE, PERTH, CANBERRA and HOBART
Belgium	Butterworth & Co. (Publishers) Ltd. 48 Rue de Namur/Namurstraat
Canada	Butterworths, TORONTO and VANCOUVER
Ireland	Butterworth (Ireland) Ltd, DUBLIN
Malaysia	Malayan Law Journal Sdn Bhd, KUALA LUMPUR
New Zealand	Butterworths of New Zealand Ltd, WELLINGTON and AUCKLAND
Puerto Rico	Equity de Puerto Rico Inc, HATO REY
Singapore	Malayan Law Journal Pte Ltd, SINGAPORE
USA	Butterworths Legal Publishers, ST PAUL, Minnesota, SEATTLE, Washington, BOSTON, Massachusetts, ORFORD, New Hampshire, AUSTIN, Texas and D & S Publishers, CLEARWATER, Florida

ISBN   0 406 01305 5
Printed in Great Britain by Ashford Colour Press Ltd., Gosport, Hampshire

Consultant Editor
DAVID VAUGHAN, Q.C.

Editors
SANDRA DUTCZAK, LL.B.
JOE NIXON, B.A.

Editorial Assistant
MARIA D'SOUZA

Produced by Butterworths European Information Services

PUBLISHER'S NOTE

With the momentum of change within the Community gathering pace it is hard to keep abreast of developments and obtain expert opinion and analysis together with original texts of legislation or cases as and when such events occur.

The *Current EC Legal Developments Series* is designed to provide the lawyer, consultant, researcher etc. with commentary and source materials of relevant practical interest on fundamental changes in Community law.

Each title in the series has a similar format presenting the full text of proposed or enacted legislation or judicial decisions under review and provides analysis and comment written by leading practitioners in the subject area under consideration.

The views expressed by the author are personal and are not intended to be applied to particular situations.

Any queries as to the nature or content of the *Current EC Legal Developments Series* or in respect of this title in the *Series* should be directed to the Managing Editor, Butterworths European Information Services, 88 Kingsway, London WC2B 6AB (071 405 6900).

Butterworth & Co (Publishers) Ltd.

PREFACE

What follows is an account of the content and progress of the European Community's rules for food products and related matters as of August 1992. Important matters, however, have been updated so as to state the law as of October 1992. It is intended to be comprehensive, although some collateral issues are described only by illustration. It includes both existing Community legislation and any formal or informal proposals for legislation which were available at the time of writing. In the spirit of harmonisation, it draws frequent comparisons with rules in the United States, Switzerland, Canada and other nations, as well as selected rules in the Member States. There are also extensive references to the literature of food science and nutrition. The law means little without some appreciation of the underlying technical and scientific problems.

The volume of Community legislation is too large for complete reproduction in appendices. The principal framework measures have, however, been listed in the appendix. In the text itself, cross-references are generally to chapters and sections.

The following terms and abbreviations are defined in the text, but it may be convenient to have a separate summary.

ACNFP
Britain's Advisory Committee on Novel Foods and Processes.

Advisory Committee
A committee of representatives of industry, unions and consumers which advises the European Commission regarding food matters.

COT
One of Britain's scientific advisory committees, more fully named the Committee on the Toxicity of Chemicals in Food, Consumer Products and the Environment.

Codex
The Codex Alimentarius Commission, sponsored by the World Health Organisation and the United Nations Food and Agricultural Organisation, which prepares recommended international rules and standards.

Committee Procedure
A mechanism increasingly used by the Community since 1985 for the adoption of subordinate legislation, with the Standing Committee for Foodstuffs or other specialised committees of national regulators performing the role of the Council.

DG III

The Directorate-General of the European Commission responsible for internal market matters, including foodstuffs.

DG VI

The Directorate-General of the European Commission responsible for agriculture.

ESC or ECOSOC

The Community's Economic and Social Committee, consisting of representatives of business, unions, the professions, and other groups.

FAC

Britain's Food Advisory Committee.

FDA

The United States Food and Drug Administration, generally responsible for food regulation apart from advertising, meat and poultry, and alcoholic beverages.

JECFA

An international committee of scientific experts established jointly by the World Health Organisation and the United Nations Food and Agriculture Organisation to study the safety of food additives.

Richmond Committee

An advisory committee established in Britain to evaluate issues relating to the microbiological safety of foods. It is known officially as the Committee on the Microbiological Safety of Foods.

SCF

The Community's Scientific Committee for Food, consisting of independent toxicologists and other scientists, and responsible for the evaluation of scientific aspects of food safety.

Standing Committee

The Community's Standing Committee for Foodstuffs, consisting of national representatives, which sometimes acts as a surrogate for the Council in the resolution of food policy matters. There are similar committees responsible for spirit drinks, plant health products, and other matters.

USITC

The United States International Trade Commission, a regulatory agency which has issued a series of reports evaluating the terms and implications of the Community's internal market programme.

White Papers
Re-appraisals of the Community's internal market programme issued by the Commission in 1985, which provided a regulatory agenda through 1992. One paper related to the internal market generally, and another specifically to foodstuffs.

Illustrative references have been made to the national rules of several Member States. These are intended simply as signposts, and not as full descriptions of national requirements. Aside from Britain, many of the references are to convenient collections of national rules. To avoid lengthy references, the following abbreviations have been used.

France	Lamy-Dehove, *Réglementation des Produits, Qualité, Répression des Fraudes* (1986 with supplements) — "Lamy-Dehove".
Italy	L. & E. Rizzatti, *Tutela Igenico-Sanitario degli Alimente Bevande e dei Consumatore* (10th ed 1990) — "Alimenti e Bevande".
Netherlands	Wet op de Voedingsraad, vol. 99 parts 1, 2, Nederlandse Staatswetten (ed. Schuurman & Jordens) (1989) — "Voedingsraad".
Spain	Codigo Alimentario (6th ed 1991) — "Codigo Alimentario".

CONTENTS

CHAPTER 1 : INTRODUCTION

For thirty years and with growing urgency, the European Economic Community has sought to harmonise the regulation of food products by its Member States. Harmonisation is one of several devices contemplated by the Treaty of Rome to promote economic development and encourage trade[1]. Its purpose is to bring national laws into sufficient conformity to eliminate technical barriers to the free circulation of services and goods, including foodstuffs, throughout the Community. Although food regulation was among the Community's earliest priorities for harmonisation, and its first food measure was adopted as long ago as 1962, most of its progress has been achieved since 1985[2]. Even now, there are significant omissions from its food measures. Some areas are not yet harmonised, and others are subject only to superficial requirements. Much has been achieved, but much more must be done before full harmonisation can be said to exist.

The Community's relatively slow pace is hardly surprising. It is simultaneously harmonising well-settled national rules regarding all the principal areas of regulatory policy, and some delays are inevitable[3]. Food policy alone presents formidable difficulties. The Community's rules for foodstuffs must encompass an extraordinary range of products and processes. Thousands of new products enter the marketplace annually[4]. Account must be taken of both traditional products, often produced locally using customary methods, and fabricated products, often produced by multinational firms using modern technologies. The Community's rules must give deference to diverse

---

1. Article 2 of the Treaty of Rome ("by ... progressively approximating the economic activities of Member States to promote throughout the Community a harmonious development of economic activities ...."). Article G of the Maastricht Treaty on European Union would rewrite Article 2, but continue to demand a "harmonious and balanced development of economic activities". Article 3 would also be rewritten, but would still require an approximation of national laws "to the extent required for the functioning of the common market".
2. For the priorities, see Dashwood, "Hastening Slowly : The Community's Path Toward Harmonization", in H. Wallace, W. Wallace and C. Webb, eds., *Policy-making in the European Community* pp177, 184 (2nd ed. 1983). The 1962 directive for food colorants was the Community's first harmonisation directive. Gray, "Food law and the Internal Market : Taking Stock", *Food Policy* p111 (April 1990).
3. CEPS, *The Annual Review of European Community Affairs 1990* pp45-46 (1991).
4. In the United States, for example, some 12,000 new products are introduced annually, and the typical supermarket offers some 20,000 products; National Academy of Sciences, Committee on Nutritional Components of Food Labeling, *Nutrition Labeling : Issues and Directions for the 1990s* pp7, 89 (1990). See also J. Burns, J. McInerney & A. Swinbank, eds., *The Food Industry, Economics and Policies* (1983); Cockbill, "Recent Developments in British Food Law", 1/91 Eur. Food L. Rev. 61 (1991).

culinary traditions and disparate regulatory approaches[1]. Its rules must accommodate changing tastes and technologies, and yet promote healthier dietary habits[2]. They must facilitate the free circulation of foodstuffs, and yet ensure their wholesomeness and quality. They must prevent any firm from obtaining undue competitive advantages[3]. They must be impartial with respect to nations, products and methods of production, and yet promote the development of the Community's poorer regions[4]. They must be at once regulatory, protective, and promotional. With these competing obligations, delays in the Community's harmonisation programme are unavoidable. Indeed, some have argued that detailed harmonisation is impractical[5].

The difficulties are magnified by the economic consequences of harmonisation. Foodstuffs are a major industrial sector in the Community, and even minor changes in national laws can cause substantial economic dislocations. The European food market now involves $600 billion in annual sales[6]. Food production provides 17 per cent of the Community's manufacturing turnover and 11 per cent of its manufacturing jobs[7]. In addition, the Community is a vigorous competitor in world markets for foodstuffs. It is a larger overall exporter of food products than the United States, and six of the world's eight leading food exporters are among its Member States[8]. In France, for example, food and drink products are the principal export sector[9]. The Community is also an important importer of foods. It received $300 million in processed foods from the United States alone in 1989, and another $870 million in soft drinks, confectionery and bakery goods[10]. Many nations, including some of the world's poorest states, rely upon the Community as a market for their agricultural commodities and foodstuffs. The economic stakes of harmonisation are high, and each year grow higher.

---

1.   For the diversity of regulatory approaches, see Hutt & Hutt, "A History of Government Regulation of Adulteration and Misbranding of Food", 39 Food DCLJ 2 (1984); A. Swinburn & J. Burns, eds., *The EEC and the Food Industries* (1984); J. Drummond & A. Wilbraham, *The Englishman's Food* (rev. ed. 1957); J. Burnett, *Plenty and Want* (3rd ed. 1989).
2.   For the need for dietary change, see, eg Merrill, "Food Labels : Couriers of Public Health", 1 World Food Reg. Rev. 18 (Aug. 1991); O. Kilgour, *Mastering Nutrition* pp281-295 (1986); Proceedings of the Tenth International Congress of Dietetics, *Dietetics in the '90s* (1989).
3.   For the Community's basic competition policies, see Articles 85 to 90 of the Treaty of Rome.
4.   For regional development, see Article 130a of the Treaty of Rome, added by Article 23 of the Single European Act. For an example of the difficulties, see Martin & Stehmann, "Product Market Integration versus Regional Cohesion in the Community", 16 ELR 216 (1991) .
5.   Food Standards Committee, *Second Report on Food Labelling* para 21 (1980); Gray, "Whither Food Regulation?", 1 World Food Reg. Rev. p33 (June 1991).
6.   *The Financial Times* (10 May 1991).
7.   Waites, et al., "Foodborne Illness : An Overview", in The Lancet, ed., *Foodborne Illness* p1 (1991).
8.   A. Daltrop, *Politics and the European Community* 174 (2nd ed. 1986); Dupuy, "La transformation des produits agricoles : 1789-1989", in Académie d'Agriculture de France, *Deux siècles de progrés pour l'agriculture et l'alimentation, 1789-1989* p225 (1990); Deboyser, "Le marché unique des produits alimentaires", 1-1991 Revue de marché unique européen p63 (1991).
9.   1 World Food Reg. Rev. 16-17 (Aug. 1991).
10.   United States International Trade Commission, *The Effects of Greater Economic Integration Within the European Community on the United States, Second Report* pp4-25, 4-29 (1990).

The difficulties of harmonisation are increased by changing public attitudes. The issues of food regulation have become controversial as well as complex. There are widespread public concerns about the safety of many foodstuffs, and those concerns are partly validated by rising incidences of foodborne diseases[1]. Technology has added to the public's fears. Additives, irradiation, biotechnology, pesticides and animal growth hormones have all provoked public debate. Health scares and chemophobia are commonplace. Some consumers and legislators reject pesticides and additives in favour of "ecological" farming and "natural" foods[2]. Others prefer the convenience or diversity of fabricated foods. Still others find health advantages in foods which technology has made lower in fats or sugars. Some consumers judge a food's healthfulness by its method of production, and others by its composition. Many value healthfulness less highly than those habits known collectively as "taste"[3].

Consumer preferences and habits are changing rapidly, and the changes are not uniform across the Community. Snack foods and irregular meal times are increasing everywhere, but frozen and many processed foods are still relatively uncommon in some Member States[4]. As in many other areas, the magnitude of change grows roughly from south to north. Assessments of the Community's rules are equally diverse. Some boast that the Community has become a "pioneer" in food regulation[5]. Others argue that the Community's rules emphasise free circulation at the expense of compositional standards, and fear a downward spiral in product quality[6]. Still others complain that the Community's rules do not adequately ensure product safety[7]. Food regulation has become a battlefield on which environmental, dietary and health issues must all be resolved.

The results of the Community's efforts are predictably mixed. Substantial progress toward harmonisation has been made, particularly in the past five years, and the changes have accelerated as 1992 has approached. Europe's food markets are more open

---

1.　See, e.g., B. Hobbs & D. Roberts, *Food Poisoning and Food Hygiene* p9 (5th ed. 1987); Miller, "The Saga of Chicken Little and Rambo", 51 J. Association of Food & Drug Officials p196 (1987); Q. Seddon, *Spoiled for Choice* pp45-48 (1991). See also below at Chapter 8, para 8.6.1.

2.　Report of the Committee of the European Parliament on Agriculture, Fisheries and Rural Development, Doc. No. A3-0311/90 at p35 (19 Nov 1990); *Report of the Committee on the Microbiological Safety of Food, Part I* (1990) at para 7.11.

3.　Farrer, "Nutritional Implications", in R. Gordon Booth, ed., *Snack Food* pp327, 343-344 (1990).

4.　Meffert, "Economic Developments Pertinent to Chilled Foods", in T. Gormley, ed., *Chilled Foods : The State of the Art* pp337, 338-341 (1990).

5.　Bangemann, "Geleitwort", 1/91 Eur. Food L. Rev. 1, 4 (1991).

6.　von Heydebrand, "Free Movement of Foodstuffs, Consumer Protection and Food Standards in the European Community : Has the Court of Justice Got It Wrong?" 16 ELR 391 (1991); Brouwer, "Free Movement of Foodstuffs and Quality Requirements : Has the Commission Got It Wrong?", 25 (1988) CMLRev 237.

7.　Resolution of the European Parliament on Food Hygiene, OJ C183 15.7.91 p52.

and more nearly integrated than ever before[1]. Most issues of food regulation are controlled by a framework of Community rules, and some issues are the subject of detailed Community requirements. For the first time, the most important determinant of national regulatory policies is the European Community[2]. Moreover, the influence of the Community's rules now reaches well beyond its present borders. It has become a major factor in regulating the world's marketplaces for foodstuffs.

Nonetheless, the Community is still far from an integrated food marketplace. Some issues are not yet governed by Community rules, and some Community rules are only general and superficial. Others are loosely drafted[3]. The transposition of Community measures into national law remains a significant problem[4]. Enforcement is still questionable and uneven. In addition, there is reason for concern about the rigidity and direction of some of the Community's policies. Some policies seem better calculated to erect than to dismantle trade barriers. Moreover, the Community has not yet identified regulatory values or goals to guide its policymaking for food after 1992. Its rulemaking is improvisational, and harmonisation seems the outer limit of its planning. Finally, the Community's procedures for regulatory decisionmaking warrant reconsideration. They promote inconsistency and make little allowance for public participation or scrutiny. Few policymaking systems are as complex, or as susceptible to impasse.

These facts should trouble everyone anxious for the Community's success. Food regulation represents a major test of both harmonisation and the Community's wider commitment to economic integration. Few regulatory areas are so important for the creation of a single European marketplace, and none exemplifies more clearly the substantial obstacles which remain. Food regulation offers an important model by

---

1.   Intra-Community trade increased more rapidly than extra-Community trade in the period from 1958 to 1987, but there was still relatively little integration. Integration has progressed more quickly in some areas of the Community than others, and particularly in northern Europe. See, e.g., A. M. Williams, *The European Community* pp57-59 (1991).

2.   S. Fallows, *Food Legislative System of the UK* p84 (1988). Some commentators see a "nearly total" transfer of sovereignty in this area to the Community. Gorny, "European Food Quality - The Prospective Importance of ISO 9.000/EN 29.000", 1/92 Eur. Food L. Rev. 13 (1992). Others believe that "subsidiarity" - the idea of decision-making at the local or national level wherever possible - is better observed in food regulation than other areas of Community law.

3.   Roberts, "European Enforcement", 1/92 Eur. Food L. Rev. 1 (1992).

4.   Most Community rules are in the form of directives to the Member States to alter their national rules, and the process of transposition has often proved slow; *Eighth Annual Report to the European Parliament on Commission Monitoring of the Application of Community Law - 1990*, OJ C338 31.12.91 p1 at p15 ("highly unsatisfactory" situation, giving "the greatest cause for concern"); *Ninth Annual Report on Commission Monitoring of the Application of Community Law - 1991*, COM(92) 136 final (12 May 1992) at p13 ("the industry with the most serious delays in transposal"). Similarly, the European Parliament has complained that transposition has occurred "only with considerable delays, major difficulties and in an incomplete form". Resolution on the completion of the internal market and the social dimension, OJ C267 14.10.91 p149 at the 2nd recital of the preamble.

which the Community's broader achievements may be measured and its difficulties identified. If the Community cannot successfully harmonise its rules for bread and cheese, it is unlikely to harmonise its rules regarding politics and politicians.

CHAPTER 2 : THE FRAMEWORK OF THE COMMUNITY'S FOOD REGULATORY POLICIES

2.1 The institutions of Community food policy

Any examination of the Community's regulatory policies must begin with the Treaty of Rome, which created and still governs the European Economic Community. The Treaty establishes a framework of goals and obligations which together make some harmonisation of national laws essential[1]. The Treaty contemplates the creation of a single internal marketplace, unhampered by discriminatory tariff or technical barriers, within which goods from all Member States may circulate freely[2]. It also demands common policies regarding competitive, social and economic issues[3]. In particular, it requires a unified approach to organising the production and marketing of agricultural products[4]. In combination, these goals demand some harmonisation of national laws, including laws for the regulation of foodstuffs. Without harmonisation, the Community cannot eliminate trade barriers, encourage agricultural stability, or ensure the unhindered circulation of goods[5]. The form and degree of harmonisation are not, however, prescribed by the Treaty. The Community is free, within broad substantive and procedural limits, to adopt any regulatory strategy which may achieve the Treaty's overall goals[6].

---

1. Articles 2, 130a, 130b of the Treaty of Rome.
2. Articles 30 to 36 of the Treaty of Rome. For the Commission's survey of the situation, see Commission Communication on the Free Movement of Foodstuffs within the Community, OJ C271 24.10.89 p3. See also P. Oliver, *Free Movement of Goods in the EEC* (2nd ed. 1988).
3. Part Three of the Treaty ("Policy of the Community").
4. Title II of Part Two of the Treaty ("Foundations of the Community"). It is significant that, unlike the articles relating to competition and other matters, the provisions relating to agriculture are found among those establishing the Community's "foundations".
5. Comparable issues may arise, for example, in the United States from the separate federal and state regulatory systems for food. For industry's views, see, e.g., McKinney, "The Impact of Federalism on Operating a Business", 44 Food D.C.L.J. 119 (1989); Nyberg, "The Need for Uniformity in Food Labelling", 40 Food D.C.L.J. 229 (1985). For the view of a state regulator, see Kirschbaum, "Role of State Government in the Regulation of Food and Drugs", 38 Food D.C.L.J. 199 (1983). For that of a "consumer", see Silverglade, "Preemption - The Consumer Viewpoint", 45 Food D.C.L.J. 143 (1990). The Community is arguably better positioned to solve such problems than the United States, where the principal answer has been federal preemption. The latter may be described as an effort to achieve harmonisation chiefly by intermittent judicial declarations. See Mitchell, "State Regulation and Federal Preemption of Food Labelling", 45 Food D.C.L.J. 123 (1990). One commentator has argued that US rules allow more discretion to its states than the Community does to its Member States; von Heydebrand, "Free Movement of Foodstuffs, Consumer Protection and Food Standards in the European Community : Has the Court of Justice Got It Wrong?", 16 ELR 391 (1991).
6. Within the framework of the Treaty of Rome, the Community's institutions are given broad discretion by the European Court to address complex economic issues. Judicial review is confined to a search for "manifest error or misuses of power" and to a determination as to whether an authority has "manifestly exceeded" its discretion; Case 204/88 *Ministère Public v Paris* [1989] ECR 4361, [1991] 1 CMLR 841, 853.

Several institutions are jointly responsible for the selection of methods to realise the Treaty's goals. Those established by the Treaty are already the subject of an extensive literature and require only brief descriptions here. The most important is the Commission of the European Communities[1]. Despite the ultimate authority of the Council and gradual changes in the role of the European Parliament, the Commission remains the originator and architect of the Community's policies[2]. It has been described as the Community's "motor", but it also exercises substantial influence over the vehicle's steering and acceleration[3]. The Commission's principal activities are formulating proposed policies, mediating among Member States and other Community institutions regarding those proposals, and overseeing the execution of existing policies and rules. It is at once a bureaucracy and a regulator, an administrative tribunal and an unelected legislature[4].

The Commission is divided into twenty-three directorates-general, each responsible for some aspect of Community affairs. Many issues may, however, be effectively addressed only by several directorates working in coordination[5]. For example, problems which affect both foodstuffs and the environment (e.g., packaging) or both foodstuffs and agriculture (e.g., primary products and pesticides) fall within the interests of two or more directorates-general. Each is principally concerned with the issues or industries for which it has been given responsibility, sometimes to regulate and sometimes to promote. Some of the jurisdictional divisions reflect bureaucratic convenience and others areas of substantive emphasis. The results are sometimes arbitrary. For example, one directorate may be responsible for the ingredient labelling of beer, while another is responsible for wine[6]. Relationships among the directorates involve competition as well as cooperation, and they sometimes evidence little enthusiasm for coordination. As a result, the European Parliament has complained of the "bureaucratic fragmentation" which often hampers the Commission's policymaking regarding foodstuffs[7].

---

1. For the Commission's basic powers and responsibilities, see Article 155 of the Treaty of Rome. For other provisions regarding its composition and role, see Treaty Establishing a Single Council and a Single Commission of the European Communities, OJ No. 152 (July 13, 1967).
2. T. Hartley, *The Foundations of European Community Law* pp 8-13 (2nd ed. 1988).
3. D. Unwin, *The Community of Europe : A History of European Integration Since 1945* p165 (1991).
4. For details regarding the Commission's size and activities, see, e.g., the Community's overall budget for fiscal year 1992, OJ L26 3.2.92 p1.
5. Food issues are largely the responsibility of DG III, which handles internal market questions, DG VI, which handles agriculture, and the Consumer Policy Service. Food labelling will reportedly be generally transferred from DG III to the Consumer Policy Service, itself formerly part of DG XI, at the end of 1992; EC Food Law p3 (May 1992). Both DG III and DG VI have numerous subsections. For details, see, e.g., *Dod's European Companion* (1991); *Eurofood* p2 (March 1991).
6. DG III is considering ingredient labelling rules for beer and cider, while wine, which is already subject to extensive rules, will be left to DG VI.
7. European Parliament Resolution on Food Hygiene, OJ C183 15.7.91 p52.

The European Parliament increasingly imagines itself as the legitimate spokesperson for its electorate. With growing forcefulness, it demands a right to formulate, or at least to guide, the Community's major policies[1]. Until recent years, these claims had little reality, and Parliament played only a modest role in the Community's decision-making. It was often a goad and sometimes a gadfly, but never a full participant in the Community's regulatory processes. By 1991, for example, the Council had adopted less than one-third of the legislative amendments suggested by the Parliament[2]. With direct parliamentary elections and the increasing authority of the Community itself, Parliament has gradually attracted more demanding legislators[3]. They have slowly forced, and are continuing to seek, a less marginal role for Parliament in the Community's governance[4]. The Parliament's powers are already a principal focus of the debate regarding the Community's future structure. The proposed Maastricht Treaty will probably prove to be only one phase of that debate, although it may significantly alter Parliament's role[5]. Even as that debate continues, food and agricultural policies are sometimes substantially affected by Parliament's contributions[6]. For example, Parliament was instrumental in 1992 in at least temporarily foreclosing a proposed footnote to draft legislation regarding sweeteners and other additives which would have created significant exceptions to harmonisation[7]. Parliament's

---

1. The role of the European Parliament falls well short of its ambitions. Its current role may be either "consultative" or "co-operative", depending upon the provisions of the Treaty of Rome which are to be implemented. For descriptions of both processes, see, e.g., F. Jacobs & R. Corbett, *The European Parliament* (1990); T. Hartley, *The Foundations of European Community Law* pp30-37 (2nd ed. 1988). For a simpler account, see, e.g., E.C. Commission, *A New Community Standards Policy* iii-vi (1990).

2. Sixth Report of the Commission to the Council and European Parliament concerning the Implementation of the White Paper on the Completion of the Internal Market, COM(91) 237 final, at p7.

3. The first Parliament to be directly elected did not begin service until 1979; see *The Times Guide to the European Parliament* p5 (1989). There have been two subsequent elections. Many parliamentary elections have, however, been contested largely on national issues. D. Unwin, *The Community of Europe : A History of European Integration Since 1945* p170 (1991).

4. A former president of the Parliament claims that a "new dynamism" in the Parliament's activities began in 1984; see *The Times Guide to the European Parliament* p5 (1989). His predecessor also perceives an "enhanced role" for Parliament, and claims that "never again" can it be "marginalised"; ibid., at p8.

5. The Maastricht Treaty on European Union would make several significant changes in Parliament's powers, including a right to request proposals from the Commission, the appointment of an ombudsman, and the power to constitute committees of inquiry to investigate violations of law or instances of maladminstration. Parliament has separately been held by the European Court to have a "common law" right to challenge the legal bases for the Council's measures; Case C-70/88 *Re Radioactive Food, European Parliament v EC Council* [1990] ECR I-2041, [1992] 1 CMLR 91.

6. Many of those contributions are made by its committees. Parliament has some 18 committees, none of them exclusively devoted to food issues, but its Social Affairs and Employment Committee now deals with general issues of health and safety legislation, while many food and consumer matters are the responsibility of its Committee on Environment, Public Health and Consumer Protection. Agriculture is entrusted to a third committee. There has also been an informal group of members concerned with food issues, known as the Land Use and Food Policy Intergroup. F. Jacobs & R. Corbett, *The European Parliament* p150 (1990). See also T. Hartley, *The Foundations of European Community Law* pp23-36 (2nd ed. 1988); N. Nugent, *The Government and Politics of the European Community* pp129-165 (2nd ed. 1991).

7. See below at Chapter 5, para 5.3.

effectiveness is likely to be increased by its efforts to assemble its own scientific and technical advisors[1].

The frustrations which still attend Parliament's activities are illustrated by a recent dispute. In 1989, the Commission proposed a Council regulation to govern the production and labelling of organic food products. Late in 1990, a committee of the European Parliament suggested significant revisions to the proposal. It did so only to discover that, reportedly under pressure from the Council, the Commission had already produced a "political compromise" which differed substantially from the original proposal[2]. The Commission evidently did not consider it necessary to submit the revision for new parliamentary comments[3]. The parliamentary committee applied its own political pressures, and a copy of the revision was finally provided. The copy was, however, provided only unofficially and only for information. The dispute is a useful reminder both of Parliament's incomplete powers and of the growing determination with which it seeks greater authority.

The third principal institution of regulatory decision-making is the Council. It consists of one ministerial representative from each of the twelve national governments, who rotate depending on the issues to be addressed at any particular session[4]. In addition, the presidency of the Council revolves among the Member States at six-month intervals in a prearranged order[5]. Each presidency enjoys significant discretion in determining the Council's agenda, and thus in governing the direction of the Council's activities. The arrangement reduces national jealousies, but also deprives the Community of the full advantages of coherent and sustained policymaking[6]. For want of an alternative, many planning and executive functions have instead devolved upon the presidency of the Commission. The Council does not have formal powers to originate internal market legislation, and its principal role is to coordinate the views of the various national governments[7]. Its control over the Commission's proposals has been eroded by qualified majority

---

1.   The Parliament has created a unit for Scientific and Technical Options Assessment ("STOA"), which will evidently draw upon outside experts; OJ C288 6.11.92 p11.
2.   Report of the Committee on Agriculture, Fisheries and Rural Development, No. A3-0311/90 (19 Nov 1990) at pp38-39.
3.   Ibid., at p39.
4.   There is, for example, an "agricultural" Council, consisting of agricultural ministers, and a "health" Council, consisting of health ministers. In 1989, the Council met formally 89 times, including ten times as the Internal Market Council; see CEPA, *The Annual Review of European Community Affairs 1990* p273 (1991). There have been some 1,500 formal Council meetings; Bull. EC 5/7-1991, point 1.7.5.
5.   Treaty establishing a Single Council and a Single Commission of the European Communities, OJ No. 152 (July 13, 1967), at art 2.
6.   Many commentators have observed the ambiguities of the Community's decision-making process, and the resulting absence of systematic policies. See, e.g., A. M. Williams, *The European Community* pp147-152 (1991).
7.   Articles 100a and 145 of the Treaty of Rome. The Council is best described as "the body where the interests of the Member States find direct expression". T. Hartley, *The Foundations of European Community Law* p13 (2nd ed. 1988).

voting under the Single European Act[1]. In addition, its supervision of subsidiary legislation is often delegated to committees of subordinate national officials[2].

The fourth principal institution is the European Court of Justice, which now is assisted by the European Court of First Instance[3]. The Court's principal role has related to the underpinnings, and not to the details or substance, of the Community's food policies. Few of the Community's rules relating to additives, labelling or other regulatory issues have been the subject of interpretation by the Court. Nonetheless, the Court's decisions regarding the free circulation of goods, and thus the limits within which Member States may impede intra-Community trade, have been major factors in establishing the pace and direction of harmonisation[4]. The Commission's harmonisation policies might have been different if the Court's decisions had been issued earlier[5]. Moreover, the Court is one forum in which the Commission seeks to compel Member States to transpose the Community's directives into national law with promptness and fidelity. The Court's success in this role has been, however, far from uniform[6].

Finally, the Treaty of Rome established an Economic and Social Committee consisting of representatives of producers, unions, professional groups, and the general public[7]. The ESC (or "ECOSOC") provides advice to the Council and Commission regarding a broad range of economic and social issues[8]. Its 189 members are distributed among the Member States roughly by population. They serve renewable four-year terms and act in their personal, and not their business or professional, capacities[9]. They are appointed by the Council upon recommendations

---

1. See below at para 2.3.
2. See below at para 2.4.
3. For general summaries of the Court's role and powers, see, e.g., L. N. Brown & F. Jacobs, *The Court of Justice of the European Communities* (3rd ed. 1989); T. Hartley, *The Foundations of European Community Law* p49 (2nd ed. 1988); N. Nugent, *The Government and Politics of the European Community* pp166-192 (2nd ed. 1991).
4. For a description of the decisions and their significance, see below at para 2.3.
5. Haigh, "Control of Food Additives and Contaminants : The EEC Situation", in G. Gibson & R. Walker, eds., *Food Toxicology - Real or Imaginary Problems?* p52 (1985). See also below at para 2.3.
6. There are several instances in which a judgment holding a Member State to be delinquent in transposing a directive has proved ineffective. Ultimately, the Court's power still consists of moral persuasion. For a summary, see Eighth Annual Report to the European Parliament on Commission Monitoring of the Application of Community Law - 1990, OJ C338 31.12.91 p1. The Maastricht Treaty on European Union would, however, give the Court, upon application from the Commission, power to impose monetary penalties upon Member States which fail to perform Community obligations.
7. Article 193 of the Treaty of Rome. For a list of former committee members from the UK and their business or professional affiliations, see S. Fallows, *Food Legislative System of the UK* p148 (1988). For the current members, see Council Decision (EEC) 90/522, OJ L290 23.10.90 p13. There are three groups within the Committee, all roughly the same size. One includes representatives of public and private employers, another national trade unions, and the third representatives of agriculture, the professions, and small or medium-sized businesses. T. Nugent, *The Government and Politics of the European Community* p211 (2nd ed. 1988).
8. Articles 197 and 198 of the Treaty of Rome.
9. Ibid., art 193.

by the Member States, and after consultation with the Commission[1]. The ESC's opinions sometimes exert influence over issues involving consumer interests or public health and safety. There are, however, recurrent complaints that it usually supports the Commission and that its effectiveness is diminishing[2].

Three other institutions were not created by the Treaty of Rome, but now play central roles in the formulation of the Community's food regulations. The Council created a Standing Committee for Foodstuffs in 1969 to facilitate cooperation between the Commission and the Member States[3]. The Standing Committee was also expected to afford the Commission easier access to the expertise of the national governments regarding food issues[4]. It consists of representatives from each of the Member States, with a representative of the Commission as its chairman[5]. The Standing Committee has been given authority under many of the Community's measures to serve as a surrogate for the Council, with powers to approve new regulatory policies and to evaluate national derogations from existing Community rules[6].

In 1974, the Commission created the Scientific Committee for Food to establish a point of systematic contact with independent scientists and other experts whom the Commission may wish to consult regarding food policies[7]. The Scientific Committee consists of as many as eighteen scientists expert in such matters as health and safety, food composition and processing, additives, processing aids, and contaminants[8]. Its members are selected by the Commission for renewable three-year terms[9]. They are not paid. Nor do they yet have any scientific support staff[10]. They may form smaller working groups, and may as needed seek the assistance of outside experts[11]. Many of its members have also served as members of national

---

1. Ibid., art 194. See also Council Decision (EEC) 90/522, OJ L290 23.10.90 p13 at the fifth and seventh recitals of the preamble.
2. See, e.g., National Consumer Council, *Food Policy and the Consumer* p26 (1988).
3. Council Decision (EEC) 69/44, OJ L291 29.11.69 p9. See also Council Directive (EEC) 85/7, OJ L2 3.1.85 p22 at the second recital of the preamble ("the Committee has the task of ensuring close co-operation between the Member States and the Commission in cases where the Council confers powers on the latter for the purpose of implementing the rules which it establishes").
4. Council Decision 69/44, OJ L291 29.11.69 p9, at the first recital of the preamble.
5. Ibid., art 1.
6. Ibid., art 2.
7. Commission Decision (EEC) 74/234, OJ L136 20.5.74 p1. For its current composition, see OJ C193 31.7.92 p5.
8. Ibid., arts 2, 3, 4, (article 3 amended by Commission Decision (EEC) 86/241, OJ L163 19.6.86 p40). The previous figure was 15. The number participating at any given time in the preparation of a report may vary, but the authorised membership is 18. The Scientific Committee may also draw upon former members and others as consultants. Many of its members are toxicologists, and it has been suggested that a wider variety of disciplines should be included. See opinion of the Economic and Social Committee, OJ C14 20.1.92 p6 at para 2.5.
9. Commission Decision (EEC) 74/234, OJ L136 20.5.74 p1, at art 6.
10. See para 14 of the explanatory memorandum that accompanied the draft of COM(91)16 final, OJ C108 23.4.91 p7. Such support has now been promised; see below at Chapter 10, para 10.2.3.
11. Commission Decision (EEC) 74/234, OJ L136 20.5.74 p1, at arts 7, 8. See also the opinion of the Economic and Social Committee regarding the use of Member State assistance on scientific questions, OJ C14 20.1.92 p6 at para 2.5.

consulting committees, and thus have helped to reconcile Community and national policies[1]. The Scientific Committee has been given increasing responsibilities for safety assessments, purity criteria, sampling and analytical methods, and other technical issues. It has prepared more than 1000 opinions, and is frequently called upon by the Commission for independent scientific judgments regarding health and safety matters[2]. The committee has become overburdened, and there are increasing demands that its expertise should be broadened and its deliberations made more public. Nonetheless, it remains the Community's principal guardian of food safety[3].

In 1975, the Commission created an Advisory Committee on Foodstuffs to permit consultations with representatives of industry, trade and consumer groups[4]. The Advisory Committee consists of thirty members, one-third of whom are "permanent" members nominated by the Commission[5]. The others are experts designated for each session, or even for particular agenda items, by the European Trade Union Conference, the Union of Industries of the European Communities, the Consumers' Consultative Council, and various agricultural and commercial groups[6]. The Advisory Committee provides views to the Commission regarding the implications of draft regulatory measures[7]. It is particularly significant in the approval of new food additives, where it serves as one judge of the technical need for new products[8]. Without proof of such a need, the Commission refuses even to consider the safety of a proposed new additive[9]. The arrangement raises potentially significant issues of conflicts of interest and barriers to innovation[10]. In addition, the Council has created several advisory committees to deal with

---

1. Haigh, "Control of Food Additives and Contaminants : The EEC Situation", in G. Gibson & R. Walker, eds., *Food Toxicology : Real or Imaginary Problems?* p55 (1985).

2. Some of the opinions are printed, often belatedly. The Economic and Social Committee has called for greater transparency in the Scientific Committee's activities, which would include more frequent and timely publications; OJ C14 20.1.92 p6 .

3. For its role, see para 3 of the explanatory memorandum issued with the Commission's proposal for a Council Directive regarding the scientific examination of questions relating to food, COM(91) 16 final, OJ C108 23.4.91 p7. See also opinion of the Economic and Social Committee regarding proposed rules for extraction solvents, OJ C106 6.8.84 p7, at para 2.1. For proposals to strengthen and alter the Committee, see below at Chapter 10, para 10.2.3.

4. Commission Decision (EEC) 75/420, OJ L182 12.7.75 p35. For the current statute, see Commission Decision (EEC) 80/1073, OJ L318 26.11.80 p28. Commissioner Bangemann has described the committee as consisting of 20 experts in equal numbers from agriculture, commerce, consumers, industry and employees. Written Question 201/90, OJ C233 17.9.90 p19. Presumably his calculation excluded the permanent members.

5. Commission Decision (EEC) 80/1073, OJ L318 26.11.80 p28, at art 2. The "permanent" members are given renewable three-year terms, but serve until they are replaced or resign.

6. Ibid., art 2 and the Annex.

7. Ibid., second recital of the preamble. The Advisory Committee may be consulted regarding "all problems concerning the harmonisation of legislation relating to foodstuffs"; art 1. The Advisory Committee evidently does not formally vote, but acts upon the basis of consensus. S. Fallows, *Food Legislative System of the UK* p85 (1988). It has been said to lack "power and effectiveness"; National Consumer Council, *Food Policy and the Consumer* p27 (1988).

8. Below at Chapter 5, para 5.1. See also Snodin, "Sweeteners : Statutory Aspects," in S. Marie & J. Piggot, eds., *Handbook of Sweeteners* pp265, 281 (1991).

9. Ibid., at pp280-281.

10. The Advisory Committee potentially may include those who manufacture a competing product, or who have some other interest in the preservation of settled arrangements.

technical issues in specialised areas. These include, for example, plant health, pesticides, animal feedingstuffs, and spirit drinks. The committees are chaired by representatives of the Commission, but consist of national regulators who help formulate technical aspects of the Community's food policies[1]. They have been assigned review responsibilities by several directives, particularly with respect to safety monitoring and national derogations from Community rules. The committees are specialised alternatives to the Standing Committee, which itself is a surrogate for the Council[2].

One institution is conspicuous by its absence. There have been recurrent proposals for a Community agency with specific responsibility for the formulation of foodstuffs policies. It might also have enforcement responsibilities. Such an agency would presumably absorb the work currently performed by the Scientific Committee and the relevant sections of the Commission. In principle, nothing would prevent it from continuing to draw upon outside scientific advice. At least for the moment, however, proposals for the creation of a Community food agency have been rejected by the Commission[3]. The gradual centralisation of food policy makes it likely that such proposals will reappear[4]. For the present, the Commission has announced that it prefers to alleviate the burdens upon the Scientific Committee by allocating more issues to national authorities[5]. It will also seek to increase the level of cooperation with international bodies, such as the Codex Alimentarius Commission, and with agencies in third countries[6]. More assistance will also be sought from international standardisation groups[7]. The proposed arrangements are a compromise, and it is unclear how successful they will prove or how long they will persist. Whether or not the new arrangements are actually implemented, the value of a specialised Community food agency will remain a continuing subject of debate.

---

1.   Various informal working groups may also be created, usually consisting of experts from the Member States. There was, for example, a working group on additives in 1990. Written Question 201/90, OJ C233 17.9.90 p19.

2.   In addition, the Community also creates special projects or groups to conduct programmes of food or agricultural research. There are, for example, now programmes related both to "consumer-led food-linked agro-industrial research and technological development", styled "FLAIR", and to "agriculture-led biotechnology-based agro-industrial research and technological development," styled "ECLAIR". For the opinion of the Economic and Social Committee regarding the programmes, see OJ C2330.1.89 p23.

3.   Below at Chapter 10, para 10.2.3.

4.   Some members of the European Parliament continue to press for a Community agency. Eurofood 6 (Jan 1992).

5.   For the Commission's proposed new arrangements, see below at Chapter 10, para 10.2.3.

6.   The Codex Alimentarius Commission was founded in 1962 to formulate suggested rules and policies for foodstuffs under the auspices of the World Health Organisation and the United Nations Food and Agricultural Organisation. Its standards were compiled in 19 volumes in 1981, and now are to be republished in 14 volumes. Only the first volume of the new edition has been issued. For the Commission's activities, see, e.g., Report of the Nineteenth Session of the Codex Alimentarius Commission (1991); 1 World Food Reg. Rev. 15 (Nov 1991); McKay, "The Codex Food Labelling Committee - Maintaining International Standards Relevant to Changing Consumer Demands", 1/92 Eur. Food L. Rev. 70 (1992).

7.   For the role of European and international standards in ensuring quality, see Gorny, "European Food Quality - The Prospective Importance of ISO 9.000/EN 29.000", 1/92 Eur. Food L. Rev. 13 (1992).

2.2   **Formative influences upon the Community's food policies**

2.2.1   **The constraints imposed by existing legislation**

The Community's principal goal with respect to foodstuffs regulation has been the creation of a single marketplace through a harmonisation of national laws. Inevitably, a major constraint upon its policies has been the national rules it has sought to reconcile. Nonetheless, harmonisation need not imply a lowest common denominator, and the Community has generally avoided such an approach[1]. Indeed, the Community's rules have often ignored limits and exceptions included in national requirements[2]. Moreover, an increasing number of Community measures relate to issues about which only a few Member States previously had rules. In such cases, the Community has formulated, and not simply harmonised, food policies. The Community's rules have been drawn from many sources, but the food policies of Germany, the Netherlands and France have been particularly important sources[3]. British law and policies have increased in influence. The food laws of these and other Member States derive from a variety of administrative traditions[4]. They differ substantially in completeness and approach, and those differences have been at once an opportunity and an impediment for the Community[5]. They have offered diverse sources and models from which the Community could select, but have also greatly increased the difficulties of reconciliation.

---

1.   See Gray, "EEC Food Law", Address to Annual Conference of European Association of Lawyers (June 1991); Gray, "The Perspective to 1992", in H. Deelstra, et al., eds., *Food Policy Trends in Europe* pp11, 13 (1991).

2.   It might be argued that the process of "approximation" under the Treaty demands some rough conformity to national laws, and that the Community may not alter preponderant national rules. This has not, however, been a limitation to which the Community appears to have adhered.

3.   Rees, "Introduction," in J. Rees & J. Bettison, eds., *Processing and Packaging of Heat Preserved Foods* pp 1, 14 (1991). The US rules have also provided important benchmarks; ibid., at p13.

4.   Because there are various national traditions, it has been argued that the gradual emergence of a Community administrative law has not been dominated by any particular set of national principles. Schwarze, "Tendencies toward a Common Administrative Law in Europe", 16 ELR 3, 17 (1991). There has instead been a "prolific interaction" between national and Community laws; ibid.

5.   For a description of the United Kingdom's rules and regulatory processes (albeit before the adoption of the 1990 Food Safety Act), see S. Fallows, *Food Legislative System of the UK* (1988). See also Scott, "Continuity and Change in British Food Law", (1990) 53 MLR 785. The Belgian system is described in C. Kestens, *L'Alimentation et le Droit* (1990); Ballon, "Le droit de l'alimentation belge : un apercu", 2-3/91 Eur. Food L. Rev. 174 (1991). For a description of the principal German rules, see H. Hummel-Liljegren, ed., *Lebensmittelrechts Handbuch* (1991); Loschelder, "Consumer Protection in the Federal Republic of Germany : A Brief Look at the German Law of Food", 6 St. Louis Univ. Pub. L. Rev. 131 (1987). For the transposition of Community rules into German law, see Eckert, "Einfuhr 'Europaischer Lebensmittel' nach Deutschland", 4/91 Eur. Food L. Rev. 313 (1991). For the French rules, see G. Cas & D. Ferrier, *Traite de Droit de la Consommation* (1986); Lamy-Dehove, *Reglementation des Produits, Qualite, Repression des Fraudes* (1986) ("*Lamy-Dehove*"). The Dutch rules are codified in the *Wet op de Voedingsraad*, 99-1, 2 *Nederlandse Staatswetten* (ed. Schuurman & Jordens) (1989) ("*Voedingsraad*"). The Italian rules are collected and annotated in L. & E. Rizzatti, *Tutela Igenico-Sanitario degli Alimenti e Bevande e dei Consumatore* (10th ed. 1990) ("*Alimenti e Bevande*"). See also G. Andreis, et al., eds., *Codice di Diretto Alimentare Annotato* (1990) (3 vols.). The basic provisions of Spanish law are set forth in the *Codigo Alimentario* (6th ed. 1991), first promulgated by Decreto No. 2484/1967, B.O.E. 248-53 (Oct 17-23, 1967) ("*Codigo Alimentario*").

Even a sketch of the histories of the national systems will suggest the barriers to harmonisation. Before the nineteenth century, basic foodstuffs were controlled by compositional standards and other rules imposed by guilds or other trade groups[1]. Their rules were sometimes supplemented by municipal or national requirements. The German rules for beer and the English assizes for bread and beer are familiar examples. By the early nineteenth century, many of those trade and local rules had become outmoded or ineffective[2]. There were many causes, including urbanisation and substantial population increases, but in essence the societal arrangements for which the rules were designed and from which they sprang had weakened or disappeared. Many of the rules were eventually abolished. Others were largely ignored[3].

The relatively open societies of the early nineteenth century permitted food adulteration and fraud to flourish[4]. Adulterated and often dangerous foods were common in both Britain and continental Europe[5]. For example, urine and picric acid were mixed with dough to create "egg" noodles. Ground coffee was mixed with chicory or sand. Green coffee-beans were darkened by lead. Confectioneries were brightened by a variety of toxic substances[6]. In 1820, a German-born scientist working in England published an influential account of the prevalence and hazards of food adulteration and contamination[7]. His descriptions aroused widespread public concerns, but few immediate regulatory responses. It was not until 1860, after lengthy pressures and additional disclosures, that England adopted the first modern regulatory statute for foods[8]. A more comprehensive English statute was adopted in 1875. Germany followed in 1879, France in 1885, and Belgium in 1890[9]. Austria began compiling a "Codex Alimentarius Austriacus" in 1891[10]. France and Switzerland adopted comprehensive statutes in 1905. The United States did so in 1906[11]. These measures often were not immediately effective, but were gradually

1.   For the English rules, see, e.g., J. Burnett, *Plenty and Want* pp86-103 (3rd ed. 1989).
2.   The English assizes were finally repealed in 1844. See Hutt, "Government Regulation of the Integrity of the Food Supply", 4 Annual Rev. of Nutrition 1 (1984).
3.   Even Hamburg's ancient purity rules for beer, which survived all challenges until the European Court, were widely violated in the nineteenth century. R. Evans, *Death in Hamburg : Society and Politics in the Cholera Years 1830-1910* p170 (1990 ed.).
4.   See, e.g., F. Filby, *A History of Food Adulteration and Analysis* (1934).
5.   J. Burnett, *Plenty and Want* 102 (3rd ed. 1989); R. Evans, *Death in Hamburg : Society and Politics in the Cholera Years 1830-1910* pp166-176 (1990 ed.)
6.   Ibid., at pp168-169. Confectionery shops were described by one German report as factories for the "professional application of poisons"; ibid., at p168. The same practices were common in the United States. J. Young, *Pure Food : Securing the Federal Food and Drugs Act of 1906* pp31-32 (1989).
7.   F. Accum, *Treatise on Adulterations of Food and Culinary Poisons* (1820).
8.   For outlines of the history, see, e.g., Gray, "The Perspective to 1992", in H. Deelstra, et al., eds., *Food Policy Trends in Europe* 11-12 (1991); du Bois, "An industry's point of view", ibid., at pp33-34.
9.   The legislation in France and Belgium was partly based on a series of French measures adopted in the revolutionary and Napoleonic periods. C. Kestens, *L'Alimentation et le Droit* pp59-68 (1990).
10.   *Report of the Nineteenth Session of the Codex Alimentarius Commission* p111 (1991).
11.   For the origins and goals of the 1906 Act, see J. Young, *Pure Food : Securing the Federal Food and Drug Act of 1906* (1989). One important factor in the Act's passage was evidence of the

strengthened by the creation of special enforcement authorities[1]. The measures themselves were frequently revised and extended in the first three decades of the twentieth century. One of the most influential of the later statutes was the Federal Food, Drug, and Cosmetic Act, adopted in the United States in 1938[2].

By the early 1960's, when the Community first began harmonising the regulation of foodstuffs, the rules of its Member States were diverse and sophisticated products of several centuries of guild or trade restrictions and several decades of national regulations. The policies embodied in those rules were rooted in national administrative histories. Special agencies, staffed by thousands of civil servants, were employed to enforce them. Complex and interdependent systems of regulators and regulated parties had developed interests in their preservation. Even where the national rules have been incomplete or unsystematic, they have provided an important predicate to the Community's measures[3]. They have sometimes provided limits and sometimes sources for the Community's rules, but they have always represented entrenched attitudes and interests to which the Community must be responsive.

The sources of the Community's rules are not limited to the national systems of its Member States. The work of the Council of Europe has offered important models regarding such issues as pesticide residues and flavourings[4]. The Codex Alimentarius Commission was established in 1962 to formulate international standards, and its recommendations have often influenced the Community's legislation[5]. Indeed, some of the Community's measures are largely restatements of Codex standards. The findings of the Joint Expert Committee on Food Additives, established by the World Health Organisation and the United Nations Food and Agricultural Organisation, have also been important[6]. Rules adopted in other nations, including the United States, have sometimes been significant influences[7].

problems in Europe; ibid. at p32. Most of the American states had previously adopted their own rules.

1. See, e.g., R. Evans, *Death in Hamburg : Society and Politics in the Cholera Years 1830-1910* pp174, 506 (1990 ed.).

2. See, e.g., Hutt, "Government Regulation of the Integrity of the Food Supply", 4 Annual Rev. of Nutrition 1 (1984).

3. The Belgian rules, for example, have been described as "un ensemble parfois désordonné". Ballon, "Le doit de l'alimentation belge : un aperçu", 2-3/91 Eur. Food L. Rev. 174 (1991), quoting Richely, "La reglementation des denrées alimentaires en Belgique en 1986", in T. Bourgoignie, ed., *L'année de la consommation 1986* p91 (1987).

4. Mestres, "L'analyse des résidus toxiques; son interet et son limites; exemple des résidus de pesticides", in R. Derache, ed., *Toxocologie et Sécurité des Aliments* p105 (1986); Gray, "EEC Food Law", Address to Annual Conference of European Association of Lawyers, p6 (June 1991).

5. For its work in labelling, for example, see McKay, "The Codex Food Labelling Committee - Maintaining International Standards Relevant to Changing Consumer Demands", 1/92 Eur. Food L. Rev. 70 (1992); van der Heide, "The Codex Alimentarius on Food Labelling", 4/91 Eur. Food L. Rev. 291 (1991).

6. See, e.g., *Report of the Nineteenth Session of the Codex Alimentarius Commission* p4 (1991).

7. Rees, "Introduction", in J. Rees & J. Bettison, eds., *Processing and Packaging of Heat Preserved Foods* pp1,13 (1991).

Food policies have become increasingly international and interdependent, and no regulatory agency can be entirely indifferent to the views of the similar agencies elsewhere[1]. The Community was a new entrant in the area of food legislation in the 1960's, but the pages on which it began writing have never been empty.

2.2.2 The impact of agricultural and industrial policies

National and international rules are not the only determinants of the Community's policies. Many institutions, industries and groups may be affected by the Community's regulatory policies, and they are predictably anxious to participate in the design of its rules. Food processors, distributors, farmers, consumers, and their institutional advocates all seek rights of participation. While they do not dictate the Community's choices, their interests provide a partial explanation for the direction and pace of the Community's efforts[2]. Their influence is enhanced by the absence of any general opportunity for the public to participate in the Commission's deliberations.

One important source of pressure is the Common Agricultural Policy[3]. From the beginning, the CAP has been the central element of Community policymaking. It is at once an economic burden, a political necessity, and an international liability[4]. Protective in purpose and effect, the CAP is defended as jealously by the Community's farmers as it is disparaged by the Community's consumers and trading

---

1. A vivid example is provided by objections filed by the Community with the Food and Drug Administration regarding FDA's proposed rules for nutritional labelling. In essence, the Community reproached FDA for departures from "international" standards. Comments of the European Community (25 Feb 1992). See also below at Chapter 3, para 3.4.

2. For an illustrative description of the influence of interest groups on a national regulatory process, see S. Fallows, *Food Legislative System of the UK* pp118-129 (1988).

3. The CAP was contemplated by, in particular, Articles 38, 39 and 40 of the Treaty of Rome. The Council is given broad decision-making powers by Article 43 to implement the agricultural policies demanded by those articles. Article 40 requires the adoption of a common agricultural policy (Article 40(2)), as well as the adoption of "all measures" needed to achieve this goal (Article 40(3)). Article 41 authorises joint measures to promote the consumption of the Community's products, and Article 42 provides that the Community's competition policies shall apply to agricultural production and trade only to the extent authorised by the Council. With respect to the application of the Community's competition policies to state aids in the agricultural area, the Council's principal step was the adoption of Council Regulation (EEC) 26/62, OJ 993 (1962). There have been many subsequent revisions. For the Commission's assessment of agricultural issues, see, e.g., the Commission's communications regarding Perspectives for the Common Agricultural Policy, COM(85) 333 final (1985), and The Future of Rural Society, COM(88) 501 final (1988). For the framework and content of the Community's agricultural policy, see, e.g., S. Ventura, *Principes de Droit Agraire Communautaire* (1967); D. Schina, *State Aids under the EEC Treaty Articles 92 to 94 96 ff.* (1987); R. Fennel, *The Common Agricultural Policy of the European Community* (2nd ed. 1987).

4. See, e.g., President Delors' address to Parliament, *The Commission's Programme for 1991*, EC Bull. Supp. 1/91 (1991) ("*The 1991 Programme*"). In response to parliamentary questions, President Delors stated that the CAP is 50 per cent of the Community's budget and that the costs are approaching "the ceiling of the resources available."; ibid., at p28. For details, see the Community's 1992 general budget, OJ L26 3.2.92 p1. Nonetheless, he defended the help given to agriculture, and explained that there are "commercial reasons" why the Community should not "yield" market share in agricultural products to the United States, although it might do so to countries of the third world. See the 1991 Programme, above at p28.

partners[1]. It has proved particularly controversial in Member States, such as Britain, which are net contributors to its costs rather than net recipients of its benefits[2]. Although large farmers have often been its principal beneficiaries[3], the CAP was intended to protect small farmers, stimulate rural development, and encourage agricultural diversification[4]. It seeks these goals through a shifting mixture of output subsidies, pricing mechanisms[5], export refunds[6] and other assistance programmes[7]. By encouraging high-cost agricultural production, the CAP compels higher consumer prices. It also stimulates incentives or prohibitions designed to promote the consumption of surplus products[8]. Similar measures have often been adopted independently by Member States[9].

---

1. See, e.g., European Consumer Law Group, "Consumer Protection in the EEC After Ratification of the Single Act," 10 J. Consumer Policy pp319, 321 (1987) (asserting "the disastrous effects of the agricultural policy ... on the interest of the consumer"). Indeed, the CAP has been described as an "absurdity which may help to explain why Britons eat so much unhealthy food". A. Coghlan, "Britain's Deadly Diet", New Scientist p29 (11 May 1991). Another commentator has placed it among the "classic monuments to human stupidity"; E. Millstone, *Food Additives* p17 (1986).

2. A vigorous attack on the CAP was provided by R. Boddy, *Our Food, Our Land* (1991), who lamented its social and economic effects upon Britain; ibid., at pp5-6. He urged unilateral withdrawal from the CAP, even at the cost of leaving the Community. For different summaries of the CAP's advantages and costs, see, e.g., A.M. Williams, *The European Community* pp119-120 (1991); A. Daltrop, *Politics and the European Community* pp172-179 (2nd ed. 1986).

3. It has been suggested, for example, that the CAP is "designed to protect a handful of mostly rich farmers." I. Stelzer, "America Hits Back with Own Market", *The Sunday Times* pp4-7 (5 May 1991). For more balanced discussions, see S. George, *Politics and Policy in the European Community* 115-129 (1985); R. Fennel, *The Common Agricultural Policy of the European Community* pp 1-14 (2nd ed. 1987).

4. Article 39 of the Treaty provides that the CAP should increase productivity, ensure a fair standard of farm living, stabilise markets, ensure the availability of supplies, and result in reasonable consumer prices. The CAP must achieve these goals without social disruptions or aggravating local differences; ibid., at Article 39(2) of the Treaty of Rome. The European Parliament has summarised the situation with the observation that "the priority aim of the CAP must be to safeguard and ensure the development of the family-based holding". Document A2-40/87, OJ C156 15.6.87 p126. See also A. Parry & J. Dinnage, *EEC Law* , chapter 15 (2nd ed. 1981).

5. See, e.g., Council Regulation (EEC) 804/68, OJ L148 28.6.68 p13, which provides for "target", "threshold" and "intervention" prices for various milk products. The regulation has frequently been amended. There are similar measures for many other products.

6. See, e.g., Joined Cases 44-51/77 *Groupement d'Intérêt Economique "Union Malt" v EC Commission* [1978] ECR 57, 59, [1978] 3 CMLR 702, 704. The assistance programmes sometimes provide greater help to particular regional products than to competing products from other Community areas. *Re Grana Padano Cheese : Denmark v EC Commission* [1991] 1 CMLR 801, decided by the European Court in 1989.

7. Import bans may also be used. One was, for example, imposed upon Chilean apples because it was feared they might have "seriously disturbed" the internal market; Case 112/80 *Firma Anton Durbeck v Hauptzolamt Frankfurt am Main-Flughafen* [1981] ECR 1095, [1982] 3 CMLR 314.

8. In early 1992, the Community held some 18 million tonnes of surplus cereals and 500,000 tonnes in beef and dairy produce. EC Agvet Briefing 15 (April 1992); Written Question 1506/91, OJ C66 16.3.92 p17. For promotional measures concerning butter and cream, for example, see Commission Regulation (EEC) 570/88, OJ L55 1.3.88 p31; Commission Regulation (EEC) 124/92, OJ L14 21.1.92 p28. Such measures are regularly endorsed by the European Parliament. See, e.g., OJ C352 31.12.85 p295; OJ C156 15.6.87 p126.

9. For example, France adopted rules as early as 1934 to prohibit the sale of milk substitutes, and justified them in part as efforts to shield milk producers and encourage a reduction of the milk surplus. The European Court eventually held, however, that the rules were forbidden by Article 30 of the Treaty; Case 216/84 *EC Commission v France* [1988] ECR 793.

An illustration of the CAP's results is the market for sugar, where the CAP has caused an average annual surplus production of some 150 per cent over the past ten years[1]. The surplus must be either added to the Community's sugar "mountain" or sold on the world market, where prices average only one-half of those in the Community. The result is an excess cost to consumers equal to one-third of the total value of the Community's production. The Community's Court of Auditors has understandably termed the programme a failure[2]. There are, however, similar arrangements for most other basic agricultural products[3]. It is hardly surprising that protectionism has been described as the CAP's "supreme" value[4].

Agricultural policy is, however, in the midst of change. It no longer stimulates a single or uniform set of pressures. A committee of the European Parliament has described the Community's rules as "ecologically and socially unacceptable", and claimed that they "threaten the survival of farmers"[5]. The committee demanded increased Community support for "ecological agriculture", and would give price and other advantages to small farmers who adopt ecological practices in their farming[6]. As this and similar proposals suggest, food regulatory policies may be substantially affected by attitudes about the future character of agriculture[7]. Food and agricultural policies are interdependent, and both are affected by changing public views regarding such matters as the environment, pesticides, other agricultural chemicals, additives, and food processing[8].

---

1. Court of Auditors Special Report 4/91, OJ C290 7.11.91 p1, at para 5.8. In response, the Commission claimed that the surplus has averaged only 127 per cent. Para 5.4 of the annex to the report.
2. The Commission responded that the programme was "working very efficiently" and a "success". At paras 5.1 and 5.4 of the annex to the report.
3. A review of the CAP's measures with respect to individual product categories is provided by R. Fennel, *The Common Agricultural Policy of the European Community* pp111-175 (2nd ed. 1987).
4. D. Unwin, *The Community of Europe : A History of European Integration Since 1945* p214 (1991). In different terms, the CAP's "fundamental" weakness has been described as a mixture of a "particular form of interventionism" and unduly high guaranteed prices. These problems are said to result from the original agreement among the Community's first six members, which gave French farmers a bargain they have subsequently been unwilling to relinquish. A.M. Williams, *The European Community* pp71-72 (1991).
5. Report of the Committee on Agriculture, Fisheries and Rural Development, No. A3-0311/90 (19 Nov 1990) at p37. The committee demanded that the "whole of agricultural and foodstuff production" should be "subject to ecological criteria".
6. Ibid., at 37-38. In contrast, see the Resolution of the European Parliament on the effects of the use of biotechnology on the European farming industry, A2-159/86, OJ C76 23.3.87 p22.
7. In part, the reasons for the impact of agricultural policies upon food rules are institutional. DG VI, which is responsible for agricultural matters, is also an important participant in the rulemaking process for foods, and its attitudes are not always the same as, or fully co-ordinated with, those of DG III, which is responsible for the internal market. See, e.g., the European Parliament's Resolution on Food Hygiene, OJ C183 15.7.91 p52.
8. Popularised accounts of the issues of ecological agriculture and food processing have important effects upon public opinion and ultimately upon regulatory policies. For pesticides, for example, see C. Robbins, *Poisoned Harvest* (1991); for processed foods, see T. Lobstein, *Children's Food* pp76-77 (1988); J. Porritt & D. Winner, *The Coming of the Greens* pp195-196 (1988).

The impact of the Common Agricultural Policy is partly reinforced and partly offset by the Community's enterprise and industrial policies. They provide strong encouragement for industrial development, particularly in the Community's less developed regions[1]. The policies also offer financial and other support in markets where Community firms do not compete effectively with their non-European rivals[2]. At the same time, the Community's industrial policies demand both the free circulation of goods and vigorous competition[3]. These goals cannot always be reconciled, and do not always produce uniform results. In the foodstuffs area, policymaking is made more complex by the number and variety of competitors, segmented into numerous product and geographical markets. The competing firms have widely differing sizes and use processing techniques and distributional systems which vary significantly among the Member States[4]. Few other industries are so diverse or include the participation of so many firms[5].

2.2.3 The impact of consumer interests and policies

A third source of pressure is the movement for consumer rights and protection[6]. Many causes might be found for the movement's importance, but among them is certainly the European Parliament[7]. A major part of Parliament's energies has been devoted to encouraging measures more sensitive to consumer claims and more

---

1.   A reduction of regional differences and improvements in the status of less favoured areas are among the Treaty's purposes, as described in its preamble. Among other steps, this led to the European Regional Development Fund. See Council Regulation (EEC) 724/75, OJ L73 21.3.71 p1. See also, e.g., *XXIInd General Report on the Activities of the European Communities 1988*, at pp227-237 (1989) (reporting on the reform of structural funds for regional development). See generally A. Parry & J. Dinnage, *EEC Law* chapter 26 (2nd ed. 1981). The Community continues to be troubled by large regional disparities in growth, income and unemployment. A.M. Williams, *The European Community* pp124-125 (1991).

2.   For example, President Delors has promised a "major effort" to "create a favourable environment for improving industrial competitiveness", including "positive adjustment policies to exploit the Community's technological and industrial potential". *The 1991 Programme*, EC Bull. Supp. 1/91, at para 19.

3.   For the Community's free circulation and competition policies, see Articles 30-36, 85-90 of the Treaty of Rome.

4.   For a survey of the European industry, emphasising north-south differences, see United States International Trade Commission, *The Effects of Greater Economic Integration Within the European Community on the United States* pp6-53 (1989). For the varying distributional systems in the Community, see Dimitrova, "Physical Distribution Today", in F. Paine, ed., *Modern Processing, Packaging and Distribution Systems for Food* p132 (1987).

5.   The number of competitors in each market sector is decreasing, as firms increase in size and the market becomes more concentrated. See "Survey of the Food Industry", *Financial Times* (10 May 1991). In 1991, mergers and acquisitions occurred in the food industry in "record" numbers. *Eurofood* p13 (Jan 1992).

6.   The Community is now in the midst of a three-year action plan to strengthen the protection given to consumer interests. EC Bull. 3-1990 at 1.1.93 (1990). The Single European Act also offers a measure of the importance now given by the Community to consumer protection. Article 100a(3), added to the Treaty of Rome by Article 18 of the Act, singled out consumer interests, along with health, safety and the environment, as deserving a "high level of protection" in proposals to complete the internal market.

7.   For the Community's own history of its protection of consumer interests, see *Consumer Policy in the Single Market* pp13-22 (2nd ed. 1991). For a more sceptical appraisal, see European Consumer Law Group, "Consumer Protection in the EEC After Ratification of the Single Act," 10 J. Consumer Policy p319 (1987). Even the Community view, however, recognises that its consumer policies "have, on the whole, fallen short of expectations". Op. cit. at p20.

protective of consumer rights. Consumer information, product quality, and health and safety are among the areas in which Parliament has shown both interest and influence. The pressures for consumer protection did not begin in the Parliament, but partly as a result of its efforts consumer groups now play larger roles in shaping the Community's food regulatory policies[1]. The Maastricht Treaty on European Union could strengthen their effectiveness[2]. In response to increasing demands, the Commission has established a Consumer Policy Service, as well as a Consumers Consultative Council to provide advice from outside groups[3]. The Advisory Committee on Foodstuffs also includes consumer representatives[4]. There are, however, recurrent complaints that these organisations are ineffective and sometimes ignored[5]. The Economic and Social Committee has, for example, described the Commission's efforts as "timid", and complained that consumer policy remains "subsidiary, secondary and indirect"[6]. In response, the European Parliament has continued to press for more stringent protective measures and a larger consumer role in policymaking[7].

The demands of consumer groups are not limited to such matters as labelling disclosures and the use of wholesome cocoa beans. Consumer rights are increasingly associated with environmental protection, and both are intermixed with a search for ecologically acceptable, "natural" food products[8]. An example is offered by a committee report from the European Parliament. The report asserted that there has been "a constant decline in the quality of foodstuffs, and ultimately the

---

1.   The Commission has accepted that consumer representatives should be consulted regarding a broad range of issues. *A New Impetus for Consumer Protection*, COM(85) 314 final (1985); *Consumer Policy in the Single Market* p33 (2nd ed. 1991). Nonetheless, it is widely argued that the role assigned to consumer interests remains too small. See, e.g., Goyens "Consumer Protection in a Single European Market : What Challenge for the EC Agenda?" (1992) 29 CMLRev. 71.

2.   The proposed Maastricht Treaty would require a "high level" of consumer protection, including "specific action" to protect consumers' health, safety and economic interests. The European Parliament has, however, expressed fears that Maastricht might reduce the protection given to consumers in some Member States. EIS, *Europe Environment* No. 384 at V-3 (March 31, 1992).

3.   For the Consumer Policy Service, see, e.g., *Directory of the Commission of the European Communities* p105 (1991). For the Consumers Consultative Council, see Decision (EEC) 90/55, OJ L38 10.2.90 p40. It includes representatives of various regional and Community consumer groups. Economist Intelligence Unit, *European Trends, Background Supplement 1990-91*, at pp66-67 (1990); National Consumer Council, *Food Policy and the Consumer* pp26-27 (1988).

4.   National Consumer Council, *Food Policy and the Consumer* p27 (1988).

5.   *Eurofood* 2 (July 1991); National Consumer Council, *Food Policy and the Consumer* p27 (1988); European Consumer Law Group, "Consumer Protection in the EEC After Ratification of the Single Act," 10 J. Consumer Policy pp319, 330 (1987).

6.   Opinion on Consumer Protection and Completion of the Internal Market, OJ C339 31.12.91 p16 at paras 2.1.1, 2.2.2.

7.   Resolution on consumer protection and public health requirements, No. A3-0060/92 (11 March 1992). The resolution calls for such steps as more complete labelling, damage remedies for consumers, and stronger rules for product liability.

8.   Consumers are apparently becoming more genuine in their demand for "natural" foods and more sophisticated as to the consequences. When one seller eliminated artificial colourings from peas in the 1970's, sales fell by 50 per cent. When another seller did it in the 1980's, there was no loss in sales. J. Burnett, *Plenty and Want* pp321-322 (3rd ed. 1989).

environment"[1]. The committee's members sought a common answer to these issues through an immediate prohibition of all "agricultural toxins"[2]. Without it, the committee predicted that a "food design" industry based upon genetic engineering might become one of Europe's largest growth sectors[3]. These fears may be thought exaggerated, but they represent a perception frequently accepted by the Community's legislators and consumers. The public debate about food policy is intensifying, and it often centres upon the intersection of science and regulation. Pesticides, additives, and biotechnology are familiar examples[4].

2.2.4   The interplay of pressures

These diverse pressures have produced discontinuities in the Community's food policies. The Community cannot with equal vigour encourage the free movement of goods, quality assurance, health and safety, agricultural protectionism, environmental improvement, industrial stimulation, consumer rights, and free competition. Compromise and conflict are inevitable. The Community must mix and qualify its goals to suit particular needs and immediate objectives[5]. This process of accommodation is familiar in any democratic system, but it is particularly complex in a political system only beginning to harmonise the attitudes of twelve stubbornly dissimilar nations. The result is regulation by compromise. Apart from subsidiary matters delegated to the Commission, each new policy must be individually negotiated. Each is a political improvisation calculated to attract a sufficient constituency to permit its adoption. The principal force favouring consistency is the cumulative persuasiveness of earlier compromises. The Community has generally avoided lowest common denominators, but the pressures in their direction are strong and persistent.

The pressures do not arise only within the Community itself. Relations with the European Free Trade Association and the new nations of central Europe are major sources of concern. Trade questions with the United States, Japan and other nations

---

1.   Report of the Committee on Agriculture, Fisheries and Rural Development, A3-0311/90 (19 Nov 1990) at p36.
2.   In the committee's estimation, such chemicals include all those "alien to the ecosystem".
3.   The committee defined "food design" as "the industrial production of food from almost any raw materials using genetic engineering and biotechnology techniques".
4.   Despite public fears about biotechnology, the Commission has devoted 100 million ECU over a five-year period to promote biotechological research. See CEPS, *Annual Review of European Community Affairs 1990* p135 (1991). For the Community's policies, see European Study Service, *Biotechnology : EEC Policy on the Eve of 1993* (1991).
5.   This is true even within individual sectorial policies. With respect to agricultural policy, for example, the Community must continually seek an "equilibrium" between "conflicting objectives." Parry & J. Dinnage, *EEC Law* p206 (2nd ed. 1981). For judicial recognitions of the same necessity, see Case 5/67 *Beus v HZA Munchen-Landsbergerstrasse* [1968] ECR 83; Case C-279, 280 & 285-286/84 *Rau* [1987] ECR 1069, [1988] 2 CMLR 704, at para 21; Case 204/88 *Ministère Public v Paris* [1989] ECR 4361, [1991] 1 CMLR 841, 848 (opinion of Tesauro AG).

are no less important[1]. Food and agricultural policies are central to many of those questions. Indeed, the Uruguay Round of multilateral trade discussions failed in 1990 largely because of disputes arising from the Community's production and export subsidies for agricultural products[2]. The Community's food regulatory policies do not fit tidily within these broader questions, but neither can they be isolated from them.

2.3   A regulatory switch in time

Prior to 1985, the Community undertook the harmonisation of food regulatory policies using a retail approach[3]. The measures which resulted from the approach have generally been termed "vertical". Under the retail approach, the Community prepared detailed compositional standards for individual foods or product categories, in which the most specific requirements were included[4]. The standards were so detailed and comprehensive that many became known, rather derisively, as "recipe laws". They provided elaborate definitions, forbade products which do not satisfy the definitions to use designated trade descriptions, restricted permissible ingredients, imposed purity criteria, required labelling disclosures, and even limited the weights or sizes in which the foodstuffs could be sold[5]. Their purpose was to ensure quality and safety, but a concern for competitive implications was never far from the regulatory surface.

The goals which underlay the vertical directives are easily understandable. The Treaty of Rome demands the free circulation of Community products, and the

---

1.   For the fears of the United States and Japan, among others, that harmonisation might result in a protectionist "Fortress Europe", see, e.g., A. M. Williams, *The European Community* p105-106 (1991). Others see such fears as "silly". Denman, "European Community Trade Issues Affecting the Food Sector in the 1990s", in G. Gaull & R. Goldberg, eds., *New Technologies and the Future of Food and Nutrition* pp113, 115 (1991).

2.   For a brief summary of the dispute, see The Economist Intelligence Unit, European Trends, No. 1, 40-41 (1991). For one account of the Community's views prior to the failure of the discussions, see the opinion of the Economic and Social Committee, OJ C337 31.12.88 p54. Such controversies are not, however, new. See e.g., Snyder, "The American-German Pork Dispute, 1879-1891", 17 J. Modern Hist. 16 (1945).

3.   A summary of the retail approach is provided by the document which marked its rejection, *Completing the Internal Market : White Paper from the Commission to the European Council*, COM(85) 310 final (14 June 1985) ("*1985 White Paper*"), as well as by the complementary paper addressed specifically to foodstuffs. See *Completion of the Internal Market : Community Legislation on Foodstuffs*, COM(85) 603 final (1985) ("*1985 Foodstuffs White Paper*").

4.   Many were adopted pursuant to a harmonisation plan formulated in 1969, revised in 1973, and finally abandoned in 1985; *1985 Foodstuffs White Paper*, COM(85) 603, at p3.

5.   The adoption of recipe laws is not limited to the Community. The United States had adopted some 200 before 1906, and now perhaps one-half of the American food supply is subject to them. Hutt, "Regulating the Misbranding of Food", 43 Food Technology 288 (1989); Merrill & Collier, "Like Mother Used to Make : An Analysis of FDA Food Standards of Identity", 74 Col. L. Rev. 561 (1974). FDA generally abandoned the approach in the 1970's. Britain and other Member States also adopted numerous compositional standards. For Spanish standards for yoghurt, for example, see the Order of July 1, 1987, B.O.E. No. 19 p1069 (July 1987). For German rules for cheese, see Ordinance of 14 April 1986.

unhindered circulation of foodstuffs could hardly be tolerated, especially in Member States which had created sophisticated regulatory systems, without assurances of quality and healthfulness. Without harmonisation, food quality and safety might be reduced to the lowest standards of the most acquiescent Member State. Indeed, even harmonisation has not protected the Community against claims that its rules tend toward homogenisation at a low level of product quality[1]. At the same time, there were apprehensions that free circulation might result in the dumping of low-cost, low-quality products. Established firms and settled interests might be eroded, and the prevention of "unfair" competition was frequently described as a policy goal. Both human safety and fair competition were thought to demand detailed and specific regulatory standards. Perhaps, too, a taste for elegant codifications encouraged such an approach.

The retail approach to harmonisation proved thoroughly unsuccessful. It required lengthy studies and interminable negotiations, in which the policy differences between Member States were often substantial. Each nation sought to shield as many of its manufacturing practices as possible from Community limitations[2]. Every rule stimulated a lengthy array of exceptions. By the early 1980's the Commission found itself falling farther and farther behind its regulatory timetable. Only a relative handful of directives had been adopted, and harmonisation seemed a receding horizon[3]. There were frequent claims of "Eurosclerosis"[4]. By 1985, it had become apparent that the retail approach could not, within any plausible time period, result in real progress. Sixteen years after its initiation, three-fifths of the 1969 harmonisation programme had not been started[5].

Even before these problems became obvious, a new approach to harmonisation had been encouraged by a series of important decisions by the European Court of Justice. Interpreting the Treaty of Rome, the Court began giving substance to the Treaty's demand for the free circulation of Community products[6]. It held that, even where

---

1. See, e.g., von Heydebrand, "Free Movement of Foodstuffs, Consumer Protection and Food Standards in the European Community : Has the Court of Justice Got It Wrong?" 16 Eur. L. Rev. 391 (1991).
2. For the "suspicion" that the Council sometimes obtains the support of Member States for proposals by promising undue license in implementing them, see Chambers, "Consolidation of Food-law Text - A Democratic Essential?", 1/91 Eur. Food L. Rev. 46, 50-51 (1991).
3. 1985 Foodstuffs White Paper, COM(85) 603, at p3.
4. A.M. Williams, *The European Community* pp79-82 (1991).
5. By 1985, measures had been adopted in only 14 of the 50 foodstuffs sectors identified in the 1969 harmonisation programme. 1985 Foodstuffs White Paper, COM(85) 603, at p3.
6. The principle of the free circulation of goods is broadly established by Articles 30 through 36 of the Treaty of Rome. In particular, quantitative restrictions on imports from other Member States, as well as other measures "having equivalent effect" to such restrictions, are prohibited by Articles 30 and 34(1) of the Treaty. Exceptions are permitted by Article 36 for reasons of public morality; public policy; public security; the health or safety of humans, animals or plants; the protection of national artistic, historic and archaeological treasures; or the protection of industrial or commercial property. Article 36 adds that such measures may not constitute a basis for arbitrary discrimination or a disguised trade restriction. See generally P. Oliver, *Free Movement of Goods in the EEC* pp166-252 (2nd ed. 1988).

national laws had not yet been harmonised, one Member State could generally not prohibit the sale of goods lawfully traded in another Member State[1]. This includes products originating in non-member countries which have entered into "free circulation" within the Community[2]. The only permissible exceptions are those authorised by Article 36 of the Treaty. Article 36 permits the use of mandatory national requirements to prevent the free circulation of Community products only to protect such basic interests as public health, consumer protection, commercial fairness, and the environment. Even in those areas, Member States are given only a narrow area of freedom. They must adopt measures reasonably proportional to their objectives, and involving the least possible interference with intra-Community trade[3]. In the foodstuffs area, national discretion is reduced still further by the repeated conclusion of the European Court that labelling disclosures are a less restrictive alternative to compositional standards and other protective measures. If

---

1.   The leading case is Case 120/78 *Cassis de Dijon* [1979] ECR 649, [1979] 3 CMLR 494, where the Court held that "any national measure capable of hindering, directly or indirectly, actually or potentially, intra-Community trade" could constitute a barrier forbidden by the Treaty of Rome. The Commission thereafter issued a communication which interpreted the opinion and provided various guidelines; OJ C256 3.10.80 p2. Among other things, the Commission inferred that a Member State may not "in principle" prohibit a product from another Member State even if the two nations have different technical or quality requirements, provided that the product "suitably and satisfactorily" fulfils the "legitimate objectives" of the receiving nation; ibid., at pp2-3. The Commission undertook to monitor national rules covering the "composition, designation, presentation and packaging" of products, as well as national technical standards; ibid., at p3. For a more recent statement, see Commission Communication on the Free Movement of Foodstuffs within the Community, OJ C271 24.10.89 p3. Numerous other decisions also interpret Articles 30 through 36 of the Treaty. The European Court of Justice has regularly held that many regulatory and inspection devices may be invalid under Articles 30 and 34(1) if they prove "equivalent" to a quantitative restriction. See, e.g., Case 51/71 *International Fruit v Produktschap voor Groeten en Fruit* [1971] ECR 1107 (import licenses); Case 8/74 *Procureur du Roi v Dassonville* [1974] ECR 837 (certificates of origin); Case 53/76 *Procureur de la Republique v Bouhelier* [1977] ECR 197, 205 (licenses and standards certificates); Case 68/76 *ECCommission v France* [1977] ECR 515 (export declarations); Case 42/82 *ECCommission v France* [1983] ECR 1013 (inspections of accompanying documents re wine imports); Case 13/77*INNO v ATAB* [1977] ECR 2115 (price controls); Case 13/78*Eggers v Freie Hansestadt Bremen* [1978] ECR 1935 (quality standards); Case 46/76*Bauhuis v Netherlands* [1977] ECR 5 (health inspections); Case C-205/89 *EC Commission v Greece* (Transcript) 19 March 1991 (health certificates for butter). These devices are not invariably invalid, but the Court has made clear that they are capable of creating trade barriers and, when they do, they may be invalidated under Articles 30 and 34(1). The issues are matters of effect and application. See, e.g., *United Foods v Belgium* [1981] ECR 995, 1029. See generally P. Oliver, *Free Movement of Goods in the EEC* at pp108-165 (2nd ed. 1988). See also, e.g., A. Parry & J. Dinnage, *EEC Law* at pp167-188 (2nd ed. 1981); Evans, "Economic Policy and the Free Movement of Goods in EEC Law" (1983) 32 ICLQ 577.

2.   Case 41/76 *Donckerwolke v Procureur de la Republique* [1976] ECR 1921 [1977] 2 CMLR 535; Case 174/82 *Officier van Justitie v Sandoz BV* [1983] ECR 2445, [1984] 3 CMLR 43.

3.   See, e.g., Case 124/81 *EC Commission v United Kingdom* [1983] ECR 203, 235, [1983] 2 CMLR 1 (British regulations for UHT milk not protected by Article 36 where less restrictive measures are available). Similarly, a ban on the importation of unpasteurised milk and cream was held a violation of Article 30, and unprotected by Article 36, where less sweeping provisions for health protection might have been adopted; Case 261/85 *EC Commission v United Kingdom* [1988] 2 CMLR 11. See also Case 40/82 *EC Commission v United Kingdom* [1982] ECR 2793, (poultry). Proportionality is a principle derived from German law, and requires any burdens or obligations which may be created to be reasonably related to the needs and importance of the goals which are sought to be achieved. It bears resemblance to the English ideas of fairness and reasonableness. See Case 104/75*Officier van Justitie v De Peijper* [1976] ECR 613, [1976] 2 CMLR 271. The principle is applicable both to Community legislation and to national legislation insofar as it is measured against Community standards. For the doctrine's origins and implications, see T. Hartley, *The Foundations of European Community Law* pp145-147 (2nd ed. 1988). For a situation where it was applied to a Council regulation, see Case 114/76 *Bela-Muhle Josef Bergman v Grows-Farm* [1977] ECR 1211, [1979] 2 CMLR 83.

imported products do not satisfy national compositional standards, the Court has held that any local interests are adequately served by informational labelling[1].

One judgment may illustrate the impact of the Court's decisions[2]. German law prohibited sausages and other charcuterie containing various non-meat ingredients. The rules applied to both German and imported products, and were justified on grounds that they helped prevent health hazards and consumer deception[3]. It was also argued that the rules protected German producers against unfair competition from low-quality foreign products. The European Court held that the German rules violated Article 30 and were not saved by Article 36 of the Treaty of Rome. It found that the rules restricted the import of foreign products lawful in their countries of origin, and held that any concerns about deception or safety could be satisfied by less restrictive requirements, including labelling obligations. If Dutch or Danish sausage contains non-meat filler, for example, it is enough if consumers are informed of the differences through labelling.

The European Court's decisions both altered the goals of harmonisation and added a new urgency to their achievement[4]. On one side, the decisions appeared to nullify many national laws protective of local products[5]. As a result, it seemed less important to eliminate those rules through vertical harmonisation. At the same time, the potential influx of new products offered additional evidence that some harmonisation was essential. Poor quality products might flood the market, and low-cost foreign producers might be advantaged in their competition with local firms[6]. There were fears of "negative integration"[7]. This did not mean a failure to

---

1.   The Court's position has been restated by a Commission official : "The path of information rather than legal prescription in matters other than safety is the only way in which diversity and liberty can be preserved". Gray, "The Perspective to 1992", in H. Deelstra, et al., eds., *Food Policy Trends in Europe* p11 (1991).

2.   *Re German Sausages, EC Commission v Germany* [1989] 2 CMLR 733, decided by the European Court in 1989.

3.   Ibid., at pp747-750.

4.   It has been observed that one implication of *Cassis de Dijon* was that there was "less need for harmonisation, and more need for vigorous enforcement of liberalisation".   Dashwood, "Hastening Slowly : The Community's Path toward Harmonisation", in H. Wallace, W. Wallace & C. Webb, eds., *Policy-making in the European Community* pp177, 197 (2nd ed. 1983).   With hindsight, it might instead be said that the Court's decisions changed the purposes and forms of harmonisation.

5.   It has been suggested that *Cassis* was an effort to give a "consumer perspective" to free circulation by insisting upon the principle of free choice, an approach which it is claimed that the Commission has not always followed. See European Consumer Law Group, "Consumer Protection in the EEC After Ratification of the Single Act," 10 J. Consumer Policy pp319, 321-322 (1987).

6.   The principal fears about the competitive advantages of imported products have usually been described in terms of reduced quality, but they have sometimes also related to lower costs of production. Article 30 of the Treaty may, however, also permit imported products to receive other advantages. When Dutch rules for fixing the prices of bread were, perhaps unexpectedly, found in some cases to produce price advantages for imports, this was held not to violate Article 30. Article 30 forbids discrimination against imports, but does not necessarily demand identical treatment for domestic and imported products; Case 80/85 *Nederlandse Bakkerij Stichting v EDAH BV* [1986] ECR 3359, [1988] 2 CMLR 113; Case C-210/89 *Re Low-Fat*

integrate, but instead integration which resulted in adverse consequences for product quality. The pressures for harmonisation were increased by the rights of all Community citizens to establish and conduct foodstuff businesses throughout the Community[1]. The European Court was making a reality of free circulation, and free circulation was thought intolerable without effective harmonisation. It was, however, a different form and degree of harmonisation than the Community had previously sought.

The Commission's reappraisal of the 1969 harmonisation programme was issued in 1985[2]. It re-evaluated harmonisation with respect to all internal market issues, including foodstuffs, but was supplemented by an ancillary document addressed specifically to food regulation[3]. The Commission acknowledged the need for a new approach to the harmonisation of national laws. It conceded that its previous efforts had sometimes been "over-regulatory", slow and inflexible[4]. It recognised that fixed and detailed regulatory requirements can stifle innovation[5]. The Commission sought methods more flexible than total harmonisation, and yet more uniform than a mutual recognition of dissimilar national standards. With respect to foodstuffs, the Commission proposed to attack the issues of harmonisation at a different level and on a more selective basis. Its new approach sought to reorganise the Community's regulation of food products on a wholesale basis, emphasising those issues which it regarded as urgent[6]. Rather than detailed vertical harmonisation through recipe laws, the Community would establish the "essential requirements" for the free circulation of goods[7].

The Commission contemplated a series of framework directives to establish basic standards and guide Member States in creating more detailed rules and procedures[8]. The Community would set the proper direction of regulatory policy and ensure that Member States, in following that direction, adhered to reasonable rules. The

---

Cheese : EC Commission v Italy [1992] 2 CMLR 1. But see Case 53/80 *Officier van Justitie v Koninklijke Kaasfabriek Eyssen* [1981] ECR 429, [1982] 2 CMLR 20.

7.   See, e.g., Opinion of the Economic and Social Committee on Consumer Protection and Completion of the Internal Market, OJ C339 31.12.91 p16.

1.   Council Directive (EEC) 68/365, OJ L260 22.10.68 p9; Council Directive (EEC) 68/366, OJ L260 22.10.68 p12. Community citizenship does not as such yet exist, but would be created by Article G of the Maastricht Treaty on European Union. In the interim, citizens of Member States enjoy rights of free travel and establishment.

2.   1985 White Paper, COM(85) p310.

3.   1985 Foodstuffs White Paper, COM(85) p603.

4.   1985 White Paper, COM(85) 310, at para 64.

5.   A desire to accommodate innovation and a recognition that compositional standards quickly become outdated were among the reasons for Britain's decision to move away from such standards. Food Advisory Committee Report on Old Compositional Orders 1 (FDAC/REP/5) (1989). In fact, however, those same standards had been recommended for elimination as early as 1970; ibid., at p2. Most were not actually abolished until July 1991. Food (Miscellaneous Revocations) Regulations, SI 1991/1231.

6.   1985 White Paper, COM(85) 310, at paras 65-72.

7.   Ibid., at para 68.

8.   As described below, the initial descriptions appeared to promise greater scope for national discretion than in fact has been given.

Commission also expected to rely more heavily on technical standardisation groups such as the Comite Européen de la Normalisation. Its goal was to replace national rules with European standards in "all areas"[1]. National rules, restricted by the framework directives and European standards, would be accepted throughout the Community on the basis of mutual recognition. In essence, the Commission sought to mix the flexibility of mutual recognition with the uniformity of harmonisation[2]. It hoped to preserve the virtues of diversity by avoiding a "straitjacket" of vertical rules[3]. Within these broad goals, the Commission sought to separate the "essential from the optional" by establishing two principal priorities[4]. First, the Community would focus upon measures designed to protect human life and health. These included measures regarding food additives, materials and articles in contact with foods, contaminants, dietary foodstuffs, and manufacturing and treatment processes[5]. Second, the Community would give priority to rules designed to ensure fair trading and the protection of consumers. These included measures regarding the labelling, presentation and advertising of foodstuffs, and for official checks and inspections[6].

An important predicate to the wholesale approach was the adoption of changes to the Treaty of Rome. Without them, unanimity would still have been required for approval of the Commission's measures. The unending rounds of national negotiations would have continued, and it would have been difficult to give expedited treatment even to subsidiary matters. Those changes were provided by the agreement of the Member States in December 1985 to the Single European Act[7]. The Act's implications are still disputed, and its provisions may be variously interpreted[8]. Among its changes was the creation of an exception to the previous

---

1.   Ibid., at paras 68-69.
2.   The Council was also urged to "off-load technical matters" by delegating more of its responsibilities to the Commission. Ibid., at para. 70. Article 155 of the Treaty was said to make "express provision" for this possibility; ibid. Article 155 defines the duties of the Commission to ensure the proper functioning of the common market, including a duty "to exercise the powers conferred on it by the Council for the implementation of the rules laid down by the latter". A corresponding power of delegation was not, however, expressly given to the Council until Article 145 of the Treaty was subsequently amended by Article 10 of the Single European Act.
3.   Gray, "The Perspective to 1992", in H. Deelstra, et al., eds., *Food Policy Trends in Europe* p11, 13 (1991).
4.   Gray, "Food Law and the Internal Market : Taking Stock", *Food Policy* pp111, 112 (April 1990).
5.   The priorities have sometimes been rather differently described. The Commission has said that the 1985 strategy was to achieve sufficient harmonisation to protect public health, provide consumers with clear labelling and protection in "matters other than health", ensure fair trading, and provide for the necessary public controls; EC. Commission, *A New Community Standards Policy* p61 (1990). See also Commission Communication on the Free Movement of Foodstuffs within the Community, OJ C271 24.10.89 p3; EC Commission, *Background Report on European Community Food Legislation* pp1-2 (6 Feb 1991).
6.   1985 Foodstuffs White Paper, COM(85) 603, at pp6-11.
7.   The Single European Act was agreed to in December 1985, executed in February 1986, and came into force in July 1987. See OJ L169 29.6.87p1.
8.   See, e.g., Pescatore, "Some Critical Remarks on the 'Single European Act'", (1987) 24 CMLRev. 9 (suggesting that the Act's adoption might actually set back the integration of the Community); D. Unwin, *The Community of Europe : A History of European Integration Since 1945* p235 (1991) (full implications of the SEA are still uncertain).

rule that the Council could adopt internal market legislation only with the Member States' unanimous approval. The Act added a new Article 100a to the Treaty, which generally permits a qualified majority of the Council to approve harmonisation directives "which have as their object the establishment and functioning of the internal market"[1]. Under Article 148 of the Treaty, a qualified majority exists if 54 of the Council's 76 votes (assigned on a weighted basis to Member States roughly according to population) favour a proposed measure[2]. As a practical matter, Article 148 permits the Commission to obtain approval of proposed internal market directives under Article 100a if they are supported by the Community's five largest members, plus nearly any two of the others[3]. Conversely, measures may be blocked by the smaller states acting unanimously, or by any two of the larger states plus nearly any of the smaller states[4]. These rules do not apply to fiscal measures, to measures relating to the free movement of persons, or to the rights of employed persons. Moreover, they must be exercised by the Council in "cooperation" with the Parliament and after consultation with the Economic and Social Committee[5].

The Single European Act was a critical step in permitting more rapid progress toward an integrated marketplace[6]. It offered two important new opportunities. First, it eliminated the need to seek unanimity among the Member States for the approval of most internal market legislation. Consensus is still essential, but a recalcitrant Member State is now less able to dictate the price of a measure's approval. Second, the Act provided a more secure basis for the delegation by the Council of subsidiary and technical matters to the Commission, the Standing

---

1. Before the Act, the governing provision for legislation which may "directly affect the establishment or functioning of the common market" was Article 100 of the Treaty, which requires the unanimous approval of the Member States. Article 100 still exists, but its relationship with Article 100a is best described as controversial. Both articles would be partly rewritten by the Maastricht Treaty. As it now stands, Article 100 encompasses measures to harmonise national rules which "directly affect" the market, leaving to Article 100a measures which "have as their object" the establishment and functioning of the market. Other provisions of the Treaty permit "qualified" or even simple majorities to decide some Community matters. See, e.g., Article 148(1) of the Treaty. Unanimity is, however, still required under Articles 51, 76, 93(2), 99, 100, 121, 165, 235, 237 and 238 of the Treaty. For the voting requirements, see T. Hartley, *The Foundations of European Community Law* p16 (2nd ed. 1988).
2. Under Article 148(2), the Member States have the following votes : Germany, France, Italy, and the United Kingdom have 10 votes each; Spain has 8; Belgium, Greece, Netherlands and Portugal have five each; Denmark and Ireland have three each; and Luxembourg has two votes.
3. If France, Germany, Italy, Spain and the United Kingdom all agree, they have a total of 48 votes. Any combination of two others, except either Denmark or Ireland plus Luxembourg, provides at least 54 votes.
4. The five largest states have a total of only 50 votes, which is insufficient to approve a measure. Two of the largest states plus any one of the smaller states except Luxembourg gives sufficient votes to block a qualified majority.
5. Some room is left by Article 100a(4) for national derogations pursuant to Article 36 of the Treaty. The latter provides a "limited right to opt out". T. Hartley, *The Foundations of European Community Law* 104 n.13 (2nd ed. 1988). A similar right is provided under Article 100b with respect to the inventory and elimination of non-harmonised national laws.
6. Deboyser, "Le marché unique des produits alimentaires", 1-1991 Revue du marché unique européen 63, 65 (1991).

Committee for Foodstuffs, and other specialised committees of national representatives[1]. This encouraged a wider use of simplified committee procedures to approve harmonisation legislation. The additional speed and greater simplicity of the new approach is, however, accompanied by significant costs. One result has been to strengthen the role of the Commission at the expense of the Member States. This is only partly balanced by the Parliament's enhanced powers, and has diminished the rigour with which the Community's proposed legislation is reviewed. Some argue that this has reduced the attention given to consumer interests[2]. It has certainly done nothing to increase the public accountability of the Community's policymakers.

These developments have not eliminated all national protectionist policies[3]. Disputes still arise, and more will undoubtedly occur after 1992[4]. Nonetheless, there is now a framework of principles favourable to free circulation and hostile to protectionism. There are also substantial impediments to unharmonised new national rules and standards[5]. Taken together, these steps have already produced important changes in the national markets for foodstuffs. Indeed, it has been argued that the changes have already gone too far, and that the Member States are unduly constrained in their efforts to ensure product quality[6]. Nonetheless, the changes will accelerate as each new directive increases the Community's regulatory momentum. Fewer questions are left to national discretion, and those questions are of diminishing significance. The central issues of food regulation are now largely entrusted to the Community. In its struggle toward harmonisation, the Community may sometimes take a step backward, but each such step is usually now accompanied by at least two steps forward.

---

1. As described above, one of the Commission's recommendations in 1985 was greater use of delegations from the Council regarding subsidiary matters. Until the SEA, however, there was some room for question as to the extent of the Council's delegational authority. Article 10 of the SEA amended Article 145 of the Treaty to provide more clearly for delegations.

2. See, e.g., S. Fallows, *Food Legislative System of the UK* pp94-95 (1988) (citing UK governmental comments and those of the Consumers in the European Community Group). The issues are important because, as Fallows rightly concludes, the Community "is, perhaps, the major factor in shaping current food legislation" in the UK ibid., at p95. The same assessment is applicable throughout the Community.

3. Some Member States persist in "hopeless" efforts to defend protectionist national rules. See The Economist Intelligence Unit, European Trends, No. 1, 37 (1991). Describing a decision of the European Court relating to an Italian rule for the minimum fat content of cheese, a commentator has suggested a rule holding national civil servants personally responsible for court costs; ibid., It seems implausible that the European Court would prove so adventurous, but the Maastricht Treaty proposes to authorise monetary penalties against Member States.

4. Additional difficulties arise from the transposition of directives into national law. Some nations are generally prompt and faithful in their adoption of the directives. Others are sometimes less so, and their failures present a significant issue in the foodstuffs area. Seventh Annual Report to the Council Regarding the Application of Community Law, COM(90) 288 final, at p16 (the delays in the foodstuff sector "are a cause for concern").   Similar apprehensions were expressed late in 1991. Eighth Annual Report to the European Parliament on Commission Monitoring of the Application of Community Law, OJ C338 31.12.91 p1 at pp14 - 15. More recently, the Commission has described the progress since June 1991 as "laggardly". Background Report on Completion of the Internal Market 1 (20 Feb 1992).

5. Below at para 2.4.

6. von Heydebrand, "Free Movement of Foodstuffs, Consumer Protection and Food Standards in the European Community : Has the Court of Justice Got It Wrong?", 16 Eur. L. Rev. 391 (1991).

2.4 The diverse patterns of regulatory policy

Changes in regulatory policy are rarely either wholly unprecedented or entirely uniform. The Community's 1985 change in regulatory direction is no exception. Examples of wholesale regulation occurred prior to 1985,[1] and examples of retail regulation have continued to occur since 1985[2]. Regulatory issues are too varied to permit any single method of response. The result is a complex and sometimes inconsistent pattern of approaches. The complexity is increased by the uneasy marriage between the Community's food and agricultural policies. Entrusted to different elements of the Commission, with distinct goals and separate constituencies, the two policies sometimes overlap and sometimes collide[3]. Coordination seems an incidental virtue. Within this evolving pattern, three forms of approach have become predominant[4]. The first was described above as regulation on a retail basis, but is more commonly termed vertical regulation. Vertical directives focus on particular products or categories, and bypass similar issues which may arise in connection with other product categories. There may, for example, be substantial areas of overlap between product categories regarding such matters as labelling, packaging and sizes, and methods of analysis. These common

1. The best example is the basic labelling directive, adopted in 1978. Below at Chapter 3, para 3.3.
2. One example, although horizontal in form, is the spirit drinks directive adopted in 1989, which effectively consists of numerous recipe laws for different spirit drinks. Below at Chapter 7, para 7.11.2. Similar rules have more recently been adopted for aromatised wines and other such beverages. Below at Chapter 7, para 7.11.1.. There are also rules and proposed rules for vertical hygiene requirements. Below at Chapter 8, para 8.6.1.
3. Food and agricultural policies are entrusted to different authorities in many countries, and the division commonly produces tensions and inconsistencies. For the complex pattern in the United States, for example, see P. Hutt & R. Merrill, *Food and Drug Law, Cases and Materials* p34 (2nd ed. 1991). Alcoholic beverages also have their own special regulatory authorities in the United States; ibid., at pp34-35. For the resulting disputes, see, e.g., Latimer, "Whither the FTC on Food Advertising?", 46 Food D.C.L.J. 503 (1991).
4. A fourth regulatory tool should also be noted, although it focuses upon production and marketing structures for basic agricultural products. Pursuant to Title II of the Treaty, the Council has adopted regulations establishing "common organisations" for the Community markets in various basic food sources. See, e.g., Council Regulation (EEC) 804/68, OJ L148 28.6.68 p13 (milk and milk products); Council Regulation (EEC) 120/67, OJ 2269 p67 (June 19, 1967) (cereals); Council Regulation (EEC) 1035/72, OJ L118 20.5.72 p1 (fruit and vegetables); Council Regulation (EEC) 2727/75, OJ L281 29.10.75 p1 (cereals); Council Regulation (EEC) 2759/75, OJ L282 29.10.75 p1 (pork); Council Regulation (EEC) 2777/75, OJ L282 29.10.75 p77 (poultry meat). Most have been frequently amended. The Council has, for example, also issued regulations setting marketing standards for eggs, including rules for the grading, marking, packing, distribution and presentation of fresh eggs. See, e.g., Council Regulation (EEC) 2772/75, OJ L282 1.11.75 p56. For their interpretation, see, e.g., Case 130/85 *Wulro BV v Tuchtgerecht Van de Stichting Scharreteieren Controle* [1986] ECR 2035, [1988] 1 CMLR 496. For labelling claims that eggs are "newly laid", see Case C-230/90 *Gutshof-Ei v Stadt Buhl* (Transcript) 25 February 1991; 1 World Food Reg. Rev. 3 (April 1992). These and similar regulations have substantial regulatory implications. For example, Council Regulation (EEC) 804/68 (relating to milk and milk products) provides for "target prices" (Article 3), "threshold prices" (Article 4), "intervention prices" for butter, skimmed milk powder and certain cheeses (Article 5), import licenses (Article 13), customs duties for products entering the Community (Article 14), limitations upon national aids (Articles 24-26), and control stamps (Article 27). See also Council Regulation (EEC) 3904/87, OJ L370 30.12.87 p1; Council Regulation (EEC) 985/68, OJ L169 18.7.68 p1; and Council Regulation (EEC) 3466/87, OJ L329 20.11.87 p8; all of which amend Council Regulation 804/68, above. Similar rules exist for many other products.

issues invite a horizontal, if not a sectorial, approach. Nonetheless, the vertical directives make no effort to look beyond the specific problems presented by the products with which they are concerned. They characteristically emphasise the importance of ensuring minimum product quality, rather than the virtues of an open marketplace and free circulation.

Many examples of the retail approach remain in the Community's legislation. They are often in the form of "recipe laws", which provide detailed compositional and other standards for specific product categories. For example, existing vertical directives relate to mineral water[1], cocoa and chocolate[2], coffee and chicory extracts[3], and fruit juices[4]. Others involve honey[5], certain sugars[6], dehydrated milk[7], and jams and jellies[8]. All of these directives were adopted in or before 1980. All have subsequently been amended, and some may eventually be replaced[9]. They represent an approach used less frequently since 1985, but the Commission has not foreclosed a return to vertical rulemaking once the 1985 harmonisation programme has been completed. Indeed, examples continue to appear. Directorate-general VI, the element of the Commission responsible for agriculture, regularly uses vertical measures to address health and safety matters arising from such products as milk and meat[10]. Other vertical measures have been adopted for spirit drinks and proposed for yellow fat products[11]. More generally, the Council has adopted regulations for product certifications which would demand compliance with compositional and other standards[12]. One result may be a general resumption of vertical rulemaking. Outside the Commission, some commentators continue to urge the advantages of vertical rules in ensuring product quality[13].

The second approach was described above as regulation on a wholesale basis. Most of these directives have been adopted since 1985, but a general labelling directive for foodstuffs was adopted as early as 1978[14]. Wholesale directives address regulatory issues horizontally. They cut across product categories to establish requirements applicable to a broad range of dissimilar products. Their principal

---

1   Council Directive (EEC) 80/777, OJ L299 30.8.80 p1.
2.   Council Directive (EEC) 73/241, OJ L228 16.8.73 p23.
3.   Council Directive (EEC) 77/436, OJ L172 12.7.77p20.
4.   Council Directive (EEC) 75/206, OJ L311 1.12.75 p40.
5.   Council Directive (EEC) 74/409, OJ L221 12.8.74 p10.
6.   Council Directive (EEC) 73/437, OJ L356 27.12.73 p7.
7.   Council Directive (EEC) 76/18, OJ L24 30.1.76 p49.
8.   Council Directive (EEC) 79/693, OJ L205 13.8.79 p5.
9.   For a statement of the Commission's intentions regarding vertical directives, see its Background Report on Community Food Legislation 4 (6 Feb 1991).
10.   Below at Chapter 7, para 7.12.
11.   Below at Chapter 7, paras 7.11, 7.13.
12.   Below at Chapter 3, para 3.8.
13.   See, e.g., von Heydebrand, "Free Movement of Foodstuffs, Consumer Protection and Food Standards in the European Community : Has the Court of Justice Got It Wrong?", 16 Eur. L. Rev. 391 (1991).
14.   Below at Chapter 3, para 3.3.

goal is to open the Community's marketplaces by establishing minimum standards for the free circulation of goods. Examples include nutritional labelling[1], other labelling and advertising claims[2], additives[3], lot markings[4], and food inspections[5]. The forthcoming hygiene directive will provide another example[6]. The product liability directive, as well as the new general safety directive, take the horizontal approach still further. They encompass a broad range of consumer goods in addition to foodstuffs[7].

The third approach is positioned between the first two. It addresses groupings of similar product categories, and creates regulatory requirements using a sectorial approach. Some sectorial measures are nearly horizontal in their scope and goals, while others provide a framework for vertical rulemaking. The directive regarding quick-frozen foods, for example, addresses the processing of foodstuffs by rapid freezing, but does not resolve all the issues which may arise from the categories of foods which may be frozen. The directive thus establishes standards for the freezing and maintenance of frozen meats, but does not address other issues which involve meats as a general foodstuff. Its goals are more nearly horizontal than vertical. The framework directive for foods intended for particular nutritional uses (sometimes known as "parnuts" products) represents another form of the sectorial approach[8]. Like the framework directive for additives[9], it prescribes basic rules for all "parnuts" products, but leaves the specific requirements applicable to individual product categories for resolution in ancillary measures[10]. The ultimate result is a structured collection of vertical measures.

The adoption of one of these approaches in a particular regulatory area does not foreclose subsequent or even concurrent use of the others[11]. They are tools and not fences. Indeed, the Community increasingly employs combinations of approaches, implemented through a variety of legislative methods, to accelerate the adoption of rules for food products. One such combination involves multiple layers of legislative measures. With respect to additives and food contact materials, for example, the Community has adopted broad framework directives which establish

---

1.   Below at Chapter 3, para 3.4.
2.   Below at Chapter 3, para 3.5.
3.   Below at Chapter 5, para 5.1.
4.   Below at Chapter 3, para 3.6.
5.   Below at Chapter 8, para 8.6.
6.   Below at Chapter 8, para 8.6.1.
7.   Below at Chapter 8, para 8.7.
8.   Below at Chapter 4, para 4.5.
9.   Below at Chapter 5, para 5.1.
10.   Below at Chapter 4, para 4.5. The Commission sometimes uses the term "daughter" directives to refer to ancillary measures intended to supplement "framework" directives. They might also be described as vertical directives or regulations designed to add specificity to horizontal directives.
11.   Labelling is an example. There is a general labelling directive which was adopted in 1978 and supplemented in 1989, but there are also other labelling requirements in separate directives for specific product categories. Below at Chapter 7.

basic horizontal or sectorial requirements. Those measures will be supplemented by directives or regulations addressed to one or more categories of products[1]. The former are horizontal, while the latter may be sectorial or vertical. The terminology matters little. It merely suggests broad differences in goals and methods. The important point is to find practical formulae for the resolution of practical issues.

One device particularly characteristic of the Community's rulemaking is the "positive" list. Such lists identify all of the substances which may be used for a particular function. Any substance omitted from the list may not be used for that function. In contrast, "negative" lists identify the substances forbidden for a particular purpose, and permit the use of all others for that purpose. The Community has employed both devices, but has increasingly preferred positive lists. It now uses them for additives, some processing aids, and some materials that come in contact with foodstuffs[2]. A positive list of flavourings has been proposed[3]. Positive lists are not peculiar to the Community; they have come into increasing use in many countries since the late nineteenth century[4]. They offer precision and guarantees of product safety, but they are also inflexible and may inhibit innovation. In the Community, additions to positive lists will prove time-consuming and difficult if they must first be approved by the Community and thereafter transposed into twelve national systems. Unless the Community devises faster methods of revision, positive lists may hamper both product development and international competition.

The Community has had greater success in accelerating other measures. Varied methods have been used. For example, framework directives are promulgated by the Council after proposals from the Commission and in cooperation with the Parliament. Ancillary matters may, however, be adopted through a simplified committee procedure[5]. The latter places the Standing Committee for Foodstuffs into

---

1. The distinctions between "directives" and "regulations" have grown increasingly inexact. Under Article 189 of the Treaty, the latter are directly applicable throughout the Community, while the former are instructions to Member States to alter their national laws. Directives frequently include (or are assumed to permit) room for national discretion, and Member States sometimes exercise greater discretion than they may actually have been afforded. The European Court has edged toward partial direct effect for directives, and the distinction between directives and regulations is thus becoming less clear. See T. Hartley, *Foundations of European Community Law* pp195-211 (2nd ed. 1988). Policy issues may also be addressed by "decisions", "resolutions" and "recommendations". For a discussion, see, e.g., Chambers, "Consolidation of Food-law Text - A Democratic Essential?", 1/91 Eur. Food L. Rev. 46 (1991).
2. In the Community's food policies, negative lists have chiefly been used in connection with materials and articles which may come into contact with foodstuffs. Below at Chapter 4, para 4.1.
3. Below at Chapter 5, para 5.2.
4. For their uses and histories, see, e.g., Sainte Blanquat & Pascal, "Les additifs", in R. Derache, ed., *Toxocologie et Sécurité des Aliments* pp247, 248 (1986); D. Marmion, *Handbook of US Colorants for Foods, Drugs, and Cosmetics* pp5-11 (3rd ed. 1991).
5. The adoption of a committee, or "simplified", procedure was one of the suggestions of the *1985 Foodstuffs White Paper*, COM(85) 603.

the role ordinarily played by the Council. Under several directives, the role of the Standing Committee may be played by one of the other specialised committees of national representatives. The Standing Committee or its surrogate has authority to approve the Commission's proposals, but if it proves hesitant the Commission may appeal to the Council. The Commission has an ultimate right to promulgate the rules as its own unless the Council is actively opposed. In other words, the Commission may act unless the Standing Committee or Council elect to prevent its action. In effect, the process is a form of legislative delegation, subject to coordinational obligations and a right of veto. The Council has formalised these procedures through a decision regarding decision-making[1]. Various delays are built into the arrangement, but they are brief by Community standards and the goal is to streamline the approval process for internal market measures.

Another important change is the imposition of limitations upon the regulatory discretion of the Member States. In particular, the Community has adopted a "new approach" to national technical standards and specifications. In 1983, the Council adopted a directive requiring Member States and their institutions involved in standardisation to give notice to the Commission of draft standards, revised standards, and technical regulations[2]. Quarterly reports must be filed, and a standing committee was created to review the proposals[3]. In 1988, the directive's requirements were made expressly applicable to standards relating to products intended for human consumption[4]. In 1989, a similar mechanism was created to monitor national proposals for new food labelling requirements[5]. All three measures have had a substantial impact upon national policymaking. Member States gave notice to the Commission of 319 standardisation proposals in 1989, another 386 in 1990, and yet another 213 in the first five months of 1991[6]. Some 42 per cent of the proposals were disapproved in 1990, and the effectiveness of nearly another four per cent was postponed by the Commission for one year to permit further consideration. The "new approach" to national standards has on several occasions been applied to proposed national rules for foodstuffs. There are, however, recurrent complaints that the Commission's rules do not ensure an adequate role for consumers in the evaluation of standards[7].

---

1. Council Decision (EEC) 87/373, OJ L197 18.7.87 p33. The decision draws subtle distinctions among several variations in the decision-making processes. Unfortunately, subsequent measures often do not indicate which variation they adopt.
2. Council Directive (EEC) 83/189, OJ L109 26.4.83 p8.
3. Articles 2(1), 5.
4. Council Directive (EEC) 88/182, OJ L81 26.3.88 p75 at Article 1(2), amending Article 1(1) of Directive 83/189, above. For a list of institutions involved in standardisation, see Commission Decision (EEC) 90/230, OJ L128 18.5.90 p15.
5. Below at Chapter 3, para 3.3.
6. Sixth Report of the Commission to the Council and the European Parliament concerning the Implementation of the White Paper on the Completion of the Internal Market, COM(91) 237 final (19 June 1991) at 15. Most of the notifications did not relate to food issues.
7. See, e.g., Organisation for Economic Cooperation and Development, *Consumers, Product Safety Standards and International Trade* p43 (1991).

The Community's use of diverse approaches to regulatory issues is a welcome departure from its pattern prior to 1985. The variability of its methods is evidence of both greater flexibility and a more realistic appreciation of the complexities of food regulation. The real concern should be whether the Community's rules are not still needlessly rigid. Much of the problem is institutional. The fact that the Community makes policy largely through directives alters the nature of its rules. Directives must first be adopted by consensus, next transposed into twelve national systems, and thereafter administered by national or local authorities. Proposals must be reviewed, often repeatedly, by Community institutions and the Member States. The arrangement invites an uneasy mixture of inflexibility and ambiguity. The Community's search for consensus promotes ambiguity, and its lack of direct enforcement authority encourages inflexibility. The ambiguities are multiplied by twelve national transposition processes. These problems are inherent in the Community's institutional structure, which combines confederalism and partial centralisation[1]. The problems are likely to be solved only by political changes reaching far beyond the regulation of foodstuffs. Until those occur, the form and sometimes the substance of the Community's food policies will be imprisoned by institutional constraints.

2.5   The direction of the Community's food policies

The Community has sought to harmonise national food regulations by issuing or proposing measures in more than thirty areas. Some have been the subject of regulation nearly since the Community's creation. Others have emerged or received new prominence since 1985. Since the 1985 White Paper, the Commission has given emphasis to five principal areas : food additives; materials and articles intended to come into contact with food; foods for particular nutritional uses; the labelling, presentation and advertising of foods for sale to the ultimate consumer; and official inspection and control mechanisms[2]. It has also adopted or proposed rules regarding such disparate issues as pesticide residues, irradiated foods, quick-frozen foods, and "novel" food ingredients and processes.

The Community's overall progress is uneven at best[3]. In several areas, substantial advances have been made. General foodstuffs labelling is the best example,

---

1.   For the ambiguities and political contradictions of the Community's structure, see, e.g., A. M. Williams, *The European Community* p147-152 (1991).

2.   For these priorities, see the Commission's Background Report on European Community Food Legislation (6 Feb 1991). For the priorities established in 1985, see above at para 2.3.

3.   This was, for example, also the conclusion of the United States International Trade Commission. *The Effects of Greater Economic Integration within the European Community on the United States* (1989). In contrast, a Commission official has seen "extraordinary" progress since 1985, and certainly the pace has accelerated. Gray, "Food law and the Internal Market : Taking Stock", Food Policy 111, 114 (April 1990).

although significant labelling issues must still be addressed[1]. In other areas, the Commission was forced to make multiple efforts before it could find acceptable requirements. Rules for infant formulae are an example[2]. In still others, the Community has adopted broad framework rules, but left the most troublesome issues for future resolution. Pesticide residues, contact materials, and additives are all examples[3]. In some instances, the Commission has devoted several years to an unsuccessful search for a formula for harmonisation. This was until recently true of infant formulae, and remains true for irradiated foods[4]. In other instances, the Community is only beginning serious efforts to resolve the relevant issues. Unfortunately, the areas of hygiene, official controls and inspections are all examples[5]. In still others, the Commission has not yet offered formal proposals. Nutritional supplements and most chilled foods are examples[6]. Nor has the Commission yet undertaken to designate the boundaries of food regulation. It has not, for example, sought in any systematic fashion to define "foods" or "foodstuffs", or to distinguish them from medicines[7].

In all these areas, there are still formidable barriers to regulatory action. The Commission must often reconcile diverse attitudes within the Commission itself, as well as among its industry and consumer advisors. Proposed rules for health and other advertising claims, for example, are reportedly under reconsideration because they have been reassigned from DG III to the Consumer Policy Service[8]. Once the Commission has successfully formulated a proposal, it must still undergo scrutiny by the Economic and Social Committee, the European Parliament, and ultimately by the Member States. Each stage may involve negotiation, and each may result in compromise. Delays are common, if not inevitable. For example, rules for health

---

1. Quantitative ingredient disclosures (sometimes known as "QUIDs") are an important example. Health claims are another. For these and other unresolved labelling issues, see below at Chapter 3, para 3.3. The Commission itself has acknowledged that "certain details" warrant supplementation or revision. Written Question 1434/91, OJ C55 2.3.92 p24.
2. The Commission proposed a directive regarding infant formulae in 1985, modified it in 1986, abandoned it, and has now at last adopted applicable rules. Some significant issues must, however, still be resolved. Below at Chapter 4, para 4.6.
3. With respect to additives, revised rules are in progress. Below at Chapter 5, para 5.1. With respect to contact materials, new rules for many plastics and films have been adopted. Below at Chapter 6, paras 6.2, 6.3.
4. Despite lengthy efforts, the Community has not yet agreed upon a proposal regarding the authorisation and control of irradiated foods. Below at Chapter 4, para 4.3.
5. The Community has adopted a framework directive regarding official controls, but it is still at an early stage in its efforts to achieve genuine harmonisation. Below at Chapter 8, para 8.6.
6. Nutritional supplements are, however, the subject of preparatory work by the Commission. Below at Chapter 3, para 3.4. For chilled foods, see below at Chapter 4, para 4.1.
7. The efforts to distinguish foods from medicines have been recurrent sources of controversy in, for example, the United States. See, e.g., *Nutrilab, Inc. v Schweiker*, 713 F.2d 335 (7th Cir. 1983); *American Health Prods. Co. v Hayes*, 744 F.2d 912 (2nd Cir. 1984). The issue is notable for its relative invisibility in Community measures. The distinctions between "foods" and other products are chiefly left to national rules, which may produce disparate results; Case C-369/88 *Compare Delattre* OJ C108 23.4.91 p2. For one example of the problems created by the issue, see the report of a working group established by Britain's Department of Health, Dietary Supplements and Health Foods (1991). Many more efforts have, however, been made to distinguish "medicines". See, e.g., P. Bogaert, *EC Pharmaceutical Law* (1992). See also C-112/89 *The Upjohn Co v Farzoo Inc* (Transcript) 16 April 1991.
8. Below at Chapter 3, para 3.5.2.

claims have been under consideration sice 1981, and a formal proposal regarding irradiated foods has existed since 1988. Neither has yet been adopted[1]. A sweeteners directive is unlikely to be adopted before 1993[2]. Few rulemaking processes anywhere in the world are as complex, or as susceptible to impasse and delay. Regulation at wholesale is simpler than regulation at retail, but it remains a difficult and often laborious process. Consensus is more attainable than unanimity, but it is still an elusive predicate to action.

The difficulties of the Community's decision-making process are one explanation for the absence of articulated regulatory goals. Despite the Commission's taste for codifications, it has shown little interest in formulating principles for the guidance of those codifications. Harmonisation has remained its principal touchstone[3]. Like the 1992 programme itself, each new measure is a political improvisation[4]. There are increasing references to consumer interests and environmental protection, but little effort has been made to integrate those sentiments into a genuine regulatory programme[5]. It is hardly surprising that the European Parliament has found the Commission's food measures to be incoherent and inconsistent[6]. The Community's failure to define regulatory values and goals for its future rulemaking is a major omission from its food policies.

---

1.   Below at Chapter 4, para 4.3.
2.   Below at Chapter 5, para 5.3.
3.   The nearest approach to the articulation of such values and goals was the *1985 Foodstuffs White Paper*, but it focused principally upon harmonisation and market integration and made no substantial effort to define other goals. Among the commentaries, the most thoughtful analyses have been provided by a senior Commission official. See, e.g., Gray, "Whither Food Regulation?", 1 World Food Reg. Rev. 33 (June 1991); Gray, "EEC Food Law", address to the Annual Conference of the European Association of Lawyers (1991).
4.   V. Wright, *The Government and Politics of France* p346 (3rd ed. 1989). Wright admires the political ingenuity of the 1992 programme, but describes it as "part myth, part rhetoric, part exhortation".
5.   Opinion of the Economic and Social Committee on Consumer Protection and Completion of the Internal Market, OJ C339 31.12.91 p16.
6.   European Parliament Resolution on Food Hygiene, OJ C183 15.7.91 p52.

CHAPTER 3 : LABELLING, PRESENTATIONAL AND ADVERTISING RULES

3.1   The issues of foodstuffs labelling

In the nineteenth century, when adulterated foods were common and dangerous, labelling was an issue of secondary importance[1]. Food labelling might be deceptive or false, but the more urgent regulatory problem was always to ensure some decent standard of purity in the composition of the foodstuffs themselves. As adulteration has been controlled, regulatory goals have expanded. Labelling issues have received a higher priority. In part, this is because processed and fabricated foods have become significant factors in most national diets. In Britain, for example, three-fourths of all foods are processed outside the home before consumption[2]. Many contain ingredients of which consumers may be unaware, and about which they would have little information even if they knew of their presence. Food composition has become more varied and less predictable. Many ingredients are artificial. One result is a series of new regulatory problems to which labelling offers a partial answer.

Those problems were first systematically addressed in the 1960's, when the Codex Alimentarius Commission established a committee regarding labelling[3]. The United States and other nations soon began re-evaluating their rules, and the Codex committee eventually proposed a series of recommended requirements[4]. All of these efforts have influenced the Commission's subsequent measures, and the

---

1.   As described above, adulteration flourished throughout the nineteenth century as regulatory standards were softened and enforcement became haphazard. For descriptions of its prevalence in Britain, see, e.g., J. Burnett, *Plenty and Want* pp86-101, 216-237 (3rd ed. 1989); J. Drummond & A. Wilbraham, *The Englishman's Food* pp289-293 (rev. ed. 1957); R. Tannahill, *Food in History* pp292-295 (rev. ed. 1988). For Germany, see R. Evans, *Death in Hamburg : Society and Politics in the Cholera Years 1830-1910* pp166-176 (1990 ed.). For the United States, see, e. g., Hart, "A History of the Adulteration of Food Before 1906", p7 Food D.C.L.J. 5 (1952); R. Lamb, *American Chamber of Horrors* (1936); W. Tucker, *Food Adulteration : Its Nature and Extent and How to Deal with It* (1903); J. Young, *Pure Food : Securing the Federal Food and Drugs Act of 1906* pp31-39 (1989).

2.   Gurr, "Lipids : Products of Industrial Hydrogenation, Oxidation and Heating", in R. Walker & E. Quattrucci, eds., *Nutritional and Toxicological Aspects of Food Processing* pp139, 152 (1988); London Food Commision, *Food Adulteration and How to Beat It* p43 (1988).

3.   For a survey of the committee's work by its former chairman, see McKay, "The Codex Food Labelling Committee - Maintaining International Standards Relevant to Changing Consumer Demands", 1/92 Eur. Food L. Rev. 70 (1992).

4.   See van der Heide, "The Codex Alimentarius on Food Labelling", 4/91 Eur. Food L. Rev. 291 (1991). Some of the American changes were based upon the 1966 Fair Packaging and Labelling Act, and others derived for the White House Conference on Food, Nutrition and Health in 1969. The latter provoked a series of FDA public hearings. For a brief history, see P. Hutt, ed., *Guide to US Food Labeling Law* paras 110 et seq. (1991).

Community's rules have in turn affected events elsewhere. Labelling has become an issue as to which international harmonisation is both widely sought and only intermittently achieved.

The issues initially related to the nature and extent of the information to which consumers should be entitled about foodstuffs. More recently, they have begun to centre upon the use of labelling to encourage changes in dietary habits. Both sets of questions arise from the greatly increased range of choices now offered to consumers. Processed and fabricated foods have multiplied the options available to consumers, but they also differ greatly in their ingredients, naturalness, and nutritional values. The differences may be masked by subtle and sometimes impenetrable labelling distinctions. Salmon "paste" may differ from salmon "spread", and both may have little in common with fresh salmon[1]. Chemistry may have contributed more to a product's composition than agriculture or fishing[2]. In the view of some consumers, one form of adulteration has been replaced by another[3]. They fear that the lawful new adulterants may be no more healthful than the unlawful adulterants they have replaced. One possible response is to limit the artificial ingredients which may be used, even if the forbidden substances are not shown to offer any hazard to human health[4].

An alternative response is to require additional labelling disclosures. If there is more actual salmon in salmon spread than paste, for example, consumers may at least be informed of the difference even if they do not elect to act upon the information. Informational labelling is important everywhere, but it has assumed special functions in the Community. Under the European Court's decisions in *Cassis de Dijon* and other cases, it has become a substitute for more restrictive national rules[5]. If imported sausage contains less meat or gin less alcohol, local compositional rules cannot be used to exclude the products. Consumers are instead given notice of the differences through labelling[6]. The effectiveness of the notices

---

1. The examples are taken from J. Burnett, *Plenty and Want* p320 (3rd ed. 1989). Any supermarket can readily provide others.
2. One of the examples cited by Burnett was a "raspberry-flavoured trifle" with 28 ingredients, including 22 additives but no raspberries; ibid., at p321, citing C. Walker & G. Cannon, *The Food Scandal, What's Wrong with the British Diet and How to Put It Right*, pXXVII (1985). It is of course true that "all food is a collection of chemicals", but every consumer rightly perceives a difference between fresh raspberries and the trifle to which Burnett referred. Compare Elton, "Allocation of Priorities - Where Do the Real Risks Lie?", in G. Gibson & R. Walker, eds., *Food Toxicology - Real or Imaginary Problems?* p3 (1985).
3. See, e.g., J. Burnett, *Plenty and Want* pp320-321 (3rd ed. 1989); London Food Commission, *Food Adulteration and How to Beat It* (1988).
4. The various positive lists of additives are steps in the direction of such limitations, although they are based largely upon safety considerations and not nutritional values. Non-safety considerations will, however, be important in the addition of new substances to the positive lists; see para 3.3, below. Other examples are the recipe laws and such national rules as the German beer purity rules.
5. For *Cassis de Dijon* and related cases, see Chapter 2, para 2.3, ante.
6. See, e.g., Case C-274/87 *Re German Sausages, EC Commission v Germany* [1989] ECR 229, [1989] 2 CMLR 733; Case C-182/84 *Miro BV* [1985] ECR 3731, [1986] 3 CMLR 545.

may be debated, but they create no impediment to trade and consumers are at least empowered to make selections on the basis of factors other than price.

The most obvious of the functions of food labelling is to promote sales. For food processors and distributors, labelling space is a scarce and valuable commodity[1]. Labelling is limited by container sizes and shapes, and the available space must be used carefully to communicate effectively. Labelling is advertising, and a well-designed label may represent the difference between competitive success and failure.

Producers are understandably troubled by governmental requirements which hamper design and absorb scarce space. Each new requirement results in new format restrictions and leaves less space for product promotion. This matters less for established brands and products sold largely by price, which rely less heavily upon labels to induce sales. It is more important for new brands or products which depend upon labelling to attract attention on crowded supermarket shelves[2]. Consumers are ill-served by requirements for the disclosure of insignificant information if they impede innovation and the introduction of new competitors.

Food labelling may also perform an educational function. There is substantial evidence that diet is associated with many forms of illness, and that changes in diet may promote public health[3]. Some of the associations are well-documented, such as the value of iodised salt in the prevention of goiter[4]. Some relate only to particular consumer populations, such as those who suffer allergic symptoms after consuming some food ingredients[5]. Other associations are more controversial, such as the suggestions that some foods help prevent some cancers, or that others help

---

1.   The costs of labelling obligations from the perspective of producers are discussed in, e.g., National Academy of Sciences, Committee on Nutritional Components of Food Labeling, Nutrition Labeling : Issues and Directions for the 1990s" p8 (1990).
2.   For an economist's evaluation of the issues, see, e.g., Schmalensee, "Advertising and Product Quality", 86 Journal of Political Economy p485 (1978).
3.   The literature regarding diet and health is vast and growing. See, e.g., Berand & Derache, "Aliments et cancer", in R. Derache, ed., *Toxicologie et Sécurité des Aliments* pp515-553 (1986); C.R. Pennington, *Therapeutic Nutrition* p242 (1988); Gibney, "Food Policy - Implications for the Nutritional Sciences", in H. Deelstra, et al., eds., *Food Policy Trends in Europe* pp19-32 (1991); Kritchevsky, "Cancer and Caloric Restriction", in R.C. Cambie, ed., *Fats for the Future* pp75-85 (1989); Carroll, "Effects of Level and Type of Dietary Fat on Carcinogens"; ibid., at pp97-108; Pariza, "Diet and Cancer", in D. Cliver, ed., *Foodborne Diseases* pp307-317 (1990); Henderson, et al., "Toward the Primary Prevention of Cancer", 254 Science pp1131, 1134-1135 (22 Nov 1991).
4.   See, e.g., R. Fernandez, *A Simple Matter of Salt* (1990).
5.   See, e.g., Joint Report of the Royal College of Physicians and the British Nutrition Foundation, "Food Intolerance and Food Aversion", 18 J. Royal Coll. Physicians 2 (1984); Lessof, et al., "Intolerance and Allergy to Food and Food Additives", in R. Walker & E. Quattrucci, eds., *Nutritional and Toxicological Aspects of Food Processing* pp345-350 (1988).

avoid heart disease[1]. There are widespread claims that foods may alleviate many other ailments[2]. The evidence regarding many associations is disputed, and the public is beseiged by hasty and conflicting claims, but there is little doubt that nutritional changes could improve the health of many of the Community's residents.

As a result, there are growing demands that food labels should perform educational and admonitory roles. It has been suggested that labels should be converted from "tools of commerce" into "instruments of public health", and that they should be "couriers" for the dissemination of nutritional messages[3]. The goal is to inaugurate "an era of preventive nutrition"[4]. One device for this purpose would be more comprehensive labelling disclosures of the nutritional properties of foods. The Community has taken modest steps in this direction, and the United States is adopting elaborate rules for this purpose[5.] A more radical device would be labelling warnings or recommendations based upon a product's role in the prevention or inducement of disease. Labels might, for example, warn against sugars or fats, or encourage the consumption of fibre. The United States and Canada require label warnings for a growing list of products, and American supermarkets have experimented with recommendations regarding the nutritional advantages of some foods. Similar steps will evidently be taken in Britain[6]. In part because of competing pressures created by the Common Agricultural Policy, the Community has been less adventurous. There are cautions against the refreezing of frozen foods and proposed notices regarding sweeteners, but the Community has otherwise shown little interest in product warnings and recommendations[7]. This may alter as pressures grow to improve public health by modifying dietary patterns[8].

---

1.   See, e.g., Henderson, et al., "Toward the Primary Prevention of Cancer", 254 Science 1131, pp1134-1135 (22 Nov 1991).
2.   For a collection of claims and assessments, see, e.g., J. Carper, *The Food Pharmacy* (1988).
3.   Merrill, "Food Labels : Couriers of Public Health", 1 World Food Reg. Rev. 18-21 (Aug 1991).
4.   Hermus, "The consequences of 100 years' evolution of dietary habits in Europe with regard to nutrition", in H. Deelstra, et al., eds., *Food Policy Trends in Europe* p67 (1991).
5.   See para 3.4, below.
6.   The United States and Canada require, for example, health warnings for saccharin, and the United States demands warnings on alcoholic beverages and other products. At least one American supermarket chain has experimented with recommendations that particular foods are helpful in providing various nutrients. They are said to be effective, especially with educated consumers. See, e.g., Schucker, et al., "The Impact of the Saccarin Warning Label on Sales of Diet Soft Drinks in Supermarkets", 2 Journal of Public Policy and Marketing p46 (1983). In Britain, The Coronary Prevention Group has developed similar labelling recommendations, and one supermarket group will reportedly adopt them; *The Times* p3 (27 March 1992); Eurofood 7 (April 1992).
7.   There are, however, various national warning requirements. For French rules for sweeteners, including table-top sweeteners, see OJ L66 18.3.88 p3664.
8.   A study by the US Federal Trade Commission suggested that the removal of restrictions on health claims in advertising provided more effective consumer notices than government-sponsored information programmes. Ippolito and Mathios, "Information, Advertising and Health Choices : A Study of the Cereal Market", 21 RAND Journal of Economics 459 (1990). See also Viscusi, et al., "Information Regulation of Consumer Health Risks : An Empirical Evaluation of Hazard Warnings", 17 RAND Journal of Economics p351 (1986).

Important questions would, however, first have to be answered. As a threshold matter, the available scientific evidence is often insufficient to justify warnings and recommendations. It makes little sense to employ food labels as educational devices unless there is confidence in the lessons they would teach. Even a few errors could nullify an entire educational programme. Second, it has been argued that such programmes may encuorage nutritional imbalances, invite consumers to treat foods as medications, and distract attention from special problems of the groups most at risk[1]. Finally, it is unclear whether food labels are an effective device for communicating nutritional messages. Any substantial number of warnings or exhortations might cause consumers to disregard labels. Even without warnings, it has been argued that consumers give little attention to labelling disclosures[2]. This is not, however, supported by surveys in Britain, France and the United States, in which consumers claimed to read labels and to wish additional labelling information[3]. It may well be that attention to labels varies by income and education[4]. If so, warnings and recommendational labels might not reach the principal audiences for which they would be intended.

Related issues arise from promotional claims which increasingly are made about food products. Some involve claims about such constituents as fats and sugars. Others involve suggestions that products are "natural" or "fresh", or that they have been produced without pesticides or other agricultural chemicals. Most claims are presumably truthful, but some offer a misleading picture of the products about which they have been made. There is little doubt that false claims should be forbidden, but it has also been suggested that even truthful claims should be prohibited if they might induce the sale of products low in nutritional value. Implicit in the suggestion is a fear that consumers cannot evaluate for themselves the quality and utility of food products. The same fear underlies arguments that compositional standards are more reliable guarantees of quality than labelling requirements. In this sense, compositional standards and informational labelling represent conflicting assumptions about consumers and the functions of regulation. One approach presumes the rationality of consumers, provided always that they

1.   Harper, "Diet and Chronic Diseases and Disorders", in D. Cliver, ed., *Foodborne Diseases* pp319, 347-349 (1990).
2.   See von Heydebrand, "Free Movement of Foodstuffs, Consumer Protection and Food Standards in the European Community : Has the Court of Justice Got It Wrong?", 16 Eur. L. Rev. 391 (1991) (citing American evidence).
3.   See, e.g., Fauconneau, "La consommation alimentaire : évolution et mutations," in Académie d'Agriculture de France, *Deux Sieécles de Progrés pour L'Agriculture et L'Alimentation, 1789-1989* p319 (1990); National Academy of Sciences, Committee on Nutrition Components of Food Labeling, Nutrition Labeling : Issues and Directions for the 1990s pp9, 94-96 (1990); Food Advisory Committee Report on Food Labelling and Advertising 1990 p61 (1991). For other American polling regarding labels, see 1 World Food Reg. Rev. 10 (April 1992); Viscusi, et al., "Informational Regulation of Consumer Health Risks : An Empirical Evaluation of Hazard Warnings", 17 RAND Journal of Economics p351 (1986).
4.   See, e.g., Schucker, et al., "The Impact of the Saccharin Warning Label on Sales of Diet Soft Drinks in Supermarkets", 2 Journal of Public Policy and Marketing p46 (1983).

have adequate information upon which to act. The other questions the ability of consumers to select sensibly among products of differing utilities.

The two approaches are not mutually exclusive. Most regulatory systems merge or blend them[1]. Unwilling or unable to decide upon their assumptions, regulators may swing from one approach to the other. In this instance, however, inconsistency is a virtue. Regulators are confronted by a wide range of products about which a great variety of claims is asserted. They can regulate those claims effectively only if they take account of dramatic differences in consumers' ages, educational attainments, and levels of nutritional sophistication. Consumer education, together with a judicious mixture of prohibitions and disclosure obligations, represents a better response than either of the two approaches alone[2].

3.2   The Community's overall approach to foodstuff labelling

One of the regulatory areas to which the 1985 White Paper assigned high priority was the labelling, presentation and advertising of foodstuffs. This was an area in which the Community had already made significant progress before 1985. Many of the Community's basic rules for food labelling derive from a directive adopted in 1978, and the Commission's subsequent efforts have chiefly involved revisions of, or supplements to, the 1978 rules[3]. The Community amended the 1978 directive in 1989 to add new labelling obligations, particularly with respect to irradiated and highly perishable foodstuffs. It also extended the 1978 rules to reach sales made to mass caterers, as well as distributional sales which occur prior to a product's ultimate sale at retail[4]. In addition, the Community has adopted rules for nutritional labelling and lot or batch markings[5]. As a result of these and other steps, the Community's basic labelling rules are now in place[6].

Nonetheless, there are still areas in which significant issues have not yet been resolved, and in which additional labelling rules may well be adopted. In a careful

---

1.   A mixture of educational programmes and prohibitions has, for example, been recommended in Britain. Food Advisory Committee Report on Food Labelling and Advertising 1990 (1991).

2.   Any measures must, however, be planned with appropriate modesty. "Careless, ill-conceived and naive nutrition education programmes" have been described as a disservice to the public and the goals of dietary improvement. Gibney, "Food Policy - Implications for the Nutritional Sciences", in H. Deelstra, et al., eds., *Food Policy Trends in Europe* p30 (1991).

3.   The directive's rules are supplemented by requirements applicable to some specific categories of foodstuffs. The supplemental rules are described below in connection with the product or category to which they relate.

4.   See para 3.3, below.

5.   For nutritional labelling, see para 3.4, below. For lot markings, see para 3.6, below.

6.   One US agency expects the uniformity of the harmonised labelling rules to benefit both Community and US producers. United States International Trade Commission, *The Effects of Greater Economic Integration within the European Community on the United States* pp6-55 (1989).

review of food labelling and advertising rules in Britain, most of which derive from Community standards, Britain's Food Advisory Committee found numerous areas for improvement[1]. Among other proposals, the FAC recommended quantitative declarations of the main characterising ingredients of foods, clearer storage and use instructions, and more complete listings of ingredients[2]. It also urged clearer formats for the presentation of required disclosures, restrictions on health claims, disclosures of post-harvest chemical treatments, and additional rules for unpackaged foods[3]. Taken together, the FAC's recommendations represent an important agenda for the Community's consideration. They are also a model of precision which might usefully guide the Commission's future proposals[4].

Some of the FAC's suggestions are already the subject of new or proposed Community legislation. For example, the Community has adopted rules for the labelling of products which claim to have been organically produced[5], and the Commission is preparing rules to restrict health and other claims made in connection with the marketing of foodstuffs[6]. It has also proposed rules for quantitative ingredient labelling. At one point, it considered rules for mandatory nutritional labelling[7]. In addition, the Council has recently adopted controversial new systems for certifications of the geographical origin or special distinctiveness of some foodstuffs[8]. The certificates may be displayed on labels or in the advertising of selected products. The other proposals mentioned above have not yet been adopted, and some are still in early stages of preparation. Some will occasion vigorous debate, and it is far from certain that all will be adopted. Taken together, they are reminders that the Community's labelling rules are still incomplete and that the uncompleted areas may prove controversial and difficult[9].

The Community's difficulties in resolving ancillary labelling issues are not unique. They are, for example, at least matched by problems in the United States. Although the Food and Drug Administration has been addressing labelling issues much longer than the Commission, FDA has not been more successful in finding satisfactory solutions[10.] Indeed, the present Commissioner of Food and Drugs argued

1. Food Advisory Committee Report on Food Labelling and Advertising 1990 (1991). The principal recommendations and findings are discussed below.
2. At paras 59, 76, 88, 100.
3. At paras 108-109, 111, 121-140, 184, 192-203.
4. The Community's rules are not always drafted with precision. Roberts, "European Enforcement", 1/92 Eur. Food L. Rev. 1, 2-4 (1992).
5. See para 3.7, below.
6. See para 3.5, below.
7. For the proposed quantitative ingredient declarations, see at para 3.3, below. The proposal for mandatory nutritional labelling has evidently been abandoned in light of the Community's 1990 nutritional labelling directive; see para 3.4, below.
8. See para 3.8, below.
9. The Commission has acknowledged that at least the "details" of its labelling rules warrant revision. Written Question 1434/91, OJ C55 2.3.92 p24.
10. American law draws a distinction between food labelling, which is governed by FDA, and food advertising, which is governed by the Federal Trade Commission. The two agencies rely on

before his appointment that the American rules are only a "patchwork" of regulatory responses to specific problems. He claimed that FDA lacks both a "coherent framework" and any "clear sense of direction"[1]. FDA has had particular difficulty in finding satisfactory rules regarding nutritional and health claims. For many years, it permitted essentially all claims which are truthful and may be substantiated[2]. More recently, it proposed a more restrictive approach, and would have limited permissible claims only to prescribed categories of situations[3]. Its proposals were overtaken by a new statute, and revised proposals have since been issued[4].

Important changes have occurred on both sides of the Atlantic regarding the increasingly controversial issues of food labelling. It should not be expected, however, that they represent any long-term resolution of the issues. Demands that labelling should encourage dietary improvements will increase, and those demands will stimulate new proposals for warnings and more detailed disclosures[5]. The debate will also continue over the effectiveness of labels both as educational devices and as notices of product quality. Labelling has become a central problem of food regulation, and the growing diversity of the marketplace will multiply the arguments for additional labelling restrictions. It has rightly been predicted that the controversies regarding labelling will continue "for many years to come"[6].

separate statutory provisions. See Wheeler-Lea Amendments, 52 Stat. 111, 114 (1938). See also P. Hutt & R. Merrill, *Food and Drug Law, Cases and Materials* p43 (2nd ed. 1991). A "label" under US law is, however, broadly interpreted and may, for example, include an accompanying booklet. *United States v 250 Jars ... Cal's Tupelo Blossom US Fancy Pure Honey*, 344 F.2d 288 (6th Cir. 1965).

1. Kessler, "The Federal Regulation of Food Labeling", p321 New Eng. J. Med. 717, 723 (1989). Dr. Kessler is now in a position to cure what in a private capacity he condemned. For one account of his efforts, see N. Tait, "FDA wages war on food labels which mislead", *Financial Times* (4 June 1991).

2. For descriptions of FDA's evolving policies, see, e.g, Hutt, "Government Regulation of Health Claims in Food Labeling and Advertising", 41 Food D.C.L.J. 3 (1986); Davis, "The New FDA Position on Health-Related Messages for Food Products and Constitutionally Protected Speech", 42 Food D.C.L.J. 365 (1987).

3. For FDA's proposals, see 55 Fed. Reg. 5176 (13 Feb 1990). More recently, the issues have been partly resolved by the Nutrition Labelling and Education Act, P.L. No. 101-535, 104 Stat. 2353 (1990). For discussions of the issues, see Kolasky, "The Impact of the Food and Drug Administration's Reproposal on Vitamins, Minerals and Other Nutritional Supplements", 45 Food D.C.L.J. 639 (1990). For an FDA explanation of the proposal, see Scarborough, "Under the Reproposed Rule, How Much Scientific Evidence Does a Company Need to Justify Its Claims and What Are the FDA's Interim Rules", 45 Food D.C. L. J. 647 (1990). For a review of the entire controversy, see Cooper, Frank & O'Flaherty, "History of Health Claims Regulation", 45 Food D.C.L.J. 655 (1990).

4. See para 3.4, below.

5. Some of these changes have already been demanded by the European Parliament. Resolution on consumer protection and public health requirements, No. A3-0060/92 (11 March 1992).

6. Pape, "The US Nutrition Labeling and Education Act of 1990", 1 World Food Reg. Rev. 25, 29 (Aug 1991).

3.3   The Community's basic rules for foodstuff labelling

In December 1978, the Council adopted a directive to harmonise national laws regulating the labelling, presentation, and advertising of foodstuffs for sale to the ultimate consumer[1] The directive has been incorporated into national law throughout the Community[2] The original directive contained significant omissions and exceptions, and the European Parliament and consumer groups soon began pressing for significant changes.   In 1987, Parliament adopted a resolution describing the 1978 directive as "unsatisfactory"[3] The resolution was a catalogue of the deficiencies of the Community's food regulations as they existed in 1987. It emphasised the lack of clarity, the urgency of more coherent standards, and the absence of uniform definitions of the "basic concepts" of food legislation[4]. Parliament argued that the 1978 directive had permitted important inconsistencies among national laws, and that they in turn had created "red tape" and a "mass of 'hidden' trade barriers"[5].

Nonetheless, there were continuing disagreements over the proper corrections for the directive's deficiencies, and the Council did not generally amend it until 1989[6]. The 1989 directive adopted new rules regarding the labelling of irradiated and highly perishable foodstuffs, and eliminated some of the national derogations permitted by the 1978 directive. It did not, however, alter the directive's basic structure or provisions. The Community has also adopted several measures which address particular labelling issues, such as nutritional labelling and lot markings[7]. The recipe laws and other vertical measures provide their own labelling rules for specific product categories[8]. Despite these amendments and supplements, the 1978 directive still provides the basic framework for the Community's labelling requirements. It remains the single most important element of the Community's efforts to create a unified market in foodstuffs. As such, it warrants detailed consideration.

---

1.   Council Directive (EEC) 79/112, OJ L33 8.2.79 p1. Although adopted in late 1978, the directive was not officially published until 1979.
2.   Eighth Annual Report to the European Parliament on Commission Monitoring of the Application of Community Law - 1990, OJ C338 31.12.991 p1 at 153. Proceedings for improper application of the directive were, however, initiated against Ireland, and for improper implementation against Spain. For the UK rules, see Food Labelling Regulations, SI 1984/1305; Food Labelling (Amendment) Regulations, SI 1989/768; Food Labelling (Amendment) Regulations 1990, SI 1990/2488, and related rules. For the Dutch rules, see Voedingsraad at p198. For the Italian rules, see Alimenti e Bevande at 167-181. For Spanish law, see Real Decreto 2058/1982, B.O.E. 207 (30 Aug 1982). For comparable US rules, see 21 C.F.R. part 101 (1991); P. Hutt, ed., *Guide to US Food Labeling Law* (1991).
3.   Document A2-235/86, OJ C99 3.4.87 p65.
4.   Ibid., at pp66-67. The Commission is now beginning to draft a measure providing such definitions.
5.   See also, e.g., Commission Directive (EEC) 83/463, OJ L255 15.9.83 p1, at the second recital of the preamble.
6.   Council Directive (EEC) 89/395, OJ L186 30.6.89 p17.
7.   For nutritional labelling, see para 3.4, below. For lot markings, see para 3.6, below. See also Council Directive (EEC) 86/197, OJ L144 29.5.86 p88; Council Directive (EEC) 88/222, OJ L28 1.2.88 p1.
8.   See Chapter 7, post.

The 1978 directive is an early example of the Community's post-1985 horizontal approach to rulemaking. Many of the features which characterise the Community's regulatory methods since 1985 may be found, at least in rudimentary form, in the 1978 directive. It was designed to act horizontally on all foodstuffs, as many post-1985 measures have been, rather than vertically on a particular category of products[1]. Like more recent framework measures, it was not intended as a comprehensive statement of all labelling requirements. While the directive contemplated detailed labelling rules, it did not itself impose all of those obligations[2]. It was instead an "initial" stage. The Council's goal was to supplement the directive by detailed rules regarding particular issues and categories of products[3]. With respect to foodstuffs generally, it has only been since 1985 that important additions have been made to the 1978 directive.

The 1978 directive does not apply to exports[4]. It does apply to all foodstuffs delivered within the Community for sale to the ultimate consumer[5]. As a practical matter, the rules are largely limited to foodstuffs sold in pre-packagings. Separate but less comprehensive rules have been established for foods, such as fresh fruits and vegetables, commonly sold without prepackaging[6]. As originally written, the 1978 directive permitted Member States to decide individually whether to apply it to foodstuffs delivered to "mass caterers"[7]. "Mass caterers" include such facilities as restaurants, hospitals, office canteens, cafes, and railway and airline catering systems. This is no longer optional, and the amended directive now imposes labelling obligations for foodstuffs sold to mass caterers. Similarly, the directive originally did not apply to sales occurring before a food's final sale to the ultimate consumer. This too was modified by the 1989 directive.

The directive includes specific labelling obligations, but also imposes a general framework of standards. In particular, it forbids any labelling, presentation or advertising which "could mislead the purchaser to a material degree"[8]. It is significant that the English version of the directive employs the word "could", which suggests that merely a potential for deception, without proof of its likelihood or actual occurrence, may be sufficient to condemn a label or advertisement. Moreover, the word "mislead" does not necessarily mean

---

1.   Council Directive (EEC) 79/122, above at the third recital of the preamble.
2.   The eighth recital of the preamble.
3.   The 1978 directive called for additional measures regarding the disclosure of alcoholic content and the regulation of various labelling and advertising claims. Only the former has thus far been adopted.
4.   Article 21. It does apply to the French overseas departments; Article 24.
5.   Article 1(1). As amended, the directive also creates labelling requirements for prepackaged products marketed (e.g., to a distributor) at a stage prior to retail. Council Directive (EEC) 89/395, OJ L186 30.6.89 p17. In such cases, some of the information may be provided in accompanying documents.
6.   See Chapter 8, para 8.1, below.
7.   Article 1(2).
8.   Article 2(1)(a).

"deceive"[1]. The standard is made potentially more onerous by the directive's failure to define a "material" degree of confusion or to indicate whether the test is subjective or objective. The directive does state, however, that the obligation "particularly" relates to claims regarding a product's properties, or any special characteristics claimed for the product[2]. The factors as to which deception is "particularly" forbidden include the product's nature, identity, properties, composition, quantity, durability, origin or provenance, and method of manufacture or production[3]. The prohibition is, in other words, comprehensive[4].

No claim may be made which attributes any effects or properties to a product it does not possess[5]. Moreover, no claim may be made regarding special characteristics if similar foodstuffs also possess those characteristics[6]. Separate rules are provided for mineral waters and products intended for particular nutritional uses, but in general the directive forbids any claim that a foodstuff has properties for preventing, treating or curing human disease[7]. These prohibitions were to have been the subject of more detailed limitations[8], but such rules have not yet been adopted. The Commission is only now attempting to add rules regarding specific labelling and advertising claims[9]. Even without them, the Community has already forbidden most claims relating to health. In this respect, its rules are more stringent than those which have until recently been used in the United States[10].

These rules are not limited to labelling. They also apply to the advertising and presentation of foodstuffs[11]. This includes their shape and appearance[12]. It also includes packaging materials, the ways in which products are arranged in shops or display cases, and the settings in which they are displayed. In other words, the prohibition against acts or practices which "could" be confusing encompasses every aspect of the ways in which foodstuffs are packaged, labelled, presented and

---

1. For an enforcement officer's complaints about the ambiguity of the rule, see Roberts, "European Enforcement", 1/92 Eur. Food L. Rev. 1, 2 (1992). The relevant provision of the UK regulations which implement the directive provides that a food's presentation shall not be such that a purchaser "is likely to be misled to a material degree". Food Labelling Regulations, SI 1984/1305, at reg 4.
2. Article 2(1)(a).
3. Article 2(1)(a)(i).
4. In the United States, an equally general prohibition is found in section 403(a) of the Food, Drug, and Cosmetic Act, which forbids labelling which is "false or misleading in any particular".
5. Article 2(1)(a)(ii).
6. Article 2(1)(a)(iii).
7. Article 2(1)(b). Nor may labelling, presentation or advertising "refer" to such properties. It should be noted that the prohibition is not dependent on falsity or deceptiveness. For mineral waters, see Chapter 7, para 7.9, post. For products intended for particular nutritional purposes (known sometimes as "parnuts" products), see below at Chapter 4, para 4.5, post.
8. Article 2(2).
9. See para 3.5, below.
10. For FDA's policies regarding health claims, see above at para 3.4.
11. Article 2(3).
12. Ibid. For other constraints upon packaging imposed by other Community legislation, see Chapter 8, para 8.1, post.

advertised. Any element of these activities may be forbidden if it encourages a product's sale and may mislead consumers[1].

3.3.1 Disclosure requirements

The directive provides a detailed list of mandatory disclosures[2]. Many must be made in labelling, and in this respect the directive is addressed particularly to pre-packaged foodstuffs. Other disclosure requirements are imposed by measures related to particular product categories, each of which is discussed below. The following disclosures are, however, the Community's basic labelling and advertising requirements for foodstuffs offered to mass caterers or the ultimate consumer.

3.3.1.1 The product's name

Each product must disclose its name[3]. This does not mean a brand or trade name. It means a name which identifies the product's nature. As a general matter, this must be any name required by applicable law[4]. "Milk chocolate," "marmalade" and "white sugar" are three of the names defined by Community law. National laws define many others. If no name is required by law, any name customary in the place of sale may be used, or any descriptive name sufficiently precise to indicate the product's "true nature"[5]. "Pizza" is a customary name, and "malted milk drink" is a descriptive but non-customary name[6].

---

1. Article 2 of the 1978 directive has been held, in conjunction with Article 30 of the Treaty, to limit national labelling and advertising rules. The European Court has held that France could not prohibit any reference in the labelling of artificial sweeteners to sugar or physical or chemical properties shared by sugar and artificial sweeteners; see Case 241/89 *SARPP Sàrl v Chambre Syndicale des Raffineurs et Conditionneurs de Sucre de France* (1990) Transcript 12 December, OJ C10 16.1.91 p9, decided by the European Court in 1990 upon reference from the Tribunal de Grande Instance in Paris. Neither Article 2 of the directive nor Article 30 of the Treaty prevents national prohibitions of misleading labelling, but national rules cannot impose needless additional burdens where confusion cannot occur; Case 94/82 *De Kikvorsch Groothandel-Import-Export BV* [1983] ECR 947, [1984] 2 CMLR 322, decided by the European Court in 1983 upon reference from the District Court in Arnhem.
2. Article 3. For partly similar Swiss rules, see, e.g., Ordinance of 26 May 1936, as amended, at Articles 13a-20.
3. Articles 3(1)(1), 5.
4. Article 5(1). The Commission is evidently studying a proposal that names defined in a European standard could be used. No such names are yet defined, although the Commission is also considering a proposal that would grant quality certifications to products which satisfy Community standards, and those standards would presumably define product names. The recipe laws already define many product names.
5. In Britain, the FAC has found that the use of customary names may result in confusion, and has urged that they should be permitted only as a supplement to legal or descriptive names; Food Advisory Committee Report on Food Labelling and Advertising 1990 (1991) at para 51.
6. The examples were suggested by P. Gaman & K. Sherrington, *The Science of Food* p251 (3rd ed. 1990).

The Commission has proposed that these rules should be modestly revised[1]. Under the proposed revisions, any name established by applicable law would be required. In the absence of such a name, the seller could use any name customary either in the place of manufacture or in the place of ultimate sale, or any descriptive name clear enough to reveal the product's "exact gnature" and to distinguish it from other products with which it might be confused. The acceptance of a name customary in the place of a product's manufacture would be new. Both customary and descriptive names could be used, provided they were not misleading to purchasers.

The ultimate purpose is to prevent confusion and deception[2]. Accordingly, no trade mark, brand or "fancy" name may be substituted for the legal, descriptive or customary name[3]. "Fancy" names are not defined, but include non-customary names which do not describe a product. Such names and marks may, however, be added to the prescribed names[4]. If confusion might otherwise occur, the name must be accompanied by an indication of the product's physical condition, or any processing treatment it has undergone[5]. For example, the label must indicate if a product is powdered or frozen. There is no express provision, as there is in the United States, for such descriptions as "sliced" or "halved", but the Community's provision may be sufficiently broad to encompass them. In particular, the label of a foodstuff treated with ionizing radiation must state that it has been "irradiated" or "treated with ionizing radiation" in one of the Community's official languages[6]. In addition, national law may, in the absence of Community rules, provide that product names must be accompanied by the names of one or more ingredients[7].

These rules may seem unequivocal, but opportunities for abuse still occur. Britain's Food Advisory Committee found that "customary" names may cause confusion, and urged that they should be permitted only as supplements to descriptive names[8]. The FAC also found that "fancy" names may cause confusion. It suggested that they

---

1. COM(91) 536 final, OJ C122 14.5.92 p12, at art 1.
2. Article 5(1).
3. Article 5(2). Similar rules are imposed in the United States by section 403 (i)(1) of the Food, Drug, and Cosmetic Act. See also 21 C.F.R. part 102 (1991).
4. Ibid. In Britain, the FAC has recommended that true names should be immediately adjacent to, and not less prominent than, any brand or fancy names. Food Advisory Committee Report on Food Labelling and Advertising 1990 (1991) at pp21, 111.
5. Article 5(3).
6. This was one of the changes made by the 1989 directive. The requirement applies to any "foodstuff" which has been irradiated, without specifically referring to ingredients. "Foodstuffs" are not defined, but the 1989 directive notes that it does not address the question of either allowing or banning the irradiation of foodstuffs "or ingredients". Ibid., at the fifth recital of the preamble. Presumably therefore the reference to foodstuffs in Article 5(3) intentionally omitted ingredients. If so, it follows that irradiated ingredients need not be identified in compound foodstuffs. The Commission has proposed a directive regarding irradiation which defines "foodstuffs" to include ingredients. For a discussion of the Commission's draft rules, see Chapter 4, para 4.3, post.
7. Article 4(c). This might include predominant flavourings (for example, "strawberry-flavoured" custard).
8. Food Advisory Committee Report on Food Labelling and Advertising 1990 (1991) at para 51.

should be permitted only in conjunction with descriptive names, and only if displayed no more prominently than those names[1]. Britain's Ministry of Agriculture, Fisheries and Food accepted both recommendations, subject to further consultations, but observed that they would require Community action[2].

In addition, there are frequently disputes about the properties or composition of products which bear a particular name. Names are shorthand indicators of a product's real or attributed characteristics, and the right to use particular names may have substantial commercial significance. Extensive legislation has long existed on these questions in several Member States. For example, French law treats "Edam" as the generic name of a type of cheese, and not as a designation of origin[3]. Cheeses sold in France as "Edam" may originate anywhere but must contain a prescribed minimum butter fat content. This is consistent with an international convention entered into by France, the Netherlands and other countries[4]. Based upon these rules, France prohibited the sale of cheese lawfully produced in Germany under the name "Edam," but with a butter fat content lower than the French standard. The European Court found that the prohibition violated Article 30 of the Treaty of Rome. France's rule could not be used to prohibit the marketing of imported cheese if the cheese's label accurately disclosed the product's butter fat content[5]. The Court noted that there was no Community legislation regarding the names of cheeses, and that in principle national rules were therefore permissible. Those rules may not, however, foreclose the sale of lawful products from other Member States if the consumer is given "proper information" regarding them[6]. This meant an unequivocal disclosure of butter fat content.

As the controversy illustrates, a product's name may result in the application of national or Community rules relating to the composition of products which use that name. In turn, those rules may demand labelling disclosures which exceed the basic requirements of the 1978 directive. They may also inhibit product development and innovation. If a product may bear a commercially valuable name only if it contains prescribed levels of fat or sugar, products with reduced levels may be obliged to adopt unfamiliar and less valuable names. For example, Italy sought unsuccessfully to prevent producers of low-fat products from using the name

---

1.   At paras 21, 111.

2.   Thomas, "United Kingdom Food Advisory Committee review of food labelling and the Government's response", 1/92 Eur. Food L. Rev. 81, 82 (1992). See also Food Advisory Committee Annual Report 1991 p2 (1992).

3.   Case 286/86 *Ministère Public v Gerard Deserbais* [1988] ECR 4907, [1989] 1 CMLR 516, decided by the European Court in 1988.

4.   Ibid., at p525. The agreement was the International Convention on the Use of Designations of Origin and Names for Cheeses, executed in Stresa in 1951. For its text, see G. Andries, et al., eds., *Codice di Diretto Alimentare Annotato* (1990), vol.2, p1414.

5.   [1989] 1 CMLR 526-528.

6.   [1989] 1 CMLR 526.

"cheese"[1]. The Italian rule was eventually invalidated under Article 30 of the Treaty as a barrier to free circulation, but similar national restrictions may hamper the introduction of other products offering dietary advantages[2].

Conversely, national laws may require products with particular characteristics to bear designated names. Such rules are generally valid, but may not impose needless additional burdens on imported products. For example, Dutch rules required products with certain properties, including specified alcohol contents, to carry the name "likeur". The European Court held that imported products could not be required to alter their labelling if they already provided information equivalent to that demanded by the Dutch rules[3]. The case was decided before the Community had adopted rules for spirit drinks, and the only issue was whether the Dutch rules were forbidden by Article 30 of the Treaty. Insofar as they required needless labelling alterations, the Court held that they were prohibited.

Another example is provided by two European Court decisions arising from a 1964 Italian law which restricted the name "aceto" to vinegars made from wine. The Italian rule required wine vinegars to carry that name, and forbade all other vinegars to do so. The European Court held in 1981 that this created a competitive advantage for products made in Italy[4]. The Italian law had an effect equivalent to a quantitative restriction upon imports and hence was prohibited by Article 30 of the Treaty. Italy amended the rule in 1982 to establish "agro" as the new generic name for vinegars, but continued to restrict "aceto" to wine vinegars[5]. In 1985, the European Court held that the new rule failed to comply with its 1981 decision because the traditional and commercially preferable name "aceto" was still largely reserved for Italian products[6].

The three decisions illustrate some of the commercial and legal issues which may arise from the selection of the name under which a product is sold in the

---

1.   Case 196/89 *The State v Nespoli* [1990] ECR I 3461, [1992] 2 CMLR 1, and Case C-210/89 *Re Low-Fat Cheese: EC Commission v Italy* [1990] ECR I 3697, [1992] 2 CMLR 1. The Court held that, despite the absence of Community compositional rules, Italy may not deny the generic name "cheese" to imported products which have a lower fat content than the minimum Italian standard. For the Italian rules, see G. Andreis, et al., eds., *Codice di Diretto Alimentare Annotato* (1990), vol 2, p1400.
2.   Such issues frequently arise in connection with yellow fat products offered as substitutes for butter. For the Commission's proposed trade description rules, see Chapter 7, para 7.8, post.
3.   Case 27/80 *Anton Adriaan Fietje* [1980] ECR 3839, [1981] 3 CMLR 722, decided by the European Court in 1980 upon reference from the District Court in Assen.
4.   Case 193/80 *EC Commission v Italy : Re Wine Vinegar* [1981] ECR 3019.
5.   Case 281/83 *EC Commission v Italy (No 2) : Re Wine Vinegar* [1985] ECR 3397, [1987] 1 CMLR 865, 871.
6.   At 872-873.

Community[1]. In an effort to clarify the issues, the Commission has issued an interpretative communication regarding name selections[2]. Where the same product is sold under different names in exporting and importing Member States, the importer is generally free to choose between the names, or indeed to employ both[3]. If, however, there are "substantial differences" between an imported product and the products sold under a particular name in an importing state, the importing state may require a different name to be used[4]. This may be done only to prevent confusion and not to give a trade advantage to domestic products. The new name cannot denigrate the imported product or discourage its sale.

The Commission offered three illustrations. The first was vinegar. Some vinegars are made by fermentation of agricultural commodities, while others are manufactured by diluting synthetic acetic acid. Two Member States permit both products to be sold under the name "vinegar". The Commission ruled that an importing Member State could legitimately prohibit use of the name "vinegar" by synthetic products, even if they can lawfully be sold under that name in the Member States where they are manufactured. Similarly, Member States may forbid imported products which do not contain live lactic bacteria to describe themselves as "yoghurt", even if that name can be used where the product is manufactured[5]. In Britain, for example, "pasteurised yoghurt" is made[6].

Member States may also forbid the name "caviar" for eggs taken from lumpfish, rather than sturgeon. In these and similar instances, national restrictions upon the names used by imported products are permissible only if those products differ in "essential characteristics" from products sold under those names in the importing state[7].

---

1. Comparable problems arise in the United States. See 21 C.F.R. sec. 102.5(a) (1991); Kleinfeld, "Common or Usual Name - Its Meaning, If Any", 16 Food D.C.L.J. 513 (1961); Sayer, "A Rose By Any Other Name", 30 Food D.C.L.J. 415 (1975).
2. OJ C270 15.10.91 p2.
3. The Commission first expressed this view in an earlier communication regarding the free movement of foodstuffs, and its 1991 interpretative communication was in essence a series of further explanations. For the earlier communication, see OJ C271 24.10.89 p3. Both communications, as well as the consequences of the European Court's decisions, are partly reflected in the Commission's proposed amendments to the rules regarding names; COM(91) 536 final, OJ C122, 14.5.92 p12. Until the proposals are adopted, the Commission's view seems an inaccurate summary of the rules regarding customary names, which currently do not permit the use of names customary in the place of manufacture but not in the place of sale.
4. OJ C270 15.10.91 p3.
5. The example is based upon a decision of the European Court that French rules limiting the name "yoghurt" to products made from fresh fermented milk could not be used to exclude imported deep-frozen yoghurts, provided they are not "substantially" different from the fresh product and are labelled to inform consumers of the differences. The French courts were left to decide whether substantial differences existed between the products; Case 298/87 *Smanor SA* [1988] ECR 4489.
6. See, e.g., du Bois, "An industry's point of view", in H. Deelstra, et al., eds., *Food Policy Trends in Europe* pp33, 38-39 (1992).
7. OJ C270 at 4. The Commission has applied this rule to permit Greece to prohibit the sale of cheeses made from cow's milk under the name "feta". Written Question 2302/87, OJ C9 p2 (1990).

3.3.1.2 A list of ingredients

Most labels must include a list of the product's ingredients[1]. There are, however, exceptions, and the form and proper degree of completeness of the lists are still matters of debate in the Community[2]. The directive defines an "ingredient" as any substance used in the manufacture or processing of a foodstuff and still present, even in an altered form, in the final product[3]. If an ingredient is itself composed of ingredients, all of those secondary substances are themselves ingredients of the final foodstuff[4]. The same rule would apply in infinite regression. Taken literally, these rules would demand very lengthy ingredient listings.

There are, however, important exceptions designed to keep ingredient lists to some reasonable length and level of detail. This avoids overcrowding and may contribute to better consumer understanding. First, any original constituents of a foodstuff separated during the manufacturing process and later reintroduced are not regarded as ingredients if they are ultimately present in their original proportions[5]. For example, fats or sugars separated during processing and afterwards recombined with the product need not be listed as ingredients unless the final product contains more or less of them than before the separation. Second, additives need not be listed if they are present in the final product only because they were in its ingredients, and serve no technical function in the final product[6]. For example, if an ingredient contains an emulsifier which remains in the final compound product, the emulsifier need not be listed if it does not perform emulsifying functions in the final product. The purpose is again to draw some reasonable line among ingredients, ingredients of ingredients, and tertiary or even more remote substances. In fact, it may be difficult to draw such distinctions. A preservative added to an ingredient will generally continue to perform a modest preservative role in the final product itself. The issues are matters of degree, and the directive does not distinguish among differing degrees. Finally, substances need not be listed as ingredients if used only as processing aids, or only as solvents or media for additives or flavourings in quantities "strictly" necessary for those purposes[7].

---

1. Articles 3(2), 6. The list must be introduced by a suitable heading which includes the word "ingredients". Article 6(5)(a).
2. Similar issues arise in the United States. For the rules imposed by or under section 403 of the Food, Drug, and Cosmetic Act, see P. Hutt and R. Merrill, *Food and Drug Law, Cases and Materials* pp74-82 (2nd ed. 1991); P. Hutt, ed., *Guide to US Food Labeling Law* (1991).
3. Article 6(4)(a).
4. Article 6(4)(b).
5. Article 6(4)(c)(i).
6. Article 6(4)(c)(ii). For carry-over additives under the Codex, see sec. 5.2, Codex Alimentarius (2nd ed. 1991). FDA has adopted a similar exception in the United States.
7. Processing aids are additives used during manufacture but removed from the completed product. They may, however, result in residues in the final product. When the residues are excessive, they become contaminants. For processing aids generally, see below at Chapter 5, para 5.9.

Ingredients must generally be listed in descending order of their weights. An ingredient's weight is usually measured at the time of its use during manufacture[1]. A substance's weight will determine its place in the ingredients list, but there is currently no Community obligation to disclose actual weights as measured either at the time of use or in the final product. As described below, however, the Commission has proposed new rules which would require some quantitative disclosures. In addition, there are various exceptions regarding the moment at which weights are measured. For example, water and other volatiles are listed in the order of their weights in the finished product, and not as of the time of their use during manufacture[2]. The purpose is to take account of any loss of volatiles during manufacturing. There is another special rule for measuring water. It may be measured simply by deducting the weights of all other ingredients from the total weight of the finished product[3]. If the result is less than five per cent of the weight of the finished product, or if water is used solely for reconstitution of a dehydrated or concentrated ingredient, water need not be listed at all. Nor need the water in a liquid medium be listed if the medium is not normally consumed[4].

There are other special rules for concentrated and dehydrated foodstuffs. Ingredients introduced in a concentrated or dehydrated form, but reconstituted during manufacture, may be listed according to their weights prior to dehydration or concentration[5]. Similarly, the labels of foodstuffs sold in dehydrated or concentrated form, but intended to be reconstituted, may list ingredients in the order of their weight in the reconstituted product, provided that a notice to this effect accompanies the ingredient list[6]. Finally, there are special rules for mixtures of fruits, vegetables, and herbs and spices where no single foodstuff "significantly predominates" in the mixture[7]. In such cases, the mixture's ingredients may be described as present simply "in variable proportion"[8].

In general, all ingredients must be listed under their specific names, in accordance with the rules described above regarding product names[9]. There are again exceptions. There are more than a dozen categories of foodstuffs which, if used as ingredients of another product, may be listed simply by category name, rather than by specific product name. The categories are identified in an annex to the directive,

1.   Article 6(5)(a).
2.   Article 6(5)(a).
3.   Articles 6(5)(a), 6(8).
4.   Article 6(8). Some in industry have suggested that similar exceptions should be adopted for other liquids used in media.
5.   Article 6(5)(a).
6.   The notice must take the form of a declaration such as "ingredients of the reconstituted product" or "ingredients of the ready-to-use product".
7.   Article 6(5)(a).
8.   Other similar expressions may also be used. The FAC found little justification for any exceptions for compound ingredients, and urged reconsideration of the existing special rules. Food Advisory Committee Report on Food Labelling and Advertising 1990 (1991) at para 88.
9.   Article 6(5)(B).

together with their definitions. They include such products as oil, fat, fish, poultrymeat, and cheese[1]. In other words, processors are not obliged to identify which kinds of oil or fish they have elected to use. The use of these generic descriptors is permissible rather than mandatory[2]. A second annex contains another series of product categories which again may be listed by category name[3]. This includes various additives and processing aids, such as colours, preservatives, antioxidents, emulsifiers, and glazing agents[4]. In these cases, the directive requires the category name to be followed either by the substance's specific name or by its EEC number[5]. For example, an ingredients list may state simply that there are preservatives, followed by the EEC numbers of the relevant substances.

Until the Community's flavouring rules, it was permissible to describe flavourings in any manner prescribed by national law[6]. There are now Community rules which restrict the manner in which flavourings may be described[7]. In addition, the Community's rules for the listing of irradiated ingredients await the adoption of more general requirements regarding irradiated foodstuffs[8]. In the interim, the Community appears to require a notice of irradiation only with respect to final products[9]. Several Member States have, however, adopted their own irradiation labelling rules[10]. There are also special rules for compound ingredients, which may be identified by their legal or customary names and listed in accordance with their overall weights[11]. In such cases, the compound's own ingredients must also be listed unless it constitutes less than 25 per cent of the finished product, or consists of additives, or is itself a foodstuff for which a list of ingredients is not required[12].

---

1. Annex I. The FAC found generic names such as "oil" and "fish" confusing and inadequate, and urged that more specific disclosures should be required. Food Advisory Committee Report on Food Labelling and Advertising 1990 (1991) at para 92. In contrast, many in the food industry have urged that the list should be lengthened. The Commission has drafted an amendment which would modestly revise the annexes. Working Document III/3630/91-EN (1991).
2. Article 6(5)(b).
3. Annex II.
4. Article 6(5)(b).
5. A "temporary" list of EEC numbers was provided for many ingredients by Commission Directive (EEC) 83/463, OJ L255 15.9.83 p1. The FAC found that ingredient lists which combine EEC numbers and names are confusing, and urged that more consistent rules should be adopted. Food Advisory Committee Report on Food Labelling and Advertising 1990 (1991) at paras 92, 96. Indeed, Spain has proposed national rules banning EEC numbers in the labelling of some confectionery products. The Commission has requested a postponement of the rules' effectiveness. Commission Decision (EEC) 91/551, OJ L298 29.10.91 p19. The use of "E" numbers for additives has become sufficiently controversial to provoke a widely sold guide in Britain and France; M. Hanssen, *The New E For Additives: The Completely Revised E Number Guide* (1987), sold in France as *E comme additifs: produits chemiques au menu* (1988).
6. Article 6(5)(b).
7. Below at Chapter 5, para 5.2, post.
8. Below at Chapter 4, para 4.3, post.
9. Article 5(3), as amended in 1989.
10. Below at Chapter 4, para 4.3, post.
11. Article 6(7).
12. The Commission is now considering changes, including a reduction of the 25 per cent rule. Paragraph 88 of the Food Advisory Committee's 1990 labelling report urged reconsideration of all the exceptions regarding compound ingredients.

Some foodstuffs are altogether exempted from the obligation to list ingredients[1]. Ingredients need not be listed for untreated fresh fruits and vegetables; carbonated water, if the fact of carbonation is clear from the product's labelling description; certain fermentation vinegars; cheeses; butter and fermented milk and cream; and products containing only a single ingredient[2]. With respect to foods consisting of a single ingredient, the Commission has proposed to limit the exception to situations where a declaration would be superfluous[3]. This might include situations, for example, where the single ingredient is invariably the same, or where it might vary but is already identified in the product's name[4]. The proposed rule would require ingredient listings unless the product's name and the name of its single ingredient were the same, or unless the product's name otherwise clearly identified the product. The Commission is also considering rules to require ingredient labelling at least of beer, and ultimately perhaps of all alcoholic beverages[5]. For the moment, only a declaration of alcoholic content is required.

With few exceptions, the Community's rules do not require any quantitative declarations regarding ingredients. In part, this reflects the technical difficulty of providing reliable weights for the ingredients in processed or fabricated products, which may vary from one container to another. Even raw agricultural products are inherently heterogeneous, and differ in composition by season, climate and the soil from which they were produced[6]. Moreover, many consumers have little interest in quantitative declarations regarding subsidiary ingredients of compound foodstuffs. Nonetheless, there are situations in which consumers wish quantitative disclosures, and some in which non-quantitative lists have little meaning. The Commission is now addressing these issues, but for the moment it is generally sufficient to declare that a product contains a particular ingredient, without disclosing how much it contains or what percentage of it the ingredient represents.

An important exception involves products whose labelling "places emphasis" upon the presence or low content of a particular ingredient "essential" to the product's

---

1. Article 6(2).
2. Under Article 6(3), special rules apply to alcoholic beverages, for which there are also now proposed ingredient labelling obligations. Those rules and proposals are described below.
3. COM(91) 536 final, OJ C122 14.5.92 p12 at art 1(3). In Britain, the proposal to impose more stringent rules for single-ingredient foodstuffs was welcomed by the FAC; Food Advisory Committee Report on Food Labelling and Advertising 1990 (1991) at para 85.
4. In its working draft of the proposal, the Commission's example of a situation where a quantitative indication would be required was pasta. Its explanation was that pasta may consist of different forms of grain. The example is based upon an Italian measure, overturned by the European Court, which restricted the name "pasta" to products made from durum wheat. See Case 407/85 *Glocken GmbH & Kritzinger v USL Centro-Sud* [1988] ECR 4233; Case 90/86 *Criminal proceedings against Zoni* [1988] ECR 4285.
5. Below at Chapter 7, para 7.11, post. Such rules are authorised but not provided by COM(91) 536 final, OJ C122 14.5.92 p12 at art 1(4).
6. National Academy of Sciences, Committee on Nutritional Components of Food Labeling, *Nutrition Labeling: Issues and Directions for the 1990's* p135 (1990).

specific properties[1]. In such cases, the minimum or maximum percentage of the ingredient used in a product's manufacture must be stated[2]. The Community has left open the possibility that it may eventually require the quantities of these ingredients to be stated by weight or volume rather than simply as a percentage[3]. The rule does not apply to ingredients used in small quantities as flavourings. Nor does it apply to products whose names are, under national rules, required to include the name of an ingredient[4]. In other words, the Community's quantitative disclosure requirement is not triggered by a national requirement regarding a product's name[5].

The Commission has now proposed amendments to the 1978 directive which would more frequently require quantitative ingredient labelling[6]. Under the proposed rules, quantitative labelling would be compulsory in three situations. First, it would be necessary where an ingredient or category of ingredient appears in a product's name or is "derived implicitly" from the name. "Tomato sauce" might be an example. "Pasta sauce" might be a product from whose name the presence of tomatoes would (sometimes wrongly) be inferred. Second, quantitative labelling would be required where an ingredient's presence is "emphasised" on a product's label. Third, it would be required where an ingredient is essential to characterise a foodstuff and to distinguish it from other products with which it might be confused. The last two rules would not, however, apply to ingredients also sold separately as foodstuffs if their drained net weight were shown and they were used in "small" quantities only as flavourings[7]. Other exceptions could be determined through a committee procedure, which could also extend the quantitative labelling obligation to additional situations and provide more detailed rules for the obligation's application. Where quantitative disclosures are required, they must be given as percentages of a given quantity of the finished product. National rules could, however, require them to be given in absolute terms.

---

1.   Article 7(1). There appear to be two conditions to the rule's application: The labelling must give "emphasis" to the ingredient's presence or low content, and the ingredient must be "essential to the specific properties of the foodstuff". It is not clear why the second condition was thought necessary. If a manufacturer elects to give "emphasis", that alone should suffice to create a disclosure obligation. The Commission's proposed rules regarding labelling and advertising claims appear to approach such a requirement. Below at Chapter 3, para 3.5.
2.   Under British rules, food labels may not emphasise an ingredient, or its "low" level, unless the minimum or maximum percentage is given. Food Labelling Regulations 1984, SI 1984/1305, at reg 20.
3.   Article 7(1).
4.   Articles 4(c), 7(1).
5.   The Commission is now considering changes which would limit the exception to situations where the national or Community rules prescribe a foodstuff's characteristics, rather than simply its name.
6.   COM(91) 536 final, OJ C122 14.5.92 p12 at art 1(5).
7.   There would also be an exception for products encompassed by the fourth and fifth indents of Article 6(5)(a) of the 1978 directive.

3.3.1.3 A statement of the container's net quantity

The labels of pre-packaged foodstuffs must generally disclose the container's net quantity[1]. This must be expressed in units of volume for liquids and units of mass for other products[2]. There are numerous exceptions. If Community or national law requires a product's label to indicate the container's "nominal", "minimum" or "average" content, this may replace the disclosure of net quantity[3]. If a product consists of multiple packages of the same size within one larger package (as, for example, snack foods are sometimes sold), the net quantity may be disclosed by stating the number of packages and the net quantity in one package[4]. Even this is not required if the number of packages and one indication of the net contents of each package can be seen from outside the overall packaging. If, however, the smaller individual packages are not themselves units of sale, the total net quantity and number of packages must be disclosed[5].

Containers of foodstuffs normally sold by number need not disclose their net quantity if the number of items is clearly visible or is disclosed in labelling[6]. For example, if fruit is sold by number regardless of the weight of each piece, it is sufficient to give the number. If a solid foodstuff is presented in a liquid medium, the label must disclose the drained net weight as well as the net quantity[7]. Liquid media are defined as mere adjuncts to the product, and include such liquids as brine, acid solutions, vinegar, sugar solutions, and fruit or vegetable juices. A net quantity need not be disclosed for foodstuffs which are subject to losses of weight or volume, and which are sold by number or weighed in the purchaser's presence[8]. Nor is a disclosure of net quantity required for products of less than five grammes or five millilitres, unless the product consists of herbs and spices[9]. Member States may establish higher threshold weights and volumes if purchasers will not be "inadequately informed." The directive offers no guidance as to when such rules may result in inadequate information. If higher thresholds are adopted, the Commission and other Member States must be given notice.

---

1. Article 8.
2. Article 8(1).
3. Article 8(2)(a).
4. Article 8(2)(c).
5. Article 8(2)(d). "Units of sale" are not defined, but presumably include units used to measure price. Perhaps they are also units which are, or may be, sold separately.
6. Article (3). Presumably it is not sufficient for this purpose if a product is normally sold by number; the particular sale involved must itself be by number.
7. Article 8(4).
8. Article 8(5)(a).
9. Article 8(5)(b).

3.3.1.4 Date of minimum durability

Labels must often provide a date of minimum durability[1]. This is the time until which a foodstuff retains its "specific properties" under conditions of proper storage[2]. Those properties are not defined, but include the product's organoleptic qualities as well as its safety and wholesomeness. For most products, the date must be preceded by the words "best before" or "best before end". The date must generally consist of a day, month and year in an uncoded form[3]. If necessary, the date must be followed by a description of the storage conditions required for such a period of durability[4]. If a product will not keep for more than three months, only a day and month need be provided[5]. If it will keep longer than three but less than 18 months, a month and year will suffice. If it will keep longer than 18 months, only a year will suffice. National derogations were permitted until the end of 1992[6].

No minimum durability date is required for many products[7]. They include fresh fruits and vegetables, wines, aromatised wines and similar products, beverages with ten per cent or more of alcohol by volume, soft drinks and fruit juices supplied in large containers to mass caterers, perishable bakery goods, vinegar, cooking salt, chewing gum, and individual portions of ice cream[8]. On the other hand, special durability dates are required for highly perishable foodstuffs likely to constitute an immediate danger to human health[9]. They must bear a date and the phrase "use by" rather than simply a "best before" date. The "use by" date must be accompanied by a description of the storage conditions which must be observed[10]. It must consist of an uncoded day and month[11]. Where appropriate, the year must also be included. Presumably this is necessary, if at all, only in the latter weeks of each year. These requirements were welcomed by Britain's Food Advisory Committee, which urged their prompt adoption in the United Kingdom[12]. This has now occurred[13].

---

1.   Article 9.
2.   Article 9(1).
3.   Article 9(2). Either the date must follow the introductory words or the words must be followed by an indication as to where on the packaging the date may be found.
4.   For the issues presented by chilled and frozen foods and the problems of storage temperatures, see below at Chapter 4, paras 4.1, 4.2.
5.   Article 9(4).
6.   Article 9(5).
7.   Article 9(6).
8.   The list is evidently intended to be exhaustive.
9.   Article 9a. This was one of the changes made by the 1989 directive.
10.   Article 9a (2).
11.   Article 9a (3).
12.   Food Advisory Committee Report on Food Labelling and Advertising 1990 (1991) at paras 68 - 71.
13.   Food Labelling (Amendment) Regulations 1990, SI 1990/2488.

3.3.1.5 Any special storage conditions or conditions of use

Aside from storage conditions needed to achieve a "best before" or "use by" date, the directive offers no guidance as to when and how storage conditions must be indicated[1]. Such rules would be complex, given the diversity of foodstuffs and the variability of their proper storage. The Community does, however, require a warning against the refreezing of quick-frozen foods[2]. The Commission is also preparing general hygiene rules, which may lead to the adoption of new provisions regarding food storage during the distributional chain[3]. Britain's Food Advisory Committee has found an "urgent need" for more precise storage instructions, and particularly regarding storage temperatures[4]. There are increasing incidences of foodborne diseases in Britain and other countries, and one source of the problem is undoubtedly improper storage.

The directive's rules for conditions of use are no more elaborate. It states simply that any special conditions of use must be disclosed, without further guidance as to when they are necessary[5]. It should be noted that the directive requires instructions for use, as well as conditions of use.

As described below, instructions for use relate to the preparation and consumption of foodstuffs, rather than their maintenance or storage.

3.3.1.6 The name or business name and address of the manufacturer or packager, or of a seller within the Community

The labels of pre-packaged products must disclose the name and address of the product's manufacturer or packager, or of a seller established within the Community[6]. The directive does not compel any particular choice among the options. This permits a product manufactured in one location to carry a seller's address in another location. Although a product's origin must be disclosed if its absence would be deceptive, some manufacturers may nonetheless take advantage of their sellers' locations to imply a different origin for their products. There are also minor exceptions to the disclosure obligation. For example, Member States may require only the name of the manufacturer, packager or seller of butter produced within their territories. The Commission must be given notice of such rules.

---

1.   Article 10.
2.   For the Community's rules regarding quick-frozen foodstuffs, see below at Chapter 4, para 4.2. There are no comparable rules for chilled foods; below at Chapter 4, para 4.1.
3.   For the proposed hygiene rules, see below at Chapter 8, para 8.6.1.
4.   Food Advisory Committee Report on Food Labelling and Advertising 1990 (1991) at paras 13, 76.
5.   Council Directive 79/112, above at Article 3(1)(5).
6.   Article 3(1)(6).

3.3.1.7 The product's place of origin or provenance

Labels must disclose a product's place of origin only if the absence of a disclosure could mislead consumers "to a material degree" regarding a product's true origins[1]. For example, a cheese usually identified with France but actually made in Denmark should be labelled as Danish. Separate directives permit Member States to require disclosures of the origins of some foodstuffs, without regard to any established risk of deception[2]. In addition, the Council has adopted Community certifications of origin for products which derive distinctive characteristics from those origins[3].

The identification of a product's origins is inevitably a controversial issue within the Community. An integrated marketplace cannot easily be created if consumers are encouraged to choose products on the basis of origin. The problems are illustrated by two decisions, one by the European Court and the other by the German Court of Appeal in Cologne. In the European Court decision, Italy was prohibited from requiring pasta labels to disclose the product's place and date of manufacture on grounds that this exceeded the provisions of the 1978 directive and impeded Community trade in violation of Article 30 of the Treaty of Rome[4]. The German decision reached quite different results[5]. It involved the marketing of Dutch chicken in Germany bearing labels entirely in German. The labels included a coded identification, but no intelligible disclosure of the products' origin[6]. The court recognised that no express claim of German origin had been made, but reasoned that labelling in German was enough to deceive consumers. It explained that some consumers prefer to purchase German rather than imported products, and that others believe German chickens to be better than Dutch[7]. The court held that the German Unfair Competition Act is not inconsistent with Germany's obligations under the 1978 labelling directive[8]. It also found that the application of German law did not impede Community trade in violation of Article 30 of the Treaty of Rome[9]. On these assumptions, it held that German law properly prohibited the sale of the Dutch chicken.

---

1.   Article 3(1)(7).
2.   See, e.g., below at Chapter 7, para 7.9.
3.   For the certification regulations, see below at para 3.8. The original proposals were reviewed, together with the English rules of product origin, in A. Painter, "The Original of Food Products", 4/91 Eur. Food L. Rev. 282 (1991).
4.   Case C-32/90 *EC Commission v Italy* OJ C224 29.8.91 p4.
5.   Case 6U 173/87 *Re Labelling of Dutch Poultry* [1990] 2 CMLR 104, decided by the Oberlandesgericht of Cologne in 1988.
6.   Ibid., at p110. The label bore a series of numbers and letters which were held to be an unintelligible disclosure of origin.
7.   Ibid., at pp112-114. It does not appear to have occurred to the court that such national perceptions and preferences (which might be described as prejudices) are themselves trade barriers.
8.   Ibid., at pp114-115.
9.   Ibid., at p114.

The two decisions illustrate both the issues which may arise from national obligations to disclose a product's origins and the diverse attitudes which may be adopted regarding those obligations. Designations of origin may be invitations to discriminate against imported products generally, or even against products from a particular Member State[1]. Systematic discrimination would hamper integration of the internal market and seems inconsistent with the goals, if not the terms, of the Treaty of Rome[2]. At the same time, some consumers may believe that products are higher in quality if they have been produced in a particular region or state. Whether or not the perceptions are accurate, it is difficult to deny consumers information which they find relevant. In some instances, the Community forbids Member States to require the disclosure of the origins of products produced within the Community, but a general policy regarding the issue has not been adopted[3].

3.3.1.8 Necessary instructions for use

Instructions for use are required whenever their absence would make it "impossible" for consumers to make appropriate use of a foodstuff[4]. Similar rules are established by other directives for particular product categories, although in some cases those rules appear to demand such instructions with greater frequency[5]. Read literally, the 1978 directive appears to require instructions only in isolated instances. In addition, the directive does not expressly distinguish between conditions of use, which are sometimes required by the rule described earlier, and instructions for use[6]. The former involve steps necessary for the maintenance, storage and preservation of a product, while the latter concern the product's actual preparation and consumption. The distinction is, however, inexact, and the directive offers no definitions or explanations.

---

1.   See, e.g., London Food Commission, *Food Adulteration and How to Beat It* pp27-28 (1988).
2.   Programmes sponsored by Member States to encourage a preference for domestic products are forbidden by the Treaty, although private programmes are permissible; compare Case 222/82 *Apple & Pear Dev. Council v K.J. Lewis Ltd* [1983] ECR 4083, [1984] 3 CMLR 733; Case 249/81 *Re "Buy Irish" Campaign: EC Commission v Ireland* [1982] ECR 4005, [1983] 2 CMLR 104.
3.   For examples of the existing rules, see below at Chapter 7.
4.   Article 3(1)(8).
5.   This was one of the areas in which Britain's FAC urged more precise labelling indications; Food Advisory Committee Report on Food Labelling and Advertising 1990 (1991) at paras 13, 76.
6.   Article 3(1)(5).

3.3.1.9 Alcoholic content

Beverages containing more than 1.2 per cent of alcohol by volume must disclose their actual alcoholic strength[1]. This rule derives from separate Community legislation, described in a later chapter[2].

3.3.1.10 Notice of irradiation

The label of any foodstuff treated by irradiation must disclose the treatment in one of the Community languages. In English, the notice reads "irradiated" or "treated with ionizing radiation"[3]. The directive does not clearly indicate whether the requirement applies to ingredients, rather than final foodstuffs, but suggests strongly that it is applicable only to the latter. Additional rules regarding irradiation have been under consideration by the Community since 1988[4].

3.3.2 Conditions of disclosure

If a product is prepackaged, the required disclosures must generally appear on packaging or an attached label[5]. Pre-packaged foodstuffs are those presented to the ultimate consumer or mass caterers in packaging which wholly or partly encloses them, such that the contents cannot be altered without opening or changing the packaging[6]. Goods wrapped at the time of sale, whether or not at the purchaser's direction, are not prepackaged. In two situations, Member States were originally given discretion as to whether the required disclosures could appear in accompanying trade documents, rather than in labelling. The first was where pre-packaged goods were marketed (for example, to distributors or retailers) prior to their sale to the ultimate consumer. The second was where pre-packaged goods were sold to mass caterers. Both provisions were modified in 1989. The directive now requires that products sold either prior to retail or to mass caterers must bear on their external packaging their names, a date of minimum durability, and the name and address of the manufacturer or packager, or of a seller located in the Community. If highly perishable, they must bear a "use by" date[7]. The other

---

1. Article 10a. For a proposed amendment that the labelling for alcoholic beverages should depend on the legislation relating to each product category, see COM(91) 536 final, OJ C122 14.5.92 p13.
2. Below at Chapter 7, para 7.11.
3. Article 5(3), as amended in 1989.
4. Below at Chapter 4, para 4.3.
5. Article 11 (1)(a).
6. Article 1(3)(b).
7. Article 11(1)(b). These provisions are "without prejudice" to the Community's rules regarding nominal quantities. The latter set tolerances for the fill of various containers, as well as other requirements intended to prevent deceptive packaging. The Community's measures in this area are discussed below. Below at Chapter 8, para 8.1.

required disclosures must be in trade documents which accompany the products or are provided to buyers at or prior to delivery[1].

The directive includes only general instructions regarding the manner in which the mandatory disclosures should be made. It states simply that the disclosures "must be easy to understand", marked in a conspicuous place, and "easily visible, clearly legible and indelible[2]." The last of these requirements is frequently repeated in other measures. The disclosures may not be obscured or interrupted by other written or pictorial matters[3]. Except for reusable glass bottles, the product's name, net quantity, and date of minimum durability or "use by" date must all appear within the same field of vision[4]. The phrase "same field of vision" is not defined by Community law, but a Guidance Note to Britain's Food Labelling Regulations defines it as "simultaneously visible under normal conditions of purchase[5]". The same rule was presumably intended by the directive. There are no Community requirements regarding the relative prominence of the disclosures, any minimal size of typescript, or any necessary format. A few such rules are provided in other measures for particular product categories, but there are no rules of general application[6].

The directive prohibits more detailed national rules concerning the manner in which the required disclosures must be made[7]. The principal exception relates to the sensitive issue of language. For products sold within their own territories, Member States must require the disclosures to be made in a language "easily understood by purchasers." They may, however, permit exceptions where other measures have been taken to inform purchasers[8]. For example, France may permit the sale of products labelled in Greek if reasonable steps have been taken to advise consumers of the label's contents. Nothing in the directive indicates what steps should be accepted as reasonable. Similar exceptions, with the same absence of definitions, are permitted under other directives relating to particular product categories.

---

1. Article 11(1)(c).
2. Article 11(2).
3. Article 11(2).
4. Articles 11(3)(b), (4), (5), (6). In essence, reusable glass bottles with the product's name marked indelibly need not include the other disclosures. There are also derogations regarding the "use by" requirement. In Britain and the Netherlands, there are additional exceptions for reusable milk bottles. Except for the last, these provisions all expire at various points.
5. Guidance Note to Regulation 35 of the Food Labelling Regulations, SI 1984/1305.
6. For one example relating to spirit drinks, see Commission Regulation (EEC) 1781/91, OJ L16 25.691 p5. In contrast, the United States prescribes print sizes, disclosure formats, and other related requirements. See 21 C.F.R. part 101 (1991); P. Hutt, ed., *Guide to US Food Labeling Law* (1991). There are, for example, rules both for "information panels" and "principal display panels".
7. Article 14.
8. The European Court has held that these provisions forbid Belgium from requiring the exclusive use of Flemish in the labelling of mineral waters sold in Belgium's Flemish-speaking areas; C-369/89 *Piageme v BVBA Peeters* (Transcript) 18 June 1991.

Labelling disclosures may be made in multiple languages, and this is increasingly the practice[1].

The absence of format requirements is a significant omission from the Community's rules. In Britain, the Food Advisory Committee found an important need for greater uniformity in the presentation of labelling disclosures[2]. Following the American pattern, it urged the adoption of a standard panel for disclosures. For disclosures not within the panel, "signposting" could direct consumers to the relevant portions of the label. A panel could ensure greater uniformity, and thus prevent unfair trading and encourage consumers to give greater attention to the disclosures. The FAC also urged larger, clearer printing to assist older and visually handicapped consumers, who understandably have difficulty reading some labelling[3]. An expert panel convened in the United States also found that standardised formats and improved legibility are essential if labels are to be helpful to consumers[4]. It warned that labelling is unlikely to affect purchasing decisions "if each label poses a new challenge to consumers"[5]. Similarly, the US Commissioner of Food and Drugs has argued that labels must present information "in a way people can understand and use"[6]. These recommendations should be considered carefully by the Community. Indeed, there is no alternative to Community action, since the labelling directive prevents independent measures by Member States[7].

In contrast, other labelling issues are entrusted to national discretion. The directive authorises Member States to adopt national rules regarding the manner in which disclosures are made for unpackaged foodstuffs, and for products packaged only at the customer's request or on shop premises for direct sale. The rationale is that unpre-packaged sales are essentially local, and that separate national rules cannot hamper Community trade. Any rules which discriminate against Community imports are forbidden by Article 30 of the Treaty of Rome, but within the Treaty's broad limits the content of the national rules is left to the Member States. They may waive some of the disclosures described above if the purchaser receives "sufficient information". In addition, the labelling directive does not override national laws which impose less stringent requirements for "fancy" packaging, such as figurines or souvenirs[8]. Containers whose largest side does not exceed ten square

---

1.   Article 14.
2.   Food Advisory Committee Report on Food Labelling and Advertising 1990 (1991) at para 108.
3.   At para 109.
4.   National Academy of Sciences, Committee on Nutritional Components of Food Labeling, *Nutrition Labeling: Issues and Directions for the 1990's* pp227, 299 (1990).
5.   At 131.
6.   Kessler, "Remarks by the Commissioner of Food and Drugs", 46 Food D.C. L.J. 21, 24 (1991).
7.   Council Directive 79/112, above at Article 14.
8.   Article 13. No explanation has been offered for this derogation. It might have been supposed that "fancy" packagings are precisely those which may often prove deceptive. Perhaps the rule represents an implicit application of the principle caveat emptor. If so, both the principle and its application are unexpected departures for the Community.

centimetres are also excluded from several of the directive's obligations[1]. It is sufficient if their labels disclose the product's name, its net quantity, and a minimum durability or "use by" date. These disclosures need not appear in the same field of vision.

In general, Member States are forbidden to hinder trade in foodstuffs which comply with the directive on the basis of national rules regarding the labelling or presentation of foodstuffs[2]. Nonetheless, Member States may still enforce non-harmonised national laws intended to protect public health; prevent fraud; protect industrial and commercial property rights; provide for indications of provenance, or registered designations of origin; or prevent unfair competition[3]. In part, these exceptions reflect the provisions of Article 36 of the Treaty of Rome.

3.3.3   Procedures for amendment and revision

As amended, the 1978 directive includes provisions designed both to control new national labelling rules and to facilitate supplementary Community rules. Those provisions illustrate the Community's increasing use of committee procedures to supervise national policymaking and expedite subsidiary legislation regarding the internal marketplace[4]. The first provision is similar to the Community's "new approach" to national technical standards, established by the Council's 1983 directive regarding standardisation[5]. The labelling directive provides that Member States may adopt new labelling, presentational or advertising rules only if they notify the Commission of their proposed measures and the reasons for them[6]. The Commission may consult the Standing Committee for Foodstuffs regarding the proposals. Alternatively, any Member State may request that the Standing Committee consider a proposal. In either case, a Member State may not go forward until three months after notification, and cannot go forward at all if the Commission rejects the proposal[7]. A frequent alternative is to order the postponement of proposed rules for periods up to twelve months. If a Member State is permitted to proceed, the Commission must initiate a procedure to determine whether the Community's own rules should be correspondingly modified.

---

1. Article 11(4). The food industry has urged that the size threshold should be increased to take account of the difficulty of labelling small containers. One industry confederation has suggested that the threshold should be 35 square centimetres. Eurofood 5 (Jan. 1992). In the United States, exceptions are permitted for packagings whose total surface area is less then 12 square inches. 21 C.F.R. sec. 101.2(c) (1991).
2. Article 15(1).
3. Article 15(2). The exception for measures designed to prevent fraud is inapplicable where such measures may impede the application of the directive's rules. The same principle would seem to apply to the other exceptions, but it is not expressly reserved with respect to them.
4. Above at Chapter 2, para 2.4.
5. Above at Chapter 2, para 2.4.
6. Article 16(2).
7. A Member State may not go forward with a proposal unless the Commission's opinion is "not negative".

An example is provided by a proposed rule for the labelling of cheeses made from unpasteurised milk[1]. Britain proposed to require the labels of such cheeses to include a statement that they were made from "untreated" or "unpasteurised" milk[2]. The proposal arose from fears about wholesomeness as the cheeses moved through lengthy distributional networks. It was transmitted to the Commission pursuant to the 1978 directive, but proved controversial because many cheeses made in France and other Member States are prepared from unpasteurised milk. The Commission consulted the Standing Committee, and eventually ruled that the proposal would hamper intra-Community trade[3]. It instructed Britain to postpone the proposed rule for twelve months to permit the consideration of a Community measure[4]. The Commission has since drafted an amendment to the 1978 directive which would require the labelling of such cheeses to declare that they are "made based on raw milk"[5]. The word "raw" is evidently thought less disturbing to consumers than "untreated" or "unpasteurised". As a separate matter, the proposal would also require labelling notices if artificial sweeteners were included in foodstuffs, and a warning against the laxative effects of polyols.

The amended labelling directive also includes a committee procedure for the adoption of subsidiary Community legislation. Under the procedure, the Commission may submit proposed measures to the Standing Committee on Foodstuffs. If a qualified majority of the Standing Committee endorses the proposal, it may be adopted by the Commission without further approval[6]. If the Standing Committee fails to express an opinion, the Commission shall "without delay" submit the proposal to the Council. If the Council either approves the measure by a qualified majority or fails to act within three months, it may be adopted by the Commission. In essence, the Commission may go forward with approval from a qualified majority in either the Standing Committee or the Council. Indeed, the Commission may go forward if a proposal has not been rejected by the Council. The arrangement is roughly a legislative delegation, subject to a right of veto[7].

---

1. For another example relating to proposed Spanish rules for confectionery labelling, see Commission Decision (EEC) 91/551, OJ L298 29.10.91 p19. For yet another relating to proposed Danish rules regarding the labelling of emulsified fats, see Commission Decision (EEC) 92/238, OJ L254 6.6.92 p48.
2. See Commission Decision (EEC) 91/333, OJ L184 10.7.91 p25, at the second recital of the preamble.
3. The fifth recital of the preamble.
4. Article 1. The issue is evidently what kinds of disclosures are appropriate regarding such cheeses, rather than whether some disclosure is needed. Some Member States apparently found Britain's disclosure formulae too close to warnings.
5. Working Document III/3631/91-EN (14 Oct 1991).
6. Council Directive (EEC) 89/395, above, at Article 12(4).
7. The arrangement is one form of the partial "off-loading" by the Council of technical matters which was contemplated by the 1985 White Paper pursuant to Article 155 of the Treaty of Rome. A more secure legal basis was later provided by the amendment of Article 145 of the Treaty of Rome by Article 10 of the Single European Act; above at Chapter 2, para 2.3.

An example is provided by a directive adopted in 1991 regarding the designation of flavourings in foodstuffs[1]. The directive was first proposed by the Commission to the Standing Committee. The Standing Committee evidently did not consider the proposal[2]. The Commission thereupon submitted it to the Council, which failed to act within the requisite three-month period[3]. In the absence of Council action, the Commission promulgated the new rules as its own directive. The 1991 directive simply conformed general food labelling to the provisions of the framework flavourings directive[4]. It amends the 1978 directive by adding a new annex which requires flavourings to be designated by the word "flavouring" or some more specific name. It also limits the descriptive word "natural", or any equivalent word, to substances and preparations permitted to be described in that fashion by the framework flavourings directive[5].

Neither the 1978 labelling directive nor its 1989 amendment eliminates other labelling requirements regarding specific product categories. The recipe laws and other Community measures contain extensive labelling requirements which are preserved by the 1978 and 1989 directives unless expressly overridden. For example, the Council has adopted a directive prescribing the names under which chocolate products may be sold, and permits labelling claims of special quality only if compositional standards are satisfied[6]. Similarly, the Commission has issued a directive regulating the indications of alcoholic strength in the labelling of beverages[7]. Another example is offered by the Council's regulation for spirit drinks, which includes labelling obligations[8]. There are also special labelling rules regarding nutritional claims and lot or batch markings. All of these rules are described in later sections.

The Community's rules for the labelling and presentation of foodstuffs are one area in which a substantial degree of harmonisation has been achieved. Some of the rules warrant revision or supplementation, but the central obligations are in place[9]. Two important challenges remain. The first is to provide official controls to ensure that the harmonised rules are observed with fidelity throughout the Community[10].

---

1.   Commission Directive (EEC) 91/72, OJ L42 15.2.91 p27. See also below at Chapter 5, para 5.2.
2.   The sixth recital of the preamble.
3.   The seventh recital of the preamble.
4.   Below at Chapter 5, para 5.2.
5.   Articles 1(1), 1(2). In Britain, the Food Advisory Committee had previously issued *Guidelines on the Use of the Word 'Natural' and Similar Terms* (1989). For a proposed reevaluation of those rules, see Consumer L. Bull. No. 66 p. 3 (March 1992). For France, see Lettre Circulaire (Dec. 20, 1970); Lamy-Dehove at 5.421.
6.   Below at Chapter 7, para 7.1.
7.   Below at Chapter 7, para 7.11.
8.   Below at Chapter 7, para 7.11.
9.   For complaints about labelling rules, most of which originate in the Community, see, e.g *London Food Commission, Food Adulteration and How to Beat It* pp33-36 (1988).
10.   The Commission now sees its "main task" as proper enforcement. EC Commission, *Background Report on Completion of the Internal Market* p4 (20 Feb 1992). For the enforcement problem generally, see below at Chapter 8, para 8.6.

The second is to formulate goals to guide the Community's future rulemaking. With harmonisation largely achieved, the Community must look beyond it to the identification of substantive labelling goals. Without them, the Community's rulemaking will inevitably remain incoherent and inconsistent. Neither challenge is restricted to labelling, and indeed labelling is not an area in which they arise most urgently, but labelling is one place among many where the Community's efforts could appropriately begin.

3.4   Nutritional labelling

The past several decades have produced substantial changes in dietary habits in all industrialised countries[1]. The Community's Member States are no exception. More food is consumed outside the home, snack foods have become common, and meal times less regular[2]. Consumers derive more energy from fats, oils, sugars and sweeteners, and less from grain. More animal protein is consumed. Less bread and fewer potatoes are eaten, but more sugar, meat and cheese. Less alcohol is consumed[3]. Many more foods are chilled or frozen[4]. Even in France, sales of fast foods quadrupled from 1984 to 1991[5]. These changes, together with radical increases in the number of processed and fabricated foods, have stimulated doubts about the healthfulness of national diets in many countries. The concerns are supported by evidence that diet and health are closely linked[6].

---

1.   The changes are described by many commentators. See, e.g., National Academy of Sciences, Committee on Nutritional Components of Food Labeling, *Nutrition Labeling : Issues and Directions for the 1990's* p7 (1990); Fauconneau, "La consommation alimentaire: evolution et mutations", in Académie d'Agriculture de France, ed., *Deux Siècles de Progrés pour L'Agriculture et L'Alimentation 1789-1989* pp311, 312-317 (1990). In the United States, the Commissioner of the Food and Drug Administration has reported "a virtual revolution in the way Americans grow, buy, and consume food". Kessler, "Responding to the Challenge: A Revitalized FDA", 46 Food D.C. L.J. 391, 392 (1991).

2.   For example, meals eaten outside the home vary from perhaps 20 per cent in Britain to 50 per cent in Sweden. See Elton, "Allocation of Priorities - Where Do the Real Risks Lie?", in G. Gibson & R. Walker, eds., *Food Toxicology - Real or Imaginary Problems?* pp3, 4 (1985). See also Waites & Arbuthnott, "Foodborne Illness: An Overview", in The Lancet, ed., *Foodborne Illness* pp1, 3-4 (1991). Germans are said to consume 30 per cent of their meals outside the home. Eurofood 10 (June 1992).

3.   Fauconneau reports that less wine is drunk even in France, but it is higher in average quality. "La Consommation alimentaire: evolution et mutations", in Académie d'Agriculture de France, ed., *Deux Siècles de Progrés pour L'Agriculture et L'Alimentation 1789-1989* p317 (1990).

4.   Meffert, "Economic Developments Pertinent to Chilled Foods", in T. Gormley, ed., *Chilled Foods: The State of the Art* pp337, 338-341 (1990). There are, however, important variations within the Community. Many are north-south differences. For example, putting aside Spain and Portugal, Italians consume only about one-fourth as many frozen foods as consumers in the Community generally and only one-eighth as many as Danes. The overall foodstuffs market continues to grow more diversified and internationalised; ibid., at pp342-344.

5.   Eurofood 10 (April 1992).

6.   See, e.g., National Academy of Sciences, Committee on Nutritional Components of Food Labeling, *Nutrition Labeling: Issues and Directions for the 1990s* p7 (1990). The Council endorsed the idea of a link between diet and cancer in its 1986 resolution regarding the European programme against cancer. See Council Directive (EEC) 90/496, OJ L276 6.10.90 p40, at the third recital of the preamble.

Consumers often wish nutritional information to make better choices among the varied foods with which they are presented. Correspondingly, manufacturers may wish to provide nutritional information to distinguish their products from those of their competitors. With these complementary incentives, many manufacturers have begun claiming nutritional properties and advantages for their products. Some of the claims are incomplete, if not deceptive, and there were frequent demands for new labelling regulations throughout the 1980's[1.] The Codex Alimentarius Commission issued guidelines in 1985, and new measures regarding nutritional labelling were adopted in 1990 in both the Community and the United States. The Community's legislation is patterned closely upon the Codex rules[2]. Nonetheless, neither the Community nor the American measure is likely to end the controversy regarding nutritional labelling.

The most comprehensive evaluation of nutritional labelling was made in the United States by an expert panel convened by the National Academy of Sciences[3]. The panel emphasised that dietary changes could promote public health and that food labelling could assist consumers in making prudent choices[4]. It urged nutritional labelling for all foods, except where impractical or unduly costly[5]. Nutritional disclosures should be provided for foods sold without prepackaging by notices at the point of sale[6]. Restaurants should provide nutritional information whenever requested by consumers[7]. The information should be periodically verified. Labelling disclosures should be standardised to facilitate their use by consumers[8].

The panel's report appeared too late to influence labelling legislation adopted by Congress in 1990, but many of its proposals are nonetheless similar to the rules in the American statute[9]. The latter is more complex and demanding than the Community's 1990 measure[10]. Unlike the Community's directive, the Nutrition

---

1.   One demand for improved rules was made by the present Commissioner of FDA before his appointment to that office. See Kessler, "The Federal Regulation of Food Labeling", 321 New Eng. J. Med. 717, 719-23 (1989).

2.   For the Codex rules, see CAC/GL 2-1985, sec. 4.2, Codex Alimentarius (2nd ed. 1991); van der Heide, "The Codex Alimentarius on Food Labelling", 4/91 Eur. Food L. Rev. 291, 293 (1991).

3.   National Academy of Sciences, Committee on Nutritional Components of Food Labeling, *Nutrition Labeling: Issues and Directions for the 1990s* (1990).

4.   At Chapter 5.

5.   At 12.

6.   At 12-13.

7.   At 13-14. The panel urged that symbols and descriptors should be used on menus to indicate nutritional properties.

8.   At 11.

9.   At IX-XI.

10. The US International Trade Commission has described the Community directive as both "much less restrictive" and less "substantive" than the new American rules. *The Effects of Greater Economic Integration within the European Community on the United States*, Third Report, 4-25, 4-26 (1990). In comments submitted to FDA, the Community has responded that the NLEA rules are too extensive and "confusing" to consumers. Comments of the European Community 9-10 (25 Feb 1992).

Labelling and Education Act of 1990 ("NLEA") requires nutritional labelling to be provided in a standardised format for most packaged and many unpackaged foods[1]. A nutritional labelling obligation generally exists even if no nutritional claims are made. There are, however, exceptions. For example, exceptions are permitted for restaurant meals, foods sold to processors or mass caterers, foods sold by small retail establishments, infant formulae, and foods containing insignificant amounts of nutrients and for which no nutritional claims are made. Special rules are provided for products whose properties may require alternative labelling methods. These include foods for special dietary use[2]. Raw agricultural products and fish are initially subject to voluntary controls, but FDA is empowered to impose mandatory labelling requirements if the voluntary arrangements prove unsatisfactory.

Permissible labelling descriptors are to be defined in regulations[3]. These are words or phrases used in a product's labelling or presentation to indicate its level of a nutrient. For example, the new rules will provide standards for determining when it may be claimed that a product is "low" in a substance, or "free" from it. Once the permissible descriptors have been designated, no others may be used without special authorisation from FDA. Similarly, FDA will issue regulations defining any health claims which will be permitted. The new statute pre-empts some of the states' previous authority regarding food labelling, but also permits them to enforce some federal requirements.

The Community's new rules for nutritional labelling differ substantially both from those recommended by the National Academy and from those imposed by the NLEA[4]. The Community's rules derive from a directive adopted in 1990 to harmonise national rules regarding the nutritional labelling of foodstuffs delivered "as such" to the ultimate consumer, or intended for restaurants, hospitals or other mass caterers[5]. The directive expressly supplements the 1978 labelling directive[6]. Unlike the NLEA, nutritional labelling is optional unless a nutritional claim is

---

1.   Nutrition Labeling and Education Act, P.L. No. 101-535, 104 Stat. 2353 (1990).
2.   Foods for "special dietary use" are essentially those described in the Community as foods for particular nutritional uses; below at Chapter 4, para 4.5.
3.   Extensive proposed rules have been published by FDA for public comment. For an analysis, see P. Hutt, ed., *Guide to US Food Labeling Law* (1991).
4.   The Community's rules are, however, closer to the guidelines issued by the Codex Alimentarius Commission. The latter require nutritional labelling only if a nutritional claim has been made, and permit the calculation of nutritional values in terms of serving sizes, or based upon 100 grammes of the product, or as percentages of a recommended daily intake of a nutrient. See van der Heide, "The Codex Alimentarius on Food Labelling", 4/91 Eur. Food L. Rev. 291, 294 (1991); National Academy of Sciences, Committee on Nutritional Components of Food Labeling, *Nutrition Labeling: Issues and Directions for the 1990's* p315 (1990). In a submission to FDA, the Community has criticised the NLEA rules as a "unilateral" deviation from international standards without a "convincing" basis. Comments of the European Community 8 (25 Feb 1992).
5.   Council Directive (EEC) 90/496, OJ L276 10.10.90 p40. See generally Mullaly, "Food Labeling Regulations for Nutrition and Irradiation in the European Economic Community", 13 Boston Coll. Int'l and Comp. L. Rev. 429 (1990).
6.   The final recital of the preamble.

made in a product's labelling, presentation, or advertising[1]. Generic advertising is disregarded for purposes of deciding whether a nutritional claim has been made[2].

"Nutritional claims" are broadly defined. They include any representation or message that a foodstuff has particular nutritional properties because of the caloric value it does or does not provide, or provides at reduced or increased levels, or because of the nutrients it does or does not contain, or contains in reduced or increased levels[3]. These claims must be made voluntarily. If other legislation has required a labelling statement regarding a nutrient, compliance does not constitute a nutritional claim. Nothing in the directive identifies the relevant legislation, but Member States are generally forbidden to adopt requirements regarding nutritional labelling, and Community legislation will therefore be the principal source of such obligations[4].

Although the Commission may initially have contemplated some mandatory nutritional labelling, the 1990 directive requires such labelling only if nutritional claims are made[5]. The only permissible nutritional claims are those relating to energy, protein, carbohydrate, fat, fibre, sodium, and various vitamins and minerals listed in an annex to the directive[6]. Among other things, the annex includes vitamins A, D, E, C, B6 and B12, calcium, thiamin, riboflavin, niacin, iron, magnesium and phosphorus[7]. In addition, if a nutritional claim is made with respect to sugars, saturates, fibre or sodium, the labelling must include their amounts[8].

---

1. Article 2(2).
2. The directive does not define "generic" advertising, but it presumably encompasses any advertising on behalf of a product category (for example, beef products) or even a particular product (for example, whole or skim milk) not conducted on behalf of a particular producer or brand.
3. Article 1(4)(b).
4. Articles 7(3), 8. In principle, the provision also includes any pre-existing national, regional or local requirements.
5. Simultaneously with its proposal of voluntary nutritional labelling in 1988, the Commission also proposed a framework for compulsory labelling when and if necessary. COM(88) 489 final, OJ C282 5.11.88 p8. The Commission's proposal would not itself have created such requirements, but would simply have provided a procedure by which the Commission could adopt requirements in light of epidemiological evidence and after consultations with the Scientific Committee for Food. The Commission's submission to FDA regarding FDA's proposed nutritional rules makes clear that it now opposes mandatory labelling. Comments of the European Community 2 (25 Feb 1992).
6. Article 3. In contrast, the NLEA requires labelling regarding a longer series of components, including among others, sodium, cholesterol, sugars, total calories and calories from fat, total carbohydrates and complex carbohydrates.
7. At the Annex.
8. Article 4(2). These requirements will take effect in 1995. Article 11 (2). The directive expressly postpones any definition of "fibre", but contemplates the adoption of a definition through a committee procedure. Article 1(4)(j). Fibre is defined as non-starch polysaccharides by Britain's Guidelines on Nutrition Labelling (1988) at Appendix 1.

If a producer does not make nutritional claims but nonetheless provides nutritional labelling, there are again minimum standards. The label must disclose the product's energy value, followed by its content of protein, carbohydrate and fat[1]. Nutritional labelling must also include the amounts of starch, polyols, mono-unsaturates, polyunsaturates, cholesterol, and any of the vitamins and minerals listed in the annex present in "significant" amounts[2]. "Significance" is defined as at least 15 per cent of a substance's recommended daily allowance. If the amounts of polyunsaturates or mono-unsaturates or cholesterol rates are given, the amount of saturates must also be given[3]. The directive designates permissible methods for calculating energy values[4], and describes the manner in which the various labelling declarations must be made[5]. The various disclosures must be made in terms of contents per 100 grammes or 100 millilitres, but they may also be made in contents per serving or portion if the number of portions in the package is stated on the label[6]. The relative advantages of disclosures by weight or serving have been disputed, and the Council has avoided any complete resolution of the issue[7].

The disclosures must reflect calculations based upon the products as sold, but may also be given for the prepared food if detailed directions are included for its preparation[8]. The declared values are to be averages based upon the manufacturer's analyses, known or actual values of the ingredients, or calculations

---

1. Article 4(1).
2. Article 4(3). Polyols are sugar alcohols. A. Bender, *Dictionary of Nutrition and Food Technology* p225 (6th ed. 1990).
3. Article 4(4).
4. Article 5. Specified conversion values are provided for protein, fat, alcohol and other substances. These add certainty, but could also prove troublesome with respect to novel foods. Some novel food ingredients are, for example, intended to reduce the caloric value of fats. A mechanism is, however, provided by Article 5 for modification of the conversion values. Similar conversion factors are provided in Regulation 37 of Britain's Food Labelling Regulations, SI 1984/1305. In the United States, the National Academy's expert panel recommended that rules should be reexamined if they may inhibit the introduction of foods or ingredients lower in fat. Mandatory conversion factors might have such a result. National Academy of Sciences, Committee on Nutritional Components of Food Labeling, *Nutrition Labeling: Issues and Directions for the 1990's* p25 (1990).
5. Article 6. One issue left in some question is the proper unit of measurement for energy. In a notice regarding implementation of the directive, Britain's Ministry of Agriculture, Fisheries and Food has suggested that kilojoules should be used before kilocalories. Notice to Interested Parties, at para 6.1 (Aug. 21, 1991). It is unlkely that most consumers know that a kilojoule equals 4.184 kilocalories, or that the latter is 1000 times greater than the calorie used for measurements in physics. V. Claudio & R. Lagna, *Nutrition and Diet Therapy Dictionary* pp31, 134 (3rd ed. 1991). The key is consistency.
6. Article 6(2).
7. See, e.g., National Academy of Sciences, Committee on Nutritional Components of Food Labeling, *Nutrition Labeling: Issues and Directions for 1990s* pp214-215 (1990). The National Academy's panel concluded that disclosures by weight are more confusing and less helpful than disclosures by servings, especially with respect to ultralight products. Canada has recently adopted requirements based upon servings; ibid. In contrast, the Codex Alimentarius rules reject servings in favour of disclosures by weight. See van der Heide, "The Codex Alimentarius on Food Labelling", 4/91 Eur. Food L. Rev. 291, 297 (1991). Britain's Guidelines on Nutrition Labelling (1988) used 100 grammes or millilitres. The Community has urged FDA to turn to metric values. Comments of the European Community 17 (25 Feb 1992).
8. Article 6(4).

from "generally established and accepted data"[1]. Disclosures regarding vitamins and minerals must also include percentages of the recommended daily allowances, as shown in an annex to the directive[2]. Declarations must be printed legibly and indelibly in a conspicuous place[3]. The information must appear in a language easily understood by purchasers, unless other measures have been taken to inform them[4]. Provisions are made for the eventual authorisation of graphic formats[5].

Member States are generally forbidden to adopt more detailed nutritional labelling requirements[6]. Nonetheless, they may continue to regulate the extent to which, and manner in which, nutritional information is given to consumers regarding non-pre-packaged foodstuffs[7]. Those issues may, however, eventually be governed by Community rules adopted through a committee procedure[8]. The nutritional labelling directive applies to imported products, but there is no indication as to how or by whom such products will be inspected[9]. This is left to national law, or measures adopted by a committee procedure under either the nutritional labelling directive itself or Community provisions for official inspections and controls[10].

A related area is not addressed by the directive or other Community legislation. There is a growing demand for dietary supplements which contain increased levels of nutrients or other special ingredients[11]. They include such products as vitamin and mineral supplements, herbal teas and powders, fortified foods, and slimming aids[12]. Health or dietary claims about the products are common, and some consumers attribute nutritional advantages to them. Most of the products are harmless, and some are conceivably helpful. Others may, if abused, present hazards to health[13]. Many are accurately labelled and avoid extravagant health

---

1.   Article 6(8). The directive offers no express order of preference, and manufacturers are evidently permitted an option. For this and other ambiguities, see, e.g., MAFF's notice to interested parties regarding Britain's implementation of the directive, dated 21 August 1991. Article 13 of Britain's Guidelines on Nutrition Labelling (1988) offers the same order of priority. Reference values is an area in which the Commission has urged FDA to join in international harmonisation. Comments of the European Community 17-18 (25 Feb 1992).

2.   Article 6(5).

3.   Article 7. This is one of the few instances in which the Community has designated format and printing requirements. There are, however, some national rules. For example, Article 14 of Britain's Guidelines on Nutrition Labelling (1988) requires all nutrition information to appear "all together in one place". It also suggests formats.

4.   Article 7(2). This exception appears regularly in the Community's legislation. Multiple languages are permissible.

5.   Article 6(3). In the absence of Community rules for graphic formats, it is unclear whether they are prohibited.

6.   Article 7(3).

7.   Articles 7(3), 8.

8.   Article 9, 10

9.   USITC, *The Effects of Greater Integration within the European Community on the United States,* Third Report, 4-54 (1990)

10.   For official controls, see Chapter 8, below at para 8.6.

11.   The most recent study of the issues was provided by a working group of Britain's Department of Health in *Dietary Supplements and Health Foods* (1991).

12.   *Dietary Supplements and Health Foods* (1991) at para 1.2.

13.   Ibid., at para 1.4.

claims, but some labelling and promotional practices are more questionable[1]. Some of the products might be regarded as medicines, and regulated as such[2]. Others might be seen as foods for particular nutritional uses, and could be regulated under the Community's rules for those foods[3]. Still others do not fit readily into the established regulatory categories. The commercial success of such products, together with the possible risks of consumer deception and to human health, have created a demand for more systematic regulatory measures[4]. In Britain, an expert committee has recommended labelling and other restrictions[5].

The Commission has promised to address dietary integrators, but draft rules have not yet appeared[6]. Directorate-General III has, however, prepared a discussion paper which explores possible regulatory steps. Issued late in 1991, the paper notes that some Member States already require prior authorisations for the marketing of diet integrators, and suggests that extensive Community rules may be necessary. Among others, the paper considers rules regarding instructions for use, purity criteria, good manufacturing practices, maximum constituent levels, and a negative list of forbidden constituents. Child-resistant closures may also be appropriate. The paper does not examine these possibilities in detail, and it is clear that the Commission has only begun its examination of the issues. In the interim, the European Proprietary Medicines Manufacturers Association (AESGP) has responded with its own proposals[7].

The 1990 directive should improve the balance of any nutritional claims which are made, and makes a start toward standardised formats for labelling disclosures. Other issues are left unresolved. Apart from rules for nutritional supplements, national rules regarding nutritional disclosures with respect to unpre-packaged foods are still not harmonised[8]. Nor is there any settled definition of fibre[9]. The

---

1.   Ibid., at para 1.5 and Appendix 2.
2.   Ibid., at paras 3.6-3.9. Although it has made various efforts to define "medicines", the Community does not yet provide rules to define "foods". For the US rules, see, e.g., *Nutrilab, Inc. v Schweiker*, 713 F.2nd 335 (7th Cir. 1983); *American Health Prods. Co. v Hayes*, 744 F.2d 912 (2nd Cir. 1984). In the United States, nutritional supplements also occupy a "gray area" in the law. Kessler, "Restoring FDA's Preeminence in the Regulation of Food", 46 Food D.C. L.J. 395, 401 (1991).
3.   At para 3.13. The Commission has stated that it does not regard "dietary integrators", which it uses as a synonym for "dietary supplements", to be "parnuts" foods. For the Community's rules regarding such foods, see Chapter 4, below at para 4.5. The Commission apparently reasons that integrators are intended for general consumption, and not for the particular needs of specific populations.
4.   There are rules in several Member States, but they embody disparate attitudes and standards. Their validity has been challenged and their status is in some cases apparently questionable; see para 3.15.
5.   *Dietary Supplements and Health Foods* (1991) at para 3.14. In the United States, the Commissioner of FDA has said that dietary supplements should be regulated because they "can harm people". Kessler, "Restoring FDA's Preeminence in the Regulation of Food", 46 Food D.C.L.J. 295, 401 (1991).
6.   Ibid., at para 3.13.
7.   EIS, European Environment, No 384 at IV-2 (31 March 1992).
8.   Articles 7(3), 8.

directive's requirements regarding claims about sugars, saturates, fibre and sodium do not become effective until late 1995. The other rules become effective in October 1993[1]. Nor are the Community's new rules as precise or detailed as those imposed by the NLEA or suggested by Britain's Food Advisory Committee[2]. They are also less comprehensive than the recommendations of the National Academy's expert panel. The 1990 directive requires the Commission to submit a report regarding its application in 1998, and it is likely that substantial changes in the Community's rules will not occur before the report's preparation[3].

3.5 The regulation of other labelling and marketing claims

The 1978 labelling directive instructed the Commission to propose additional rules regarding two issues. They were rules for the disclosure of alcoholic content and a non-exclusive list of health or other claims which should generally be prohibited or restricted in the labelling, presentation or advertising of foodstuffs[4]. Rules regarding the disclosure of alcoholic content were adopted with reasonable promptness[5]. In 1981, the Commission prepared a list of labelling and advertising claims which should be restricted or forbidden, but the measure was never adopted. Member States evidently found it insufficiently precise[6]. Nine years later, the Commission circulated a preliminary working draft of a new proposal. Several revisions have followed. The draft provoked substantial questions and the Commission has now reportedly abandoned it, but it nonetheless warrants description as the Commission's most recent effort to resolve an important issue of regulatory policy. In addition, the Commission's draft should be compared to suggestions made by Britain's Food Advisory Committee and requirements imposed in the United States by the 1990 nutritional labelling statute. Before describing the draft, however, it is useful to examine the Community's broader prohibitions against deceptive advertising.

---

9.   Article 1(4)(j).
1.   Article 11(2).
2.   For the NLEA, see above at Chapter 3, at para 3.4. For the FAC's recommendations, see Food Advisory Committee Report on Food Labelling and Advertising 1990 (1991) at Appendix V.
3.   Council Directive (EEC) 90/496, above at Article 11(3). See also the ninth recital of the preamble.
4.   When the 1978 directive was adopted, the Codex Alimentarius was completing proposed rules regarding food claims, and its work suggested the feasibility of similar Community rules. See Codex Alimentarius sec. 4.1 (2nd ed. 1991); CAC/GL 1-1979 (Rev.1-1991); van der Heide, "The Codex Alimentarius on Food Labelling", 4/91 Eur. Food L. Rev. 291, 293 (1991).
5.   Below at Chapter 7, at para 7.11.
6.   Working Document II/9081/90-Rev. 1 (1990) at 3.

3.5.1   General restrictions upon advertising content

The Commission proposed a directive for the control of misleading advertising as early as 1978[1]. The proposal addressed comparative advertising as well as unfair and deceptive claims. The issues proved controversial, with Member States particularly divided over the merits of comparative advertising[2]. No directive was adopted until 1984, and it dealt only with deceptive advertising[3]. Comparative advertising was left for the Member States to prohibit or not, as they individually found appropriate. The 1984 directive broadly defines "advertising" to include all representations made in connection with a business, profession, trade, or craft to promote the sale of goods or services[4]. Labelling, product presentations, and advertising in all media are included. Advertising is "misleading" if it deceives, or is likely to deceive, those to whom it is addressed or whom it reaches. The deception must be likely to influence the economic behaviour of the advertisement's recipients, or to injure a competitor of the advertiser[5]. The deception must either encourage the purchase of a product or service, or discourage the purchase of a competing product or service.

An advertisement's potential deceptiveness is judged in light of all its features[6]. This includes claims regarding the product's uses, fitness, manufacture or results. It also encompasses information about the product's price, the methods by which the price was calculated, and other terms or conditions under which the product is sold. Relevant features also include the advertiser's identity, assets, special qualifications, or distinctiveness. In other words, an advertisement may be found misleading based upon all the information it contains, or fails to contain, regarding any attribute of the product or its advertiser likely to influence the product's sale or the sale of a competing product. The burden of proof is upon the advertiser to establish that his advertisements are not misleading[7].

The 1984 directive consists principally of requirements for the establishment of national systems for the regulation of advertising[8]. Member States were required to

---

1.   The history of the Commission's efforts is recounted in the explanatory memorandum which accompanied COM(91)147 final (21 June 1991), at para 3.4.
2.   The 1978 proposal was, however, supported by the Economic and Social Committee and European Parliament. See OJ C70 21.3.78 p1; OJ C49 24.2.92 p35, at para 1.1.
3.   Council Directive (EEC) 84/450, OJ L250 19.9.84 p17. The directive has been adopted in all the Member States except Italy and, in large measure, Belgium. See COM(91) 147 final, above at 5. See also OJ C49 24.2.92 p35, at para 1.4.
4.   Council Directive 84/450, above at Article 2(1).
5.   Article 2(2). There is no provision exempting puffery or hyperbole.
6.   Article 3.
7.   Article 6.
8.   Before the 1984 directive, the European Court held that Member States may not discriminate against foreign products in applying national advertising rules; Case 314/81 *Procurer de la Republique v Waterkey* [1982] ECR 4337, [1983] CMLR 145, decided in 1982 by the European Court upon reference from the Tribunal de Grande Instance of France.

adopt rules allowing legal actions against misleading advertising either in national courts or before administrative authorities[1]. The tribunal must be empowered to order the cessation of misleading advertising and even to prevent its publication[2]. The future publication of misleading advertising may be prohibited without proof of actual loss or damage, intentional behaviour, or even negligence. It is, in other words, a broad authority to police the content of all advertising[3]. National rules must also permit expedited proceedings for immediate relief against deceptive claims on at least an interim basis[4]. They must include a power to compel corrective advertising. None of these rules forecloses industry codes for self-regulation or more stringent national rules[5].

The Commission has now reopened the issue of comparative advertising, about which it failed to obtain agreement in 1984. Several Member States prohibit comparative advertising, and others have adopted substantial restrictions[6]. The Commission has proposed a directive to amend the 1984 directive and generally authorise comparative advertising. "Strict limitations" would be imposed[7]. The only permissible comparisons would be those which are objective, relevant, verifiable and fairly chosen[8]. The comparisons could not be misleading or confusing, and could not denigrate a competitor or his products[9]. References could be made to third-party comparative testing only with the third party's consent, and only if the advertiser accepted responsibility for the testing's adequacy[10]. The 1984 directive's requirements regarding regulatory procedures would be extended to include comparative advertising, but the power of Member States to adopt more stringent standards would no longer include an option to prohibit comparative

---

1.   Article 4(1).
2.   Article 4(2).
3.   There is no express exception for political advertising, although "advertising" is defined to include claims in connection with a trade, business craft or profession intended to promote the supply of goods or services. Article 2(1). Commissioner van Miert has excluded political, corporate and institutional advertising. Written Question 171/91, OJ C315 5.12.91 p5.
4.   The accelerated procedures may, at the option of the Member States, result in either interim or final decisions.
5.   Articles 5, 7.
6.   A summary of the national rules is contained in the Commission's explanatory memorandum which accompanied COM(91) 147 final; ibid., at pp13-19. Several Member States, including Belgium and Germany, forbid even truthful comparisons. In others, there are either significant restrictions or the law is unclear. Comparative advertising is generally permitted in the United States, Canada and Scandinavia; ibid., at pp13-21. For a recent decision illustrating the Belgian rules, see *Federation Royale de l'Industrie des Eaux et des Boissons Refraishissantes v S.A. Procter & Gamble Benelux*, A.C./3.853/92, decided in Brussels on 30 March 1992.
7.   COM(91) 147 final, above at 9.
8.   Article 3a(1).
9.   The limits upon this are unclear. All unfavourable comparisons are to some degree denigrating, and the Commission's restriction may therefore invite distinctions based upon the forcefulness of an advertisement. Would it, for example, be permissible to claim that one product is "better" than another, but not that it is "much better"?
10.   Article 3a (2).

advertising[1]. The burden of proof to justify an advertisement would still be upon the advertiser[2].

The Commission's proposal is scarcely a strong endorsement of comparative advertising, although it assumes that comparisons may sometimes represent a healthy form of competition[3]. Comparisons may stimulate innovation and provide the basis for more reasoned choices by consumers. Nonetheless, the Commission and some Member States remain convinced of the need for rigid controls. Even the Economic and Social Committee, which generally endorses comparative advertising, has urged stringent limitations. They include special rules for mail order sales. More generally, the ESC has demanded rules against "innuendo (or any wording which could be construed as innuendo), implied comparisons, shock tactics, or gratuitous insinuation"[4]. Implicit in these concerns is scepticism that consumers can be relied upon to distinguish puffery from fact. The issues are controversial, but the Commission is likely to continue to press both for a limited approval of comparative advertising and for broader restrictions upon deceptive advertisements[5].

3.5.2 The draft restrictions upon food advertising claims

The Commission's 1990 draft rules for the prohibition or limitation of food claims do not address comparative advertising. Nor do they suggest new prohibitions against deceptive advertising in general. The draft proposal instead provides non-exhaustive lists of claims permitted only under specified conditions and other claims which would be entirely prohibited because they are misleading to consumers[6]. A committee procedure could add new claims, or otherwise reformulate the lists[7]. If the rules were adopted, they might eventually be applied to foodstuffs sold to mass caterers, but they would initially reach only foods intended

---

1.   Proposed Article 7(2).
2,   Council Directive (EEC) 84/450, above at Article 6.
3.   COM(91) 147 final, above at 6-9. The advantages to consumers of comparative advertising were also accepted by UNICE, the Union of Industrial and Employers' Confederations of Europe, in a position paper issued in April 1992. UNICE urged, however, that strict controls should be imposed. Its Belgian delegation would instead have imposed a general prohibition against comparative advertising, subject to specific exceptions.
4.   OJ C49 24.2.92 p35, at para 2.14. The ESC did not explain how these broad prohibitions could be reduced to the precise rules it otherwise believes necessary. At para 2.6.
5.   The Commission's proposal states that the rules against misleading advertising are incomplete and that additional restrictions are needed, quite apart from comparative advertising. Ibid., at 5. Belgium and other Member States opposed to comparative advertising are apparently now arguing that questions of deception should be "resolved" before comparative advertising is addressed.
6.   Working Document III/9081/90-Rev. 1, above at 3, 9, 13-14. For varying definitions of "claims", as well as CIAA proposals for their regulation, see EC Food Law p5 (July 1992).
7.   Ibid., at pp3, 9.

for sale to the ultimate consumer. The draft proposal would entirely forbid the following claims in the labelling, presentation and advertising of such foods[1]:

(a)   Claims relating to measurable characteristics of a product which cannot be substantiated;

(b)   claims likely to bring other foodstuffs into disrepute[2];

(c)   claims that a balanced diet of everyday foodstuffs cannot provide adequate quantities of all nutritive substances[3];

(d)   claims that an everyday foodstuff contains all of the necessary nutritive elements in adequate quantities for a balanced diet;

(e)   claims that a foodstuff has acquired nutritive value from the addition of substances which in fact were added for technical or organoleptic reasons;

(f)   claims of endorsements or approvals by the medical, paramedical or pharmaceutical professions[4];

(g)   claims involving a medical or similar association, or a medical instrument, or the human body or a human organ intended to illustrate a bodily function[5];

(h)   claims linking diet and health; and

(i)   claims which imitate product names protected by Community law, even if preceded by words such as "type", "kind" or "imitation"[6].

Moreover, the Commission's draft proposal would permit the following claims only if fully substantiated and subject to appropriate verification[7]:

(a)   claims suggesting that a product is superior or exclusive in its possession of measurable factors. These claims would be permitted only with a precise indication of the nature or limits of the

---

1.   Ibid., at pp13-14.
2.   Such a rule might forbid or greatly inhibit comparative advertising, although it might merely forbid comparisons which are not truthful or are misleading.
3.   Britain's FAC would also forbid claims relating to deficiency diseases, although it recognised the desirability of rules regarding the usefulness of some foods for preventing chronic diseases. Food Advisory Committee Report on Food Labelling and Advertising 1990 (1991) at paras 125 - 129.
4.   Some reconciliation with the framework directive for foods for particular nutritional uses, below at Chapter 4, para 4.5, or one of its proposed "daughter" directives, might prove necessary. In general, the Community resists the authorisation of endorsements. It was more accommodating with respect to mineral waters. Below at Chapter 7, at para 7.9. The 1990 proposal would not forbid endorsements by persons in non-medical occupations, such as film or rock stars. In contrast, the FAC has proposed a prohibition of all testimonials. Food Advisory Committee Report on Food Labelling and Advertising 1990 (1991) at para 140.
5.   This provision seems particularly opaque, although presumably it would, for example, apply to references to human kidneys in the labelling of mineral waters, compare above at Chapter 7, para 7.9, diagrams of the human digestive system, or similar labelling or advertising devices.
6.   This provision would be linked to the new Community designations based upon geographical origins or product distinctiveness. Below at Chapter 3, para 3.8. It might, for example, forbid "imitation Serrano ham" or "Beaujolais-type wine".
7.   The Commission has not explained how or when verification might occur. The FAC has urged that it is generally preferable to impose strict criteria for determining permissible claims, rather than to require premarketing approvals. Food Advisory Committee Report on Food Labelling and Advertising 1990 (1991) at paras 133-134.

product's asserted degree of superiority or exclusivity, and only if otherwise consistent with Community legislation;

(b)   claims that a product is "natural". These claims would be permitted only for products found in nature, which have not been subjected to any treatment other than cold treatment, mechanical extraction or mixing, and which were without any additives or chemical product additions[1]; or only if a product had undergone no treatment other than pasteurisation or sterilisation, and was presented in a medium consisting only of water and salt[2].

(c)   claims of increased or reduced content of a nutriment, another substance, or energy[3]. These claims would be permitted only if the addition or reduction amounted to a change from the original level of at least 30 per cent, and the content was indicated in the same field of vision as the product's name[4].

(d)   claims of a low level of a nutriment, or another substance or material. These claims would be permitted only if the reduction from the original level amounted to at least 50 per cent, and the content was indicated in the same field of vision as the product's name.

(e)   claims regarding the absence or non-addition of a nutriment, another substance, or energy. These claims would be permitted only if another nutrient or substance was not added to provide, or which had the effect of providing, the same properties; or unless the other substances were disclosed in characters of the same size as the claim.

(f)   claims regarding the absence of alcohol. These claims would be permitted only if alcohol were in similar products, and the foodstuff had an alcoholic strength lower than 0.1 per cent by volume.

(g)   claims related to the low level of alcoholic content; These would be permitted only if similar foodstuffs generally had a higher content, and the product had between 0.1 per cent and 1.2 per cent of alcohol by volume.

---

1.   Some reconciliation with the rules for organic products, below at para 3.6, would presumably be attempted. The FAC also found abuses in this area, including statements which it regarded as "inaccurate and misleading". Food Advisory Committee Report on Food Labelling and Advertising 1990 (1991) at Appendix IV.

2.   An earlier version permitted claims made in "traditional culinary terms". This has evidently been abandoned. For the Community's rules regarding "natural" flavourings, see below at Chapter 5, para 5.2.

3.   "Energy" refers to caloric levels.

4.   In Britain, the FAC has suggested that the word "reduced" should be permissible if the reduction is at least 25 per cent from the original level. Food Advisory Committee Report on Food Labelling and Advertising 1990 (1991) at para 121.

(h)   claims relating to a product's organic production. These would be permissible only if the product conformed to the Community's rules for such products[1].

(i)   claims relating to newness. These would be permitted only if the new characteristic were clearly designated.

In addition, the Commission is evidently considering whether to permit claims that a product has religious or ritual significance, has received awards or honours, or is from a farm or is "artisanal", only if the claims can be substantiated[2].

The Commission's draft rules are best evaluated by comparisons with the proposals of Britain's Food Advisory Committee and the rules imposed in the United States by the Nutritional Labelling and Education Act. The FAC's proposals provide a list of nutritional claims and detailed conditions for their use[3]. For example, a claim that a food has "reduced fat content" would be permissible only if its fat content were no more than three-quarters of that in a similar food typical of those for which no such claim is made. In addition, the claim could not be made without a nutritional declaration in the product's labelling. Similar rules are offered for some sixteen other possible nutritional claims[4]. One suggestion would impose substantial new obligations upon producers and retailers. The FAC suggests that where nutritional claims are made in advertising, they should be substantiated in the advertisements themselves. For reasons of space alone, such a requirement would be likely to discourage many nutritional claims. Many of the FAC's proposals are now embodied in draft rules prepared by Britain's Ministry of Agriculture, Fisheries and Food[5].

The proposed rules in the United States are still incomplete in important respects, but already are more comprehensive than the Commission's proposals. For example, the NLEA permits a labelling claim relating a food to a disease or health-related condition only if there is "significant scientific agreement" that the claim is supported by the "totality of publicly available scientific evidence"[6]. Only evidence which satisfies "generally recognised scientific procedures" may be considered. In addition, claims which characterise the level of any nutrient in a

---

1.   Below at para 3.7.
2.   In Britain, the FAC has suggested that the label or advertisement should contain sufficient information to permit the verification of any claims. Food Advisory Committee Report on Food Labelling and Advertising 1990 (1991) at para 121. The Commission does not suggest such a requirement.
3.   Food Advisory Committee Report on Food Labelling and Advertising 1990 (1991) at Appendix V, p76.
4.   Ibid., at pp82-88.
5.   Draft Food Labelling (Amendment) (Nutrition Claims) Regulations, issued March 4, 1992. For existing rules see Food Labelling (Amendment) Regulations, SI 1990/2488, at regs 36-38 and Schs 6 and 7.
6.   21 U.S.C. sec. 343 (r)(3)(B)(i).

food are permitted only in accordance with regulations issued by FDA[1]. There are many other rules, including limitations upon claims that a particular nutrient has been removed, or that a food contains particular levels of cholesterol or saturated fats.

Food health claims present difficult questions of balance and degree, and judgments may differ as to the proper requirements. The important fact is that both the FAC and the NLEA recognise acknowledge the complexity of the issues and the necessity for precision in their resolution. Unlike the Commission's draft, they have not sought to reduce the issues to a handful of ambiguous axioms. Perhaps in an unsuccessful search for clarity, the Commission has failed to take adequate account either of the varied claims which may be made or of the careful distinctions which must be drawn among them. It is hardly surprising that the Commission has reportedly abandoned its 1990 draft, and now is searching for more satisfactory rules[2].

3.6   Lot markings

In 1989, the Council adopted a directive requiring foodstuff labels to include indications or marks identifying the production or manufacturing lot to which the foodstuff belongs[3]. The directive recognises that lot markings may facilitate preventive steps when particular batches of foodstuffs become actual or potential health hazards[4]. It also states that the harmonisation of national rules may prevent barriers to the free circulation of goods and facilitate international trade[5].

A "lot" is a batch of sales units produced or packaged under "practically the same conditions"[6]. Those "conditions" are not characterised in terms of time or an uninterrupted manufacturing process. At least in principle, multiple or broken processing runs might still produce a single "lot". By comparison, FDA defines a "lot" as products "produced under conditions as nearly uniform as possible" or, in the

---

1.   21 U.S.C. 343(r)(2)(A). Proposed regulations have now been issued. For an analysis, see P. Hutt, ed., *Guide to US Food Labeling Law* (1991).

2   See, e.g., *New York Times* (19 Feb 1992). The change in direction reportedly occurred because responsibility for the measure has been reassigned from DG III to the Consumer Policy Service. The latter is said to regard the 1990 proposal as too rigid. It has drafted a new proposal and is surveying consumer groups for their views.

3.   Council Directive (EEC) 89/396, OJ L186 30.6.89 p.21. By the end of 1991, only Belgium and Britain had transposed the directive. Eighth Annual Report to the European Parliament on Commission Monitoring of the Application of Community Law, OJ C338 31.12.91 p1, at p142. For the British rules, see Food (Lot Marking) Regulations 1992, SI 1992/1357.

4.   The third recital of the preamble.

5.   The seventh and eighth recitals of the preambles. The Codex Alimentarius Commission proposed rules for date-marking in 1981, but they are now "somewhat obsolete". van de Heide, "The Codex Alimentarius on Food Labelling", 4/91 Eur. Food L. Rev. 291, 294 (1991).

6.   Council Directive (EEC) 89/396, above at Article 1(2).

absence of a manufacturer's code, as a day's production[1]. As a practical matter, however, products in a "lot" are likely under the Community's definition to have been produced roughly at the same time and during a single manufacturing run.

As a general matter, a foodstuff may not be marketed without an identification of its batch or lot[2]. There are, however, numerous exceptions. They include many agricultural products, unpre-packaged products, those packaged only at the point of sale for immediate sale or at the purchaser's request, and those sold in small packages or containers[3]. The latter are excluded if the largest side of their packaging does not exceed ten square centimetres[4]. Agricultural products delivered for storage or processing, or merely transported to a producers' organisation, are also excluded. An amendment to the 1989 directive excludes individual portions of ice cream if the lot is shown on the ice cream's overall package[5]. In addition, Member States may until 1997 exempt glass bottles intended for re-use[6]. Finally, products with a date of minimum durability or a "use by" date need not include a lot marking if the date consists at least of an uncoded day and month[7]. Since the 1989 amendment to the 1978 labelling directive frequently requires such dates, this permits the omission of lot markings from many products[8].

Each product's lot number is determined by its producer or packager, or by the first seller established within the Community[9]. The lot number must be preceded by the letter "L", unless it is clearly distinguishable from other labelling indications without use of the letter[10]. The marking must be easily visible, clearly legible, and indelible. The Community does not require any specific size of print.

The directive's requirements were scheduled to become effective in 1991, but there were many complaints to the Commission that this was impractical. Special packaging and labelling machinery is needed in some instances, and there were claims that it could not always be delivered promptly. The Commission eventually recommended a delay until mid-1992[11]. The Economic and Social Committee

---

1.   21 C.F.R. sec. 103.3 (1991).
2.   Article 2(1).
3.   Article 2(2). This same size exception is found in the 1978 labelling directive. Above at para 3.3.
4.   The size limitation excludes relatively few products, and some in the food industry have urged a higher threshold size.
5.   Council Directive (EEC) 91/238, OJ L107 274.91 p50, amending Article 2(2) of the 1989 directive. In essence, this makes the lot markings directive consistent with the 1978 labelling directive, as amended. Above at para 3.3.
6.   Article 2(3). Such bottles must, however, be indelibly marked. They must also be without a label, ring or collar.
7.   Article 5.
8.   Above at para 3.3.
9.   Article 3.
10.   Article 4.
11.   COM(91) 297 final, OJ C219 22.8.91 p11.

accepted the delay "while deploring the reasons for it"[1]. A delay was granted until July 1, 1992, with the additional provision that products either labelled or on the market at that time could continue to be sold[2].

3.7   The designation and control of organically produced foodstuffs

A major development in food marketing over the past decade has been the increasing demand for "organic" or "natural" products[3]. Because of fears about food additives and pesticides, some consumers seek products manufactured with fewer additives or grown with fewer agricultural chemicals. They do so despite the absence of evidence that reduced uses of pesticides and other agricultural chemicals result in higher product quality[4]. The market shares of these products are still small, although realistic calculations are made difficult by the ambiguity of the terminology and the freedom with which "naturalness" is claimed[5]. Whatever the actual market shares, many consumers profess to prefer natural products[6]. It is less certain how many are prepared to travel farther or to pay more for such products, or how much more[7]. Nonetheless, food producers of every description now find it commercially desirable to claim that their products are "natural", "organic" or "ecologically beneficial". Some of the claims are undoubtedly justified. Others are questionable, if not misleading[8]. A study in Germany found that many households which believed they were obtaining organic foodstuffs were in fact often purchasing ordinary products[9]. Most of the food products in Germany which claim to be organic are reportedly not organic at all[10]. There is a growing public demand for organic products, but few standards or restrictions which permit consumers reliably to identify products which actually have those origins and properties[11].

---

1.   OJ L40 17.2.92 p12.
2.   Council Directive (EEC) 92/11, OJ L55 11.3.92 p32.
3.   The changes may be accelerating. A committee of the European Parliament has anticipated a rapid and worldwide increase in the demand for "ecologically produced products" through the year 2000. Report of the Committee on Agriculture, Fisheries and Rural Development, A3-0311/90 (19 Nov 1990) at p35.
4.   The absence of proven quality differences is recognised by the opinion of the Economic and Social Committee regarding a proposed Council regulation to encourage organic farming methods. See CES (91) 136 regarding COM(90) 366 final (30 Jan 1991). Nonetheless, the ESC also suggested, rather inconsistently, that improvements in environmental practices "could have a positive impact on product quality"; ibid., at p7.
5.   The current demand is probably one per cent of the total foodstuffs market in northern Europe, and perhaps less elsewhere. A3-0311/90 (19 Nov 1990).
6.   In Germany, from one-third to one-half of consumers profess some interest in organic foodstuffs; ibid.
7.   In France there are growing numbers of special marketplaces for organic products, with prices reportedly 10 to 100 per cent higher than ordinary foodstuffs; *The Independent* (28 December 1991) p29.
8.   Parliament's Committee on Agriculture, Fisheries and Rural Development has complained of the widespread persistence of "pseudo-organic" products and the "deplorable level of consumer deception". A3-0311/90, above at pp35, 38.
9.   The survey reported that a large part of the total food expenditures of households which consider that they purchase organic foodstuffs is in fact spent on non-organic products; ibid., at p35.
10.   The estimated percentage of sham products ranged from 50 to 90 per cent; ibid.
11.   The Council has adopted a voluntary scheme of "ECO-labels" for Community products, but it excludes foods; Council Regulation (EEC) 880/92, OJ L99 11.4.92 p1.

In 1989, the Commission proposed to provide such standards through a Council regulation to control the organic production of agricultural products and to impose uniform designations for organic foodstuffs[1]. The Commission's proposal provoked both enthusiasm and discontent. One committee of the European Parliament concluded that the proposal met a genuine need, and should be implemented and even extended "as soon as possible"[2]. It thought new rules were needed to encourage ecological farming and the consumption of products produced by methods beneficial to the environment[3]. A second committee, with responsibilities chiefly for agriculture, was markedly less enthusiastic[4]. It agreed that new measures were needed, but was strongly critical of the Commission's more general agricultural and consumer policies[5]. It complained that they reflect an "unbalanced interpretation" of the Treaty of Rome[6]. It claimed that the Community's policies are marked by "ecological contradictions" and "the greatest possible sympathy for the interests of the chemical industry[7]." The committee sought changes in agricultural and food policies to encourage ecological farming and reductions in agricultural chemicals and food additives[8]. Both committees offered detailed suggestions for revising the 1989 proposal[9].

In 1991, the Commission substantially modified its 1989 proposal[10]. The modifications did not quiet the debate, but the revised proposal was finally issued by the Council as a regulation in June 1991[11]. The regulation observes that some Member States had already adopted rules, and that uniform Community rules were needed to protect organic farming, enhance the credibility of organic products, and ensure fair competition[12]. The regulation establishes standards for organic farming

---

1.   COM(89) 552 final, OJ C4 9.1.90 p4. There are comparable efforts in the United States. For a summary of the regulatory developments, see P. Hutt & R. Merrill, *Food and Drug Law, Cases and Materials* pp59-60 (2nd ed. 1991).
2.   Report of the Committee on Environment, Public Health and Consumer Protection, A3-0311/90 (19 Nov 1990) at p40. Because the Commission's proposal related only to products of vegetable origin, the committee urged the Commission to "complement" the proposal with a regulation regarding products of animal origin; ibid., at p42.
3.   The committee suggested that the regulation should be reevaluated after two years.
4.   Report of the Committee on Agriculture, Fisheries and Rural Development, A3-0311/90, above at p35.
5.   The committee saw an urgent need for regulation both to prevent consumer deception and unfair trade practices.
6.   The committee argued that the Community's basic agricultural policies had remained essentially unchanged, and that the changes now being "forced" involved price reductions and "survival of the fittest"; at pp35-36.
7.   Ibid., at p37. The committee asserted that ecological farming remained a "market niche", while "massive" assistance was given to genetic engineering and biotechnology. Ibid. It urged changes to encourage ecological farming and "natural" food products.
8.   It urged "the avoidance of all possible food additives" and a "fundamental change" in agricultural policy; ibid at p 38.
9.   Ibid., at pp24-33, 43-55.
10.   COM(91) 112 final, OJ C101 18.4.91 p13.
11.   Council Regulation (EEC) 2092/91, OJ L198 22.7.91 p1. Britain's Ministry of Agriculture, Fisheries and Foods has issued guidance notes for its interpretation.
12.   The fourth and fifth recitals of the preamble.

and offers special marketing designations for foodstuffs produced in compliance with those standards. It is to be enforced by a new inspection system[1].

The regulation applies to unprocessed agricultural products which consist "essentially" of ingredients of plant origin[2]. It does not apply to animals, animal products, or foodstuffs containing ingredients of animal origin. These are exempt until rules for the production and inspection of animals and animal products are adopted[3]. The Commission promised to propose rules for organic animal products by July 1992[4].

The regulation applies to products for which claims of organic production are made. In the draft proposal, organic production would have been claimed whenever a product's labelling, advertising or commercial documents included the terms "organic" or "biodynamic". It would also have been claimed whenever it was asserted that a product had been produced without synthetic pesticides, soil conditioners or fertilisers, or that its production complied with the regulation's standards[5]. As adopted, the regulation emphasises only the last of these tests[6]. It is enough if a product bears indications suggesting that its producers have complied with the regulation's standards. The regulation permits such claims only if a producer or importer has actually agreed to comply with its standards, including periodic inspections[7]. In general, a product's labelling and advertising may claim organic production only if its ingredients of agricultural origin have been produced in accordance with rules set forth in the regulation's annex. Any non-agricultural ingredients must be limited to those listed in the annex, and the product cannot have been irradiated. Other forbidden treatments will eventually be identified[8]. Despite these rules, as much as five per cent of a final product may be non-organic if those ingredients are not organically produced in sufficient quantities in the Community.

Nonetheless, the labelling of other products may refer to organic production if at least 50 per cent of their agricultural ingredients satisfy the regulation's standards, and if they otherwise conform to the limitations described above[9]. In such cases, however, comprehensive claims of organic production may not be made. Instead, claims may only be made in the product's list of ingredients, and only with respect

---

1. The fifth and thirteenth recitals of the preamble.
2. Article 1.
3. Article 1(a).
4. Article 1(2).
5. COM(89) 552 final, above at Article 2.
6. Articles 1(1), 2. The change was presumably for simplicity, although arguably it may permit claims which approach those controlled by the regulation to escape restriction.
7. Article 5.
8. The annexes were included in the regulation, but left uncompleted.
9. Article 5.

to the particular ingredients which satisfy the regulation's requirements. Moreover, ingredients must still appear in descending order of weight. Partial claims of organic production may not be given undue prominence. The organic ingredients cannot, for example, be listed in a different colour, style or size of lettering[1]. These rules may be supplemented by requirements established through a committee procedure involving a standing committee of national representatives[2]. In essence, however, the regulation permits only two options, and products which do not fully comply with the regulation may claim organic production only in their lists of ingredients, and may do so only without special emphasis[3].

The rules of organic production are set forth in an annex to the directive[4]. At least two calendar years must normally have passed since the last application of any forbidden agricultural chemicals[5]. The quality of the soil must be maintained by crop rotation or composted organic material[6]. Some discretion is left for the use where necessary of organic or mineral fertilisers listed in an annex[7]. Pests, diseases and weeds must be controlled by crop rotation, mechanical cultivation, protection of the pests' natural enemies, flame weeding, or the selection of plant species and varieties[8]. A limited variety of plant protection products may, however, be used if there is an immediate threat to a crop[9]. Seeds treated with forbidden chemicals may be used only if untreated seeds cannot be obtained[10]. A committee procedure may add other protection products to the permissible list if they are "essential" and natural alternatives are unavailable[11]. Even if a protection product is permitted, it may not be placed in direct contact with the seed, crop, or crop products. The only exceptions are where contact occurs outside the growing season of the edible parts and does not leave chemical residues[12]. The use of all plant protection products is subject to environmental constraints. They may not contribute to any unacceptable effects on, or any contamination of, the environment[13]. The permissible products may also be subjected to conditions of use, compositional

---

1. The format requirements are in addition to the obligations of the 1978 labelling directive. Above at para 3.3.
2. Article 5(7). New conditions and limitations may be applied to both permissible ingredients and permissible preparatory products. The two lists would be included in Annex VI to the regulation.
3. No incentive is given to a producer to increase the use of organic ingredients from zero to (say) forty per cent, and little additional encouragement is given even to those who reach 90 per cent.
4. Annex I.
5. Para 1, Annex I.
6. Para 2, Annex 1.
7. The penultimate sentence of para 2, Annex 1. Any organic or mineral fertilizers identified in Annex II may be used only to the extent that adequate crop nutrition and soil conditioning are not possible through crop rotation or the use of composted organic materials.
8. Para. 3, Annex I.
9. Annex II (B). The permissible products include, for example, sulphur, stone meal, sodium silicate and sodium bicarbonate.
10. Article 6(2). Proof of unavailability must be given to the inspecting authority.
11. Article 7(1).
12. Article 7(1).
13. No explanation is given either of "unacceptable effects" or of "contamination".

standards, or other requirements to be decided upon through a committee procedure[1].

Producers who claim organic production must submit to regular inspections[2]. Member States must either designate public inspection authorities or establish a special inspection system operated by approved private bodies[3]. Private bodies may be approved only if they adopt standardised inspection procedures. Moreover, they must be capable of imposing appropriate penalties, have adequate resources to perform their responsibilities, and be independent of those subject to their inspections[4]. Public authorities must ensure that private bodies act objectively and effectively, and must withdraw approvals from those which do not[5]. Whether or not private bodies are used, information obtained in an inspection may be disclosed only to the firm involved and the relevant public authorities[6]. If an inspection reveals an "irregularity", all claims of organic production must be removed from the lot or production run[7]. If there is a "manifest infringement", or an infringement with "prolonged" effects, the operator must be prohibited from asserting organic production for a fixed period to be agreed upon with the Member State[8]. There are no provisions for monetary fines or notices to consumers to penalise producers who falsely claim organic production.

Those who produce or import organic products for marketing within the Community are required to give notice to each Member State in which this occurs. They must also submit to the national inspection systems[9]. Member States must maintain lists of those who have submitted to inspections, and must permit reviews of the lists by "interested parties"[10]. Products which conform to the regulation's requirements may display a Community designation of organic production[1]. In English, for

---

1.   Article 7(2). The rules are to be adopted through a procedure involving a new standing committee.
2.   Article 8(1). A list of the information needed for registration is set forth in Annex IV to the proposal. The requirement is evidently limited to notification, and does not compel pre-marketing clearance, although the notifying firm is immediately subject to inspection. The provision was originally labelled "other inspection measures", and followed another provision labelled "regular inspection system". The relationship between the two systems was opaque. The uncertainties are generally resolved in the final regulation.
3.   Article 8(1).
4.   Article 9(5).
5.   Article 9(6).
6.   Article 9(7)(b). The provision suggests that the names of producers who falsely claim organic production could not be disclosed to the public. The regulation's prescribed sanction is simply to withdraw the right to make labelling claims.
7.   Article 9(9)(a).
8.   Article 9(9)(b). No description is given of a "manifest infringement", but the word "manifest" may carry some connotation of "intentional" or "deliberate". Nor are "prolonged effects" defined, but presumably more than a single lot or production run would have to be affected.
9.   Article 9(1). The 1990 amendment to the original proposal added a specific requirement that the notifying firm must submit to inspections.
10.   Article 8(3). The original proposal would have demanded annual publication of lists. There is now no publication requirement. The lists will evidently not disclose the names of firms whose approval has been suspended or withdrawn. There is no indication as to whether consumers or competitors will be "interested parties".

display a Community designation of organic production[1]. In English, for example, the product's label or advertising may state "Organic Farming - EEC Control System[2]." The products must be packed and transported to the point of retail sale in closed packaging[3]. Their labelling and advertising may not suggest that the Community designation indicates any superior organoleptic, nutritional or salubrious qualities[4]. Member States must take "whatever action is required" to prevent fraudulent use of the Community's designation, as well as other labelling abuses[5]. On the other hand, Member States may not restrict the marketing of products which satisfy the regulation's requirements on grounds related to their production, labelling or presentation[6].

Products imported from third countries are subject to special requirements[7]. They may claim to have been produced organically only if their country of origin is first approved for that purpose by the Commission. Approval will require evidence satisfactory to the Commission that a country imposes restrictions equivalent to those demanded by the regulation[8]. Imported products must be accompanied by certificates indicating that they have resulted from a system of production, and were subject to a system of inspection, equivalent to those under the regulation[9]. Without certificates, imported products may not be marketed within the Community upon the basis of organic production. Given the absence of similar controls in most areas of the world, a strict interpretation of this requirement could prove a substantial barrier to foreign products[10].

The Commission issued a regulation early in 1992 providing rules for third-country products[11]. The rules require third-country producers to provide forecasts of the types and quantities of products to be exported to the Community. They also demand evidence of foreign rules of production and inspection systems. The Commission may require on-the-spot inspections, and may designate its own local

---

1. Article 10(1).
2. Annex V.
3. Article 10(1)(d). It is not expressly required that the products be sold at retail in closed packaging.
4. Article 10(2). The European Parliament's Committee on Environment, Public Health and Consumer Protection has observed that ecological farming relates to methods rather than results, and that there is no scientific evidence that ecological methods produce better products. A3-0311/90, above at 41.
5. Article 10(6).
6. Article 12. The proposal was amended to add a reference to labelling.
7. Article 11. The provision is among the few not altered by the Commission. Parliament's Committee on the Environment, Public Health and Consumer Protection urged that domestic and imported products should be subjected to the same "strict" standards. A3-0311/90, above at p42.
8. Article 11(1).
9. Article 11(1)(b).
10. Some systems are, however, developing outside the Community. See, e.g., Rimmer, "The Development of Canadian Standards for Organic Production", 1 World Food Reg. Rev. 13 (Oct. 1991). For Australian rules, see 1 World Food Reg. Rev. 3 (April 1992).
11. Commission Regulation (EEC) 94/92, OJ L11 17.1.92 p14.

inspectors to conduct them. Authorisations to claim organic production within the Community may be suspended or withdrawn whenever violations are found. Many of these provisions have, however, proved premature, in that little effort has yet been made by third countries to seek approval as sources of organic products[1]. Accordingly, the Council has adopted rules delaying the approvals list and instead permitting temporary three-year authorisations by Member States[2].

The Council's regulation is unlikely to preclude further controversies regarding organic foodstuffs. It assures consumers more reliable information regarding the actual origins and properties of foodstuffs offered for their selection, but its sanctions for violations may well prove inadequate. Nor are there yet rules for products of animal origin. Moreover, the regulation's controls fall short of the demands in Parliament for basic changes in the Community's agricultural and food policies[3]. These would involve reorientations of the Common Agricultural Policy which would far exceed any proposals yet made by the Commission. They would also involve fundamental changes in food processing and reductions in the use of additives[4].

3.8 Protective and promotional measures for distinctive foodstuffs

Late in 1990, the Commission issued two proposals to give special protection to producers of selected food products. One was designed to create two certificates attesting to the geographical origins of some products, and the other to create certifications of product distinctiveness. The certificates could be displayed on the labels or in advertisements for the products. Less distinctive products, or those with diverse or multiple geographical origins, would be denied certification. Both proposals were adopted as Council regulations in July 1992[5].

Although the regulations have general application, it is likely that only traditional foodstuffs will qualify. Indeed, the regulations are less regulatory than promotional. They are designed to ensure that selected traditional products are given protected positions in the Community's marketplace. They are said to

---

1.   Council Regulation (EEC) 2083/92, OJ L208 25.7.92 p15, at the second recital of the preamble.
2.   Article 1. Notices of national approvals would be given to the Commission.
3.   The Commission has, however, proposed a Council regulation to encourage improved environmental practices in the Community's agriculture. See COM(90) 366 final.
4.   A senior Commission official has observed that "the progress of food science and technology has undoubtedly been a major contributor to improved human health and longevity, yet science-based innovation is the focus of suspicion". Gray, "Whither Food Regulation?" 1 World Food Rev. Rep. 33, 34 (June 1991). Nonetheless, the European Parliament has continued to urge reductions in additives. Resolution No. A3-0060/92 (11 March 1992).
5.   Council Regulation (EEC) 2082/92, OJ L208 24.7.92 p9; Council Regulation (EEC) 2081/92, OJ L208 24.7.92 p1.

represent the first stages of a general programme to maintain "product quality"[1]. Ironically, the Commission has elsewhere warned that any provision which has the effect of crystalising consumer habits around the national manufacturing tradition, so as to confer a competitive advantage on domestic products, is incompatible with the Treaty[2]. Re-phrased in terms of Community law, the warning is applicable to the Council's regulations.

These are not the Community's first ventures in product promotion. It has, for example, adopted extensive promotional measures regarding alcoholic beverages, and made recurrent international efforts to protect the names used for wines and spirit drinks[3]. Similarly, the Council adopted a regulation in 1977 to expand the Community's markets for milk, butter and other milk products[4]. Its goal was to increase consumption of the Community's excess milk production. The measures have been judged a success and largely remain in effect[5]. Nonetheless, the European Parliament has continued to demand additional measures "to promote butter sales and reduce the butter mountain[6]." Accordingly, the Commission issued another regulation in 1991 to increase consumer "awareness" of milk and milk products, authorise an information programme, and initiate other efforts to promote the sale of milk products[7]. These measures have resulted in a relatively high consumption of butter in northern Europe, and widespread use of butter in food manufacturing[8]. These efforts are offspring of the Common Agricultural Policy, which encourages high-cost production and compels expenditures to dispose of the resulting surpluses[9]. The pressures to encourage consumption of the Community's agricultural surpluses may sometimes override concerns about dietary consequences[10].

---

1.   See, e.g., OJ C326 16.12.91 p36; Written Question 2177/91, OJ C141 3.6.92 p10.
2.   XXIst General Report on the Activities of the European Communities 1987, at 358 (1988). The statement is essentially a summary of the European Court's holding in Case 178/84 *EC Commission v Germany* [1987] ECR 1227, [1988] 1 CMLR 780.
3.   See, e.g., *International Herald Tribune*, p11 (24 July 1991). For the Community's rules regarding wines and spirit drinks, see Chapter 7, below at para 7.11..
4.   Council Regulation (EEC) 1079/77, OJ L131 26.5.77 p6. For amendments, see, e.g., Regulation (EEC) 3660/90, OJ L362 27.12.90 p44.
5.   Commission Regulation (EEC) 1657/91, OJ L151 15.6.91 p45 at the first recital of the preamble.
6.   Document B2-1339/85, OJ C352 31.12.85 p295.
7.   Commission Regulation (EEC) 1657/91, above. For other promotional and implementational measures, see Commission Regulation (EEC) 1632/91, OJ L150 15.6.91 p23; Commission Regulation (EEC) 465/92, OJ L53 28.2.92 p8.
8.   Berger, "Problems and Opportunities in Market Development for Oils", in R. Cambie, ed., *Fats for the Future* pp217, 226-229 (1989).
9.   For the impact upon food policies created by the CAP, see above at Chapter 2, para 2.2.2. Another example at the national level is the practice in several Member States of levying higher taxes on margarine than butter, in an effort to encourage butter consumption. Eurofood 3 (August 1991).
10.   One example is rapeseed oil, which is used in the manufacture of margarine and other products. Under CAP encouragement, rapeseed oil is produced in the Community at a cost three times higher than its market price. Berger, "Problems and Opportunities in Market Development for Oils", in R. Cambie, ed., *Fats for the Future* pp217, 225 (1991). At the same time, the Community has, for reasons of suspected health hazards, limited the content of erucic acid (which is found in rapeseed oil) in margarine; below at Chapter 7, at para 7.6.

3.8.1 The certifications of product distinctiveness

The Commission's first proposal was for a Council regulation to create a new system of Community certificates of specific character for foodstuffs[1]. As adopted, the regulation recognises that some producers take, or would like to take, marketing advantage of the distinctive characteristics of their products. Those characteristics may derive from special raw materials or methods of production[2]. Varieties of ham, sausage or cheese might be examples. Some beers might also be illustrations[3]. The regulation is designed to facilitate promotional efforts by adding a Community endorsement of the products' distinctiveness. It permits associations of producers although not individual firms, to seek certificates of "special character" for their products. The certificates will be granted by the Community, and will indicate that a product possesses characteristics which "clearly" distinguish it from other products in the same category[4]. A product's "specific character" may be shown by national or other compositional or processing standards, provided that those standards were intended to define a product's specific features[5]. In any case, the product must be made using traditional raw materials, or have a traditional composition, or be produced by traditional methods of processing[6].

Requests for certification will first be submitted to national authorities. If endorsed by national officials, they will be forwarded to the Commission[7]. After inviting comments and objections, the Commission will determine whether the product genuinely possesses distinguishing features[8].

If necessary, disagreements are to be resolved among the Member States. When a certificate is granted, a trade description and product specification will be assigned. Only foodstuffs which satisfy the specification may use the trade description, and only the protected products may include the designated product

---

1.   Council Regulation (EEC) 2082/92, OJ L208 25.7.92 p9. For the initial proposal, see COM(90) 2414 final, OJ C30 6.2.91 p4. For modest revisions, see COM(92) 28 final, OJ C71 20.3.92 p14. The Community has also adopted a programme which "Eco-labels" to some products, but food and drink products are excluded; Council Regulation (EEC) 880/92, OJ L99 11.4.92 p1. In addition, the Commission is reportedly considering proposals to permit regional authorities to create special criteria for locally produced products, including foodstuffs. Eurofood 15 (April 1991). The idea has been described as a potentially fertile source of trade barriers; ibid.
2.   The sixth recital of the preamble.
3.   The regulation applies to the agricultrual products listed in Annex II to the Treaty of Rome, plus those in an annex to the regulation. The latter includes beer.
4.   Article 2(1).
5.   Article 2(1).
6.   Article 4(1).
7.   Article 7(2). National authorities would make an initial screening. Article 7(3).
8.   Articles 8, 9. Objections must be filed within six months. Article 9(1). This appears to be the only instance in the food regulatory area where the Commission proposes to solicit public comments regarding a prospective ruling. Comments are, however, permitted only by those demonstrating a "legitimate" economic interest. Comments are to be submitted to Member States.

names in their labelling, presentation and advertising[1]. In some cases, permission may be given to use a Community symbol. Use of the trade description will be contingent upon compliance with rules governing the foodstuff's production. An inspection system will ensure adherence to the rules[2].

As the Economic and Social Committee has observed, the product specifications may be sources of substantial controversy[3]. The certifications are meaningless without them, but they also mean that minor changes in processing or ingredients will result in losses of certification[4]. Moreover, products closely similar to those already certified must either be denied a significant competitive advantage or be granted their own certifications on the basis of minor distinctions. If multiple certifications of similar products are denied, the Commission must favour only one by selecting among them. One policy is likely to confuse consumers, while the other invites national or regional rivalries for the Commission's protection. Not surprisingly, the ESC concluded that the programme, while "well-intentioned", has "fundamental defects"[5].

The regulation permits countries outside the Community to apply for Community certificates on behalf of their producers. Approval is, however, contingent upon reciprocity, and third countries may be awarded Community certificates only if they offer comparable protection for Community products. Third countries are obliged to adopt standardisation and inspection arrangements equivalent to those in the Commission's proposal[6]. The original proposal would have authorised the Commission to enter into agreements with third countries creating reciprocal rights of inspection, but this provision was omitted from the final regulation[7].

There are already many national designations of product distinctiveness, and an important issue is how those national measures will be reconciled with the

---

1. Articles 15 (1).
2. Article 14. National inspection authorities are be required to be impartial and expert. Article 14 (3).
3. OJ C40 17.2.92 p3 at paras 2.3-2.5.
4. There are provisions for modifications of the product specifications, but they may be blocked by any producer who objects. In such cases, the only remedy for producers seeking a modification is to apply for a different certificate. Article 11 (5).
5. At para 2.
6. Article 16. The demand for comparability of inspection systems seems unaccountable. If Ruritania regards its sausages as distinctive, and legally denominates them as such, why should the Community care if Ruritania does not enforce its denomination within Ruritania by an elaborate inspection process? Its failure to do so may diminish the credibility of Ruritanian sausage among the Community's consumers, but that hardly hurts the Community, or the Community's own sausage makers. The Community's interests are to ensure that sausages sold as "genuine Ruritanian" within the Community actually are Ruritanian, and conversely that Ruritanian sausages are not passed off as German or Danish. It has no need to demand a web of third-country inspection measures in Ruritania or elsewhere.
7. COM(90) 2414 final, at Article 20.

Commission's regulation[1]. The Commission recognises that confusion might result. Nonetheless, the regulation states merely that the Member States are obliged to take "appropriate measures" to prevent abuse of the certificates and any confusion with national designations[2]. At a minimum, this requires legal protection against fraudulent use of the certificates and imitation of the protected products[3]. A standing committee will manage the programme[4]. The original proposal contemplated that the Community would offer financial support to promote the marketing of certified foodstuffs. This would have included the distribution of information to consumers[5]. This was intended to help "stabilise" the Community's agricultural markets[6]. The same goal is reflected in the regulation's recitals, but there is no specific authorisation for promotional assistance[7].

3.8.2   The certifications of geographical origin

The Commission simultaneously proposed a Council regulation regarding geographical indications and designations of origin[8]. The final regulation is again more promotional than regulatory. It notes that Member States already have designations of origin for some foodstuffs, and that those programmes had successfully promoted the marketing of registered products[9.] It claims that a uniform Community system will encourage fair competition and promote consumer acceptance of the designations[10]. Aside from wine and spirit drinks, the certificates are available for most foodstuffs and agricultural products, whether or not they are processed[11]. The regulation is without prejudice to the Community's rules regarding such matters as labelling, health issues, quality standards, and inspection programmes[12].

---

1.   The Economic and Social Committee has observed that the Community's programme is based upon national schemes, and particularly the French rules. OJ C40 17.2.92 p3 at para 1.
2.   Article 18. See also Article 14.
3.   Article 14 (4). This presumably contemplates changes in national law, and in that respect the measure is more nearly a directive than a regulation.
4.   Article 19. It was suggested in the European Parliament that the committee's members should make public declarations of their interests, and that the committee should meet publicly. OJ C326 16.12.91 p35 at pp38-39, 42.
5.   COM(90) 2414 final, at Article 24. The idea raises possible issues of discrimination against uncertified products in the same product category.
6.   COM(90) 2414 final, at Article 24(3).
7.   Council Regulation (EEC) 2082/92, above at the second recital of the preamble.
8.   Council Regulation (EEC) 2081/92, OJ L208 24.7.92 p1. For the proposal, see COM(90) 2415 final, OJ C30 6.2.91 p9. For the general issue of disclosures of origin, see below at para 3.3.
9.   The sixth and seventh "whereas" clauses. For the French rules, see Vincent, "La certification et la normalisation en France: historique, situation actuelle et perspectives", 4/91 Eur. Food L. Rev. 263 (1991); 1 World Food Reg. Rev. 14 (April 1992).
10.   The seventh recital of the preamble
11.   Article 1(1). Complete lists of the eligible products are given in annexes to the regulation and Annex II to the Treaty of Rome. See also Written Question 3098/91, OJ C183 20.7.92 p29.
12.   Article 1(2).

Two new designations are created. The first is a protected geographical indication, and the second a protected designation of origin[1]. Protected geographical indications allow use of the name of a region, place, or occasionally a country. The geographical designations will be followed by the letters "PGI"[2]. They will be available for products originating in that region, place or country with a quality or reputation attributable to their geographical environment and the processing or preparation which occurs there[3]. Protected designations of origin also allow use of the name of a region, place, or occasionally a country. They will be followed by the letters "PDO"[4]. They would be restricted to products originating in that region, place or country whose quality or characteristics are "essentially or exclusively" a result of that geographical environment, and whose production, processing and preparation all occur there. No more precise distinctions are drawn between the two proposed certifications. Presumably, the designations are chiefly distinguished by the degree of exclusivity with which the designated products are associated with a particular location. The extent to which raw materials are derived from that location, or processing occurs there, will determine which designation will be appropriate[5]. The differences are, however, subtle and perhaps impenetrable to most consumers, and this is an area in which extensive changes in the proposals were urged[6].

Protected products will be assigned mandatory specifications[7]. These include a designation of the geographical area from which the products are required to come, their physical characteristics, preparatory methods, labelling obligations, and other requirements. For purposes of both designations, the specified methods will include any "authentic" and unvarying local methods of production or processing[8]. It follows that innovations in processing, whether or not they cause any change in a product's physical or organoleptic characteristics, will cause a loss of certification. Changes in the specifications may be requested, but only by a Member State[9]. New national inspection systems will ensure compliance with the specifications[10].

---

1.   Articles 2(2), 4.
2.   Article 2(2)(b).
3.   Article 2(2)(b). Parma ham from Italy or serrano ham from Spain might be examples. Traditional designators which satisfy the same standards may also be used. Article 2(3).
4.   Article 2(2)(a).
5.   The European Parliament suggested that some flexibility should be shown regarding the origins of raw materials, and that geographical areas should be defined in some cases to include adjacent areas of production. OJ C326 16.12.91 p35. For the Commission's minor changes in response to the suggestions, see COM(92) 32 final, OJ C69 18.3.92 p15. Some flexibility is permitted in the final regulation by Article 2(4).
6.   The United Kingdom and others proposed that the designations should be combined and simplified. See Consumer L. Bull. No. 57 at pp6-7 (June 1991); EIS, Europe Environment, No. 383 at IV-S (17 March 1992). Other proposals would have eliminated protected geographical indications, leaving only protected designations of origin.
7.   Article 4.
8.   Article 4(2)(e).
9.   Article 9.
10.   Article 10. Private bodies approved by national authorities may perform the inspections. Article 10(2).

Applications must generally be made on behalf of associations of producers. In exceptional cases, a natural or legal person may also seek protection for a product[1]. After an initial screening by national authorities, the applications will be submitted to the Commission[2]. Other Member States and any persons with a "legitimate economic interest" may submit comments or objections[3]. Such persons will presumably include producers of competing products, but it is less clear whether consumer groups are included. Countries outside the Community may seek Community protection for their products, but only if they offer comparable protection to Community products and have created analogous inspection systems[4]. The country of origin will have to be disclosed on the product's label[5].

The regulation requires Member States to adopt protective measures for the certified products. These include legislation to prevent the copying, misuse or evocation of the designations[6]. Member States may continue to permit product names including words such as "style", "type" or "imitation", but only for a period of five years and only where they have already been permitted for five years[7]. The geographical indications and designations of origin could not become "generic names"[8]. This is presumably an effort to override national laws which might permit common "use of the designations. The original proposal would have permitted the Commission to offer financial support to promote the protected products and provide information regarding them to consumers[9]. Like the Commission's proposal for certifications of product distinctiveness, the geographical certifications are intended to promote the "stability" of the Community's agricultural markets[10].

---

1. Article 5. The conditions for individual applications are to be set through a committee procedure, using a new advisory committee. Articles 5(1), 15.
2. Article 5(5).
3. Article 7. Member States are, however, permitted to allow comments from those with "legitimate interest", presumably even if those interests are not economic. Member States will provide comments directly to the Commission. Comments from private persons will be sent to their Member States, which will take account of them in their own comments to the Commission.
4. Article 12.
5. Article 12(2).
6. Article 13 (1). The regulation resembles a directive in its call for changes in national law. This would also trigger the Commission's proposed rule against advertising claims which evoked product names protected by Community law, even if accompanied by such words as "like" or "imitation". Above at para 3.5. The European Parliament suggested that claims of "type" or "like" products should be permitted. OJ C326 16.12.91 p35 at proposed Article 14 (1a).
7. Article 13(2). The true origin must be disclosed and such products may not be sold under those labels in Member States where the use of such words is forbidden.
8. Article 13(3). This is one of the elements of the proposal criticised by some Member States and members of the European Parliament. Various exceptions were suggested. See, e.g., OJ C326 16.12.91 p35.
9. COM(90) 2415 final, at Article 15.
10. COM(90) 2415 final, at Article 15 (2); Council Regulation (EEC) 2081/92, above at the second recital of the preamble.

3.8.3 The search for product quality

The Commission's proposals for Community certifications of geographical origin and product distinctiveness understandably proved to be controversial[1]. They stimulated a "north-side divide" among the Member States, with some northern states opposing the proposals as unnecessary and protectionist[2]. Members of the European Parliament expressed similar objections[3]. Commentators called the proposals "anticompetitive" and "unworkable"[4]. Some of the objections presumed extravagant applications of the proposals, under which familiar products might be made only in places with which their connections are remote[5]. In contrast, other observers argued that the proposals were steps toward assurances of product quality[6]. They expressed fears that the European Court's decisions regarding free circulation have undermined national compositional standards and encouraged low-quality products[7]. Implicit in those concerns are doubts about both the tastes of consumers and the quality of processed and fabricated foods. The debate regarding the Commission's proposals was sometimes characterised as a dispute over free circulation and product quality, and sometimes as a choice between technology and traditional craftsmanship[8]. Adoption of the regulations was a major victory for proponents of local traditional producers, but there is still little evidence of any actual prospect of lower product quality, or that traditional products warrant special protection. It has not yet been shown that existing trademark rules do not offer adequate protection, or that new designations will assist consumers in selecting better foodstuffs[9].

---

1. The general literature on regulation and product quality is immense and growing. See, e.g., Allen, "Regulation and Product Quality", 15 RAND Journal of Economics 311 (1984); Schmalensee, "Advertising and Product Quality", 86 Journal of Political Economy p485 (1978).
2. See, e.g., Eurofood 5 (March 1991); EC Food Law 2 (May 1992). It is reported that the proposals were formulated without prior consultations with any representatives of industry.
3. See, e.g., interview with Ken Collins, MEP, 1 World Food Reg. Rev. 19 (Dec. 1991).
4. Painter, "The Original of Food Products", 4/91 Eur. Food L. Rev. 282, 286 (1991).
5. Frankfurters, Cornish pasties and cheddar cheese were often used as examples. Parliament proposed that products should be excluded if their connections with a particular area are remote and attenuated. OJ C326 16.12.91p35. The Commission agreed to exclude products whose links with their regions of origin have been lost.
6. See, e.g., Deboyser, "Le marché unique des produits alimentaires", 1-1991 Revue du marché unique européen 63, 72-78 (1991).
7. For complaints that quality is declining, see von Heydebrand, "Free Movement of Foodstuffs, Consumer Protection and Food Standards in the European Community: Has the Court of Justice Got It Wrong?" 16 Eur. L. Rev. 391, 394 (1991); Brouwer, "Free Movement of Foodstuffs and Quality Requirements: Has the Commission Got It Wrong?", 25 CMLRev. 237 (1988).
8. For the view that the Community's rules should be neutral with respect to forms of food and processing, see Gray, "The Perspective to 1992", in H. Deelstra, et al., eds., *Food Policy Trends in Europe* pp11, 17 (1991). On the other hand, some members of the European Parliament accepted the regulations as alternatives to compositional standards, although they regard the latter as preferable. See, e.g., EIS, Europe Environment No. 377, pIV-6 10 (Dec 1991).
9. One issue is whether changes in processing technology are not in fact desirable because they may produce foods lower in fats or sugars, and thus contribute to dietary improvements. It has been argued in the United States that compositional standards (which are the essence of the Commission's proposals) have proved a "disincentive, or at least a discouragement, to product innovation", and that this has impeded nutritional improvements. National Academy of Sciences, Committee on Nutritional Components of Food Labeling, *Nutrition Labeling : Issues and Directions for the 1990s* p323 (1990). For an earlier appraisal, see Austern, "Food Standards: The Balance Between Certainty and Innovation", 24 Food D.C.L.J. 440 (1969).

The debate over product quality is unlikely to cease with the Council's regulations. France is, for example, preparing an "inventory of culinary heritage" which would place food specialities on a protected basis similar to that for national architectural monuments[1]. The Commission has reportedly drafted another quality standards programme which includes quality labels that could be displayed by producers who comply voluntarily with Community standards[2]. In essence, the plan would extend the regulations to include products without the geographical or other distinctive properties necessary for certification under those regulations. The idea has not yet been issued as a proposal and, if adopted, may require a formidable apparatus of new vertical standards.

1.   1 World Food Reg. Rev. 14 (April 1992). It is unclear how this might work in practice, or indeed whether it would work at all.
2.   The Commission is considering additional proposals intended to enhance produce "quality". Written Question 2177/91, OJ C141 3.6.92 p10.

CHAPTER 4 : SECTORIAL MEASURES

An important area of priority for the Community since 1985 has been the adoption of measures to harmonise national rules regarding various distinctive categories of foodstuffs. The foods in these categories are characterised chiefly by diversity. Some are made distinctive by their intended purposes, and others by their methods of processing or manufacture. The most important of the former are foods for particular nutritional uses, sometimes termed "parnuts" products. The latter include quick-frozen and chilled foods, irradiated foods, and "novel" food ingredients derived from biotechnological techniques. The Community's existing or proposed measures which address these foods are neither wholly vertical nor entirely horizontal. For want of a better label, they have become known as sectorial measures. They include some of the most controversial food issues now before the Community.

The Community's record of achievement in this area is undistinguished. Despite lengthy efforts, it did not adopt a directive regarding quick-frozen foods until December 1988[1]. There are still very few rules for chilled foods, although they are increasingly important in the diets of the Community's residents. It adopted a framework directive regarding foods for particular nutritional purposes in 1976, but the measure proved unsatisfactory and the Community did not agree upon a replacement until 1989. Aside from infant formulae, the Commission has still not proposed rules for most categories of "parnuts" foods[2]. It has adopted rules for infant and follow-on formulae, but the Commission's first proposal regarding those products failed. It did not find acceptable rules until 1991, after several years of debate. The Commission has made lengthy efforts to authorise irradiated foods, but it still has not overcome the political and public sensitivities which surround irradiation[3]. The issue is unlikely to be resolved quickly, and any measure which is adopted is unlikely to prove conclusive. There is a draft regulation regarding novel food ingredients and processes, but no measure has yet been adopted[4].

---

1.   Below at para 4.2.
2.   Below at para 4.5.
3.   Below at para 4.3.
4.   Below at para 4.4.

In all, the Community has harmonised only a small fraction of the national rules for sectorial products. More progress will undoubtedly be made, but full harmonisation is not likely to occur, if at all, until well after 1992. The omissions are significant deficiencies of the internal market programme, but they cannot in fairness be regarded as surprising. Irradiation, biotechnology and many "parnuts" foods have all provoked substantial public debate. Similar controversies have arisen in other parts of the world, and repeated scientific studies have failed to resolve the disputes. Many of the concerns which surround food processing, including the public's apprehensions regarding human safety and the environment, have centred upon sectorial issues. Even where the public debate has been less vigorous, as it has with respect to chilled and quick-frozen foods, complex technical and commercial issues must still be resolved.

4.1 Chilled foods

Chilled foods have become an important element of the diets of the Community's consumers[1]. Average consumption varies among the Member States, but in some areas chilled foods are more widely consumed than foods sold at ambient temperatures. In all states, they represent a substantially larger proportion of national diets than frozen foods[2]. In some nations, the growth in sales exceeds five per cent annually[3]. In Britain, sales grew in real terms by 95 per cent from 1985 to 1990[4.] These calculations are complicated by varied definitions of chilling, but such foods may conveniently be described as perishable products maintained at temperatures near freezing and below $8^{0}C$[5]. Consumers commonly regard them as "fresh", but in fact they are chilled as a method of preservation[6]. Chilling produces small changes in nutritional levels[7,] but chilled foods have still dramatically increased the range of foodstuffs available to the Community's consumers[8].

---

1. Useful summaries of the issues presented by chilled foods are contained in the proceedings of technical meetings sponsored by the Commission under its COST research programmes. See, e.g., T. Gormley, ed., *Chilled Foods : The State of the Art* (1990); T. Gormley & P. Zenthen, eds., *Chilled Foods : The Ongoing Debate* (1990).
2. Meffert, "Economic Developments Pertinent to Chilled Foods", in T. Gormley, ed., *Chilled Foods : The State of the Art* pp337, 338-341 (1990).
3. Bogh-Sorensen & Olsson, "The Chill Chain", in T. Gormley, ed., *Chilled Foods : The State of the Art* p245 (1990).
4. Eurofood 10 (April 1992).
5. A similar definition is used by the Institute of Food Science and Technology. See Walker & Stringer, "Microbiology of Chilled Foods", in T. Gormley, ed., *Chilled Foods : The State of the Art* p269 (1990).
6. Chilling merely delays the rate of spoilage. B. Hobbs & D. Roberts, *Food Poisoning and Food Hygiene* p166 (5th ed. 1987).
7. Bognar, et al., "Nutrient Retention in Chilled Foods", in T. Gormley, ed., *Chilled Foods : The State of the Art* pp305, 330-331 (1990).
8. T. Gormley & P. Zenthen, eds., *Chilled Foods : The Ongoing Debate* p1 (1990). The advantages of chilled products are illustrated by fish products, which are otherwise among the most perishable of all foods. See Whittle, et al., "Chilled Fish and Fishery Products", in T. Gormley, ed., *Chilled Foods : The State of the Art* pp87-89 (1990).

The benefits of chilled foods are accompanied by significant disadvantages. Like frozen foods, they require special care in their transport and storage. Integrated controls over time and temperature are essential to maintain quality and wholesomeness[1]. Any prolonged interruptions in temperature controls during transport, in retail display cabinets, or in domestic refrigerators may produce spoilage. Deteriorations in product quality can cause substantial risks of food-borne illness[2]. It is widely agreed that there are weaknesses in the chill-chains which link production and consumption, but differing views as to the points of special weakness[3]. The difficulties are increased by the fact that appropriate temperature levels vary by product[4]. As a result, there is still insufficient information regarding the shelf lives of many products[5]. Packaging may also affect both shelf lives and the extent of any nutritional changes produced by chilling[6]. In all, chilled foods present complex technical questions to which reliable answers are only gradually being found[7].

The regulatory controls for chilled foods are correspondingly incomplete. There is an international Agreement on the Transport of Perishables which includes temperature controls, but its recommendations differ from the national rules in, for example, Denmark and Germany[8]. In the Community, little has been done to harmonise the differences in national controls. There is as yet no comprehensive Community measure regarding food hygiene, and almost nothing addressed to the special issues presented by

---

1. See Bogh-Sorensen & Olsson, "The Chill Chain", in T. Gormley, ed., *Chilled Foods : The State of the Art* pp245, 262 (1990).
2. It has, for example, been argued that cook-chill products (which are cooked by the processor and thereafter chilled for preservation during transport and storage) are "inherently unsafe", particularly in light of purchasing patterns described by the author as the "supermarket culture". R. Lacey, *Unfit for Human Consumption* pp128, 220 (1991). For a different view, although one which observes that food poisonings in England and Wales remain at a "high level", see B. Hobbs & D. Roberts, *Food Poisoning and Food Hygiene* pp9, 166 (5th ed. 1987).
3. The weak link has been described by two authors as the retail display cabinet, while another has emphasised transport and domestic refrigeration. All three authors would undoubtedly accept that all of the points are potential weaknesses. Compare James & Bailey, "Chilling Systems for Foods", with Williams, "Chilled Combined Foods and Chilled Meats", both in T. Gormley, ed., *Chilled Foods : The State of the Art* pp26, 242 (1990).
4. T. Gormley & P. Zenthen, eds., *Chilled Foods : The Ongoing Debate* p15 (1990). For example, it remains unclear how long cooked bakery goods may be held without chilling before transport. Some products may be held for two hours, while others might have to be chilled more promptly. See, e.g., Consumer L. Bull. No. 55 at 3-4 (April 1991). For the specific issues of snack foods, see Persson, et al., "Refrigeration and Snack Foods", in R. Gordon Booth, ed., *Snack Food* pp301-326 (1990).
5. Williams, "Chilled Combined Foods and Chilled Meats", in T. Gormley, ed., *Chilled Foods : The State of the Art* pp225, 242 (1990).
6. Bognar, et al., "Nutrient Retention in Chilled Foods", in T. Gormley, ed., *Chilled Foods : the State of the Art* pp305, 330-331 (1990); Gac, "Propriétés générales des emballages pour produits refrigérés, congelés et surgelés", in G. Bureau & J. L. Multon, eds., *L'Emballage des Denrées Alimentaires de Grande Consommation* pp583-598 (1989).
7. A review of the issues reported only "scanty" knowledge about the problems of chilled foods, including their nutritional qualities. T. Gormley & P. Zenthen, eds., *Chilled Foods : The Ongoing Debate* pp5-10 (1990).
8. Bogh-Sorensen & Olsson, "The Chill Chain", in T. Gormley, ed., *Chilled Foods : The State of the Art* pp245, 248 (1990).

the different methods of chilling foods[1]. Temperature controls have, however, been imposed upon retail display cabinets for frozen foods, and similar controls are likely to follow for chilled food cabinets[2]. Commercial difficulties may result in regulatory compromises, as they have for frozen foods, but at least some start is likely to be made. Other issues may be reserved until additional technical evidence is obtained. The Community has sponsored or proposed research programmes regarding chilled foods, and more general research regarding the effects of processing on food quality and nutritional values[3]. These and similar steps should eventually provide a reliable basis for resolving the issues of chilled foods.

4.2   Frozen foods

Although freezing is an ancient method of food preservation, many Community consumers have only recently begun using frozen foods regularly[4]. Consumer use of frozen foods still varies widely among the Member States[5]. Progress in the Community's regulation of those products has been correspondingly slow. The Commission proposed a directive to harmonise national legislation regarding quick-frozen foods in 1984, but the European Parliament and the Economic and Social Committee objected that the proposal was incomplete and undemanding[6]. In some respects, the proposed rules were less rigourous than those in some Member States. It was not until December 1988 that the Council finally adopted a directive[7]. It applies to all foodstuffs which have

---

1.   The Commission has proposed a framework measure regarding food hygiene standards. Below at Chapter 8, para 8.6. Specific hygiene rules have been adopted for chilled minced beef. Below at Chapter 7, para 7.12. In addition, there are national rules regarding such matters as temperature controls. See, e.g., Food Hygiene (Amendment) Regulations 1991, SI 1991/1343.

2.   Among others, the Richmond Committee in Britain has urged the adoption of minimum temperature performance controls. Report of the Committee on the Microbiological Safety of Foods, Part 1, at 85. The costs of such controls will, however, be high. In Britain, the costs of complying with temperature controls imposed by the Food Hygiene (Amendment) Regulations 1991 have been estimated at 300 million pounds. *The Times* p10 (28 March 1991). For the rules relating to retail cabinets for frozen foods, see below at Chapter 4, para 4.2.

3.   For the Commission's research programmes relating to chilled foods, see, e.g., T. Gormley, ed., *Chilled Foods : The State of the Art* (1990); T. Gormley & P. Zenthen, *Chilled Foods : The Ongoing Debate* (1990). For broader research regarding the effects of food processing, see, e.g., opinions of the Economic and Social Committee, OJ C40 17.2.92 p24; OJ C23 30.1.84 p1,. See also Council Decision (EEC) 84/304, OJ L151 7.6.84 p46.

4.   M. Jul, *The Quality of Frozen Foods* p1 (1984).

5.   Danes consume eight times more frozen foods than Italians, and Italians consume only one-fourth of the average in the Netherlands. Meffert, "Economic Developments Pertinent to Chilled Foods", in T. Gormley, ed., *Chilled Foods : The State of the Art* pp337, 338-341 (1990). In Britain, sales of frozen foods have diminished since 1988, as consumers have switched to chilled and microwaveable foods. The latter may be stored at ambient temperatures. *Eurofood* p10 (Jan. 1992).

6.   For the Parliament's reactions, see OJ C175 15.7.85 p296. For the opinion of the Economic and Social Committee, see OJ C12 16.1.89 p1.

7.   Council Directive (EEC) 89/108, OJ L40 11.2.89 p1.

undergone "quick-freezing"[1], whose temperature after thermal stabilisation is maintained at -18° C or lower, and which are marketed in a way indicating that they have those characteristics[2]. Most frozen foods sold to consumers are quick-frozen, but some national laws continue to distinguish between quick-frozen and other frozen foods[3]. Only quick-frozen (or "surgelé") foods are encompassed by the directive. Ice creams and edible ices are excluded[4]. So too are products which have been frozen, but thawed before sale[5].

The directive's purpose is to ensure the quality and safety of quick-frozen products until they reach the consumer. This demands that all microbiological activity be suspended until the product's consumption[6]. In technical terms, this involves a complex mixture of time, temperature and packaging[7]. The directive does not, however, address most of these complexities. It is concerned almost exclusively with temperature[8]. It requires that product temperatures be maintained at -18°C or lower, with short upward fluctuations during transport, local distribution or in retail cabinets[9]. Under the directive, "possibly brief" upward fluctuations of 3° C or less are permitted during transport[10]. Temperature requirements involve difficult commercial issues, and the Commission recognised that some existing equipment cannot satisfy the requirements. There are particular problems with respect to retail cabinets and local distributional

---

1.　　There are various alternative methods, including "block", "blast", "immersion" and "contact" freezing. See, e.g., F. Paine & H. Paine, *A Handbook of Food Packaging* pp211-214 (1983); P.J. Fellows, *Food Processing Technology: Principles and Practice* pp375-400 (1988).

2.　　Council Directive (EEC) 89/108, above at Article 1(2). For a similar definition of quick freezing, but prescribing a thermal stabilisation period of no more than two hours, see A. Bender, *Dictionary of Nutrition and Food Technology* p238 (6th ed. 1990).

3.　　See, e.g., *Lamy-Dehove* at pp6-450, et seq. See also M. Jul, *The Quality of Frozen Foods* pp207-208 (1984). The French alternative to quick-frozen is "congelé".

4.　　Council Directive (EEC) 89/108, above at Article 1(2).

5.　　Article 1(2). Attention to the problems presented by thawed products was, however, one of the recommendations of the Economic and Social Committee. OJ C104 1985 p17 at para 2.2.

6.　　Council Directive (EEC) 89/108, above at the ninth recital of the preamble.

7.　　M. Jul, *The Quality of Frozen Foods* pp112-148 (1984).

8.　　Jul argues that regulators are unduly preoccupied with temperature controls, and that different levels of controls are feasible. M. Jul, *The Quality of Frozen Foods* p137 (1984). The Agreement on the Transport of Perishables also sets differentiated temperature controls; ibid., at 175. Jul suggests that rigid temperature controls are unlikely to benefit consumers and require substantial energy expenditures; ibid., at pp176, 186. Their chief advantage may be regulatory simplicity.

9.　　Article 5 (1). FDA does not impose specific temperature requirements, although it generally requires compliance with good manufacturing practices, and prohibits thawing. There is, however, a U.S. code of recommended practices for frozen foods which includes temperature and monitoring provisions. M. Jul, *The Quality of Frozen Foods* p175 (1984). U.S. producers fear that the Community's more specific requirements may create non-tariff trade barriers. USITC, *The Effects of Greater Economic Integration within the European Community on the United States* pp6-58 (1989). For Swiss law, see Ordinance of 26 May 1936, as amended, at Article 11(2).

10.　The word "possibly" is unexplained and perhaps inexplicable. Perhaps it is intended as a synonym for "occasional" or "irregular". Swiss law allows similar temperature fluctuations for short periods. Ordinance of 26 May 1936, as amended, at Article 11(2).

networks[1]. The directive takes account of those problems by a compromise between safety considerations and commercial demands. It permits Member States to authorise temperature tolerances of as much as 6° C for such equipment[2]. The tolerances are to expire in December 1996, but the Commission may "if appropriate" make further proposals regarding temperatures in retail cabinets by January 1993[3]. Whether or not they grant tolerances, Member States must ensure the adequacy of transport and display equipment through random official checks[4]. Despite the recommendations of the Economic and Social Committee, there are no provisions for monitoring breakdowns in refrigeration systems, or for research into the feasibility of such monitoring[5]. There was originally no provision regarding permissible load lines for open retail sale cabinets, but the Commission has since adopted such rules[6]. An official certificate of compliance cannot be required as a prerequisite to the marketing of a quick-frozen product[7].

Raw materials must be of "sound, genuine and merchantable quality." They must also have the "required degree of freshness"[8]. Processing must be conducted promptly, and appropriate equipment must limit chemical, biochemical and microbiological changes "to a minimum[9]." The only authorised cryogenic media are air, nitrogen and carbon dioxide, although dichlorodifluoromethane (R12) may be permitted by Member States until 1993[10]. Purity criteria for cryogenic media are to be established through a committee procedure involving the Standing Committee for Foodstuffs[11]. The positive

---

1. The tenth, eleventh and twelfth recital of the preamble. See also Article 5(2). This is consistent with the general industry perception, although loadings and transfers are perhaps more serious problems. M. Jul, *The Quality of Frozen Foods* p179 (1984). The Codex Alimentarius Commission has also proposed rules on the handling of frozen foods during transport; ibid., at pp268-269.

2. Article 5(2). Tolerances are generally limited to 3° C, but, if and to the extent Member States decide, they may reach 6° C for retail display cabinets. The Commission must be informed of such decisions. For eight years, Member States may also authorise tolerances for local distributional systems of as much as 6° C. Article 5(3). These tolerances depart from the views of the Economic and Social Committee, which urged "strict temperature levels rather than to adapt the rules to fit inappropriate equipment." OJ C104 p18 (1985) at para 2.5.1.

3. Article 5(2)(b).

4. Article 6.

5. OJ C104 p18 (1985) at para 2.5.2.

6. Council Directive (EEC) 89/108, above at para 2.6.2. Under the Commission's rules, retail storage cabinets must have a visible thermometer which measures temperatures at the maximum load line. Derogations are permitted for relatively small chambers. Commission Directive (EEC) 92/1, OJ L34 21.2.92 p28.

7. Article 6(2).

8. Article 3(1). The word "required" does not mean that there are Community freshness requirements; presumably the word is used as a synonym for "requisite" or "suitable". The freshness of the unfrozen product is an important determinant of the quality of the frozen product, and manufacturers are generally anxious to freeze products as promptly as possible.

9. Article 3(2).

10. Article 4.

11. Articles 4, 12.

list of cryogenic media is one area in which the directive followed the recommendations of the Economic and Social Committee[1].

The directive does not contain specific packaging obligations, but provides simply that prepackaging must be suitable to prevent contamination and drying[2]. With respect to labelling, it applies the 1978 directive as amended[3]. It supplements the 1978 directive by requiring the words "quick-frozen," or the equivalent in other Community languages, to be added to the product's sales name. It also requires a phrase similar to "do not refreeze after defrosting[4]." There must be a date of minimum durability, as well as a reference from which the product's lot or batch may be identified[5]. Labels must indicate the period for which the product may be stored, as well as the temperature and equipment needed for proper storage[6].

The labels of products not encompassed by the 1978 labelling directive (that is, products not sold to mass caterers or the ultimate consumer) must nonetheless include many of the disclosures demanded by that directive. Their labels must disclose their sales names; net quantities in terms of mass; a lot or batch reference; and the name or business name and address of the manufacturer or packer, or of a seller established in the Community[7]. These must appear on the product's packaging or container, or on a label[8]. Sampling and monitoring procedures were adopted in 1992, using a committee procedure involving the Standing Committee for Foodstuffs[9]. Member States are forbidden to prohibit the

---

1. OJ C104 p18, (1985) at para. 2.4.
2. Article 7. This applies to foodstuffs intended for supply to the ultimate consumer. Contrary to the recommendation of the Economic and Social Committee, there is no express provision regarding packaging "sweating". See OJ C104 p18 at para 2.7. By one estimate, packaging is, next to the quality of the raw materials themselves, the most important factor in a product's ultimate quality. M. Jul, *The Quality of Frozen Foods* pp128 (1984). To be effective, packaging must be impermeable to water-vapour, oxygen and volatile flavour substances. Id. at 134. For a description of the role and characteristics of packaging for frozen foods, see, e.g., F. Paine & H. Paine, *A Handbook of Food Packaging* pp207-218 (1983).
3. Article 8(1). This applies to foodstuffs intended for supply without further processing to the ultimate consumer or to mass caterers.
4. The Economic and Social Committee suggested a phrase such as "never refreeze a defrosted product." OJ C104 p18 (1985) at para 2.9.3. This is one of the few areas in which a warning label has been required by the Community.
5. This provision is not expressly reconciled with the lot marking directive and its exceptions, below at Chapter 3, para 3.6, but presumably overrides the exceptions.
6. Article 8. Contrary to the recommendation of the Economic and Social Committee, there is no requirement for a "star" system for marking products. Such a system was suggested by European standardisation groups to identify products which have not been properly stored. OJ C104 p18 (1985), at para 2.9.1. By one estimate, date labelling is based upon inadequate data and unduly conservative. M. Jul, *The Quality of Frozen Foods* pp253-255 (1984).
7. Article 9(1).
8. Article 9(2).
9. Article 11. For the rules, see Commission Directive (EEC) 92/2, OJ L34 11.2.92 p30.

marketing of products which comply with the directive, insofar as those prohibitions are based upon manufacturing specifications, product presentation or labelling[1].

The directive represents a useful harmonisation of national rules regarding an important category of processed foods. Substantial questions may, however, be asked about certain of its policies. As the Economic and Social Committee observed with respect to the Commission's initial proposal, the directive's rules are less rigourous than those which previously existed in some Member States[2]. The lengthy derogations for temperature controls are questionable compromises between health considerations and commercial demands. In addition, the directive makes no effort to encourage methods of identifying foodstuffs which have been inadequately stored or maintained. Finally, it does not address issues presented by frozen foods which have not been quick-frozen, or frozen foods thawed before sale. The latter may create safety hazards, and the absence of regulatory constraints is a significant omission from the Community's rules[3].

4.3 Foods and ingredients treated with ionising radiation

The Community's difficulties in resolving the issues of chilled and quick-frozen foods are substantially exceeded by its problems regarding food irradiation. Few disputes regarding food regulation have proved so resistant to compromise. The treatment of foods and food ingredients with ionising radiation is a method of preservation, intended to delay the effects of micro-organisms[4]. All preservative methods produce changes in the colour, texture or nutritional properties of foodstuffs, but irradiation causes fewer and less serious modifications than its alternatives[5]. Nonetheless, high radiation doses may cause significant nutritional losses[6]. Irradiation is especially suitable for herbs and spices, but may also be appropriate for poultry, some other meats,

---

1. Article 10.
2. OJ C104 p17 (1985) at para 1.3. The rules are, however, generally consistent with the code of practice adopted by the Codex Alimentarius Commission.
3. OJ C104 p17 (1985) at para 1.5. Several Member States already have adopted labelling requirements for such products. M. Jul, *The Quality of Frozen Foods* pp268-269 (1984). Thawed products are often sold without prepackaging, which itself is not generally addressed by Community legislation.
4. For descriptions of the processes, uses and advantages of irradiation, see, e.g., DHSS Advisory Committee on Irradiated and Novel Foods, Report on the Safety and Wholesomeness of Irradiated Foods (1986); D. Robins, *The Preservation of Foods by Irradiation* (1991); P.J. Fellows, *Food Processing Technology: Principles and Practice* pp186-195 (1988); Elias, "Wholesomeness of Irradiated Food", in R. Walker & E. Quattrucci, eds., *Nutritional and Toxicological Aspects of Food Processing* pp103-112 (1988).
5. D. Robins, *The Preservation of Food by Irradiation* p13 (1991).
6. Elias, "Task Force on Irradiation Processing - Wholesomeness Studies", in C. Felix, ed., *Food Protection Technology* pp349, 353 (1987).

and some vegetables[1]. It is a particularly valuable weapon against food contamination in developing countries[2]. It is not a new process. The first patent was issued in the United States in 1921, and the process has been the subject of extensive technical and scientific study for several decades[3]. An International Consultative Group on Food Irradiation, representing some 32 countries, has existed since 1984[4]. Irradiation is approved by seven of the Community's twelve Member States, and more than 20 other countries[5].

Nonetheless, food irradiation continues to provoke widespread debate. Many legislators and consumers question its long-term safety[6]. It has been argued that irradiation may hide contamination and permit the sale of older, lower quality foods[7]. Those concerns have not been reduced by scientific reviews which have repeatedly approved irradiation under appropriate conditions of use. An expert committee convened by WHO and FAO conducted lengthy studies of irradiation, and concluded that it is safe under proper restrictions[8]. The committee's conclusions were accepted by the Codex Alimentarius Commission, which issued standards for irradiated foods and a code of practice for irradiation facilities[9]. In 1986, an advisory committee in Britain

---

1.   DHSS Advisory Committee on Irradiated and Novel Foods, Report on the Safety and Wholesomeness of Irradiated Foods (1986).

2.   An English member of the European Parliament has described irradiation as the "number one tool against increasing food contamination, which is a growing threat in Western Europe". Interview with Dr. Caroline Jackson, MEP, 1 World Food Reg. Rev. 22, 23 (July 1991). For its value in developing countries, see Elias, "Wholesomeness of Irradiated Food", in R. Walker & E. Quattrucci, eds., *Nutritional and Toxicological Aspects of Food Processing* pp103, 110 (1988). The World Health Organisation has urged irradiation's approval largely because of its value in poorer countries. See 1 World Food Reg. Rev. 21 (Dec 1991).

3.   D. Robins, *The Preservation of Food by Irradiation* p11 (1991). One of the principal scientific proponents of irradiation has repeatedly described the evidence of its safety as "impressive". Elias, "Wholesomeness of Irradiated Food", in R. Walker & E. Quattrucci, eds., *Nutritional and Toxicological Aspects of Food Processing* pp103, 110 (1988); Elias, "Task Force on Irradiation Processing - Wholesomeness Studies", in C. Felix, ed., *Food Protection Technology* pp353, 357 (1987).

4.   Report of the Nineteenth Session of the Codex Alimentarius Commission p5 (1991). For the Codex rules, see Codex Standard 106-1983, Codex Alimentarius (2nd ed. 1991).

5.   D. Robins, *The Preservation of Food by Irradiation* pp41-65 (1991). It was authorised in the United States in 1981. P. Hutt & R. Merrill, *Food and Drug Law, Cases and Materials* p329 (2nd ed. 1991). There are, however, moratoria or bans in some states. See, e.g., Lear's p34 (July 1992). For the Japanese rules, see Ministry of Health & Welfare, *Food Sanitation Law, Food Addives in Japan* p32 (1981).

6.   The diverse attitudes of consumer groups are illustrated in the hearings regarding irradiation before the House of Lords Select Committee on the European Communities. See Irradiation of Foodstuffs, Session 1989-1990, 4th Report (HL Paper 13) (1989). Evidence of consumer attitudes is also provided by surveys summarised by D. Robins, *The Preservation of Food by Irradiation* pp75-81 (1991).

7.   For these and other concerns, see T. Webb & T. Lang, *Food Irradiation : The Myth and the Reality* pp11-19, 83, 120 (1990). See also London Food Commission, *Food Adulteration and How to Beat It* pp190-233 (1988).

8.   D. Robins, *The Preservation of Food by Irradiation* p39 (1991).

9.   Ibid., at p40. See Codex Alimentarius sec. 8 (2nd ed. 1991).

reached similar conclusions[1]. In 1989, a committee of the House of Lords heard extensive evidence regarding irradiation and again concluded that, under proper conditions, it may be employed safely[2].

In response, some legislators and consumer groups point to a report issued by a committee of the British Medical Association, which suggested a full-scale study of the issues[3]. Similar uncertainties were expressed in Australia[4]. Those fears are shared by several Member States. Germany, for example, has declined to approve any irradiation. Even before the Commission proposed to authorise irradiation, the European Parliament adopted a resolution complaining of the absence of long-term studies, and concluding that irradiation's safety was still unproven[5]. The debate is vigorous and emotional, and for many consumers irradiation has become a symbol of technology's uncertainties and hazards.

In 1988, the Commission rekindled the controversy by proposing a Council directive to harmonise national rules regarding irradiation[6]. The proposal was less a harmonisation than an authorisation, for it would have instructed Member States which do not permit irradiation to allow its use for a substantial list of foodstuffs. The proposal was quickly criticised by consumer groups and in the European Parliament[7]. The Commission amended the proposal in 1989 to eliminate several foods from the list for which irradiation would be authorised[8]. It also strengthened the proposed labelling obligations and agreed that any issues "likely" to affect public health should be reviewed by the Scientific Committee for Food. The Commission also agreed that the Scientific Committee's opinions would be published, together with the basis for those opinions[9].

The changes have done little to facilitate agreement within the Council. In May 1990, a compromise was suggested which would have eliminated all products from the

---

1. DHSS Advisory Committee on Irradiated and Novel Foods, Report on the Safety and Wholesomeness of Irradiated Foods (1986).
2. Irradiation of Foodstuffs, Session 1989-90, 4th Report (HL Paper 13) (1989).
3. T. Webb & T. Lang, *Food Irradiation : The Myth and the Reality* p125 (1990).
4. Bradgate & Howells, "Food Law in the United Kingdom", 46 Food D.C.L.J. 447, 461 n.111 (1991).
5. Document A2-216/86, OJ C99 p68 (April 13, 1987).
6. COM(88) 654 final, OJ C366 31.12.88 p7.
7. For a description of the controversy, see Scott, "Continuity and Change in British Food Law", 53 Mod. L. Rev. 785, 799 (1990).
8. COM(89) 576 final, OJ C303 2.12.89 p5. Strawberries, papayas, mangoes, bulbs and tubers, and frogs' legs were removed from the authorised list. The amendment also revised the proposal's recitals and abandoned a proposed logo.
9. Article 12.

authorised list except herbs and spices[1]. Other foods would have required temporary national authorisations, which would have been subject to Community review through the Standing Committee for Foodstuffs. This would have avoided any formal review of the additions by the European Parliament. Later in 1990, it was instead suggested that existing national authorisations should remain in effect until 1996, when they would lapse unless endorsed by the Standing Committee after evaluation by the Scientific Committee. This would essentially have postponed harmonisation for several years. Both suggestions failed to win sufficient support within the Council. In these circumstances, it is far from clear that the Commission's amended proposal will provide the basis for any measure which might eventually be adopted[2]. Nonetheless, it is useful to examine that proposal, as well as the rules in France and Britain, to illustrate the approaches to irradiation which have been taken within the Community.

The Commission's proposal would control virtually all irradiation of foodstuffs. The only exceptions would be foods exposed to low radiation doses from measuring or inspection devices and foods prepared under medical supervision for patients requiring sterile diets[3]. With those exceptions, irradiation would be permitted for eight categories of foodstuffs[4]. These would include dried fruits, pulses, dehydrated vegetables, cereal flakes, dried herbs and spices, prepared shrimps and prawns, deboned poultrymeat, and arabic gum[5]. Each category would be assigned a maximum permissible dose of radiation, ranging from one to ten kilograys. The advisory committee which reviewed these issues in Britain found that ten kilograys will not prejudice a product's safety[6]. Products could be irradiated in stages or at multiple processing points, but the total dosage could not exceed the maximum levels[7]. Only prescribed radiation sources could be used, and instructions would be given for the

---

1.   Herbs and spices are particularly appropriate for irradiation because of their rapid spoilage rates. Indeed, the Commission has observed that the alternative to irradiation is treatment by ethylene oxide, which may leave harmful residues. See COM(89) 576 final, above at the new fourteenth recital of the preamble

2.   In response to a Parliamentary question, Commissioner Bangemann has said that the Commission proposal would impose "strict controls" upon irradiation. Written Question 1082/89, OJ C125 12.5.80 p32. It is likely that any measure eventually agreed upon would do so.

3.   No. 88/C336/06, above, at Article 1. The provision relating to measuring and inspection devices includes limitations upon doses and energy levels. Article 1(2) (a).

4.   Annex I, as amended.

5.   No description is given of the kind or degree of "preparation" needed to bring shrimp and prawns within the authorisation.

6.   DHSS Advisory Committee on Irradiated and Novel Foods, Report on the Safety and Wholesomeness of Irradiated Foods (1986) at para 2.1. As described below, some nations permit higher doses, although there is evidence that they result in nutritional losses.

7.   Article 4(1).

calculation of dosages[1]. Validation measurements and random dosimeter sampling would be required[2].

Even within these limits, irradiation would be permitted only if several conditions were satisfied[3]. Irradiation would be authorised only to meet a "reasonable technological need" and only if it offered benefits to the consumer[4]. It could not be a substitute for compliance with health rules or good manufacturing practice[5]. In general terms, irradiation could not be used if it presented any hazard to human health[6]. Finally, it would have to serve one of four purposes[7]. It could be used to destroy pathogenic organisms, to reduce spoilage, to prevent premature ripening or sprouting, or to disinfect foodstuffs. These criteria would guide any amendments to the list of foodstuffs for which irradiation would be authorised[8].

One of irradiation's features is that nothing in a product's quality or appearance reveals whether it has occurred[9]. This is a significant advantage, but it also means that processors could market products without any disclosure that irradiation has been conducted. Labelling is therefore both valued as a device to warn consumers and yet discounted as an effective guarantee of consumer protection[10]. Consumer groups demand labelling if irradiation is approved, but also deny that labelling offers adequate protection. Whatever labelling's weaknesses, the Commission has proposed detailed obligations[11].

As a threshold matter, labels would include the notice of irradiation already demanded by the 1978 labelling directive, as amended[12]. The proposed directive would extend this requirement to include foodstuffs not intended for sale to consumers, as well

---

1.   Annex II.
2.   Annex III, as renumbered by the amended proposal.
3.   Annex IV, as renumbered by the amended proposal.
4.   Para 1 of Annex IV.
5.   The phrase "health rules" is not explained. Presumably it refers to any applicable rules of hygiene or wholesomeness.
6.   In the view of those who question the adequacy of the existing scientific data, this would effectively prohibit all food irradiation. It is likely, however, that the Commission sees this as a reassurance rather than a standard.
7.   Para 2 of Annex IV.
8.   Article 3(1). It appears that the criteria would be intended less as a limitation upon the uses of irradiation, as those uses would be authorised by the directive (defining, for example, when prepared shrimp could be irradiated) than as a guide to future authorisations.
9.   See, e.g., P. Seddon, *Spoiled for Choice* p129 (1990).
10.   See, e.g., T. Webb & T. Lang, *Food Irradiation : The Myth and the Reality* pp82-83 (1990).
11.   Adequate labelling was one of the European Parliament's demands in its 1987 resolution regarding irradiation. Document A2-216/86 (April 13, 1987) at para 4.
12.   Article 5(1).

as food ingredients[1]. As described above, the labelling directive does not unequivocally require a notice of irradiation regarding ingredients included in compound foodstuffs[2]. The proposal would require labels of compound foodstuffs containing irradiated ingredients either to include a general declaration of irradiation or to reveal each of the irradiated ingredients[3]. Labels would also identify the particular facility which performed the irradiation, and provide a lot or batch number[4]. The irradiation facility could be identified by name or reference number. The requirement of a lot or batch number would presumably override the exception in the lot marking directive for labels containing a "best before" or "use by" date[5].

The proposal offers no specific instructions regarding packaging, but there would be a general obligation to use packaging "appropriate for the purpose"[6]. In contrast, specific limitations would be imposed upon irradiation facilities. They would be individually approved by national authorities[7]. They would also be obliged to comply with the Joint FAO/WHO Recommended International Code of Practice prepared by the Codex Alimentarius Commission[8]. National approval would be required before irradiation could begin. National authorities would issue facility reference numbers and conduct continuing programmes of inspection[9]. They would be expected to withdraw or modify a facility's approval if there were deficiencies in its methods or activities. The names and reference numbers of approved facilities would be published by the Commission in the Official Journal[10]. Irradiation facilities would be obliged to maintain records regarding each lot of products, including the consignee, packaging, and data regarding controls and validations[11].

---

1.   Article 5(2), as amended.
2.   Some ambiguity about ingredients is also left by the proposal, which would apply the 1978 directives to foods intended for sale to the ultimate consumer, while imposing a specific requirement that notice be given of ingredient irradiation with respect to other foods. Articles 5(1), (2), as amended.
3.   Article 5 (2) (3), as amended. The provision appears to assume that a notice of ingredient irradiation is required by the 1978 labelling directive.
4.   Article 5(2).
5.   For the exception in the lot marking directive for products with a "best before" or "use by" date, see above at Chapter 3, para 3.6.
6.   Article 9. For a discussion of packaging issues, see Nielsen, "Use of Irradiation Techniques in Food Packaging", in F. Paine, ed., *Modern Processing, Packaging and Distribution Systems for Food* pp52-61 (1987).
7.   Article 6(2).
8.   Article 6(3).
9.   Article 6(2).
10.   Articles 6(4), 5.
11.   Article 7.

The proposed directive would prohibit the importation of irradiated foods into the Community unless they complied with its rules[1]. Information similar to that required for products irradiated within the Community would have to be provided for imported products. This would include the identity of the irradiation facility, a lot number, the date of irradiation, the packaging used during treatment, and validation and control data. This information would appear in documents accompanying each consignment[2]. Irradiation facilities would have to be supervised locally in a fashion equivalent to the proposed directive. The fact and degree of supervision would have to be "officially confirmed" by the country in which irradiation occurred. In addition, the Commission could seek inspection rights regarding irradiation facilities outside the Community[3]. Details of the arrangements would be published in the Official Journal[4].

The Commission's proposals may usefully be compared to the French and British legislation. The French rules have been revised on several occasions, but originate from a 1970 decree which created a framework of requirements for irradiation and the control of irradiation facilities[5]. The list of products for which irradiation is authorised is shorter than the Commission's proposed list. It includes, for example, strawberries, onions, shallots, poultrymeat, arabic gum, dehydrated vegetables, cereal products, herbs and spices[6]. Irradiated products must bear a notice of irradiation in their labels, as well as in accompanying sales documents[7]. Imported products must satisfy requirements equivalent to the French rules regarding maximum dosage, the supervision of irradiation facilities, and other matters[8]. The Commission's proposed rules are, in other words, generally similar to those which have existed in France for more than 20 years.

In turn, the French rules are similar to those in several other Member States. The longest list of approved products is in the Netherlands, which includes egg powder, malt, rice and rye breads[9]. Belgium approves irradiation for a list of products similar to that in France. Denmark, Italy and Spain have approved irradiation only for

---

1. Article 8.
2. Article 8(1).
3. Article 8(2). The Commission would be authorised to enter into "arrangements" with other countries for mutual notification of irradiation plants and the creation of inspection rights. There is no express requirement that importations would be permitted only from irradiation facilities actually inspected by the Commission.
4. Article 8(4).
5. The relevant materials are summarised in *Lamy-Dehove* at 6-380 et seq.
6. These and other products were authorised for irradiation by orders issued at various dates between 1982 and 1986. *Lamy-Dehove* at 6-390. Strawberries were added in 1989. Journal Officiel, No. 5 6.1.89 p224.
7. *Lamy-Dehove* at 6-387.
8. At 6-395.
9. D. Robins, *The Preservation of Food by Irradiation* p45 (1991).

potatoes and a few other foodstuffs. The maximum permissible dosages are generally similar to those proposed by the Commission, although Denmark authorises 15 kilograys for herbs and spices. The United States permits irradiation of a small list of foodstuffs, with maximum dosages of as much as 30 kilograys.

The British rules are more recent. Irradiation was a major focus of debate during consideration of the Food Safety Act in 1990[1], and several efforts were made in Parliament to prohibit all food irradiation[2]. The efforts failed, and the 1990 Act is silent regarding the issue. Nonetheless, an advisory committee to the Ministry of Health and Social Services generally endorsed the findings of the Codex Alimentarius Commission, which had approved irradiation with some limits and for some purposes[3]. Similar approval was given by the House of Lords Select Committee on the European Communities[4]. Regulations have now been issued in Britain authorising some uses of irradiation[5].

The British regulations adopt the outlines of the Commission's amended proposal with respect to the licensing, inspection and control of food irradiation plants[6]. Irradiation plants must be licensed, and licenses may be granted only by joint action of Britain's food and health authorities[7]. If irradiation occurs outside Britain, the authorities must be satisfied that the foreign facility maintains standards similar to those demanded in Britain[8]. The list of foodstuffs for which irradiation is permitted is broadly similar to the Commission's proposed list, but there are significant additions. The British list includes fruit, vegetables, cereals, bulbs and tubers, spices and condiments, poultry, fish and shellfish[9]. This is more inclusive than the French and Commission lists, and also more extensive than the recommendations of the House of Lords Select Committee.

---

1.   Food Safety Act of 1990, Eliz. II c.16 (1990).
2.   For a review of the debate, see Scott, "Continuity and Change in British Food Law", 53 Mod. L. Rev. 799-800 (1990).
3.   DHSS Advisory Committee on Irradiated and Novel Foods, Report on the Safety and Wholesomeness of Irradiated Foods (1986) at para. 2.2. See also Scott, "Continuity and Change in British Food Law", 53 Mod. L. Rev. 785, 799 n.95 (1990).
4.   House of Lords Select Committee on the Irradiation of Foodstuffs, Irradiation of Foodstuffs, Session 1989-1990, 4th Report (HL Report 13) (1989).
5.   Food (Control of Irradiation) Regulations, SI 1990/2490; Food Labelling (Amendment) (Irradiated Food) Regulations, SI 1990/2489.
6.   SI 1990/2490, at regs 3 and 9, and sch 1.
7.   Regulation 2 and Schedule 1.
8.   Regulation 6(a) (ii) and Schedule 2. The first license was issued in June 1991; *Financial Times* (13 June 1991).
9.   SI 1990/2490, at reg 2(2) (c).

The references to fruit and vegetables are not limited to dried or dehydrated products, the poultrymeat need not be deboned, the shellfish are not limited to "prepared" shrimp and prawns, and the reference to fish is new. The House of Lords Select Committee found that irradiation is particularly suited for herbs, spices, poultrymeat, shrimps and prawns. Maximum irradiation doses are prescribed for each of the products. These range from 0.2 to ten kilograys, and are generally similar to those proposed by the Commission[1]. Irradiation is subject to general conditions which again are similar to those urged by the Commission[2]. Re-radiation is forbidden, and irradiated foods must be segregated from other foodstuffs at the irradiation facilities[3]. Extensive records regarding the irradiation process must be maintained[4]. The British regulations also impose special labelling requirements[5]. Labels of foods prepackaged for sale to consumers or catering establishments must indicate that the products have been "irradiated" or "treated with ionising radiation"[6]. Ingredient lists of compound foods must indicate if the ingredients have been irradiated. Foods which are not prepackaged, as well as those sold for immediate consumption in a catering establishment, need not indicate if they have been irradiated[7].

These developments will not close the controversy regarding irradiated foods. The approval of irradiation in France and six other Member States did not reduce the concerns in Bonn or Strasbourg, and its approval in London does not appear to have diminished concerns about its safety in Britain. Indeed, civil service canteens and prisons have reportedly declined to use irradiated foods[8]. At the Community level, the disagreements among Member States and within the European Parliament seem continuing and fundamental[9]. Long efforts are likely to be required before any compromise can be found.

---

1.   SI 1990/2490, at reg 2(2) (e).
2.   Schedule 1, para 3(2).
3.   Schedule 1, paras 8, 9.
4.   Regulation 3 and Schedule 1.
5.   This is consistent with the views both of the DHSS Advisory Committee and of the House of Lords Select Committee.
6.   SI 1990/2489, at regs 4, 10.
7.   Regulation 7.
8.   The civil servant responsible for canteens reportedly declared that "we will not knowingly use irradiated foods", but attributed the judgment to the fears of his customers rather than any concerns among the authorities themselves; *The Times*, p2 (11 March 1991).
9.   As noted above, Germany reportedly opposes all irradiation. The European Parliament includes many who are sceptical of irradiation, but it would evidently approve the irradiation at least of herbs and spices. Fuster, "The Implementation of the EC Commission's White Paper of 1985", 1 World Food Reg. Rev. 10, 11 (1991).

4.4 Novel food ingredients and processes

There have been more changes in foodstuffs over the past several decades than collectively occurred during the previous several centuries[1]. Many food ingredients are now made artificially from chemical sources, or have been given new properties through biotechnology or processing innovations[2]. Some "novel" foods offer important advantages over traditional foodstuffs in nutritional content, caloric levels, or other characteristics. They have, however, provoked substantial public concerns. Some consumers fear that they mark a decline in food quality, and others question their safety. In response, some regulators suggest that special regulatory controls should be adopted, at least for products involving biotechnology. In Britain, a special advisory committee provides expert scientific guidance regarding novel foods and processes[3]. In contrast, other regulators have argued that genetically engineered products may generally be regulated in the same fashion as conventional products[4]. In the United States, FDA has declined to seek new legislative authority to regulate ingredients and processes involving biotechnology[5]. Its existing authority is thought adequate for any special regulatory measures which may prove necessary[6]. This option is not available in the Community, where there is no residual regulatory framework upon which the Commission could rely. Without specific Community legislation, novel food ingredients and processes would be left for regulation by non-harmonised national laws. Given the public's apprehensions about synthetic and biotechnological products[7], as well as the

1. Hermus, "The consequences of 100 years' evolution of dietary habits in Europe with regard to nutrition", in H. Deelstra, et al., eds., *Food Policy Trends in Europe* p67 (1991).
2. One commentator has suggested that traditional classifications will become "obsolete" as foods become more "functionally designed and tailor-made" as a result of novel technologies; ibid. at p73.
3. The Advisory Committee on Novel Foods and Processes was established by the Department of Health in 1988, but a predecessor committee had performed a similar role since 1984. See Guidelines on the Assessment of Novel Foods and Processes 1-3 (1991); Annual Report of the Advisory Committee on Novel Foods and Processes (1991).
4. Vettorazzi, "Safety Aspects of Genetically Engineered Food Products", in F. Paine, ed., *Modern Processing, Packaging and Distribution Systems for Food* pp215-216 (1987); WHO, Strategies for Assessing the Safety of Foods Produced by Biotechnology (1991); Report of the Nineteenth Session of the Codex Alimentarius Commission 15 (1991); Eurofood 4 (March 1992). Novel foods have been the subject of consultations between FAO and WHO, and some international consensus may result from those efforts. Gray, "Whither Food Regulation?", 1 World Food Reg. Rev. 33, 35 (1991).
5. *International Herald Tribune* p3 (27 May 1992). See also McCowin, "Genetically Engineered Foods and Ingredients - Legal Considerations", in C. Felix, ed., *Food Protection Technology* pp331, 334-335 (1987); Frank, "Food Additive Models for the Regulation of Recombinant DNA Technology Under the Federal Food, Drug, and Cosmetic Act," 45 Food D.C.L.J. 169, 171 (1990); Rulis, "The Food and Drug Administration's Food Additive Petition Review Process," 45 Food D.C.L.J. 533, 541 (1990).
6. FDA has recently reaffirmed the view that special controls are not needed. 57 Fed. Reg. 22984 (May 29, 1992); Kessler, et al., "The Safety of Foods Developed by Biotechnology", 256 Science 1747 (26 June 1992); Gershon, "Genetically engineered foods get green light", p357 Nature p352 (4 June 1992). Labelling is still demanded by some commentators. See, e.g., Washington Post p. B11 (5 June 1992). See also Maryanski, "Special Challenges of Novel Foods (Biotechnology)", 45 Food D.C.L.J. 545 (1990).
7. A committee of the European Parliament has, for example, declared that the "dangers and risks" of biotechnology demand "a ban on the use of... high risk technologies and a consistent decision not to use them". Report of the Committee on Agriculture, Fisheries and Rural Development, Document A3-0311/90 (Nov 1990) at 38. For a review of the new technologies, see Bescancon, "Techologies

principle of free circulation, the Commission is compelled to seek a Community framework for the regulation of such products[1].

In 1989, the Commission drafted a regulation to harmonise national rules regarding "novel" ingredients and processes[2]. The Commission's draft has since been revised, and a formal proposal has been made[3]. The draft is largely designed to regulate foods which contain genetically modified ingredients, or which are themselves made through biotechnological processes[4]. The actual scope of the proposal is, however, considerably broader. The Commission initially intended to propose a directive, but more recent drafts have changed the proposal's form to that of a regulation. As a result, the measure would have direct effect without need for implementing national legislation. In the Commission's view, the "smooth running" of the internal market demands that novel products should be controlled at the Community level, which requires a regulation[5]. Perhaps the Commission fears that the transposition of a directive might be unnacceptably slow, or that there might be undue national variations. An important implication of the Commission's choice of a regulation is that the Community's approvals of new products would be immediately effective throughout the Member States.

A "novel" food is one not previously used to a "significant" degree for human consumption, or produced by processes that result in significant changes in its composition, nutritional value, or intended uses[6]. This includes all new or modified products, and not merely those involving biotechnology or new synthetic ingredients. As originally drafted, the proposal contained a more detailed list of relevant changes. These included changes in a product's digestibility, stability, or hygienic quality. It also included a product's content of substances derived from new strains of food organisms. Each would have provided a separate and sufficient basis for finding a process to be "novel". Any modified process which, for example, altered a product's

---

alimentaires et qualitiés nutritionnelles de l'aliment", in Académie d'Agriculture de France, ed., *Deux Siécles de Progrés pour L'Agriculture et L'Alimentation*, pp1789-1989 331, 337 (1990).

1. The use of biotechnology has been described as "essential" for the European food industry. Gautier, "The Food Industry in France and in the European Community", in G. Gaull & R. Roddberg, eds., *New Technologies and the Future of Food and Nutrition* p129 (1991). Moreover, it is no longer a small-scale activity. As early as 1986, there were 150 companies in the United States alone. P. Hutt & R. Merrill, *Food and Drug Law, Cases and Materials* p330 (2nd ed. 1991).
2. Draft proposal III/3562/89-EN-Rev. 4.3 (1989). There are subsequent revisions.
3. COM(92) 295 final, OJ C190 29.7.92 p3.
4. See, e.g., Article 6. For a description of biotechnology and the various approaches encompassed by the term, see, e.g. USITC, *The Effects of Greater Economic Integration within the European Community on the United States*, Second Report, 4-49 (1990). For a glossary and other background, see ACNFP, Guidelines on the Assessment of Novel Foods and Processes (1991) at 4-5, 22-24.
5. The third recital of the preamble.
6. Article 1. A similar definition is provided by section 18(1) of Britain's 1990 Food Safety Act.

digestibility or other properties would have been "novel", whether or not it involved biotechnology[1]. Although the proposed list of relevant changes has been shortened, it is likely that the Commission would still expect any substantial change in a foodstuff or process to bring it within the proposed regulation. The Commission's proposal excludes food additives, irradiated foods, flavourings and extraction solvents insofar as they are encompassed by other directives[2].

Those who wish to market a food containing a novel ingredient or a foodstuff produced by a novel process would be required to comply with pre-marketing requirements, including the preparation of a safety and nutritional assessment. Under the original proposal, they would have been required to establish a product "dossier[3]." The latter was not defined, but would presumably have consisted of relevant compositional and safety data. The dossiers would have been available for national inspection[4]. Later versions do not refer to dossiers, but it is unlikely that any substantial change is intended. The draft invited preliminary consultations with the Scientific Committee whenever it would be involved in the reviewing process.

Two alternative mechanisms would be created to evaluate new products. Under earlier versions of the proposal, a series of guidelines and questions would have directed manufacturers to the proper mechanism[5]. In essence, the questions would identified products which do not involve biotechnology and for which the technology has already been reviewed in published scientific writings. If a product or process involved scientific work published through a peer-review process, and did not involve live organisms or new biotechnological techniques, it would have been subject to a simplified review procedure. The guidelines and questions have now been eliminated, but the underlying principles remain unaltered. All products and processes would now be subject to the simplified procedure except those involving the consumption of viable organisms or whose safety is not established by "generally accepted scientific data"[6].

---

1. The ACNFP's definition is equally sweeping, but excludes "minor process modifications" and other changes which do not produce "significant" toxicological or nutritional alterations in food. Guidelines on the Assessment of Novel Foods and Processes (1991) at 4. It concedes that comprehensive guidance cannot be given as to what foods and processes should be deemed "novel"; ibidd., at p5. There appears to be no de minimis exception in the Commission's proposal, although its proposed series of guidance questions would have the effect of excluding some minor changes.
2. The ACNPP also excludes such substances from its definition of novel foods and processes; ibid., at p4.
3. The original Article 4(1).
4. The original Article 4(2).
5. Annex I.
6. Article 4.

Under the simplified approval process, products and processes would be presented for review by independent scientific experts[1]. Lists of experts would be designated by the Member States, and a producer would select from the lists[2]. Under the original proposal, the expert would have been asked whether the product was "equivalent" to currently consumed foods. If it was, a summary dossier would have been sent to the Commission, and the product would have been approved for marketing[3]. In later drafts, the expert would apply criteria set forth in an annex to the regulation. The criteria require a proposed product to be safe at its intended level of use, not misleading to consumers, and not nutritionally disadvantageous as compared to any foodstuffs the product would replace. If the expert found that a product satisfied these criteria, a notification would be sent to the Commission. Member States and the Commission would be permitted a period for objections. If none were made, the product would be approved for marketing throughout the Community. Most novel foods and processing methods would be reviewed in this way.

A different mechanism would apply to products not receiving an approval under the first mechanism, or not the subject of generally accepted scientific data, or involving the consumption of live organisms. In these situations, approval would be obtained through the Commission and Standing Committee, after consultations where appropriate with the Scientific Committee for Food[4]. Producers would be required to submit special applications for marketing approval based upon safety and nutritional evaluations. Under earlier drafts, applicants could request confidentiality for their submissions. This was eliminated from the final proposal, but detailed rules for implementation of the proposal would be separately adopted[5]. The Commission will solicit the views of the Member States regarding applications, and the Scientific Committee would conduct an assessment of the proposed product if questions of public health were involved[6]. If it deemed them appropriate, the Scientific Committee could require additional studies or data. In an earlier draft, decisions regarding approval

---

1.   Article 5.
2.   The proposal does not expressly indicate who would make the selection or if there would be restrictions on the choice, beyond the fact that it would be made from a list approved by national authorities. Presumably the manufacturer would decide among those qualified in a relevant specialty.
3.   The proposal originally stated that only a summary dossier would be needed if a new product were "equivalent or better" to similar foods in nutritional value, digestibility, hygienic quality, stability, "or" its content of undesirable substances. The disjunctive suggested that equivalence would have been required only with respect to the particular property which rendered the food "novel".
4.   Articles 5 (2), 6, 8.
5.   Article 5 (4), 6(6), 10. Confidentiality requests could have been based upon competitive considerations, including trade secrets.
6.   Article 6, 8.

would have been required within six months of the application[1]. Later versions contain no timetable. The Commission would issue a decision based upon the Scientific Committee's evaluation, in which it could establish a trade name and labelling requirements for the new product[2].

If an application involved genetically modified organisms which were the subject of an authorisation under Community law, this fact would be included in the application[3]. In such cases the safety evaluation would have to include an environmental risk assessment[4]. Any decision likely to have an effect on human health could be adopted by the Commission only after consultations with the Scientific Committee[5]. Member States could suspend or restrict temporarily the marketing of foods which, although in compliance with the proposed regulation, were believed by them to endanger human health[6]. "Detailed" grounds for such a belief would be required[7]. National actions would be reviewed by the Standing Committee for Foodstuffs, which could either override them or alter the Community's rules to conform to the new evidence[8].

The draft regulation is by no means certain of adoption, and there may be substantial modifications before it is accepted. The proposal may face substantial opposition in the European Parliament, which has proven to be suspicious of biotechnology and uneasy about food safety[9]. Parliament may well demand either special labelling rules or additional preconditions to approval. One possible requirement might be a threshold inquiry into the technical need for new products. The Community already demands proof of technical need for proposed new food additives before it will consider their safety[10]. It would be surprising if less rigourous constraints were imposed upon novel products and processes. Since FDA has proposed to treat biotechnological foods without special constraints, any additional requirements could increase the differences between U.S. and Community food policies.

1.   Although the original proposal did not expressly authorize it, one possible decision presumably might have been to defer approval pending further evaluations.

2.   Article 6(3). There is, however, evidently no general plan to require the labelling of all products containing genetically modified organisms. Written Question 2929/91, OJ C141 3.6.92 p33.

3.   Article 7(1). For the Community's rules regarding the release of genetically modified organisms into the atmosphere, see Council Directive (EEC) 90/220, OJ L117 8.5.90 p15.

4.   Article 7(2).

5.   Article 8. Since the likelihood of such an effect is a question only the Scientific Committee can answer, the result would presumably be to require most issues to be referred to the Committee.

6.   Article 9(1).

7.   No further indication is offered as to the nature of the evidence, but presumably it would have to exceed mere suspicion, and certainly could not be a generalised concern about biotechnology.

8.   Article 9(2).

9.   Perhaps in response to such concerns, which are not confined to the Parliament, the Commission has created a new Biotechnology Coordination Committee to review biotechnological issues, including those in the foodstuffs sector. Eurofood at 4 (April 1991).

10.   For the rules regarding proposed new additives, see below at Chapter 5, para 5.1.

The Commission is evidently anxious not to impose elaborate requirements upon products which represent only modest changes in existing technology[1]. The Commission's device for this purpose would, however, itself represent a novel departure from the Community's previous methods. As described above, it would employ a screening mechanism involving independent experts selected from lists compiled by the Member States. Since the expert's approval would be tantamount to marketing authorisation throughout the Community, firms are likely to search carefully for undemanding sources of review. In these circumstances, it is questionable whether the experts' judgments would be credible to the European Parliament and public.

The difficulty is the absence of an alternative. Since the Commission has declined to propose a Community food agency, there are insufficient Community resources to screen all of the products and processes which would be defined as "novel". The Commission might have suggested the use of national authorities, but its proposal asserts that regulation at the Community level is necessary for the "smooth running" of the internal market[2]. Unable to perform the work itself and having foreclosed assistance from the Member States, the Commission is left with the appraisals of experts whose judgments may be suspect. A better solution might be a new expert committee, subordinate to the Scientific Committee, which could perform the screening functions. In important or disputed cases, its views could be reviewed by the Scientific Committee. Such an arrangement might be less expeditious than the Commission's proposal, but it could also provide a more credible and consistent review process.

A useful comparison is the report of Britain's Advisory Committee on Novel Foods and Processes[3]. Although it adopted a broad definition of novel foods and processes, the ACNFP recognised that many minor changes in food processing are safe and desirable[4]. It acknowledged that some forms of novelty warrant greater scrutiny than others, and suggested a "decision-tree" requiring different levels of research and information regarding different products and processes[5]. These would range merely from nutritional studies through to an extensive battery of research programmes. The Commission's

---

1.　　The growing restrictions are already said to inhibit research and development. Brill, "Plant Genetic Engineering and the Food Industry", in G. Gaull & R. Goldberg, eds., *New Technologies and the Future of Food and Nutrition* pp45, 48 (1991). In the Commission's view, relatively few products would require detailed review by the Scientific Committee.
2.　　The third recital of the preamble.
3.　　For an example of a product reviewed by the ACNFP and Food Advisory Committee, see Food Advisory Committee Annual Report 1991 p3 (1992).
4.　　Report on the Assessment of Novel Foods and Processes (1991) at p4.
5.　　At pp8-9. In December 1991, the ACNFP supplemented its report with draft guidelines on the conduct of taste trials for novel foods or foods produced by novel processes.

draft proposal also previously included a similar decision-tree, but its version was simpler and offered fewer levels of requirements. The ACNFP system is complex, but offers the important virtue of imposing requirements tailored to each level of risk and each degree of novelty. It would, however, require substantial Community or national resources to administer the various levels of requirements. For the moment, the Commission has foreclosed any possibility of providing those resources.

4.5   Foods for particular nutritional uses

Foods for particular nutritional uses (known sometimes as "parnuts" foods) encompass a great variety of specialised foodstuffs. Some are particularly designed for infants and young children. Others are intended for those whose physical conditions demand special diets, or dietary supplements[1]. Diabetics and persons with gastro-intestinal maladies are among those who require specially formulated foodstuffs. Still other products are intended for consumers who engage in strenuous exercise, or who are interested in weight reduction or control. These diverse products present distinctive regulatory problems. Their labels and advertisements commonly include health-related claims or claims regarding their levels of nutrients or other substances. Their purity, as well as their effectiveness for their intended purposes, may require special protective measures.

An example is offered by low calorie diet foods sold for the control of overweight and obesity. Overweight is increasingly common in Britain and other Community states[2]. Many consumers seek methods of weight control, and low calorie diet products are now marketed directly to the public[3]. There is little evidence regarding the long-term consequences of diets consisting principally of such products, but the products may certainly be abused and, if abused, may result in ill-effects[4]. In the United States, FDA requires such products to carry warning labels emphasising that they should be used only temporarily and only under proper supervision[5]. In Britain, an expert advisory committee has urged the adoption of compositional standards and marketing controls[6]. The Community has not yet addressed the issues. Like other "parnuts" foods, these

---

1.   The Commission has taken the view that dietary supplements should not be regulated as "parnuts" products, but should instead be subject to their own regulatory regime as "dietary integrators." Above at Chapter 3, para 3.4.
2.   Committee on Medical Aspects of Food Policy, Working Group on Very Low Calorie Diets, *The Use of Very Low Calorie Diets in Obesity* p1 (1987). For the risks of obesity, see, e.g., R. Karanek & R. Marks-Kaufman, *Nutrition and Behavior* pp241-265 (1991).
3.   *The Use of Very Low Calorie Diets in Obesity* (1987) at p7.
4.   Ibid., at p19.
5.   Ibid., at p6. For the US rules, see 21 C.F.R. part 105 (1991).
6.   Ibid., at pp24-29.

products may invite compositional requirements, labelling obligations, and even marketing restrictions. Like the others, they occupy a twilight area between medicines and ordinary foodstuffs[1].

The issues created by "parnuts" foods have not been susceptible to prompt or uncomplicated solutions. Indeed, the Community has made two efforts merely to find a framework of principles within which they may be considered. The Council first adopted a directive regarding such foods in 1976[2]. The 1976 directive defined "parnuts" foods as those which, because of special composition or processing, are clearly distinguishable from products intended for normal consumption[3]. They must also be, and be marketed as, useful for the particular nutritional needs of special populations, including infants and young children[4]. The 1976 directive imposed labelling requirements, and promised that purity criteria, sampling procedures, and methods of analysis would later be provided[5]. It did not address the separate issues presented by individual categories of "parnuts" foods. The directive was frequently amended and became the subject of growing dissatisfaction[6]. Clarity alone eventually required a new measure[7]. Nonetheless, it was not until 1989 that the Council finally replaced the 1976 directive with a new framework directive for "parnuts" products[8].

Like its 1976 predecessor, the 1989 directive does not provide detailed requirements for specific product categories. Instead, it creates general standards applicable to the entire sector of "parnuts" foodstuffs. They are eventually to be supplemented by ancillary measures applicable to the most important categories of such products[9]. Many of the general standards closely parallel those imposed by the 1976 directive[10]. "Parnuts" products are again defined as foods with a special composition or derived

---

1.   As noted above, the Community's regulations have not yet sought to define "foods". Greater efforts have been made to define medicines. P. Bogaert, *EC Pharmaceutical Law* (1992). Similar efforts have been made in the United States. Above at Chapter 2, para 2.5.
2.   Council Directive (EEC) 77/94, OJ L26 31.1.77 p55.
3.   Article 1(2).
4.   For additional nutritional requirements, see Article 1(2) (b).
5.   Article 8.
6.   See Council Directive (EEC) 89/398, OJ L186 30.6.89 p27, at the first and second recital of the preamble.
7.   The 1976 directive was repeatedly amended, including as recently as 1985, see Council Directive (EEC) 85/7, OJ L2 3.1.85 p22, and the Council evidently recognised the confusion this created. Article 14 of the 1989 directive repealed the 1976 directive.
8.   Council Directive (EEC) 89/398, above.
9.   Among others, the list includes infant and follow-on formula, low-energy and energy-reduced foods, dietary foods, and gluten-free foods. Article 4 and Annex I. The Commission has begun the preparation of an ancillary directive regarding foods with modified sodium content. It would, for example, determine when foods could claim to be either "low" or "very low" in sodium. EC Food Law 3 (May 1992).
10.   Council Directive (EEC) 89/398, above at Articles 1, 2.

from a special manufacturing process which makes them both "clearly distinguishable" from other foodstuffs and suitable for their claimed purposes[1]. They must be marketed in a fashion designed to indicate that suitability[2].

A particular nutritional use is one which fulfils the special requirements of one or more designated populations. Those populations include infants or young children, persons with disturbed digestive processes or metabolisms, or persons with a special physiological condition who may benefit from the controlled consumption of certain substances[3]. Only products intended for those populations may be characterised by labelling or advertising as "dietetic" or "dietary"[4]. Labels and advertisements for products intended for general consumption are forbidden to use such terms[5]. The directive contemplates, however, that future rules may eventually permit ordinary foodstuffs to indicate their suitability for particular nutritional uses[6]. As a general matter, the labelling and presentation of foods intended for particular nutritional uses may not claim any properties for the prevention, treatment or cure of human disease[7]. Some exceptions may eventually be permitted by future rules. The prohibition does not preclude the dissemination to physicians, nutritionists or pharmacists of "useful" information about the products and recommendations regarding their usage[8]. No indication is offered as to who would judge the information's "usefulness" or by what standards. The information must be intended exclusively for such professional groups.

The 1978 labelling directive, as amended, is generally applicable to "parnuts" foodstuffs[9]. Additional labelling rules are also provided by the 1989 directive. Labels must state the particular "parnuts" designation under which the product is sold, accompanied by a description of its nutritional characteristics[10]. If the product is one for which an ancillary directive is to be adopted, but this has not yet occurred, the label must disclose the compositional elements or manufacturing processes which give the product its special characteristics. The label must also state the product's available energy value[11]. If a product is sold for use by infants in good health, it must

---

1.   Article 1(2).
2.   Presumably this does not require an advertising campaign, but would be satisfied by a labelling or presentational statement claiming suitability for a particular nutritional purpose.
3.   These provisions are repeated from Article 1(2) (b) of the 1976 directive. There is no indication as to the respects in which physiological conditions must be "special", or how "special" they must be.
4.   Article 2(1).
5.   Article 2(2) (a).
6.   Articles 2(2) (a), 2(3). A committee procedure will decide when this will be permissible. The Standing Committee for Foodstuffs will be used for the procedure; Article 13.
7.   Article 6(1).
8.   Article 6(2).
9.   Article 7.
10.   Article 7(2).
11.   Article 7(3).

display a reference to this purpose[1]. "Parnuts" foods may be sold at retail only in a prepackaged form, and the packaging must completely cover the product[2]. Derogations from the prepackaging rule may, however, be permitted by national laws for "purposes of the retail trade". In such cases, the product must still be accompanied by the requisite disclosures[3]. It is not clear how this would occur, or what standards would be applied to judge the adequacy of the disclosures. Presumably leaflets or posted notices might be used.

An important departure from the 1978 directive is a new system of national labelling reviews[4]. Except for products for which ancillary directives will be issued, labelling must be submitted to national authorities when a product is first placed on the market in each Member State[5]. National authorities may require the manufacturer or importer to provide proof of compliance with the directive, including the features of its composition or manufacture which give the product its particular characteristics[6]. This includes substantiation of any nutritional claims made for the product[7]. Nonetheless, Member States may not prohibit trade in a product unless they have "detailed grounds" to believe that it does not satisfy the directive's requirements, or that its consumption may endanger public health[8]. In such cases, the Member State may temporarily suspend trade in the product[9]. If the Commission agrees with the assessment, it will initiate appropriate Community measures. If it does not, it may override or modify the suspension[10].

The directive includes a committee procedure for the adoption of subsidiary rules. The procedure is similar to that included in the 1978 labelling directive as amended[11]. The Commission will use the procedure to promulgate detailed rules regarding the

---

1.   Article 7(2).
2.   Article 8. Prepackaging requirements are not common, but they have, for example, also been applied to organic foods. Above at Chapter 3, para 3.7.
3.   Article 8(2). The "purposes" of the retail trade are not defined, but presumably the goal is to leave undisturbed any practice of selling such products in unpackaged form.
4.   Article 9.
5.   Article 9(1). The provision calls for notification and not pre-marketing clearance. There is no express provision for foods already on the market when the directive was adopted.
6.   Article 9(3). References to readily available publications may suffice.
7.   The provision does not refer to advertising claims, although this may arguably be unnecessary given the general scope of the substantiation requirement.
8.   Article 11. The provision does not apply to the products listed in Annex I to the directive. Among others, they include infant and follow-on formulae, baby foods, low-energy and low-sodium foods, and special dietary foods. In those cases, the rules are reserved until ancillary directives are adopted. This has thus far occurred only with respect to infant and follow-on formulae.
9.   Article 11(1).
10.   Articles 11(2), (3). A committee procedure involving the Standing Committee for Foodstuffs is to be used.
11.   Articles 12, 13.

composition, labelling, presentation and advertising of specific "parnuts" products[1]. The subjects are to include baby foods; low-energy and energy-reduced foods intended for weight control; dietary foods for special medical purposes; low-sodium foods; gluten-free foods[2]; foods intended as a response to the expenditure of intense muscular effort; and foods for diabetics[3]. Infant and follow-on formulae were also included, but are already the subject of an ancillary directive. The procedure will not, however, create rules regarding the use of additives in these products. Rules regarding additives must be submitted to the Council and European Parliament for approval in the usual way[4].

4.6   Infant and follow-on formulae

Few issues have provoked such prolonged debate as infant and follow-on formulae. They are generally made from cows' milk or soya protein, and are used throughout the world as a substitute for breast feeding[5]. They were for some years accepted by many mothers as a welcome alternative, and were often used when breast feeding would have been feasible. There is now substantial evidence that breast feeding is superior and that mothers should breast-feed whenever possible. In essence, mother's milk provides a balanced diet at the correct temperature and in the right quantity. It transmits the mother's protective antibodies to the baby, while avoiding hazards of contamination which may accompany the reconstitution of infant formulae. Finally, breast feeding is emotionally preferable for both mother and child. On the other hand, dioxins have been found in human milk at levels which exceed the recommended intake for babies[6]. In Britain, however, an expert advisory committee has concluded that the benefits of breast feeding outweigh any risks from dioxins[7].

Breast feeding is not always possible, and infant and follow-on formulae provide essential alternatives when it is not. The regulatory question is how best to permit the

1.   Article 4 and Annex I.
2.   Gluten-free foods are formulated without wheat or rye protein especially for persons with coeliac disease. A. Bender, *Dictionary of Nutrition and Food Technology* p126 (6th ed. 1990). For the functions and content of such diets, see, e.g., C.R. Pennington, *Therapeutic Nutrition* pp257-258 (1988).
3.   Annex I.
4.   Article 4(1) (g). For a general description of the processes for adoption of a Council directive, see, e.g., T. Hartley, The Foundations of European Community Law pp30-36, and especially pp32-35 (2nd ed. 1988).
5.   For the uses and disadvantages of infant formulae, see, e.g., B. Fox & A. Cameron, *Food Science, Nutrition and Health* p316 (5th ed. 1989); R. Gaman & K. Sherrington, *The Science of Food* pp144-145 (3rd ed. 1990); D. Kilgour, *Mastering Nutrition* p231 (1986).
6.   Department of the Environment, Dioxins in the Environment, Pollution Paper No. 27 (1989). The Community has not adopted dioxin rules, although it suggested limits on their emission in 1989. Written Question 2533/91, OJ C55 2.3.92 p56.
7.   Committee on Toxicity of Chemicals in Food, Consumer Products and the Environment, Steering Group on Chemical Aspects of Food Surveillance, *Dioxins in Food*, Appendix I (1992).

marketing of infant formulae without misleading mothers about their disadvantages or unduly encouraging their use. The issues have been made more controversial by the marketing programmes of some manufacturers. The United States began addressing these problems in 1980, when Congress adopted the Infant Formula Act[1]. The Act followed a series of product recalls which raised substantial issues about the products' composition and labelling[2]. The Act gives FDA considerable discretion to control the manufacture, composition and labelling of infant milks. FDA has since adopted implementing regulations, but its rules have provoked litigation and dissatisfaction among consumer groups[3].

Matters have proved no simpler in the Community. In Britain, the Food Advisory Committee recommended legislation as early as 1981[4]. The Commission first proposed Community legislation regarding infant formulae in 1984[5]. The Commission's proposal would have imposed compositional and labelling requirements, as well as some restrictions upon advertising claims. It would not, however, have imposed substantial limitations upon other marketing practices[6]. The 1984 proposal was thought insufficiently stringent, and was ultimately revised in 1986[7]. The 1986 amendment was more rigourous than its predecessor, and would have given greater prominence to the International Code of Marketing of Breast-Milk Substitutes, adopted by the World Health Congress in 1981[8]. It would also have required more emphasis upon the benefits of breast feeding[9]. This was supplemented by a Council resolution adopted in 1986, which announced that the Community would control "so far as it is able" the marketing of breast-milk substitutes in developing countries[10]. As the resolution suggests, much of the debate regarding infant formulae has involved marketing practices in developing countries. The modified proposal failed, and no other Commission proposals to regulate infant formulae were offered for nearly five years. After the adoption of the framework "parnuts" directive, the Commission announced that its first ancillary

1.   P.L. No. 96-359, 90 Stat. 1190, codified at 20 U.S.C. sec. 350a (1991).
2.   P. Hutt & R. Merrill, *Food and Drug Law, Cases and Materials* p177 (2nd ed. 1991).
3.   The regulations are set forth at 21 C.F.R. parts 106, 107 (1991). They were challenged unsuccessfully in *FORMULA v. Schweiker*, 593 F. Supp 346 (D.D.C. 1984). For a discussion of the issues, see Levin, "The Infant Formula Act of 1980: A Case Study of Congressional Delegation to the Food and Drug Administration", 47 Food D.C.L.J. 101 (1987).
4.   Food Advisory Committee, Report on Infant Formulae (1981) at para 45. French rules derive from a 1976 order, supplemented in 1988. Journal Officiel No 135 p7848 (June 10, 1988).
5.   COM(84) 703 final, OJ C28 30.1.85 p3.
6.   Article 9. The proposal would have applied to exports outside the Community, unless the law of the importing country otherwise provided.
7.   COM(86) 364 final, OJ C285 12.11.86 p5.
8.   WHO, International Code of Marketing of Breast-Milk Substitutes (1981). A description of the Code and the events which provoked it is provided by A. Chetley, *The Politics of Baby Foods* (1986).
9.   COM(86) 364 final, at Article 1.
10. Council resolution on the marketing practices for breast-milk substitutes in developing countries by Community-based manufacturers, OJ C285 12.11.86 p19.

measure would relate to infant and follow-on formulae[1]. It promised stringent controls, and indeed said that the new restrictions would be even more rigourous than those imposed upon tobacco products.

In May 1991, the Commission adopted a directive regarding the control of infant and follow-on formulae[2]. Consistent with the Commission's earlier announcement, the directive imposes substantial restrictions upon the composition and marketing of the products. There are, however, several issues, some of them difficult or controversial, for which the Community postponed the adoption of rules. First, compositional requirements for formulae made from protein sources other than cows' milk or soya are deferred until they prove necessary[3]. Similarly, microbiological standards and maximum contaminant levels were judged to present complex problems and deferred to a "later stage[4]." Finally, the Commission delayed any rules regarding exports to third countries[5].

A major goal of the 1991 directive is to encourage Member States to adhere to the International Code of Marketing of Breast-Milk Substitutes[6]. The Code represents a major effort by WHO and UNICEF to promote breast feeding[7]. It generally forbids the advertising or promotion of breast-milk substitutes, including sampling, point-of-sale advertisements, and discounts[8]. It discourages hospital demonstrations of breast-milk substitutes unless they are "necessary"[9]. Labelling must give warnings of the advantages of breast feeding and may not "idealise" infant formulae[10]. Here again, most of the concerns centred upon marketing practices in the poorest countries, where a risk of contamination from polluted water is often added to the other disadvantages of infant formulae.

Under the 1991 directive, infant formulae are defined as foodstuffs especially intended for infants during their first four to six months of life, and which are expected to satisfy

---

1. *Financial Times* p7 (14 Feb 1991). See also the Commission's Background Report, European Community Food Legislation (6 Feb 1991). The next proposal for an ancillary directive is likely to involve energy-reduced foods; ibid. As described above, however, a proposal regarding modified-sodium products is in preparation. *EC Food Law* p3 (May 1992).
2. Commission Directive (EEC) 91/321, OJ L175 4.7.91 p35.
3. The second recital of the preamble.
4. The fourth recital of the preamble.
5. The thirteenth recital of the preamble.
6. Article 1.
7. UNICEF reported in 1984 that contaminated and misused infant formulae had contributed to many infant deaths throughout the world. UNICEF, The State of the World's Children 1985 (1984); A. Chetley, *The Politics of Baby Foods* (1986).
8. WHO, International Code of Marketing of Breast-Milk Substitutes (1981), at Article 5.
9. Article 6.5.
10. Article 9.

the infants' entire nutritional requirements during that period[1]. Follow-on formulae are products intended for infants over four months, and which are to be progressively supplemented by other foodstuffs[2]. Compositional criteria are provided for both products[3]. They include minimum and maximum levels of protein, lipids[4], carbohydrates, vitamins, and minerals. Sesame and cotton seed oils, as well as certain fats, are prohibited[5]. The products may be made only from designated ingredients, or from other ingredients whose suitability is established by "generally accepted scientific data"[6]. Additives are to be the subject of a separate Council directive[7]. Microbiological and purity standards are reserved for later consideration, but in general the products may not contain any substance in a quantity which may endanger the health of infants[8]. Only products which conform to these requirements may be marketed as infant and follow-on formulae, and no product other than infant formulae may be marketed for the nutritional needs of healthy infants during the first six months of life[9]. Rigourous labelling requirements are imposed[10]. The labels of both products are required to bear a series of mandatory disclosures, and are also subject to various prohibitions. For infant formulae, labels must state that the product is suitable for infants when they are not breast-fed, with a statement as to the superiority of breast feeding. There must also be a statement that infant formulae should be used only upon the recommendation of an independent person qualified in medicine, nutrition or pharmacy, or of a professional engaged in maternal and child care[11]. These statements must be preceded by words similar to "important notice"[12]. If iron has not been added, there must be a statement that the total iron requirements of infants over four months

---

1. Commission Directive 91/321, above at Article 1(2) (c).
2. Article 1(2) (d). This is one difference with Codex and the WHO International Code, which define follow-on formulae in terms of the sixth month onwards. The World Health Assembly voted in 1986 that follow-on milks are generally unnecessary.
3. Article 4 and Annexes I, II.
4. Lipids is a general term including such organic compounds as fats, oils and waxes. A. Bender, *Dictionary of Nutrition and Food Technology* p166 (6th ed. 1990). For a discussion of their roles in food and nutrition, see B. Fox & A. Cameron, *Food Science, Nutrition and Health* pp42-69 (5th ed. 1989).
5. Annex I, para 3.1; Annex II, para 3.1. The prohibited fats are those containing more than 8 percent trans-isomers of fatty acids. In the United States, FDA has not adopted similar prohibitions and evidently questions their necessity. USITC, The Effects of Greater Economic Integration within the European Community on the United States, First Report, 6-59 (1990).
6. Articles 3(1), 3(2).
7. Article 5 (2). A proposed positive list of permissible additives for use in infant and follow-on formulae is contained in an annex to the Commission's suggested new rules for preservatives and a miscellany of other additives. See Working Document III/9049/90, at Annex V (1990), and subsequent revisions. The annex also provides some proposed conditions of use. See also Food Advisory Committee, Report on the Review of the Use of Additives in Foods Specially Prepared for Infants and Young Children (1992).
8. Commission Directive (EEC) 91/321, above at Article 6(1).
9. Article 2.
10. Article 7. Names for the products in the Community's official languages are provided. In English, they are "infant formulae" and "follow-on" formulae unless they are made entirely from cows' milk protein. In such cases, the designated names are "infant milk" and "follow-on milk"; Article 7(1).
11. Articles 7(2) (a), 7(4).
12. Article 7(4).

must be met from other sources[1]. Labels must state the available energy value and the product's content of proteins, lipids and carbohydrates[2]. Labels must also give the average quantity of each mineral and vitamin[3]. Where applicable, the levels of choline, inositol and carnitine must be disclosed[4]. There must be instructions for preparation and a warning against contamination and other preparatory hazards[5].

The labelling, presentation and advertising of infant formulae may not discourage breast-feeding[6]. Such terms as "humanised" and "maternalised" are forbidden. Pictures of infants or other pictures or text which idealise the product are forbidden[7]. Graphic representations may be used to illustrate proper methods of preparation. The products may claim certain special compositions, such as "iron enriched" or "low sodium", only if they satisfy designated compositional requirements[8]. Infant formulae may be advertised only in baby care and scientific publications, and the advertisements may include only factual information[9]. No effort may be made to stimulate a belief that infant formulae are equivalent to breast-feeding. These rules may be made more stringent by the Member States, which may elect even to prohibit all advertising. No point-of-sale advertisements, samples, or promotional gifts may be used at the retail level or through hospitals or health workers[10]. The practice of some manufacturers of providing low-cost or free samples to nurses, physicians and hospitals is prohibited.

The rules for follow-on formulae are nearly as severe. Their labels must bear a statement that they are suitable only for infants aged over four months[11]. They must state that the products should form only part of a diversified diet and that they are not a substitute for breast milk during the first four months of life. Labels must disclose the available energy value and the content of proteins, lipids and carbohydrates[12]. They must also state the average quantities of vitamins and minerals, as well as any quantities of choline, inositol or carnitine[13]. There must be instructions for preparation

---

1.   Article 7(2) (b).
2.   Article 7(2) (d).
3.   Article 7(2) (e).
4.   Choline and inositol are both classed as vitamins, but only choline is thought to be an essential dietary factor. Carnitine is found in animal tissues, and is evidently involved in fat metabolism. A. Bender, *Dictionary of Nutrition and Food Technology* pp53, 64, 144 (6th ed. 1990). For carnitine, see also B. Fox & A. Cameron, *Food Science, Nutrition and Health* p160 (5th ed. 1989).
5.   Article 7(2) (f).
6.   Article 7(3).
7.   Article 7(5).
8.   Article 7(6) and Annex IV.
9.   Article 8(1).
10.   Article 8(2).
11.   Article 7(2) (c).
12.   Article 7(2) (d).
13.   Article 7(2) (e).

and a warning against preparatory hazards. The labels, presentation and advertisements of follow-on formulae may not discourage breast-feeding[1].

The directive also imposes new informational obligations upon the Member States[2]. They must ensure that "objective" information regarding infant and child feeding is provided to mothers and those engaged in the field of child nutrition[3]. The informational materials must reflect the benefits of breast-feeding, the disadvantages of partial bottle-feeding, and the difficulty of changing from bottle-feeding to breast-feeding[4]. Any materials prepared by manufacturers or distributors of infant or follow-on formulae may be distributed only upon request, and only with the approval of national authorities. The materials may not refer to a proprietary brand, but may bear a company's name or logo[5]. Any free or low-priced supplies of infant formulae may be used only for infants who must be fed by bottle, and only as long as bottle-feeding is required[6].

As the Commission promised, the 1991 directive imposes restrictions upon the marketing of infant and follow-on formulae unequalled among food products. The only parallels among lawful products relate to tobacco and pharmaceutical drugs. In addition, the directive prescribes the terms of informational and educational programmes which must be conducted by the Member States. Here again, there are few situations in which the Commission has instructed the Member States, not merely to distribute informational materials, but also what those materials must contain. These unusual measures reflect the intense controversy which surrounds the marketing of infant formulae, particularly in the world's poorest nations. The principal remaining step, which the Commission deferred until a separate directive, was to determine what restrictions should be placed upon the export of infant and follow-on formulae to third countries[7]. The Council has since adopted rules for export products, which do little more than compel compliance either with the 1991 directive or with "applicable world standards" established by the Codex Alimentarius Commission[8]. There is also a proposed Council resolution which would reiterate the Community's willingness to help enforce international standards[9].

---

1. Article 7(2) (f).
2. The propriety of informational requirements as part of an internal market measure has been questioned by, e.g., Lange, et al., "New Developments", 4/91 Eur. Food L. Rev. 403, 406 (1991).
3. Article 9(1).
4. Article 9(2).
5. Article 9(3).
6. Article 9(4).
7. The thirteenth recital of the preamble.
8. Council Directive (EEC) 92/52, OJ L179 1.7.92 p129.
9. COM(91) 441 final, OJ C124 16.5.92 p15. For revisions, see OJ C155 20.6.92 p19.

CHAPTER 5 : THE REGULATION OF FOOD ADDITIVES

Few issues of food regulation provoke such public and legislative anxiety as the control of additives. The term "additives" is itself one source of confusion[1]. It is sometimes used broadly to include contaminants and other substances added unintentionally to foodstuffs. This encompasses, for example, migrations of the constituents of food packagings. Using this approach, additives in the United States are termed either "indirect" or "direct"[2]. In Europe, it is more common to describe the former as contaminants, and to restrict "additives" to substances used intentionally to perform a technical function in the processing or preservation of foodstuffs[3]. This includes substances employed to alter texture, colour or other organoleptic properties. A more important source of controversy is the number and volume of additives. The concern over additives has naturally grown as their uses have increased[4]. By one estimate, there are 3,850 additives in use in Britain, which together add four kilogrammes to each Briton's average annual food intake[5].

Another source of concern are the additives which, after receiving regulatory approval, have subsequently been banned from some of the world's marketplaces. For example, the sweetener cyclamate was approved by most regulatory authorities and entered into widespread use throughout the world. After those approvals, it was withdrawn from the market for safety reasons in the United States and Britain. It reportedly may now be approved once more in both countries[6]. It continues to be used in many other nations. Each of the successive changes may have been prudent in light of the scientific evidence then available, but the

---

1. For various definitions which have been used, see Saint Blanquat & Pascal, "Les additifs", in R. Derache, ed., *Toxocologie et Sécurité des Aliments* pp247-249 (1986).
2. See 21 USC. sec. 201(s); 21 C.F.R. sec. 170.3 (e) (1991). See also Rulis, "De Minimis and the Threshold of Regulation", in C. Felix, ed., *Food Protection Technology* pp29-36 (1987).
3. This is the Codex definition; *General Principles* sec. 2(3), *Codex Alimentarius*, vol. 1 (2nd ed. 1991). The European Court has taken a different view of additives in animal feedingstuffs. *Denkavit Futtermittel GmbH v Land Nordrheinwestfalen* [1987] 3 CMLR 585. Swiss law also refers to "indirect" additives. Ordinance of May 26, 1936, as amended, at Article 2(1)(a). It also refers to contaminants and excessive residues as "substances étrangères". Article 7a(2)(a). For substances not regarded as additives, see Article 9a(2).
4. J. Burnett, *Plenty and Want* p321 (3rd ed. 1989).
5. Ibid., citing E. Millstone, *Food Additives* p40 (1986). More than 3000 of the total are flavourings. Q. Seddon, *Spoiled for Choice* p84 (1990). A government estimate is that there are more than 3000 flavourings and more than 300 other additives, including 20 colorants. MAFF, *About Food Additives* (1991). By a third estimate, the number is approaching 4000. R. Taylor, *Food Additives* p11 (1980).
6. Below at para 5.3; O'Brien, et al., "Intense Sweeteners", in S. Marie & J. Piggott, eds., *Handbook of Sweeteners* pp104, 109-110 (1991). For FDA's recent views and steps regarding cyclamate, see P. Hutt & R. Merrill, *Food and Drug Law, Cases and Materials* p328 (2nd ed. 1991). Some colorants offer similar examples of regulatory inconsistency. See, e.g., E. Millstone, *Food Additives* pp121-124 (1986).

impression to many consumers and legislators is one of indecision or even incompetence. This impression is strengthened by the bewildering array of national controls for additives. Many consumers cannot understand why scientific and safety questions have provoked so many regulatory inconsistencies[1].

These and other factors have given additives a "poor reputation" among legislators and consumers[2]. Many believe that additives are inadequately regulated. Others are concerned that their risks have not been fully revealed to the public[3]. They point to the allergic reactions suffered by some consumers, and express fears that additives may present long-term hazards to public health[4]. Indeed, their concerns reportedly may reach "almost to hysteria"[5]. It seems to matter little that many food additives have been in common use for lengthy periods, and that most regulators estimate the health risks from food contamination to be many times greater than any risks from additives[6]. Nor does it appear to matter that additives have broadened the choice of foodstuffs, prolonged their durability, and reduced their costs[7]. Much of the world's food supply is, for example, already lost through microbial spoilage. Without preservatives, those losses would be greatly increased[8]. These benefits cannot excuse any genuine risks to human health, but they should temper our appraisal of additives.

Concerns about additives greatly complicate the food regulatory process everywhere, but the most severe difficulties are presented in the United States. The regulatory issues there are in part controlled by the Delaney Clause[9]. The

1. More than 100,000 conditions of use for additives are said to have been adopted by Member States. Gray, "EEC Food Law", address to the Annual Conference of the European Association of Lawyers (June 1991), at page 9. For the Italian rules, for example, see G. Andreis, et al., eds., *Codice di Diretto Alimentare Annotato* (1990), vol. 1, pp 293-327.
2. B. Fox & A. Cameron, *Food Science, Nutrition and Health* p385 (5th ed. 1989).
3. The issues have, however, been debated at length. For an early example, *see* Hutt, "Public Policy Issues in Regulating Carcinogens in Food", 33 Food D.C.L.J. 541 (1978).
4. For the health issues, see., e.g., R. Kanarek & R. Marks-Kaufman, *Nutrition and Behaviour : New Perspectives* pp131-145 (1991). A committee of the European Parliament, for example, has expressed misgivings about all products which are not "ecological" and "natural". It demanded a return to "small-scale ecological farming" and the avoidance of "all possible food additives". Report of the Committee on Agriculture, Fisheries and Rural Development, No. A3-0311/90 (19 Nov 1990) at p38. Parliament itself has called for reductions in additives to the lowest practicable levels. No. A3-0060/92 (11 March 1992).
5. B. Fox & A. Cameron, *Food Science, Nutrition and Health* at p385 (5th ed. 1989).
6. See, e.g., Q. Seddon, *Spoiled for Choice* pp24-25 (1990); P. Hutt & R. Merrill, *Food and Drug Law, Cases and Materials* pp176-177 (2nd ed. 1991). See also Foster, "Perennial Issues in Food Safety", in D. Cliver, ed., *Foodborne Diseases* pp369-381 (1990); Elton, "Allocation of Priorities - Where Do the Real Risks Lie?", in G. Gibson & R. Walker, eds., *Food Technology - Real or Imaginary Problems?* pp3-4 (1985).
7. B. Fox & A. Cameron, *Food Science, Nutrition and Health* p385 (5th ed. 1989); MAFF, *About Food Additives* p1 (1991).
8. R. J. Taylor, *Food Additives* p19 (1980). Food preservation "has been and always is a necessity". Derache, "La conservation des aliments", in R. Derache, ed., *Toxocologie et Sécurité des Aliments* p403 (1986).
9. The Delaney Clause is codified at 21 USC. sec. 348(c)(3)(A) for food additives, 376(b)(5)(B) for colour additives, and 360b(d)(1)(H) for animal drugs. FDA must approve the use of additives unles they are "generally regarded as safe by qualified experts" ("GRAS") or were approved

clause is three interrelated statutory provisions which together forbid the use of substances which induce cancer in man or animals[1]. In most cases, health and safety questions about additives arise from programmes of animal testing. Animal testing has not, however, always proven reliable in predicting the risks of human cancer, and the Delaney Clause has therefore sometimes been an unduly rigid regulatory standard. The complications are increased by decisions of federal appeals courts demanding the clause's rigorous interpretation[2]. It is likely that the Delaney Clause was intended as a statement of regulatory policy, rather than a scientific standard, and indeed such a policy was adopted by FDA before the clause was enacted[3]. The principal difficulty created by the clause is not its content, but its embodiment in a statutory instruction[4].

Nothing directly comparable to the Delaney Clause exists in Community law. The Community has, however, adopted or proposed several measures which include broad declarations that no substance may be used in foodstuffs if it may threaten human safety[5]. These are intended as declarations of regulatory policy but, like the Delaney Clause, they are written as legislative prohibitions. The Community may eventually regret their adoption. Even so, it has retained greater flexibility than has been permitted to the FDA to approach additives on the basis of realistic appraisals of the available scientific evidence. In principle, the Community remains free to make risk assessments which in the United States might be foreclosed by the Delaney Clause[6]. It is far from clear, however, that the difference in principle has resulted in genuine differences in regulatory results.

---

for use prior to 1958. The latter are called "prior-sanctioned" substances. For a recent description of FDA's process, see Rulis, "The Food and Drug Administration's Food Additive Petition Review Process", 45 Food D.C.L.J. 533 (1990). The process includes "action" and "tolerance" levels for direct and indirect additives. For a judicial interpretation of FDA's obligations, see *Young v.Community Nutrition Institute*, 476 US 974 (1976).

1. For a review of the Delaney clause's implications, see Geyer, "Searching for a Workable Interpretation of the Delaney Clause", 43 Food D.C.L.J. 797 (1988). For a description of its background, see P. Hutt & R. Merrill, *Food and Drug Law, Cases and Materials* pp868-877 (2nd ed. 1991).

2. *Public Citizen v Young*, 831 F.2d 1108 (D.C.Cir. 1987); *Les v Reilly*, No. 91-70234 (9th Cir. 1992). See also Gelbert, "A Limit on the Food and Drug Administration's Discretion to Use Quantitative Risk Assessment for Permanently Listing Colour Additives - Public Citizen v Young", 45 Food D.C.L.J. 551 (1990). For FDA's efforts to apply a de minimis exception under the clause, see, e.g., 353 *Nature* 289 (26 Sept 1991).

3. Hutt, "Public Policy Issues in Regulating Carcinogens in Food," 33 Food D.C.L.J. 541 (1978). For another viewpoint, see Blank, "The Delaney Clause: Technical Naivete and Scientific Advocacy in the Formulation of Public Health Policies," 62 Calif. L. Rev. 1084 (1974).

4. The Delaney Clause is the subject of recurrent efforts for modification or repeal. For recent efforts, see 353 *Nature* 289 (26 Sept 1991).

5. Such declarations may be found, for example, in the rules regarding smoked foods, below at para 5.4, and the proposed rules regarding irradiated foods, above at Chapter 4, para 4.3.

6. A major objection to the Delaney Clause has been its substitution of an inflexible legislative standard for administrative discretion in dealing with subtle technical issues. See, e.g., Blank, "The Delaney Clause: Technical Naivete and Scientific Advocacy in the Formulation of Public Health Policies," 62 Calif. L. Rev. 1084 (1974).

The Community has encountered its own difficulties in regulating additives. Its problems have arisen in part from the number and variety of additives, in part from disagreements regarding the relevant scientific evidence, and in part from the magnitude of the harmonisation process itself. Some observers believe that another source of difficulty is the Community's method of harmonisation. It has elected a regulatory approach which is "both broader in scope and more restrictive than that in the United States"[1]. The Community has sought to prepare positive lists of the principal categories of additives using a definition that literally encompasses even baking soda and salt[2]. The Commission has permitted itself a narrow basis for the exclusion of traditional products but, unlike the United States, it has generally declined to approve additives on the basis of long use and widespread approval. It is, however, preparing proposed measures which are closer in result to the American rules[3]. On both sides of the Atlantic, the regulation of additives has for different reasons been a problem without final or satisfactory solutions.

The Community has sought to harmonise national rules for the regulation of additives since 1962, when a directive relating to colorants was adopted. Despite the adoption of other significant measures, the Community's overall progress before 1985 was slow and incomplete. Many national rules regarding the uses of additives either remained unaffected or were subject only to partial limitations. More progress has been made since 1985. After lengthy efforts, a new framework directive for additives was adopted late in 1988. A new flavourings directive quickly followed. A sweeteners directive is, however, now unlikely to be adopted before 1993. A new directive regarding colorants has been proposed. New measures regarding other categories of additives are in preparation, and they include a proposal to authorise many additives for any technical purpose on a *quantum satis* basis[4]. This would be a helpful simplification of national rules, and a welcome departure from the Commission's frequent rigidity. In the interim, many categories of additives are still regulated at the Community level only by early and unsatisfactory directives[5]. When new rules are adopted, it is unclear whether they will include satisfactory mechanisms for the approval of future products or the continuing revision of the positive lists. For the moment, it can only be said that the Community has at least created a framework within which the issues may be addressed systematically.

---

1. USITC, *The Effects of Greater Economic Integration within the European Community on the United States, Second Report* p4-51 (1990).
2. This is USITC's assessment of the breadth of the Community's definition of "additives," but it is difficult to reconcile with Article 1 of the framework additives directive, which does not define many traditional products as "additives"; below at para 5.1.
3. Below at para 5.1.
4. *Quantum satis* permits the use of as much of a substance as necessary to achieve a particular technical purpose, consistent with good manufacturing practices.
5. These include colouring materials, preservatives, emulsifiers, anti-oxidants, and a miscellany of other additives. There are of course numerous national rules. For a general description of the British regulations with respect to additives, see S. Fallows, *Food Legislative System of the UK* p21 (1988).

Food additive issues cannot be decided by the Community without reference to regulatory developments elsewhere. FDA had adopted extensive rules regarding additives, and its decisions remain one benchmark of regulatory judgment[1]. With the growing international trade in foodstuffs, some harmonisation of the rules of the major trading countries is becoming commercially more urgent[2]. The recommendations of international advisory groups, such as the Codex Alimentarius Commission, are often influential upon the Community's policy making. So too is the work of the Council of Europe[3]. The evaluations of the FAO/WHO Joint Expert Committee on Food Additives (JECFA) help to guide the work of the Community's Scientific Committee for Foods[4]. As a practical matter, the scientific and policy judgments which regulate the worldwide market for processed foods are principally made by the Community, FDA and the Codex Alimentarius Commission. Their decisions are sometimes stubbornly inconsistent, but their regulatory obligations grow increasingly inter-dependent.

5.1   The 1988 framework rules for additives

Food additives have been a frequent subject of Community legislation for thirty years. Among other early steps, the Council adopted directives regarding colourings in 1962[5], preservatives in 1963[6], antioxidants in 1970[7], and general food additives in 1974[8]. The Scientific Committee for Food adopted guidelines for safety assessments of additives in 1980, which the Commission urged the Member States to transpose into national legislation[9]. The Commission adopted methods of analysis for verifying compliance with purity criteria for additives in 1981[10]. Many of these rules were frequently revised or supplemented. Nonetheless, the measures were often undemanding, and resulted in little real harmonisation of national laws. Tens of thousands of national conditions of use for additives were left unharmonised[11].

---

1.   See, e.g., Rees, "Introduction," in J. Rees & J. Bettison, eds., *Processing and Packaging of Heat Preserved Foods* pp1, 13 (1991).
2.   American exports to the Community of processed foods alone were some $300 million in 1989. USITC, *The Effects of Greater Integretion within the European Community on the United States, Second Report*, pp4-25, 4-29 (1990). The Community is now an even larger exporter of food products than the United States; above at para 5.9.
3.   See, e.g., Snodin, "Sweeteners: Statutory Aspects," in S. Marie & J. Piggott, eds., *Handbook of Sweeteners* pp265, 283-286 (1991).
4.   See, e.g., Mestres, "L'analyse des résidus toxiques; son interet et son limites; exemple des résidus de pesticides", in R. Derache, ed., *Toxcologie et Sécurité des Aliments* pp105 (1986).
5.   Council Directive (EEC) 2645/62, OJ 11.11.62 p279.
6.   Council Directive (EEC) 64/54, OJ L161 27.1.64 p64
7.   Council Directive (EEC) 70/357, OJ L157 18.8.70 p31.
8.   Council Directive (EEC) 74/329, OJ L189 12.7.74 p1.
9.   Commission Recommendation (EEC) 80/1089, OJ L320 27.11.80 p36. The 1980 guidelines are found in the tenth series of the reports of the Scientific Committee for Food.
10.   First Commission Directive (EEC) 81/712, OJ L257 10.8.81 p1.
11.   See, e.g., Opinion of the Economic and Social Committee, OJ C328 22.12.86 p5. The ESC noted that apart from amendments no directives regarding additives had been issued during the previous twelve years, and that "no progress" had been made regarding conditions of use for additives; at para 1.1. It acknowledged, however, that the issues are "sensitive" and "difficult"; at paras 1.3, 1.4.

The Commission proposed a new general directive regarding additives in 1986[1]. The proposal was, however, extensively criticised by the Economic and Social Committee and the European Parliament[2]. The ESC noted that the Commission's previous efforts had produced little progress, and that virtually nothing had occurred for more than a decade. It argued that a more "flexible" approach was needed[3]. After a series of specific objections, the ESC concluded generally that the Commission's proposal offered few solutions to the deficiencies of the Community's legislation. Indeed, it feared that the proposal "could give rise to considerable difficulties"[4] .

In December 1988, the Council finally adopted a new directive for the harmonisation of national laws regarding additives for use in foodstuffs intended for human consumption[5]. The 1988 directive is in large measure a confirmation of the ESC's criticisms. In most areas, it did not attempt to resolve all the relevant questions, but simply acknowledged the need to harmonise national laws through a "comprehensive" future directive[6]. The Council conceded that comprehensive rules might have to be "drawn up in stages"[7]. The 1988 directive was merely one such stage, in which lists and categories of additives were compiled for future regulation[8]. Nonetheless, the 1988 directive also established general principles to guide the design of those future stages[9]. Those principles are its chief contribution to the Community's food policies.

The 1988 directive applies to a lengthy list of substances, provided that they are used as ingredients during the manufacture of foodstuffs, and provided further that they are still present, even if in an altered form, in the final product[10]. "Additives" are substances not normally consumed as a food and not ordinarily used as characteristic ingredients of food[11]. To distinguish them from contaminants and

---

1.   Proposal for a Council Directive, OJ C116 16.5.86 p2.
2.   See, e.g., Opinion of the Economic and Social Committee, OJ C328 22.12.86 p5.
3.   Ibid., at para 1.2. The ESC offered no indication of what alternative approach it preferred, or how increased flexibility should be balanced against harmonisation.
4.   At para 1.4. Among other steps, the Committee urged prompt publication of the opinions of the Scientific Committee for Food; at para 1.5.
5.   Council Directive (EEC) 89/107, OJ L40 11.2.89 p27. For the French transposition, see Journal Officiel No. 287 p16096 (Dec 9, 1991); Journal Officiel No. 151 pp8620 (July 1, 1992).
6.   Council Directive (EEC) 89/107, above at the third recital of the preamble.
7.   The use of stages is appropriate only "where necessary," although any possibility of avoiding their use now seems remote; Article 3(1).
8.   The fourth recital of the preamble.
9.   The fifth to tenth recitals of the preamble.
10.   Article 1(1). By comparison, the 1974 German foodstuffs law defines additives as substances added to foodstuffs to alter their characteristics, to create specific properties, or to produce specific effects. Processing aids are excepted. See *Die Gesetz Uber die Verkehr mit Lebensmitteln* [1974] I BLBI. 1945, at sections 2, 11(2). For other definitions, see Saint Blasquat & Pascal, "Les additifs", in R. Derache, ed., *Toxocologie et Sécurité des Aliments* pp248-249 (1986).
11.   The latter part of this definition would exclude such traditional products as salt and baking soda. The important word "characteristic" is left undefined, perhaps wisely, but may invite disputes regarding some traditional ingredients. Baking soda is "characteristic" of some foods,

processing aids, additives must be added intentionally to achieve a "technological" purpose, and must be expected to remain, directly or indirectly, in the final foodstuff[1]. The following categories of additives are specifically encompassed by the framework directive[2]:

Colours

Preservatives

Anti-oxidants

Emulsifiers

Emulsifying salts

Thickeners

Gelling agents

Stabilisers, including foam stabilisers

Flavour enhancers

Acids

Acidity regulators

Anti-caking agents

Modified starches

Sweeteners

Raising agents

Anti-foaming agents

Glazing agents, including lubricants

Flour treatment agents

Firming agents

Humectants

Sequestrants

Enzymes, where used as additives

Bulking agents

Propellant gases

Packaging gases

In total, the categories will encompass more than 500 substances, all of which will be reviewed by the Community before approval[3]. Nonetheless, several categories of substances fall outside the directive. In particular, the directive does not apply

---

although not others, but so too are many colourings and flavourings. The Community might sensibly have borrowed the US system of granting blanket approval to substances "generally regarded as safe". Alternatively, it might have compiled lists of all substances approved throughout the Community at some fixed date, and granted them approval. This again has been a shortcut in the United States. As described below, the Commission's proposed approval of many additives on a *quantum satis* basis approaches such a rule.

1. Article 1(2). For another definition, see A. Bender, *Dictionary of Nutrition and Food Technology* p5 (6th ed. 1990).

2. Article 1(1) and Annex I. Definitions of the principal additives are included in the Commission's draft of a "daughter" directive relating to miscellaneous additives. Working Document III/9049/90-Rev.1, revised by Working Document III/3624/91/EN.

3. Written Question 1600/91, OJ C55 2.3.99 p33. This represents an increase in the numbers individually approved by many Member States. For Codex definitions of the various functional classes, see sec. 5.1, Codex Alimentarius (2nd ed. 1991).

to substances used to protect plant products against blights or pests, flavourings encompassed by the separate flavourings directive[1], or substances added to foodstuffs as nutrients[2]. The Commission is also now considering whether to create exceptions for other substances. They include cooking salt, blood plasma, edible gelatin, novel food ingredients, fat substitutes, release agents, some enzymes, microbial cultures, and some starch products[3]. Each of the categories encompassed by the directive will ultimately be the subject of a positive list of permissible substances[4]. A substance not included in the positive list applicable to its "principal function" in a particular food will be forbidden for that use in that food[5]. In other words, a substance approved for one use cannot be used "principally" for another use, unless it is also included in the positive list applicable to that use[6]. Future directives will list foodstuffs in which the additives may be included, and may place quantitative or other limits on particular additives[7]. As a guide for those limitations, general criteria for the approval of additives are included in an annex to the directive.

Additives may be approved only if "a reasonable technological need" for their use has first been demonstrated. Such a need is one which cannot be satisfied by other means which are economically and technically practicable[8]. In addition, an additive may not present any hazard to health or safety at its proposed level of use. Moreover, additives may not be used to mislead consumers about the quality of raw materials or processing. To demonstrate a "reasonable technological need", a food additive must serve one of the following purposes:

(a)   to preserve the nutritional quality of the food;

1.   For the flavourings directive, see below at para 5.2.
2.   Council Directive (EEC) 89/107, above at Article 1(3).
3.   Working Document III/9049/90-Rev. 1. A more recent version revises the list.
4.   USITC has expressed concern that the Community's positive lists may exclude additives approved in the US but not in general use within the Community. It also expressed concern that the lists are not developed in an "open environment" where third-country producers have opportunities to be heard, and that there is no prompt procedure for obtaining approvals of new additives. USITC, *The Effects of Greater Economic Integration within the European Community on the United States* pp6-57 (1989).
5.   Council Directive (EEC) 89/107, above at Article 2(2). Additives may, however, be authorised for several functions by inclusion in more than one positive list. The Commission is now contemplating a blanket approval for all purposes of some basic additives on a *quantum satis* basis.
6.   This rule may stimulate arid disputes about what is, or is not, a substance's "principal function" in a food. Presumably the essence of the rule is that approval for one use does not imply approval for another use, and that substances employed for multiple purposes must be approved for each. As written, however, it is open to the interpretation that a substance approved for its "principal" use may also be used for subsidiary purposes, even if not approved for those purposes.
7.   Article 3.
8.   Annex II, para 1. This provision may hamper the approval of new additives, given the number and variety of those already approved. It has, however, been described in the European Parliament as a safety guarantee. Report of the Committee on the Environment, Public Health and Consumer Protection, A3-0080/91 at 17-18 (March 26, 1991). A similar practice has been followed in Britain. R. Taylor, *Food Additives* p17 (1980).

(b)   to provide necessary constituents for foods manufactured for consumers with special dietary needs;

(c)   to enhance the "keeping quality" or stability of a food, or to improve its organoleptic properties[1], so long as this does not change the nature, substance or quality of the food in a fashion which may deceive the consumer; or

(d)   to assist the manufacture, processing, preparation, treatment, packing, transport or storage of food, so long as the additive is not used to disguise faulty raw materials, undesirable or unhygienic practices, or other impermissible techniques during the food's processing, transport or storage[2].

The precise regulatory significance of these criteria is unclear. Insofar as a particular additive is authorised by a positive list, and is employed in accordance with any conditions of use established by that list, the criteria are presumably satisfied. If so, the criteria are guidelines for the approval of new substances or for the general revision of the positive lists, and not restrictions upon additives already included in the positive lists. In contrast, proposed additives developed after a positive list has been adopted (for example, a new preservative developed after the revised positive list for preservatives) may be approved only if existing products cannot, singly or in combination, perform the same functions. It is not clear whether proof of lower cost or greater efficiency would satisfy the criteria[3].

The framework directive also includes extensive labelling requirements. The packagings of additives not intended for sale to the ultimate consumer must provide a lengthy series of disclosures[4]. These include:

(a)   any name required by Community law for the substance and its EEC number; or, if there is no number, a description sufficient to prevent confusion;

(b)   for each additive sold in a mixture, its name and EEC number, listed in descending order of weight[5];

(c)   either the words "for use in food" or the words "restricted use in food", or some more specific reference to the additive's intended purpose;

1.   Organoleptic properties are those which affect a bodily sense, especially aroma and taste. A. Bender, <i>Dictionary of Nutrition and Food Technology</i> p205 (6th ed. 1990).
2.   Council Directive (EEC) 89/107, above at Annex II, para 2.
3.   Matters are clearer in Britain. The Food Advisory Committee declared before the directive that it would assess need in light of six criteria. They are whether the product would help maintain wholesomeness, permit a food to be presented in a more attractive manner, permit added convenience, extend dietary choice, meet a need for nutritional supplementation, or offer an economic advantage. See MAFF Food Facts Information Sheet, No.7, <i>Additives</i> (1986). For applications of Britain's rules, see <i>Food Advisory Committee Annual Report 1991</i> pp3-4 (1992). France has created a Commission de Technolgie Alimentaire to judge technical need. <i>Lamy-Dehove</i> at pp5-4; Journal Officiel (2 Aug 1989).
4.   Council Directive (EEC) 89/107, above at Articles 7(1), 7(2). That is to say, the provision is addressed to additives sold to processors or other intermediaries, and does not encompass substances covered by the 1978 labelling directive, as amended.
5.   For limitations, see Article 7(1)(a) at the second indent.

(d)   any special conditions of storage or use, if their absence would "preclude" the product's appropriate use[1];

(e)   any necessary directions for use;

(f)   an indication of the product's batch or lot;

(g)   the name or business name and address of the manufacturer or packager, or of a seller established in the Community;

(h)   the percentage of any component which is subject to any quantitative limitation, or adequate information to permit compliance by a purchaser with any quantitative limit;

(i)   the net quantity; and

(j)   anything further which may be demanded by a future comprehensive directive[2].

In addition, there are special rules for substances used to facilitate the storage, sale, standardisation, dilution or dissolution of additives.

There are no detailed rules regarding the presentation or format of the mandatory disclosures. The directive states simply that the required information must be provided conspicuously, legibly and indelibly[3]. The disclosures may appear in consignment documents, rather than labelling, if the the additive is intended for food manufacture. In such cases, the product's package or container must state conspicuously that the product is "intended for the manufacture of foodstuffs and not for retail sale"[4].

Additives intended for sale to consumers are also subject to labelling rules. They must bear the name under which they are sold, or a description sufficient to avoid confusion[5]. Their labels must also contain the information required in items (a) through (g) and (i) and (j) listed above[6]. In addition, there must be a "use by" or "best before" date similar to that required by the 1978 labelling directive, as amended. In other words, their labels must include all the items listed earlier except information regarding any applicable quantitative limitations. The latter are evidently deferred until the Community adopts rules regarding quantitative ingredient labelling[7]. Again, the directive provides simply that the required information must be stated conspicuously, legibly and indelibly[8].

---

1.   The word "preclude" is a substitute for the test of "impossibility" used in the 1978 labelling directive. Above at Chapter 3, para 3.3.1. The new test is presumably intended to result in more frequent labelling disclosures regarding special conditions of use or storage.

2.   Article 7(1).

3.   Article 7(1).

4.   Article 7(2).

5.   Article 8. The name must include the relevant EEC number, if one exists. Article 8(1). For the Commission's list of "temporary" EEC numbers, see above at Chapter 3, para 3.3.1.

6.   Articles 8(a), 8(d).

7.   Above at Chapter 3, para 3.3.1.

8.   Article 8.

The directive also includes provisions to facilitate a more comprehensive measure, or series of measures, addressing particular categories of additives. The proposed directives will provide positive lists of permissible additives, lists of foodstuffs in which they may be used, and any conditions for their use. The last may include, where appropriate, limits on the technical purposes of their use[1]. The directives will also provide rules for carrier substances and solvents, including purity criteria where necessary[2]. The directives are to be adopted by the Council under Article 100a of the Treaty, in co-operation with the Parliament[3].

Another series of directives would not necessarily require action by the Council[4]. Using a committee procedure involving the Standing Committee for Foodstuffs, other directives will provide purity criteria, methods of analysis to ensure compliance with the criteria, rules for sampling, and any other rules needed to ensure compliance with the criteria in Article 2 and Annex II of the framework directive. These measures may not be adopted unless the Commission first consults the Scientific Committee regarding any implications for human health[5].

The Commission has declared that it is considering additional labelling legislation regarding food additives and foodstuffs containing additives[6]. It has already proposed an amendment to the basic additives directive which would give broadened effect to a footnote originally offered in connection with the proposed sweeteners directive[7]. The proposed amendment would allow Member States to forbid the use of additives in "traditional" products produced within their own territories[8]. They could not forbid the production of non-traditional foodstuffs using additives in conformity with Community rules. Any issues regarding these arrangements would be considered by the Standing Committee for Foodstuffs. The Commission would be obliged to take "utmost account" of the views of the Standing Committee.

5.2   Flavourings

Flavourings are among the earliest and most traditional food additives. Pepper, for example, was one of the first subjects of international commerce in foodstuffs[9]. With

---

1.   Article 3(2). These may be provided in one comprehensive directive or in stages. Article 3(1). Based upon current proposals, stages are contemplated.
2.   Articles 3(2)(a), (b).
3.   Article 3(2)(c). In other words, a simplified committee procedure may not be used.
4.   Council action could, however, be sought if a qualified majority of the Standing Committee failed to adopt a Commission proposal. Article 11(3)(b).
5.   The sixth recital of the preamble and Article 6.
6.   Explanatory memorandum accompanying COM(92) 255 final, at 4 (17 June 1992).
7.   Below at para 5.3.
8.   COM(92) 255 final, at 6 (17 June 1992).
9.   See, e.g., Q. Seddon, *Spoiled for Choice* pp83-84 (1990).

the appearance of fabricated and processed foods, the sources of flavourings have become more diverse and their commercial significance has increased. New flavourings have been developed from both natural and artificial sources, and the production of flavourings has become a significant sector of the food industry[1]. Some artificial flavourings are identical to those in nature, and some natural flavourings are reinforced by artificial substances. As many as 3000 different flavourings are now available[2].

Because of their number and traditional use, there were no comprehensive regulations of flavourings until the 1960's, and many countries, including Britain, still have no rules specifically for them[3]. In 1960's FDA began what in essence is a positive list of flavourings. Many flavourings are sold in the United States on the basis that they are "generally regarded as safe" ("GRAS"), but FDA's approval process has resulted in the availability of fewer flavourings in the United States than in Europe[4]. In the 1970's, Germany and Italy developed dual systems of positive lists for artificial flavourings and negative lists for flavourings made from natural sources[5]. France also began distinguishing among natural, artificial, and reinforced flavourings[6]. The latter include natural substances to which artificial strengthening has been added[7]. It also became common to distinguish artificial substances which are identical to substances found in nature. In the same period, the Council of Europe began preparing lists of permissible flavourings[8].

The Commission first proposed a directive regarding flavourings in 1980[9]. The issues proved more complex than the Commission had first appreciated, and no directive was actually adopted until 1988[10]. In the course of considering the Commission's proposal, the European Parliament adopted a resolution acknowledging the growing trade in flavourings, and urging a system of mixed positive and negative lists according to the source of the flavouring[11]. The 1988

1. For the size and growth of the flavouring industry in the Community and elsewhere, see, e.g., Ashurst, "Introduction", in P. Ashurst, ed., *Food Flavourings* pp1-16 (1991); Elkes, "Europe 1992: Its Impact on Nontariff Trade Barriers and Trade Relations with the United States", 44 Food D.C.L.J. 563, 577-83 (1989).
2. P. Gaman & K. Sherrington, *The Science of Food* p250 (3rd ed. 1990); Q. Seddon, *Spoiled for Choice* p84 (1990); MAFF, *About Food Additives* p1 (1991).
3. MAFF Food Safety Directorate Information Bulletin No.20 (1991).
4. Ashurst, "Introduction", in P. Ashurst, ed., *Food Flavourings* p16 (1991).
5. Ibid., at p17.
6. France's distinction between artificial and natural additives ultimately is based upon the decree of 15 April 1912, but the key measure was adopted in 1973; *Lamy-Dehove* above at p5-401.
7. For reinforced flavourings, see Lettre Circulaire (20 Dec 1971); *Lamy-Dehove* above at p5-421.
8. Le Bourhis, "Les aromes", in R. Derache, ed., *Toxocologie et Sécurité des Aliments* pp467, 484 (1986). For the impact of the Council's lists in France, see Lettre Circulaire (20 Dec 1971).
9. OJ C144 13.7.80 p9. See also OJ C103 24.4.82 p7.
10. Council Directive (EEC) 88/388, OJ L184 15.7.88 p61.
11. Resolution of the European Parliament, OJ C66 15.3.82 p116, at paras 3, 4. For a similar view, see Le Bourhis, "Les aromes", in R. Derache, ed., *Toxocologie et Sécurité des Aliments* pp467, 486 (1986).

directive does not expressly reject a negative list for natural flavourings, but its goal is a positive list of all permissible flavourings and sources[1]. Nonetheless, the 1988 directive is not intended as a complete resolution of all the relevant issues; it is simply a framework measure designed as a "first step" toward harmonisation[2]. It includes purity criteria, labelling obligations, and other requirements which provide a basis for the eventual elimination of differences in national laws.

Simultaneously with the directive, the Council published a decision announcing a plan for an inventory of flavouring sources and substances used in the preparation of flavourings[3]. The inventory will provide the basis for the proposed positive list[4]. It is also expected to facilitate other regulatory measures concerning the production of flavourings and source materials[5]. The inventory was compiled after consultations with the Member States, but assistance was also obtained from the food industry[6]. The inventory is to be regularly updated by the Commission[7]. Although the inventory was to have been completed during 1990, it has not yet publicly appeared[8]. In essence, however, an inventory now exists, and the Commission has prepared a draft measure which would create a positive list. If the positive list is adopted, one commentator predicts that the impact upon the flavourings industry could be "profound"[9].

An important threshold problem is to decide what should be regulated as flavourings. The 1988 directive defines flavourings as substances and preparations intended for use in foodstuffs to "impart odour and/or taste". The directive is also applicable to source materials used for the production of flavourings[10]. It does not apply to edible substances intended to be consumed as such[11]. Nor does it apply to

---

1.   In contrast, Canada regulates flavourings on the basis of a negative list. Health Protection Branch, *Health Protection and Food Laws* p76 (4th ed. 1985).
2.   Council Directive (EEC) 88/388, above, at the fourth recital of the preamble.
3.   Council Decision (EEC) 88/389, OJ L184 15.7.88 p67.
4.   Elkes, "Europe 1992: Its Impact on Non-tariff Trade Barriers and Trade Relations with the United States", 44 Food D.C.L.J. 563, 581 (1989).
5.   Council Decision 88/389, above, at the second recital of the preamble.
6.   Article 1(1). See also Elkes, "Europe 1992: Its Impact on Nontariff Trade Barriers and Trade Relations with the United States", 44 Food D.C.L.J. 563, 581 (1989).
7.   Council Decision 88/389, above, at Article 1(2).
8.   Article 1(1). It was to have been issued within twenty-four months of June 1988; ibid. It apparently now exists, but will not be published. Consumer L. Bull. No. 66 p7 (March 1992). Both the inventory and the positive list raise questions of the confidentiality of industry research, and of protecting innovation in flavouring substances and production. The Commission has expressed a willingness to grant some measure of confidentiality. Elkes, "Europe 1992: Its Impact on Nontariff Trade Barriers and Trade Relations with the United States", 44 Food D.C.L.J. 563, 582 (1989).
9.   Ashurst, "Introduction", in P. Ashurst, ed., *Food Flavourings* p23 (1991).
10.   Council Directive (EEC) 88/389, above, at Article 1(1). "Flavourings" include flavouring substances and preparations, process flavourings, smoke flavourings, and mixtures of these. Article 1(2)(a). In general, a "flavouring substance" is a chemical substance with flavouring properties which is obtained by physical processes, chemical synthesis or isolated by chemical processes (whether or not identical chemically to a natural animal or vegetable substance). Article 1(2)(b).
11.   Article 2.

substances which have exclusively a sweet, sour or salt taste. Finally, the directive does not apply to materials of vegetable or animal origin with inherent flavouring properties, where they are not used as flavouring sources[1].

Flavourings may not contain any substance in a toxicologically dangerous quantity[2]. More specifically, they may not exceed designated limits for arsenic, lead, cadmium, and mercury[3]. Nor may they exceed limits for other substances listed in two annexes to the directive[4]. The annexes include such substances as benzopyrene, agaric acid, aloin and coumarin. Maximum limits and various exceptions are provided.

The directive also includes labelling requirements. Flavourings intended for sale to the ultimate consumer must comply with the 1978 labelling directive, as amended[5]. Others may not be marketed unless they bear the following information[6]:

(a)   The name or business name and address of the manufacturer or packer, or of a seller established in the Community;

(b)   either the word "flavouring" or some more specific name or description (for three years, Member States were permitted to maintain the use of any more specific local names)[7];

(c)   either the words "for foodstuffs" or a more specific reference to the foods for which the substance is intended;

(d)   if the product is a compound, a list in descending order of weight of the categories of flavouring substances and preparations included in the product, classified in terms set forth in the directive[8];

(e)   where flavourings have been mixed with other substances to dissolve or dilute them, a list in descending order of weight of those products; the list may use EEC numbers where they exist;

(f)   the maximum quantity of each component subject to any Community or national quantitative limit, or information sufficient to allow the purchaser to observe any such limit;

1.   The rule invites disputes as to the principal purpose for which a substance is used, when in fact a substance may be used both as, for example, a colorant and as a flavouring.
2.   Article 4(a).
3.   Articles 4(a)-(c). In each case, specific quantitative limits are provided. The European Parliament urged the adoption of even lower limits. Document A2-236/87, OJ C94 11.4.88 p68, at p70.
4.   Annexes I, II.
5.   For the rules regarding foodstuffs encompassed by the 1978 labelling directive, as amended, see Commission Directive (EEC) 91/71, OJ L42 15.2.91 p25.
6.   Article 9(1).
7.   Within three years from July 1988, decisions were to have been made about continuing to permit these local names. No such decisions have yet appeared.
8.   The list is in order of weight, but need not include the actual or nominal weight of each ingredient. For the more general issue of quantitative ingredient labelling, see above at Chapter 3, para 3.3.1.

(g)   an indication of the lot or consignment; and

(h)   the nominal quantity, expressed in units of mass or volume[1].

The information must be visible, legible and indelible. It may be provided in accompanying trade documents, rather than in labelling, if a product's packaging indicates that it is intended for food manufacture and not retail sale[2]. In such cases, the documents must be supplied with or prior to the product's delivery, and the words "intended for the manufacture of foodstuffs and not for retail" must appear on the container. The disclosures must be made in a language readily understandable by purchasers. Multiple languages are permitted.

Consistent with its rules regarding organic foods, the Community has imposed restrictions upon the use of such words as "natural" or "from nature" to describe flavourings[3]. They may not be used in a product's labelling or presentation, or in advertisements, unless specific standards are satisfied. All "natural" flavouring preparations must be derived from vegetable or animal origins. They must be obtained by use of physical, enzymatic or microbiological processes, or by "traditional food-preparation processes"[4]. No guidance is offered as to what processes will be deemed traditional[5].

The directive applies to flavourings and foodstuffs which contain flavourings either produced within or imported into the Community[6]. It does not apply to products exported from the Community[7]. Member States were required to permit flavourings which comply with the directive within two years of its adoption. After three years, they were also required to forbid flavourings which do not comply with the directive[8]. Until a positive list of flavourings is actually adopted, this essentially requires the Member States only to enforce the purity criteria and labelling requirements. The directive contemplates ancillary directives relating to special categories of flavourings (e.g., those derived from animal or vegetable sources not normally considered as foods) and any additional measures needed to protect public health or trade[9]. In the interim, any existing national rules are preserved[10].

---

1.   Article 9(1).
2.   Article 9(3).
3.   Such rules existed in France, for example, as early as 1971. Lettre Circulaire (20 Dec 1971).
4.   Council Directive (EEC) 88/389, above at Article 9(2).
5.   In an earlier proposal, "traditional" processes were defined to include at least drying, torefaction and fermentation. See Document A2-326/87, OJ C94 11.4.88 p68 at p70. Presumably the provision as adopted is no more narrow. For a similar Codex definition, see Codex Alimentarius, vol. 1, sec. 5.6 at 1.2 (2nd ed. 1991).
6.   Article 11(1).
7.   Article 11(2). For the general issue of exports, see below at Chapter 9, para 9.3.5.
8.   Article 13.
9.   Article 5.
10.   Article 12(2).

The directive includes procedures for both temporary national derogations and the adoption of supplementary requirements[1]. Member States may temporarily restrict trade in a substance if they have "detailed evidence" that it constitutes a danger to public health[2]. There is no indication as to what kinds or quantities of evidence must be offered, although the word "detailed" suggests a relatively high standard of proof. The Standing Committee for Foodstuffs and the Scientific Committee for Food are assigned roles in the review of national actions and the formulation of any supplemental Community rules[3]. A simplified committee procedure is used, similar to that in the 1978 labelling directive[4]. The procedure permits the Commission to adopt measures with the approval of a qualified majority of the Standing Committee for Foodstuffs. Absent that, proposals may be adopted by the Commission if the Council fails to reject them within a three-month period.

An example of the new rulemaking process was provided by a directive issued by the Commission in 1991 relating to the labelling of flavourings and source materials[5]. The directive was originally proposed to the Standing Committee, which failed to adopt an opinion. It was thereafter submitted to the Council, which did not act within the requisite three-month period[6]. In these circumstances, the Commission was entitled to issue the new rules as its own directive[7]. The Commission's directive added a new article to the 1988 flavourings directive, providing labelling requirements for flavourings intended for sale to the ultimate consumer[8]. They cannot be marketed unless their labels include either the word "flavouring" or some more specific name or description[9]. Their labelling must also include the words "for foodstuffs," or some more specific reference to the foods for which they are intended.

Several other disclosures are also required. With minor variations, they are essentially restatements of the 1978 labelling directive, as amended. They include a date of minimum durability; any special conditions of storage or use; instructions for use if their omission might permit an inappropriate use;[10] the net quantity; the

---

1.   Articles 7, 8, and 10.
2.   Article 8(1).
3.   Articles 7, 8, and 10. The Scientific Committee for Food is to be consulted before any measures are adopted which "may have effects on public health." This was one of the amendments proposed by the European Parliament. Document A2-326/87, OJ C94 11.4.88 p68 at p71.
4.   Article 10.
5.   Commission Directive (EEC) 91/71, OJ L42 15.2.91 p25.
6.   The third and fourth recitals of the preamble.
7.   The fourth recital of the preamble.
8.   As noted above, Article 9 of the 1988 directive related only to products not intended for sale to the ultimate consumer.
9.   Commission Directive (EEC) 91/71, above, at new Articles 9a(1)(a), (b).
10.   In earlier measures, the Community required such instructions where their absence would make appropriate use "impossible", or would "preclude" appropriate use. Above at Chapter 3, para 3.3.1. In effect, the Commission has now reversed the presumption. It is not clear whether this represents a general change of attitude, or simply a belief that flavourings are more likely to require instructions for use.

name and address of the manufacturer or packer, or of a seller established within the Community; and a batch or lot mark or indication[1]. If the product is a mixture of substances, a list must be included in descending order of weight of the flavourings and other substances contained in the mixture[2]. Terms such as "natural" may be used in a flavouring's labelling or presentation only if it has been solely, or "almost solely",[3] extracted by physical, enzymatic or microbiological processes, or by traditional food preparation processes[4]. This information must be provided in a language easily understood by purchasers, unless other measures have been taken to ensure that the purchasers are properly informed[5]. There is no indication as to the form or terms in which consumers may otherwise be informed, and the issue is evidently left to the discretion of Member States. The disclosures may be provided in multiple languages.

A related directive was issued simultaneously by the Commission to regulate the designations of flavourings in the lists of ingredients on the labels of foodstuffs[6]. The proposal had also been submitted to the Standing Committee, which failed to adopt an opinion, and thereafter to the Council, which failed to take any action[7]. The directive was therefore promulgated by the Commission itself[8]. It conforms the 1978 labelling directive to the provisions of the 1988 flavourings directive, including the latter's rules for the use of terms such as "natural"[9].

The Commission has subsequently prepared a working draft of a positive list of flavouring substances[10]. The draft regulation is based in part upon guidelines issued by the Scientific Committee for the evaluation of chemically-defined flavourings[11]. The proposed list is an amalgam based upon findings of the Council of Europe, FDA, and the Flavours and Extracts Manufacturers Association, as reviewed by the Scientific Committee. The list includes both approved flavourings

---

1. The date of minimum durability must conform to the 1978 labelling directive, as amended, and the batch marking must conform to Council Directive (EEC) 89/396, OJ L186 30.6.89 p21. Above at Chapter 3, para 3.6. The net quantity must be stated in units of mass or volume.
2. No quantitative declarations are required of a mixture's ingredients. It should be noted, however, that this represents a more stringent requirement than that imposed for mixtures by the 1978 labelling directive, which permits various exceptions. Above at Chapter 3, para 3.3.1.
3. The phrase "almost solely" is not given quantitative limits.
4. Article 9a(2). Traditional processes are not defined.
5. Article 9a(3).
6. Commission Directive (EEC) 91/72, OJ L42 15.2.91 p27. It is also discussed above in connection with the labelling directive. Above at Chapter 3, para 3.3.2.
7. The sixth and seventh recitals of the preamble.
8. The seventh recital of the preamble.
9. Article 1 amends the 1978 labelling directive to add a new Annex III which governs the designation of flavourings in the lists of ingredients for the labels of foodstuffs. The Annex conforms general foodstuff labelling to the 1988 framework flavourings directive.
10. The most recent version at the time of writing was Working Document III/3515/EN-Rev.5 (15 June 1992). Other flavouring materials would be the subject of subsequent legislation. In Britain, proposed new regulations for flavourings are also in draft form.
11. *Guidelines for the Evaluation of Flavourings for Use in Foodstuffs: 1. Chemically Defined Flavouring Substances*, adopted at the Committee's 81st plenary session (9-10 Dec 1991).

and those only provisionally approved. The latter would be finally approved or disapproved within five years. As a transitional matter, existing national authorisations would be retained for five years. Unlike most of the Community's positive lists, the proposed regulation would create a specific mechanism for the list's revision. A committee procedure involving the Standing Committee for Foodstuffs would be used.

5.3   Sweeteners

Sweeteners provoke both social and scientific controversy. Many consumers blame natural sugars for obesity and other health problems, and some commentators see evidence of "saccharophobia" in newspapers and magazines. Sugar is certainly the ingredient most often watched for by consumers on food labels, as well as the ingredient they seek most often to avoid[1]. Nonetheless, some commentators declare sugar to be man's most efficient food, providing more pleasure than "any other single substance"[2]. Perhaps as a result, the Community has had harmonised rules regarding various natural sugar products for more than a decade[3]. It has, however, not yet resolved the sensitive public and regulatory issues surrounding artificial sweeteners. The latter have assumed increasing commercial importance as consumer demand has grown for low-calorie, reduced-energy foodstuffs[4]. Confectionery, pastry, beverages and numerous other products now contain artificial sweeteners[5]. Some contain "bulk" sweeteners, which are chiefly hydrogenated sugar products[6], but many include "intense" artificial sweeteners, such as saccharin and aspartame[7]. As the name suggests, small quantities of "intense" sweeteners provide high levels of sweetness. Acesulfame K, for example, is 200 times sweeter than sucrose[8].

1.   Fischler, "Attitudes toward Sugar and Sweetness in Historical and Social Perspective", in J. Dobbing, ed., *Sweetness* pp83-98 (1987); Lecos, "Food labels and the sugar recognition factor", *FDA Consumer* p3 (April 1980); R. Kanarek & R. Marks-Kaufman, *Nutrition and Behaviour : New Perspectives* p169 (1991).

2.   Rozin, "Sweetness, Sensuality, Sin, Safety and Socialization: Some Speculations", in J. Dobbing, ed., *Sweetness.*, at pp99, 109 (1987).

3.   Below at Chapter 7, para 7.2.

4.   One commentator has observed a "marked change in eating habits" as patterns of living and working "have changed beyond recall". Farrer, "Nutritional Implications", in R. Gordon Booth, ed., *Snack Foods* pp327, 328, 343-344 (1990). See also Hermus, "The Consequences of 100 Years' Evolution of Dietary Habits in Europe with regard to Nutritiom", in H. Deelstra, et al., eds., *Food Policy Trends in Europe* p67 (1991).

5.   Worldwide sales of aspartame, for example, rose by more than 40 times from 1981 to 1987, and the sales of all intense sweeteners nearly doubled from 1974 to 1987. Lindley, "Sweetener Markets, Marketing and Product Development," in S. Marie & J. Piggott, eds., *Handbook of Sweeteners* p186, 190-191 (1991); Leroy, "Les Edulcorants", in R. Derache, ed., *Toxocologie et Sécurité des Aliments* pp447-465 (1986).

6.   For descriptions of sucrose, non-sucrose carbohydrate sweeteners, and sugar alcohols, see S. Marie & J. Piggott, eds., *Handbook of Sweeteners* at pp33-103 (1991).

7   O'Brien, et al., "Intense Sweeteners," in S. Marie & J. Piggott, eds., *Handbook of Sweeteners* pp104-115 (1991).

8   Lipinski, "Acesulfame K", in L. Nabors & R. Gelardi, eds., *Alternative Sweeteners* pp11, 15 (2nd ed. 1991). For a table of relative sweetness, see Nabors & Gelardi, "Alternative Sweeteners: An Overview"; ibid., at p3.

Intense sweeteners are generally artificial, and some have provoked widespread public debate regarding their long-term safety[1]. As a result of the controversy, the Commission began to formulate harmonised rules for artificial sweeteners as early as 1984[2]. It did not, however, succeed in formally proposing such rules until 1990[3]. No rules have yet been adopted, but the Community now appears to be moving toward their adoption. Late in 1991, the Council adopted a common position which was expected to provide the basis for a directive regarding sweeteners. Elements of the proposal encountered substantial opposition in the European Parliament, and it may now be 1993 before a directive can be adopted[4]. The directive has, however, since been reproposed by the Commission[5].

The Commission's initial proposal followed two reports regarding sweeteners issued by the Scientific Committee for Food. In the first, the committee found considerable inconsistencies among the rules of the Member States[6]. It observed that the consumption of natural sugars has risen substantially, and that diets might be significantly improved by sweeteners other than sugar[7]. It reviewed the available safety data and suggested guidelines for the use of artificial sweeteners. In its second report, the Scientific Committee re-examined the safety data and provided new ingestion limitations for many intense sweeteners[8]. No effort was made to identify the foodstuffs for which particular sweeteners should be authorised. The SCF sought instead to establish overall acceptable daily intakes of the sweeteners for which it had adequate safety data. In both reports, it recognised that public health would be improved by reductions in sugar consumption, but also encouraged limitations upon the uses of artificial sweeteners because of concerns about their long-term safety[9]. Its ambivalent endorsements of artificial sweeteners provided the bases for the Commission's proposed rules.

---

1.   For the role of artificial sweeteners and the controversy which surrounds them, see, e.g., Nabors & Galardi, "Alternative Sweeteners: An Overview", in L. Nabors & R. Gelardi, eds., *Alternative Sweeteners* pp1-10 (2nd ed. 1991); S. Marie & J. Piggott, *Handbook of Sweeteners*, (1991); B. Fox & A. Cameron, *Food Science, Nutrition and Health* p379 (5th ed. 1989). Four intense sweeteners are now approved for use in Britain: aspartame, acesulfame K, saccharin, and thaumatin; ibid. NHDC (a natural high-potency sweetener developed in the United States from fruit) is likely to be added. Cyclamate was prohibited in 1970. J. Burnett, *Plenty and Want* p321 (3rd ed. 1989).
2.   *Reports of the Scientific Committee for Food*, Sixteenth Series, EUR 10210 (1985).
3.   COM(90) 381 final, OJ C242 27.8.90 p4. For an amended version, see COM(91) 195 final.
4.   The controversy is described below. See also *EC Food Law* p2 (May 1992).
5.   COM(92) 255 final (17 June 1992).
6.   *Reports of the Scientific Committee for Food*, Sixteenth Series, EUR 10210 (1985).
7.   Ibid., at p2. The committee found that reductions in sugar consumption are appropriate on dietary and health grounds; ibid. This same conclusion has more recently been stated in Britain by a report issued by the Department of Health. *The Health of the Nation*, CM 1523 (1991) at pp68-69. In the Community, the conclusion has also been endorsed by the Economic and Social Committee. Some scientists are less confident. See, e.g., Drewnowski, "Sweetness and Obesity", in J. Dobbing, ed., *Sweetness* pp177-192 (1987); Rolls, "Sweetness and Satiety", ibid., at pp161-173.
8.   *Reports of the Scientific Committee on Food*, Twenty-first Series, EUR 11617 (1989).
9.   Some research suggests, however, that low calorie sweeteners are often accompanied by increases in subsequent food intake. R. Kanarek & R. Marks-Kaufman, *Nutrition and Behaviour : New Perspectives* p201 (1991).

The Commission's proposed directive would form one part of the comprehensive directive, or series of directives, contemplated by the 1988 framework additives directive[1]. It would encompass all substances used to impart a sweet taste to foods except foodstuffs with natural sweetening properties, such as sugar and honey[2]. Under the Council's common position, it would also include table-top sweeteners for use in coffee, tea or other foodstuffs. The proposal contains a draft positive list of all the sweeteners which would be permitted, with maximum permissible levels and lists of the foodstuffs for which each sweetener would be authorised[3]. The uses of some sweeteners would be closely limited, but sorbitol, mannitol, isomalt, maltitol, lactitol and xylitol would be authorised for use in a wide range of desserts, cereals, jams and confectionery on a *quantum satis* basis[4].

Several other sweeteners would be subject to maximum levels of use in particular foods. These include acesulfame K, aspartame, cyclamate, saccharin, thaumatin, and neohesperidine dihydrochalone (NHDC)[5]. The first four are artificial sweeteners; the last two are derived from naturally occurring substances[6]. All six would be subject to specific quantity and product limitations. Acesulfame K could, for example, be used in various listed products in maximum levels ranging from 200 mg/kg (in sweet-sour vegetable and fish preserves) to 2000 mg/kg (in sugar-free chewing gum). Similarly, aspartame could be used at a maximum level of 600 mg/l in sugar-free water-based flavoured drinks, 1000 mg/kg in breakfast cereals, and 2000 mg/kg in sugar-free confectionery. There would be many other such limitations.

---

1.   COM(90) 381 final, at Article 1(1).
2.   Articles 1(2), 1(3), 1(4). The most commonly used bulk sweeteners are sucrose, derived from sugar beets or sugar cane, other non-sucrose carbohydrates, and sugar alcohols such as sorbitol. See S. Marie & J. Piggott, eds., *Handbook of Sweeteners* pp33-103 (1991). For the Community's vertical directives regarding honey and certain sugars, see below at Chapter 7, paras 7.2, 7.3.
3.   Article 2 and the Annex. Some of the sweeteners in the proposed positive list are still not approved for use in, for example, the United States; USITC, *The Effects of Greater Economic Integration within the European Community on the United States, Third Report*, pp4-28 (1990).
4.   COM(90) 381 final, at the Annex. The principal foodstuff for which the listed sweeteners would not be authorised would be water-based flavored non-alcoholic drinks; ibid. Cola drinks are a major example. All of the listed products are sugar alcohols derived by hydrogenation from glucose or fructose. Billaux, et al., "Sugar Alchols", in S. Marie & J. Piggott, eds., *Handbook of Sweeteners* pp72-75 (1991). The principle of *quantum satis* means without fixed or definite limit, but appropriate for the need. The Economic and Social Committee has defined the principle to mean "the amount necessary to achieve the required effect by good manufacturing practice"; OJ C120 6 5.91 p9.
5.   Cyclamate, NHDC and lactitol were all opposed in the European Parliament. Report of the Committee on the Environment, Public Health and Consumer Protection, A3-0080/91 at 19 (March 26, 1991).
6.   A. Bender, *Dictionary of Nutrition and Food Technology* p2, 23, 82, 153, 193 and 250 (6th ed. 1990). The US currently approves the use of only three high-intensity sweeteners: saccharin, aspartame and acesulfame K. For aspartame, see 46 Fed. Reg. 3282 (24 July 1981); 46 Fed. Reg. 50947 (16 Oct 1981). For its uses, see 21 C.F.R. sec. 172.804 (1991). Cyclamate raises difficult issues because it is prohibited in the US and Britain, but JECFA, the joint FAO and WHO expert advisory committee, has endorsed its safety and Britain and the US may still change their positions. See Bopp & Price, "Cyclamate", in L. Nabours & R. Gelardi, eds., *Alternative Sweeteners* pp71-95 (2nd ed. 1991). But see Food Advisory Committee Annual Report 1991 p7 (1992).

Virtually all of the intense sweeteners have been subject of debate, but the controversy surrounding saccharin has been particularly bitter and prolonged. Much of the dispute has occurred in the United States, where the debate over the possible health consequences of saccharin's use has continued for more than a decade. Saccharin was developed in the United States in the nineteenth century, and has been commercially available for nearly a century[1]. It is now authorised for use by some 90 countries, but increasing questions about its long-term safety provoked substantial controversy beginning in the 1970's. It became the most widely tested of all food additives[2]. Questions about its hazards led to a proposed ban by FDA, repeated congressional hearings, studies by the Office of Technology Assessment and the National Academy of Sciences, and ultimately to a legislative moratorium on regulatory action[3]. In effect, Congress declined to permit FDA to prohibit saccharin's use. The dispute provides a long and acrimonious example of the misunderstandings which may arise from the intersection of science, regulatory policy and public opinion.

Cyclamate has provoked nearly as much controversy. It was developed in the United States in 1937 and became commercially popular in the 1960's, when it was often used in combination with saccharin[4]. In 1969, there were reports of bladder tumours in rats fed with high dosages of cyclamate and saccharin, and cyclamate was subsequently banned by FDA in 1970. Britain took similar steps to forbid it[5]. Extensive research and repeated applications have not yet reversed the prohibitions, although both FDA and Britain are reportedly again considering cyclamate's approval[6]. The Joint FAO/WHO Expert Committee on Food Additives has found cyclamate to be safe, and it is now widely used throughout the world.

---

1.   O'Brien, et al., "Intense Sweeteners," in S. Marie & J. Piggott, eds., *Handbook of Sweeteners* pp105-107 (1991). It is several times less expensive than sucrose and most alternative sweeteners. See Mitchell & Pearson, "Saccharin", in L. Nabors & R. Gelardi, eds., *Alternative Sweeteners* pp127, 133 (2nd ed. 1991).

2.   Clayson, et al., "Control of Food Additives and Contaminants: The Canadian and United States Position", in G. Gibson & R. Walker, eds., *Food Technology - Real or Imaginary Problems?* pp57, 60 (1985).

3.   The original (and frequently extended) moratorium legislation was the Saccharin Study and Labeling Act, P.L. No. 95-203, 91 Stat. 1451 (1977). One consequence was a label warning. For its effects, see Schucker, et al., "The Impact of the Saccharin Warning Label on Sales of Diet Soft Drinks in Supermarkets", p2 J. of Pub. Policy & Marketing 46 (1983). For disparate views about the general controversy, see, e.g., Hutt, "Individual Freedom and Government Control of Food Safety: Saccharin and Food Additives", 329 Annals N.Y. Acad. Sci. 221 (1979); Cooper, "Saccharin - Of Risk and Democracy", 40 Food D.C.L.J. 34 (1985); Schultz, "The Bitter Aftertaste of Saccharine", 40 Food D.C.L.J. 66 (1985); E. Millstone, *Food Additives* pp126-130 (1986).

4.   O'Brien, et al., "Intense Sweeteners," in S. Marie & J. Piggott, eds., *Handbook of Sweeteners,* pp109-110 (1991); Bopp & Price, "Cyclamate", in L. Nabors & R. Gelardi, eds., *Alternative Sweeteners* pp71-76 (2nd ed. 1991).

5.   The safety of cyclamate and other sweeteners was subsequently reconsidered in Britain by the Food Additives and Contaminants Committee. See *Report on the Review of Sweeteners in Food* (1982).

6.   In Britain, the Food Advisory Committee and COT supported a ministerial announcement in 1991 that the ban should not be lifted; *Food Advisory Committee Annual Report 1991* p7 (1992).

Events in the Community have been less dramatic. In the midst of the American controversy, the Scientific Committee for Food announced that it endorsed a "temporary" daily ingestion level for saccharin proposed by the Joint FAO/WHO Expert Committee on Food Additives[1]. The Scientific Committee suggested that purity criteria should be adopted, and recommended that saccharin should not be used in foods intended for young children. It also urged that children and pregnant women should be encouraged to limit their ingestion of saccharin[2]. These recommendations were endorsed by the Commission, which suggested that they should be embodied in national rules[3]. Neither the Council nor the Commission has, however, adopted measures compelling such steps. Because of the controversy which surrounds artificial sweeteners, the Community was instead content to leave their control to national discretion. As a result, the Member States have adopted diverse and often inconsistent rules. For example, Britain has banned cyclamate while other Member States permit its use, and only Belgium appears to have approved neohesperidin dihydrochalone (NHDC). Denmark forbids lactitol[4].

The Commission's 1990 proposal would greatly reduce the areas of national discretion. The only permissible sweeteners would be those listed in the proposal's annex, and they could be employed only under conditions of use prescribed by the annex[5]. Although the proposal does not address the issue, new sweeteners could apparently be authorised only through an amending directive, without provision for a committee process[6]. A complete repetition of the Community's legislative process would be required, including a proposal from the Commission, readings in the European Parliament, and reviews by the Council[7]. The absence of a simplified committee procedure is intended to reassure Parliament and the public that new sweeteners could not be authorised without public scrutiny[8].

---

1. Commission Recommendation (EEC) 78/358, OJ L103 15.4.78 p32.
2. At para 1.1
3. Some were eventually adopted in France and Spain. Journal Officiel No. 66 p3664 (18 March 1988); B.O.E. No. 16 p1791 (10 Oct 1986). For later but similar British recommendations, see Food Advisory Committee Annual Report 1991 p5 (1992).
4. Report of the Committee on the Environment, Public Health and Consumer Protection, A3-0080/91 at 19 (26 March 1991).
5. COM(90) 381 final, above at Article 2. In addition, sweeteners could not be included in foods intended for infants and young children "except where specially provided for." Article 2(3). The proposal does not indicate where special provisions would be made, but the language leaves open the possibility of either Community or national legislation.
6. The proposal contains no provisions for additions to the positive list, and the only references to a committee procedure would involve decisions about labelling and as to whether a sweetener may be used in a particular foodstuff.
7. The legislative process is briefly described in, e.g., T. Hartley, *The Foundations of European Community Law* pp30-36 (2nd ed. 1989); EC Commission, *A New Community Standards Policy* ppiv-v (1990).
8. The approval of new sweeteners is a major point of dispute in the European Parliament. See Report of the Committee on the Environment, Public Health and Consumer Protection, A3-0080/91 at 18-19 (26 March 1991).

Apart from the products approved for virtually all foodstuffs, sweeteners would be authorised for use only in designated foods. As originally drafted, the lists of foods for which sweeteners would have been approved contained significant omissions. There was, for example, no express provision for the use of table-top sweeteners, such as saccharin, although the Council is now prepared to authorise them[1]. Nor would all snack foods have been included, although there were provisions for bakery goods, desserts, confectioneries, and edible ices[2]. The limitations were contrary to the views of the Economic and Social Committee, which emphasised the advantages of reduced sugar consumption and urged wider approvals for artificial sweeteners to help achieve those reductions[3]. Some of the omissions were attributed to the absence of adequate supporting data[4]. Most have now been eliminated in the draft measure accepted by the Council.

The Council's draft would also impose various labelling obligations. Table-top sweeteners would be required to disclose the sweetening substance used in their manufacture[5]. Table-top sweeteners containing polyols would have a warning that "excessive consumption may induce laxative effects"[6]. Those containing aspartame would bear a warning that they contain "a source of phenylalanine". Similar but more extensive warning rules have existed in France since 1988[7]. Other Community labelling obligations could be added through a committee procedure involving the Standing Committee for Foodstuffs[8].

The Council's draft also included a footnote designed to accommodate concerns regarding beer in Germany and perhaps other states[9]. It would have permitted Member States to prohibit the use of sweeteners in alcohol-free beers or those with an alcohol content no greater than 1.2 percent of volume, provided they were brewed by "traditional" processes in the Member State's own territory[10]. This was said to be without prejudice to the Community's principles of free movement and

---

1. As first drafted, Article 2(4) would have applied the maximum levels only to ready-for-consumption foodstuffs prepared according to a manufacturer's instructions. This was evidently because table-top sweeteners were not thought to be "additives". Opinion of the Economic and Social Committee, OJ L120 6.5.91 p9, at para 2.2.
2. For a description of the political and policy debates regarding snack foods, see, e.g., *Eurofood* at p15 (May 1991). The Commission later accepted the use of sweeteners in potato crisps and other snack foods popular in Britain; *The Independent* (23 July 1991).
3. OJ C120 6.5.91 p9, at paras 3.5, 3.8, 21.
4. *Eurofood* at p15 (May 1991). At least some of the concerns have been resolved. *Eurofood* at p4 (August 1991); *The Independent* (23 July 1991).
5. COM(90) 381 final, above at Article 5(1). The disclosure would take the form of a statement that the product is a "...-based table-top sweetener", with the insertion of the particular sweetener.
6. Article 5(2). Such a warning was urged by the European Parliament. Report of the Committee on the Environment, Public Health and Consumer Protection, A3-0080/91 at 20 (26 March 1991).
7. Journal Officiel No. 66, p3664 (March 18, 1988).
8. COM(90) 381 final, above at Article 6.
9. At the Annex.
10. It should be observed that the process, and not the product, was required to be "traditional". Low-alcohol beers are certainly not traditional in Germany, and the proposed derogation seems chiefly protective in purpose.

establishment. The footnote reflected an uneasy compromise, and many members of the European Parliament were anxious for its deletion. BEUC, the European consumers organisation, also opposed it[1]. If adopted, the footnote could have represented an important precedent for other national derogations regarding other additives and foodstuffs[2]. In an unusual display of authority, however, Parliament succeeded in forcing the footnote's abandonment. The result was at least a temporary victory both for harmonisation and for parliamentary authority[3]. The Commission has, however, proposed a broader version of the footnote as an amendment to the basic additives directive, and reproposed a sweeteners directive[4].

Whatever the ultimate form of the directive, the debate regarding artificial sweeteners is likely to continue. New intense sweeteners are under development, and may eventually stimulate new disputes[5]. Moreover, sweeteners obviously satisfy an increasing consumer demand for low or reduced calorie foodstuffs. There is substantial evidence that many consumers ingest too much sugar, and that their diets would be improved if those amounts were reduced[6]. At the same time, there are still many consumers who question the long-term safety of artificial sweeteners[7]. Some are concerned about all additives, and particularly those which are artificial[8]. Until the scientific evidence is more complete and more widely accepted, any Community rules are likely to remain a source of controversy.

5.4   Preservatives

Preservatives have been used for centuries to prolong the durability and protect the safety of foodstuffs. Salting, sugar, alcohol, spices, and smoking are familiar examples of traditional preservation methods[9]. Preservatives have, however, become more varied and commercially more important as the food industry itself

---

1.   EIS, *Europe Environment* No. 384 (31 March 1992) at iv-2; *Eurofood* p6 (April 1992).
2.   *Eurofood* p2 (Dec 1991). The Commission evidently intended to include similar footnotes in other additives measures.
3.   *EC Food Law* p2 (May 1992). For the Commission's subsequent efforts to find new formulae for the footnote, see *Europe*, No. 5753 (n.s.) p11 (19 June 1992).
4.   COM(92) 255 final (17 June 1992).
5.   O'Brien Nabors, et al., "Intense Sweeteners", in S. Marie & J. Piggott, eds., *Handbook of Sweeteners* p114 (1991).
6.   In the United States, the consumption of sucrose trebled between 1900 and 1972, and is still double its level in 1900. R. Kanarek & R. Marks-Kaufman, *Nutrition and Behaviour : New Perspectives* pp170-171 (1991). For one of many appraisals that sugar consumption remains too high, see Coghlan, "Britain's Deadly Diet", *New Scientist* p29 (11 May 1991). For a similar report about the German diet and the reluctance of Germans to alter it, see A. Tuffs, "Germany: Food Matters", 337 *The Lancet* p1336 (1 June 1991).
7.   For a similar view in the United States regarding saccharin, see Schultz, "The Bitter Aftertaste of Saccharin", 40 Food D.C.L.J. 66 (1985).
8.   For such concerns, see, e.g., B. Fox & A. Cameron, *Food Science, Nutrition and Health* pp379-385 (5th ed. 1989); Q. Seddon, *Spoiled for Choice* pp82-90 (1990).
9.   For the role of preservatives, including traditional salting and smoking, see, e.g., B. Fox & A. Cameron, *Food Science, Nutrition and Health* p335 (5th ed. 1989); C. Catsberg & G. Kempen - van Dommelen, *Food Handbook* p59 (1990).

has grown more complex and international[1]. Durability has become a significant factor in food marketing, in part because some processed foods deteriorate more rapidly than equivalent traditional products[2]. In addition, the distance and time which separate a food's processing from its consumption have increased. Distributional networks have become longer and more complex. Food markets, which once were local and seasonal, are often now international. Preservatives have made these changes possible, and also have helped to reduce the real costs of foodstuffs. Longer shelf-lives mean that distributors may make fewer and larger deliveries, and that retailers lose fewer products through spoilage[3].

Preservational methods have also changed. Chilling and quick-freezing have partly replaced canning. Irradiation is increasing in importance. A growing range of chemical preservatives is used[4]. Most chemical preservatives may be used with safety, but some are toxic and may create substantial hazards for human health. For example, milk was once protected by formalin, a solution of formaldehyde[5]. In response to these changes and hazards, the Community began harmonising national rules for the regulation of chemical preservatives as early as 1963[6]. Although frequently amended, the 1963 directive is still in effect[7]. The Commission has, however, proposed new rules for the regulation of chemical preservatives[8].

The 1963 directive applies to both preservatives and foodstuffs containing preservatives produced within the Community. It also applies to products imported into the Community. It does not apply to export products[9]. The directive created a positive list of preservatives which may be used to protect foodstuffs intended for

---

1. For a description of modern preservation methods, see, e.g., D. Shapton & N. Shapton, *Principles and Practices for the Safe Processing of Foods* pp305-375 (1991).
2. The tendency of some processed foods to deteriorate more rapidly has been recognised by the European Court with respect to some cheeses; See *Officier van Justitie v Koninklijke Kaasfabriek Eyssen BV* [1982] 2 CMLR 20, decided by the European Court in 1981 upon reference from the Gerechtshof of Amsterdam.
3. Without preservatives, contamination would "inevitably" increase and food costs rise. Lessof, et al., "Intolerance and Allergy to Food and Food Additives", in R. Walker & E. Quattrucci, eds, *Nutritional and Toxicological Aspects of Food Processing* p345 (1988).
4. For example, benzoic and sorbic acids may be used to preserve shrimp and mustard, biphenyl to prevent moulds on citrus fruit, and sulphurous acid to prevent browning in pre-processed potatoes and vegetables. C. Catsberg & G. Kempen-van Dommelen, *Food Handbook* p59 (1990).
5. Many other toxic chemicals have also been used. B. Fox & A. Cameron, *Food Science, Nutrition and Health* pp337-338 (5th ed. 1989).
6. Council Directive (EEC) 64/54, OJ 27.1.64 161 p64. The directive was adopted late in 1963 but not officially published until 1964. As of 31 December 1990 the directive had been adopted by all Member States except Italy. *Eighth Annual Report to the European Parliament on Commission Monitoring of the Application of Community Law*, OJ C338 31.12 91 p1, at p113. For UK rules, see Preservatives in Food Regulations, SI 1989/553; Preservatives in Food (Amendment) Regulations, SI 1989/2287. For the Dutch rules, see *Voedingsraad* at p314. For Spanish rules, see, e.g., *Codigo Alimentario* at chap. 33. For French rules, see *Lamy-Dehove* at p5-5.
7. See, e.g., Council Directive (EEC) 85/172, OJ L65 6.3.85 p22; Council Directive (EEC) 85/585, OJ L372 31.12.85 p43. There are numerous earlier amendments.
8. COM(92) 255 final (17 June 1992).
9. Council Directive (EEC) 64/54, above at Article 10. For the issue of the application of safety rules to exports, see below at Chapter 9, para 9.3.5.

human consumption against deterioration caused by micro-organisms[1]. Oxidation is another source of food deterioration, but anti-oxidants are regulated under separate Community rules[2]. In a few instances, preservatives may be employed only under specific conditions of use, but those issues are generally left to national law[3]. The only preservatives originally subject to Community limitations were sodium nitrite, sodium nitrate and potassium nitrate. The first may only be used in a mixture with sodium chloride, while the last two may be used either alone or in a mixture with sodium chloride. Additional restrictions have since been imposed on other preservatives.

The 1963 directive does not override national rules in several areas. For example, a Member State may forbid the domestic use of any preservative in the directive's positive list if there is no "technological reason" for its use in foodstuffs produced and consumed in the Member State's own territory[4]. In essence, Member States are not obliged to permit a preservative if feasible alternatives exist[5]. Special derogations are also permitted for several foodstuffs. Member States may authorise the use of hexamethylene tetramine in semi-preserved fish and fishery products, and in caviar and other fish eggs[6]. Limitations are, however, imposed upon the maximum residue levels of hexamethylene tetramine in the foods as they are actually marketed[7]. States may also retain laws permitting the use of formaldehyde in Grana Padano cheese[8].

The 1963 directive does not affect national laws regarding foodstuffs which have preservative properties, including vinegar, edible oils and sugar[9]. Nor does it affect national rules regarding nisin[10], products used for the coating of foodstuffs, products

1.   Article 1 and the Annex.
2.   Below at para 5.7.
3.   Council Directive (EEC) 64/54, above at the Annex.
4.   Article 2(2).
5.   The Council adopted a definition of "technological reasons" in the 1988 framework additives directive which presumably would now be applied to interpret the 1963 preservatives directive. Above at para 5.1.
6.   Article 5(1). As described below, this authorisation is continued by the proposed positive list in the Commission's draft of new rules for preservatives. A maximum level is included.
7.   Hexamethylene tetramine (or hexamine) is used with benzoic acid (found naturally in cloudberries and other products) as a preservative. A. Bender, *Dictionary of Nutrition and Food Technology* pp33, 135 (6th ed. 1990).
8.   Article 5(2). Limitations upon maximum levels in the final products are imposed. The derogation permits the retention of such rules, and not their enactment. For the scientific issues, see Resmini, "Detection of Combined Formaldehyde in Gran Padano and in Provolone Cheese", in R. Walker & E. Qattrucci, eds., *Nutritional and Toxicological Aspects of Food Processing* pp83-92 (1988). He recommends a prohibition.
9.   Article 6(a). Sodium chloride and ethanol are also included, but the entire list is only illustrative of the permissible products.
10.   Nisin is an antibiotic found naturally in cheese. It is used to prolong storage life or as a processing aid for some foods. A. Bender, *Dictionary of Nutrition and Food Technology* p196 (6th ed. 1990). Its use as a processing aid is outside the scope of the 1963 directive. The European Court has sustained under Article 36 of the Treaty Dutch rules which forbade nisin in products for domestic consumption but permitted it in export products. This was held to be a matter of national discretion, even though other Member States had permitted its use in all

used to protect plant products against harmful organisms[1], anti-microbial products used for the treatment of drinking water, and anti-oxidants[2]. With these exceptions, no preservatives beyond those in the positive list may be authorised by Member States[3]. Member States may, however, suspend the use of a permitted preservative for one year if its use might endanger human health[4].

The directive also imposes restrictions on materials used for the smoking of foodstuffs[5]. Wood or plants used for smoking must be in a "natural state". Materials which are impregnated, coloured, gummed, painted or treated "in a similar manner" are all excluded. The directive provides generally that smoking must not create "any" risk to human health. Since it is widely argued that the consumption of large quantities of smoked foodstuffs over a long period may be harmful, the latter requirement is evidently only hortatory[6].

The directive has frequently been revised to extend the effectiveness of national derogations, authorise new preservatives, or change the status of existing substances[7]. The most important changes were made by a 1965 directive regarding labelling[8]. Under the 1965 directive, labels of preservatives must disclose the name and EEC number of the substance, and the name and address of the manufacturer, or of a seller "responsible" for the product within the meaning of applicable national law[9]. Labels must also include the words "for foodstuffs (restricted use)". If the product is a mixture, its label must include the mixture's name and the percentage of the preservative which is included. Member States may require this information to be provided in their official languages. The 1963 directive was also supplemented by another directive in 1965, which established purity criteria for preservatives in

products; Case 53/80 *Officier van Justitie v Koninklijke Kaasfabriek Eyssen BV* [1981] ECR 409, [1982] 2 CMLR 20.

1. National laws regarding plant protective products are, however, subject to separate Community rules. See below at Chapter 8, para 8.3..
2. Articles 6(b)-(f). This list is evidently exhaustive. For rules relating to anti-oxidants, see below at para 5.7.
3. Article 1.
4. Article 4(1). Acting upon a proposal from the Commission, the Council may, in response to a national suspension order, amend the Annex by directive, but this requires a unanimous decision; ibid., at Article 4(2). This provision was adopted prior to the Single European Act, above at Chapter 2, para 2.3, and thus prior to Article 100a of the Treaty. The Council may, however, extend the suspension for an additional year by qualified majority. Council Directive (EEC) 64/54, above at Article 4(2).
5. Article 3. For recommendations regarding smoked foods by the Council of Europe, see Resolution AP (85) 2 (17 Jan 1985).
6. B. Fox & A. Cameron, *Food Science, Nutrition and Health*, p337 (5th ed. 1989). On the other hand, it has been argued that smoked products and artificial smoke preparations present small risks unless consumed in quite large quantities. Netter & Sternitzke, "The Influence of the Phenolic Fractions of Smoke Condensates on Drug Metabolism", in R. Walker & E. Quattrucci, eds., *Nutritional and Toxicological Aspects of Food Processing* pp51, 59 (1988).
7. For some of the amendments, see, e.g., Council Directive (EEC) 85/172, OJ L65 p22 (6 March 1985); Council Directive (EEC) 85/585, OJ L372 31.12.85 p43.
8. Council Directive (EEC) 65/659, OJ 222 28.12.65 p3263.
9. Council Directive (EEC) 64/54, above, at Article 9, as amended by Council Directive (EEC) 65/659, above.

the 1963 directive's positive list[1]. The 1965 directive has itself been amended on several occasions[2].

As described above, the 1988 framework directive contemplated ancillary directives relating to various categories of additives, including preservatives[3]. Pursuant to the 1988 directive, the Commission issued a working document in 1990 which proposed new rules for antioxidants, preservatives, and "miscellaneous" additives. The draft has since been revised, but currently includes all additives except colorants and sweeteners[4]. A great variety of substances and products would not, however, be regarded as additives. In earlier versions, they included foodstuffs with additive properties, cooking salts, flavourings and smoke solutions, substances used to treat drinking water, blood plasma, edible gelatin, certain pectin products, novel food ingredients, fat substitutes, and dextrins[5]. The proposed list of exclusions has since been shortened to include substances used to treat drinking water, pectin products, chewing gum bases, various starches, blood plasma, gelatin, amino acids, and ammonium chloride[6]. Flour treatment agents would be handled in separate legislation.

An annex to the revised proposal would generally permit the use for all purposes of a positive list of additives[7]. The list includes such substances as acetic acid, carbon carbonates, lecithins, and pectins. These and many others could be used in virtually any product for any technical purpose on a *quantum satis* basis, provided that good manufacturing practices were followed and the level were no greater than necessary to achieve the intended purpose[8]. Nonetheless, the additives in the proposed annex would not be authorised for use in such products as unprocessed foodstuffs, honey, chocolate, jams, mineral waters, coffee, tea, virgin oils, certain milks and sugars, butter, infant formulae, follow-up formulae, and weaning foods[9]. A committee procedure would resolve any disputes about whether a foodstuff falls within these categories[10].

1. Council Directive (EEC) 65/66, OJ L22 92.65 p1.
2. Most recently, see Council Directive (EEC) 85/585, OJ L352 13.12.85 p1. As of December 31, 1990, it had been adopted throughout the Community; *Eighth Annual Report to the European Parliament on Commission Monitoring of the Application of Community Law*, OJ C338 31.12.91 p1 at p133.
3. Above at para 5.1.
4. COM(92) 255 final (17 June 1992). For an earlier version, see Working Document III/3624/91/EN.
5. Pectin consists of plant tissues and is used as a setting agent and for other processing purposes. A. Bender, *Dictionary of Nutrition and Food Technology* p214 (6th ed. 1990). Dextrins are mixtures of soluble compounds formed by partial breakdowns of starch; ibid., at p86.
6. Article 1(4).
7. Article 2(2).
8. Annex I. This would be subject to limitations under national law for traditional products; COM(92) 255 final (17 June 1992); above at para 5.3.
9. Article 2(3).
10. Article 5.

Other proposed annexes would list substances authorised only for particular purposes. One list includes preservatives approved only for certain foods and, in many cases, only subject to maximum levels[1]. This includes such substances as sorbates, sulphur dioxide, sulphites, nisin, and sodium nitrite. The maximum levels would apply to foodstuffs as they are actually marketed, and would thus include any additives in ingredients and any substances occurring naturally[2]. Additives would be permitted in compound foods if they are allowed in its ingredients but, conversely, a substance containing additives could be used as an ingredient only if the final food conformed to the proposed directive[3]. The directive would be without prejudice to separate measures for sweeteners and colorants[4]. If adopted, it would repeal the 1963 preservatives directive[5].

Important changes may be made in the Commission's proposal before a replacement is found for the 1963 directive. As it stands, the proposal includes several useful innovations. It would be a welcome simplification of national rules to create a list of foodstuffs which, because of long evidence of their safety, were freed from additive regulation. Similarly, inconsistent national conditions of use would be reduced if some well-accepted additives were approved upon a *quantum satis* basis for use whenever appropriate. Supplemental lists would be needed of additives approved only for specific purposes and under particular conditions, but arid disputes could be avoided about national rules and the "principal" purpose for which an additive was used in a particular product. Finally, although the proposed rules regarding maximum permissible levels need clarification, they are evidently intended to permit some degree of flexibility.

5.5   Colouring materials

Dyes and pigments have been used in foodstuffs for centuries to impart pleasing colours[6]. A Paris edict regulated the colouring of butter in 1396, and some French wines were coloured as early as 1860[7]. The earliest colorants were often spices and fruit products, which may originally have been used because of their flavouring properties, but which were also soon valued because of the attractive colours they added to foodstuffs. Turmeric and saffron are examples. In addition, most foods are

---

1.   Annex II.
2.   Article 2(6).
3.   Article 3.
4.   Article 4. Until its rejection by the European Parliament, the proposed footnote in the sweetener directive preserving various national rules would also have evidently been included in the preservatives directive; above at para 5.3; *Eurofood* 6 (April 1992). See also above at para 5.1.
5.   Article 9.
6.   Summaries of the uses and significance of colouring materials in foodstuffs may be found in, for example, B. Fox & A. Cameron, *Food Science, Nutrition and Health* p378 (5th ed. 1989); N. Light, *Longman Illustrated Dictionary of Food Science* pp78-83 (1989).
7.   D. Marmion, *Handbook of US Colorants for Foods, Drugs, and Cosmetics* pp3-6 (3rd ed. 1991).

now processed before their presentation to the consumer, and processing may alter natural colourings. Canned peas and strawberries, for example, would be less attractive to consumers, and indeed might be thought "unnatural", if colourings were not added[1]. Other changes in colouring may be sought before processing begins. For example, substances may be added to fish food and poultry feed to brighten egg yolks and the flesh of salmon and trout[2]. The great variety of colouring materials now available means that processors may exercise considerable imaginativeness in altering or accentuating the colours of processed foods. In some instances, this may be done to disguise the deficiencies of processing methods or raw materials.

Traditional colouring materials were of natural origin. They included cochineal and carotene, for example, as well as turmeric and saffron[3]. Silver, gold and even aluminium are still used for the decoration of cakes and other desserts. Titanium dioxide is used in confectioneries, icings and sugar syrups. More recently, a broad range of synthetic dyes has been developed. Most are entirely safe, but some are toxic in large quantities and a few are thought carcinogenic[4]. Colorants were widely used in the nineteenth century to mask adulteration or poor quality[5]. As a result, regulators have long sought to restrict the choice and quantities of pigments and dyes used in foodstuffs, as well as the foods in which they are permitted. The risks of colorants were a major factor stimulating the 1906 food and drug statute in the United States, and the creation of what amounted to a positive list beginning as early as 1907[6]. Several European governments began prohibiting some colorants by the end of the nineteenth century[7]. Similarly, the Community's earliest regulatory measure with respect to foodstuffs was addressed to colouring materials.

In 1962, the Council adopted a directive to harmonise national laws regarding the use of colouring materials in foodstuffs intended for human consumption[8]. The

---

1.   B. Fox & A. Cameron, *Food Science, Nutrition and Health* p378 (5th ed. 1989).
2.   Ibid., at p375.
3.   Ibid., at p378. Turmeric is a spice and colorant which gives a yellowish hue to meat, rice and other dishes. R. Igoe, *Dictionary of Food Ingredients* p140 (2nd ed. 1989). Carotene is a red pigment found in carrots and yellow maize. The related products carotenoids and zanthophylls are used as pigments. A. Bender, *Dictionary of Nutrition and Food Science* pp53-54 (6th ed. 1990). Cochineal is a red pigment produced from insects found in Central America and the West Indies; ibid., at p69.
4.   There is an extensive literature. For the risks of, for example, erythrosine, see the proceedings of the 33rd meeting of the Joint FAO/WHO Expert Committee on Food Additives, *Toxicological Evaluation of Certain Food Additives and Contaminants* p39 (1989).
5.   Colorants provided many of the examples of dangerous foodstuffs collected by Accum in the early nineteenth century. D. Marmion, *Handbook of US Colorants for Foods, Drugs, and Cosmetics* p5 (3rd ed. 1991).
6.   Ibid., at p6-14.
7.   Ibid., at p6-7. See also Q. Seddon, *Spoiled for Choice* p85 (1990); R. Taylor, *Food Additives* pp26-28 (1980).
8.   Council Directive (EEC) 2645/62, OJ L279 11.11.62 p1. As of 31 December 1990, the directive had been adopted by all Member States; *Eighth Annual Report to the European Parliament on Commission Monitoring of the Application of Community Law*, OJ C338 31.12.91 p1 at p113. For the UK rules, see Colouring Matter in Food Regulations, SI 1973/1340; Colouring Matter in Food (Amendment) Regulations, SI 1987/1987, and prior amended provisions. See also Annex I to the

directive still provides the Community's basic rules regarding colourings, although new rules have now been proposed by the Commission. As it has in subsequent measures, the Council stated in 1962 that its principal consideration was human health, but that it had also given attention to economic and technical needs[1]. The directive was intended to preclude deception, eliminate trade barriers, and prevent unfair competitive conditions[2]. It applies to all foodstuffs produced for use within the Community. It also applies to imported products, whether or not processed, intended for use within the Community[3]. The directive does not directly address products intended for export, although it is specifically inapplicable to the French overseas departments[4]. The directive's references to the "use" of colorants suggests, however, that it is applicable to foodstuffs coloured within the Community, even if they are ultimately consumed elsewhere[5].

The 1962 directive generally prohibits Member States from authorising any colorants other than those listed in annexes[6]. The annexes are divided into lists of colourings for both mass and surface colouring (e.g., cochineal), those for surface colouring only (e.g., aluminium), and those for certain uses only. The designated uses of the approved colourings may not be subject to any "general prohibition" by the Member States[7]. The measure's overall effect was to reduce the colorants previously permitted by Member States by some 40 percent[8].

Nonetheless, the directive originally preserved existing national authorisations for the use of certain colourings not included in the positive lists[9]. Those colourings were to have been reviewed by the Community and, if found harmless and useful, could have been added to the positive list[10]. The derogations have now expired. The directive still permits the use of foodstuffs which have a subsidiary colouring property, such as paprika and saffron[11]. They are, however, permitted only if "natural" and used because of their aromatic, sapid or nutritive properties rather than any "subsidiary" colouring properties[12]. The directive left undisturbed any

---

various transitional rules were provided. For the Spanish rules, see, e.g., *Codigo Alimentario* at 4.31.07. For the French rules, see *Lamy-Dehove* at p5-30.

1. Council Directive (EEC) 2645/62, above at the first recital of the preamble.
2. The second recital of the preamble. Such recitals have become routine in the Community's food regulatory measures.
3. Article 1(4).
4. Article 14.
5. Article 1(1).
6. Article 1(1) and Annex I.
7. Article 1(2).
8. Gray, "The Perspective to 1992", in H. Deelstra, et al., eds., *Food Policy Trends in Europe* pp11, 12 (1991).
9. Council Directive (EEC) 2645/62, above at Article 2(1) and Annex II. The annex contained a list of colourings which could be used for a period of three years, as well as a list of permissible dilutants and solvents for those colourings.
10. Article 2.
11. Article 3.
12. This requirement seems curious, and perhaps unenforceable. For example, paella and other Spanish rice dishes contain saffron. Is this for taste or for its pleasing colour? And does it

than any "subsidiary" colouring properties[1]. The directive left undisturbed any national rules for the colouring of hard-boiled eggs and tobacco, or for the stamping of external parts not usually consumed with foodstuffs[2]. The latter include, for example, egg shells, citrus fruit skins, and cheese rinds[3]. Member States are specifically permitted to authorise the use of pigment rubine and burnt umber for colouring cheese rinds[4]. Moreover, they may specify the foodstuffs in which colorants in the two annexes may be used, as well as conditions for their use. The result is to leave national rules largely unharmonised[5].

Accordingly, the inclusion of a colorant in the Community's positive lists does not always eliminate trade barriers to products in which the colorant has been used. An example is offered by a European Court decision regarding colourings in lumpfish roe[6]. German producers sought to sell roe in Belgium which contained colorants permitted in Germany and included in the 1962 directive's positive lists[7]. The colorants were not approved in Belgium for roe, although they were approved for other purposes. The Court assumed that they might have been authorised by Belgium for roe if a suitable application had been filed with the national authorities[8]. In the absence of such an application, Belgium prohibited the sale of the German roe. In submissions to the Court, the Commission acknowledged that national approvals were not forbidden by the 1962 directive, but argued that denials which restricted the sale of products imported from other member states were inconsistent with Article 30 of the Treaty, and were not saved by Article 36[9]. The Court preliminarily sustained the Belgian ruling. Nonetheless, it also held that in applying its local rules Belgium must give weight to any technical or organoleptic needs for the colorants. In addition, Belgium must take account of the findings of the Scientific Committee in deciding whether the colorants create safety hazards[10]. In the Court's view, the 1962 directive provided strong evidence of the absence of substantial risks to human health. Widespread use of the colorants in roe, together with the absence of evidence of safety hazards, placed heavy burdens on Belgium to justify restrictions upon imported products.

---

1. This requirement seems curious, and perhaps unenforceable. For example, paella and other Spanish rice dishes contain saffron. Is this for taste or for its pleasing colour? And does it matter? As described below, however, the requirement is essentially repeated in the Commission's proposals for new rules.
2. Article 4. This authorisation depends upon the existence of appropriate national rules. It would not be, however, under the Commission's proposed new rules.
3. Article 4(b).
4. Article 7.
5. Article 5. The formulation of Community-wide lists of foodstuffs in which colorants may be used, as well as conditions of their use, would have been a formidable effort, but the absence of such lists has permitted substantial trade barriers. As described below, the Commission is now attempting to provide such lists.
6. Case 247/84 *The State v Motte* [1985] ECR 3887, [1987] 1 CMLR 663, decided by the European Court in 1985 upon reference from the Cour d'Appel in Brussels.
7. Ibid., at p681. The colorants were cochineal red and indigotin. At 665. The products also contained a preservative, hexamethylene tetramine, which was not authorised in Belgium.
8. Ibid., at p677-680.
9. Ibid., at p679.
10. Ibid., at p682.

The directive provides a positive list of products to dilute or dissolve colourings[1]. The permissible products include, for example, sodium carbonate, sodium chloride, glucose, starches, and water[2]. It also imposes special labelling obligations. Colourings may be marketed only if their labels disclose the name and address of their manufacturer or a seller established within the Community, an EEC number, and the words "colouring matter for foodstuffs"[3]. It was originally sufficient if these statements were provided in two Community languages, one of Germanic and the other of Latin origin, but Member States may now require them in their official languages[4].

An annex to the directive provides purity criteria[5]. The directive also contemplated methods of analysis to verify the purity of colorants[6]. Those methods were not designated by the directive itself, and indeed were not provided until 1981[7]. Finally, the 1962 directive is specifically applicable to colourings used in chewing gum[8]. Gum was the only foodstuff to which such express treatment was given. The 1962 directive has since been amended on several occasions, principally to revise the positive lists[9].

These rules are now under reconsideration. Draft revisions were suggested in 1985, and amended in 1988 and 1989[10]. In 1990, in accordance with the framework additives directive, the Commission issued a working document which again suggested revisions in the 1962 directive[11]. The draft has since been issued as a formal proposal[12]. It has already proved controversial in the European Parliament, which may press for reductions in the number of approved colourants. In part, the new proposal is based upon reports from the Scientific Committee for Food, which made an appraisal of colourings in 1983 and again 1989[13]. In its later report, the SCR recommended yet another study to establish additional specifications for colourings[14].

---

1. Council Directive (EEC) 2645/62, above at Article 6. A separate list of dilutants and solvents is provided in Annex II for the colourings included there.
2. The list also includes sodium sulphate, lactose, sucrose, dextrins, ethanol, glycerol, sorbitol, edible oils and fats, and beeswax.
3. Article 9(1). EEC numbers were provided in Annex I of the directive.
4 Article 9(2), as amended.
5. Article 11 and Annex III.
6. Article 11(2).
7. First Commission Directive (EEC) 81/712, OJ L257 10.9.81 p1.
8. Article 10.
9 Council Directive (EEC) 65/469, OJ 178 26.10.65; Council Directive (EEC) 67/653, OJ 263 30.10.67; Council Directive (EEC) 70/358, OJ L157 18.7.70 p136; Council Directive (EEC) 76/399, OJ L108 26 4.76 p19; Council Directive (EEC) 78/144, OJ L44 15.2.78 p20; Council Directive (EEC) 81/712, OJ L257 10.9.81 p1.
10. COM(85) 474. See also P. Deboyser, *Le droit communitaire relatif aux denrées alimentaires* p118 (1989).
11. Draft Proposal for a Council Directive on Colours, No. III/9266/90 - Rev 1. For a revised version, see Working Document III/3624/91/EN.
12. COM(91) 444 final, OJ C12 18.1.92 p7.
13. *Reports of the Scientific Committee for Food*, Twenty-first Series, EUR 11617 (1989).
14. Ibid., at 2.

Under the Commission's proposal, colours are substances which add or restore colour in foodstuffs, are not separately consumed as foodstuffs, and are not "normally" used as "characteristic" ingredients of foods[1]. They include natural as well as artificial substances. They do not include foodstuffs or flavourings used in compound foods because of their aromatic, sapid or nutritive properties, even if they have a "secondary" colouring effect[2]. Paprika and saffron might be examples. Nor do they include colorants for egg shells, stamping meat, and inedible external parts of foodstuffs. A new positive list of colourings would be created, together with a separate list of colours permitted only for certain uses[3]. The latter includes designated foodstuffs and proposed maximum levels[4]. Canthaxanthin, for example, could be employed only in cooked sausages and only up to 30 mg/kg. There would also be a list of foodstuffs to which only specified colours could be added[5]. In butter, for example, only carotene and annatto could be used as colorants. Yet another list would contain foodstuffs to which no colours could be added except insofar as specifically authorised by the proposal[6]. They include, for example, bread, pasta, tomato paste, and coffee. A final list would permit the use of designated colorants on a *quantum satis* basis in all foodstuffs except those specifically excluded by the proposed directive[7]. A committee procedure involving the Standing Committee for Foodstuffs would resolve any disputes and modify the annexes as needed[8]. The proposed conditions of use would be reviewed by the Commission after five years[9].

5.6   Emulsifiers, stabilisers, thickeners and gelling agents

Food technology requires a great variety of additives to achieve the textures and consistencies demanded by fabricated and processed foodstuffs. For example, emulsifiers are used to make suspensions from oils or fats and water. They are important in the manufacture of salad creams and mayonnaise, but may also be added to such products as ice creams[10]. Stabilisers are added to increase the durability of the emulsions[11]. Thickeners, gelatine and other gelling agents may alter the consistency of foodstuffs. A manufacturer may, for example, wish "creamy" or spreadable products. Bulking agents may be added[12]. These and other

---

1.   COM(91) 444 final, above at Article 1(2).
2.   Article 1(3).
3.   Annexes I, IV.
4.   Annex IV.
5.   Annex III.
6.   Annex II. British law already prohibits the use of colorants in some foods. See Colouring Matter in Food (Amendment) Regulations 1987, SI 1987/1987, and prior amended regulations.
7.   Annex V.
8.   Articles 4, 6.
9.   Article 7.
10.   For the roles of emulsifiers, see B. Fox & A. Cameron, *Food Science, Nutrition and Health* pp61-64, 377-378 (5th ed. 1989); C. Catsberg & G. Kempen-van Dommelen, *Food Handbook* (1990).
11.   G. Fox & A. Cameron, *Food Science, Nutrition and Health* pp61, 377-378 (5th ed. 1989).
12.   One common substance is polydextrose, although a warning label is now required in the United States above prescribed levels. See, e.g., Smiles, "The Functional Applications of Polydextrose", in G. Charalambous & G. Inglett, eds., *Chemistry of Food and Beverages : Recent Developments* pp305, 321 (1982).

"creamy" or spreadable products. Bulking agents may be added[1]. These and other substances may be made from natural or artificial sources. Gums, starches and pectin may be used, as well as artificial products such as superglycerinated fats[2]. The commercial importance of the products, as well as the wide variety of foodstuffs in which they are used, have made them inevitable subjects of regulatory control.

The Council first adopted a directive to harmonise national laws regarding emulsifiers, stabilisers, thickeners and gelling agents in 1974[3]. The directive states that differences in national laws may hinder the free movement of goods and result in unfair competition[4]. It recognises that considerations of public health must be given priority, but that attention must also be given to possible consumer fraud and economic and technical needs[5]. Significantly, the directive encourages additional scientific research regarding health effects[6]. The latter recital is by no means routine in the Community's food legislation. No specific explanation was offered for its inclusion, but the Scientific Committee has subsequently conducted a review of the health implications of emulsifiers and related products[7]. Partly as a result, revised rules for the use of such products are now in preparation by the Commission. Although frequently amended, the 1974 directive remains incomplete, and the Commission's new rules will seek to resolve some of the questions left unanswered in 1974.

The 1974 directive creates two positive lists of emulsifiers and similar substances authorised for use within the Community[8]. The first is a list of substances permanently approved for use, although in some instances they may be used only under prescribed conditions[9]. In general, however, the directive does not provide

---

1.   One common substance is polydextrose, although a warning label is now required in the United States above prescribed levels.   See, e.g., Smiles, "The Functional Applications of Polydextrose", in G. Charalambous & G. Inglett, eds., *Chemistry of Food and Beverages : Recent Developments* pp305, 321 (1982).

2.   Pectins are natural plant tissues derived from fruits and vegetables. Superglycerinated fats are artificial fatty substances, the most commonly used of which is glyceryl monostearate (GMS). They are used as emulsifiers or stabilisers, or to provide protective coatings. See A. Bender, *Dictionary of Nutrition and Food Technology* p273 (6th ed. 1990); B. Fox & A. Cameron, *Food Science, Nutrition and Health* p61 (5th ed. 1989).

3.   Council Directive (EEC) 74/329, OJ L189 12.7.74 p1. For the UK rules, see Emulsifiers and Stabilisers in Food Regulations 1989, SI 1989/876; Emulsifiers and Stabilisers in Food (Amendment) Regulations 1992, SI 1992/165. For the Dutch rules, see *Voedingsraad* at p438. For the French rules, see *Lamy-Dehove* at p5-132.

4.   Council Directive (EEC) 74/329, above at the first recital of the preamble.

5.   The third recital of the preamble.

6.   The fifth recital of the preamble.

7.   *Reports of the Scientific Committee for Food*, Twenty-first Series, EUR 11617 (1989) at p49.

8.   Council Directive (EEC) 74/329, above at Article 2(1) and Annex I; Article 3(1) and Annex II. Emulsifiers are in essence defined as substances which permit a uniform dispersion, thickeners as those which increase viscosity, and gelling agents as those which give foodstuffs the consistency of a gel. Article 1. See also Case 304/84 *Ministère Public v Müller* [1986] ECR 1511, [1987] 2 CMLR 469 (emulsifiers in pastry).

9.   Article 2(1) and Annex I. Annex I includes such substances as lecithins, alginic acid, sodium alginate, agar, guar gum, pectin, glycerol, sucroglycerides, and stearyl tartrate. Lecithins are

rules regarding permissible conditions of use. Instead, it promised that lists of foods in which the approved substances may be used, as well as conditions of use, would be adopted "as soon as possible"[1]. In 1980, six years after the directive's adoption, the European Parliament again urged the addition of conditions of use "as soon as possible"[2]. None has yet appeared, although they form part of the Commission's new draft proposals. The second positive list includes substances which originally were approved only for five years[3]. This period has since been repeatedly extended. Annex II includes such substances as karaya gum, sorbitan monopalmitate, and sorbitan monolaurate[4]. It originally included ghatti gum and xanthan gum, but the first has since been prohibited and second moved to Annex I[5]. Procedures are included for revising the positive lists, and for the adoption of detailed purity criteria[6]. The 1974 directive itself provides general purity criteria. These include limits on the permissible amounts of arsenic, lead, copper and zinc, as well as a general rule that a toxicologically dangerous amount of any substance may not be included[7]. More detailed purity criteria were adopted in 1978[8].

The 1974 directive does not apply to a lengthy series of products. It is inapplicable to foodstuffs which have natural emulsifying, stabilising, thickening or gelling properties. These include eggs, flour and starches[9]. Nor does it apply to emulsifiers used in release agents[10]. Nor is it applicable to acids, bases or salts used to change or stabilise pH; to blood plasma, modified starches, or edible gelatine; to hydrolysed food proteins and their salts[11]. Finally, it is not applicable to products containing pectin and derived by prescribed processes from fruit products. Until

fatty substances derived from soya, peanuts and corn. A. Bender, *Dictionary of Nutrition and Food Technology* pp161-162 (6th ed. 1990).

1.   Article 4.
2.   Resolution of the European Parliament, OJ C4 7.1.80 p65.
3.   Article 3(1).
4.   For a toxicological examination of karaya gum, see Proceedings of the 33rd Meeting of the Joint FAO/WHO Expert Committee on Food Additives, *Toxicological Evaluation of Certain Food Additives and Contaminants* p97 (1989). The European Parliament proposed to ban it as early as 1980; OJ C4 7.1.80 p65 at p66. The Commission is now proposing the approval of karaya gum for designated purposes and subject to quantitative limits.
5.   For xanthan gum, see, e.g., Teague, et al., "Recent Developments in the Application of Xanthan Gum in Food Systems", in G. Charalambous & G. Inglett, eds., *Chemistry of Foods and Beverages : Recent Developments* pp265-292 (1982).
6.   Articles 7, 10.
7.   Article 6(1)(a).
8.   Council Directive (EEC) 78/663, OJ L223 7.8.78 p7; Council Directive (EEC) 82/504, OJ L230 2.8.82 p35; Council Directive (EEC) 90/612, OJ L326 26.10.90 p58; Commission Directive (EEC) 92/4, OJ L55 29.2.92 p96.
9.   Council Directive (EEC) 74/329, above at Article 9.
10.   Release agents are applied to tins, enamels and plastic films to prevent food from adhering to them; A. Bender, *Dictionary of Nutrition and Food Technology* p242 (6th ed. 1990). Presumably such agents may eventually be regulated under the rules applicable to materials in contact with foodstuffs.
11.   Hydrolysed proteins are chemically altered in a manner such that, for example, cane sugar may be made into glucose and fructose; A. Bender, *Dictionary of Nutrition and Food Technology* p141 (6th ed. 1990); R. Igoe, *Dictionary of Food Ingredients* p72 (2nd ed. 1989)

1987, Member States were also permitted to authorise foodstuffs containing polyoxyethylene and certain other substances[1].

The exceptions may appear self-explanatory, but they have sometimes produced controversy. In 1978, for example, the Italian Ministry of Health limited the use of animal gelatine to particular products and within specified quantitative limits[2]. The Commission argued to the European Court that the Italian order prevented the sale of products lawfully traded elsewhere in the Community, and hence violated Article 30 of the Treaty[3]. Italy claimed in response that gelatine was encompassed by the 1974 directive, and that its exclusion from the directive's limitations meant that Member States could adopt whatever rules they deemed appropriate[4]. In essence, Italy claimed that the directive removed gelling agents from Article 30 and left the use of gelatine to national discretion. It argued that the Council had simultaneously occupied the field and yet permitted it to be regulated in part as Member States elected. The European Court had little difficulty in rejecting the argument, and held that the Italian order violated Article 30[5]. The dispute is largely a tribute to the ingenuity of Italy's counsel, but it also illustrates the willingness of national authorities to search for justifications for national rules even within the Community's harmonisation measures.

The labels of approved substances must include the name and address of their manufacturer, or of a seller established within the Community[6]. They must also disclose the name and EEC number of the substance, and the names and EEC numbers of any components mixed with the substances, including the percentages of those components[7]. In addition, their labels must state "for foodstuffs (restricted use)." There are also special labelling rules for sorbitol and sorbitol syrups[8]. Any official language of the Community may be used, although Member States are permitted to demand their own official languages[9].

---

1. For this former derogation, see Council Directive (EEC) 86/102, OJ L88 3.4.86 p40. Polyoxyethylene compounds are chiefly used as emulsifiers for bakery goods. A. Bender, *Dictionary of Nutrition and Food Technology* p225 (6th ed. 1990).
2. *Re Gelatin in Sweets, EC Commission v Italy* [1986] 2 CMLR 274, decided by the European Court in 1984.
3. Ibid., at p277, 281.
4. Ibid., at p277-278.
5. Ibid., at p288-289.
6. Council Directive (EEC) 74/329, above at Article 8(1). The designated seller must be "responsible" within the meaning of national law.
7. Ibid. There are not yet any general Community requirements for quantitative disclosures, but the 1974 directive's requirement for percentage disclosures is more rigorous than the general obligations imposed by the 1978 labelling directive, as amended.
8. Articles 8(1)(d), 8(2). Sorbitol is a sugar alcohol formed from fructose and found in plums and other fruit. It is less sweet than sucrose, and is thus used in diabetic foods. A. Bender, *Dictionary of Nutrition and Food Technology* p261 (6th ed. 1990). The rules relating to sorbitol must now be read in light of the proposed sweeteners directive.
9. Article 8(4).

The directive has been repeatedly amended since 1974, generally to revise the two positive lists. Despite the original five-year limitation upon its effectiveness, much of the 1974 "temporary" list remained in effect at least through 1991[1]. The European Parliament expressed "regret" at the repeated extensions as early as 1980, but its concerns evidently had little influence upon the Commission[2]. The Commission has, however, now proposed a new directive which would revise the rules for preservatives, anti-oxidants and miscellaneous additives. These include emulsifiers, stabilisers, thickeners and gelling agents[3]. The new measure is based in part upon an appraisal of emulsifiers made by the Scientific Committee late in 1988[4]. Revised positive lists would be created, and the 1974 directive would be repealed[5]. The substances "temporarily" approved in 1974 would either be forbidden or permanently authorised for use. Karaya gum, for example, would be authorised up to maximum levels in several product categories, and on a *quantum satis* basis in dietary supplements[6]. In the interim, Britain has adopted its own revised rules for emulsifiers and stabilisers based upon an extensive report by the Food Advisory Committee[7].

5.7   Anti-oxidants

The preservative agents described in an earlier section are intended to protect foodstuffs against spoilage or deterioration because of bacteria, moulds and yeasts. They do not offer protection against deterioration or rancidity because of oxidation[8]. Fatty products, which include bakery goods and many other foodstuffs, are readily susceptible to discoloration and spoilage through oxidation. To provide protection against oxidation, food processors employ anti-oxidants in such products as cheese spreads, vegetable oils and chewing gums. They may also prevent the discoloration of some fruits[9] and even plastic packaging materials[10]. Anti-oxidants occur naturally in fats, but their levels must be increased to provide the protection demanded for processed foods[11].

---

1.   Council Directive (EEC) 89/393, OJ L186 30.6.89 p13. This is the latest in a series of extensions, and prolonged the effectiveness of the "temporary" list until 31 December 1991. No further extension has been sought, presumably because the Commission expects soon to propose a new directive. The list was revised by Council Directive (EEC) 80/597, OJ L155 23.6.80 p23.

2.   OJ C4 7.1.80 p65. By 1985, the Parliament was evidently resigned to the situation, and another extension was approved without comment. OJ C46 18.2.85 p91.

3.   COM(92) 255 final (17 June 1992). For a more complete description of the draft, see above at par 5.4.

4.   *Reports of the Scientific Committee for Food*, Twenty-first Series, EUR 11617 (1989) at 49.

5.   COM(92) 255 final (17 June 1992), at 33.

6.   COM(92) 255 final (17 June 1992) at Annex IV.

7.   Emulsifiers and Stabilisers in Food (Amendment) Regulations 1992, SI 1992/165; Food Advisory Committee, Report on the Review of the Emulsifiers and Stabilisers in Food Regulations (1992).

8.   The role and nature of anti-oxidants are described by B. Fox & A. Cameron, *Food Science, Nutrition and Health* p343 (5th ed. 1989).

9.   Ibid. For the use of diphenyl to prevent fruit spoilage, see also A. Bender, *Dictionary of Nutrition and Food Technology* p89 (6th ed. 1990).

10.   B. Fox & A. Cameron, *Food Science, Nutrition and Health* p376 (5th ed. 1989). The anti-oxidants used for this purpose are not those approved for use in foodstuffs.

11.   Ibid., at p343.

Anti-oxidants were among the earliest subjects of Community foodstuffs regulation. The Council adopted a directive in 1970 for the approximation of national laws regarding anti-oxidants for use in human foodstuffs[1]. The directive has been amended on several occasions, but continues to provide the Community's basic rules regarding anti-oxidants. Revised rules are, however, in preparation by the Commission as part of its proposed directive for preservatives and miscellaneous additives. The 1970 directive prohibits the authorisation by Member States of any anti-oxidants other than those in a positive list in the directive's annex[2]. The annex is divided into lists of anti-oxidants, anti-oxidant substances which also perform other technical functions, and substances which increase the anti-oxidant effect of other products[3]. They may be diluted or dissolved only in substances listed in part IV of the annex[4]. Anti-oxidants are defined as products used to prevent the deterioration of foodstuffs because of oxidation, including such problems as fat deterioration and colour changes.

Despite the positive lists, Member States were originally permitted to retain national laws which authorised other anti-oxidants. These included synthetic beta-tocopherol, calcium disodium ethylene diamine tetra-acetete, propyl gallate, and L-ascorbic acid esters[5]. These exceptions have expired, but some of the substances were transferred to the directive's positive list. Member States are, however, permitted to suspend the use of any substance in the positive lists for as long as one year if it might endanger human health[6]. This permits consideration of the issue by the Community, and the adoption of any appropriate Community legislation. This is subject to extension for an additional year by a qualified majority of the Council, but the Council can amend the permanent list to add or delete substances only by acting unanimously[7].

The 1970 directive provides several criteria of purity, including limitations on the permissible content of arsenic, lead, copper and zinc[8]. More generally, the directive prohibits any "measurable trace" of any other toxicologically dangerous element.

1.   Council Directive (EEC) 70/357, OJ L157 18.7.70 p31. For the British rules, see Antioxidants in Food Regulations 1978, SI 1978/105; Antioxidants in Food (Amendment) Regulations 1991, SI 1991/2540. For the Dutch rules, see *Voedingsraad* at p225. For Spanish rules, see, e.g., *Codigo Alimentario* at chap. 33. For the French rules, see *Lamy-Dehove* at p5-50.

2.   Council Directive (EEC) 70/357, above at Article 1 and the Annex.

3.   Article 1 and the Annex.

4.   Article 1.

5.   Article 2. These were originally permitted for a period of only three years. The last such derogation finally expired at the end of 1986, some 16 years after the creation of the "temporary" list. Council Directive (EEC) 81/962, OJ L354 9.12.81 p22.

6.   Article 3.

7.   Article 3(1). The provision regarding changes to the permanent list was adopted before the addition of Article 100a to the Treaty by the Single European Act.

8.   Article 4(a).

This includes heavy metals "in particular", but other substances are potentially also encompassed. As methods of scientific detection continue to improve, this prohibition of any "measurable trace" becomes steadily more stringent. Methods of detection often outrace the technical ability to remove trace substances. The directive also stated that the Council would subsequently adopt more specific purity criteria, as well as methods of analysis and sampling to verify compliance with the criteria[1]. The Standing Committee for Foodstuffs was given a consultative and approval role in this process[2]. Purity criteria and analytical methods were eventually provided in 1978[3].

The 1970 directive also imposes special labelling obligations. Labels of anti-oxidants are required to disclose the name and address of the product's manufacturer, or of a seller established within the Community[4]. Labelling must also include the name and EEC number of the substance, and the words "for foodstuffs (restricted use)"[5]. If the product is a mixture, the label must disclose the names, EEC numbers and percentages of substances in the mixture[6]. These statements were originally to have been given in at least two Community languages, one of Germanic and one of Latin origin. Member States may now require them in their own official languages[7].

National rules regarding the foodstuffs in which anti-oxidants may be used, as well as other conditions for their use, were left undisturbed[8]. The absence of rules regarding conditions of use is a major omission from Community legislation, but they are an important feature of the new measure upon which the Commission has been working. The existing directive does not apply to substances or foodstuffs containing anti-oxidants intended for export from the Community[9]. It does apply to substances and foodstuffs imported into the Community[10]. The directive has been amended on several occasions to revise the positive lists[11].

---

1.   Article 5.
2.   Article 6.
3.   Council Directive (EEC) 78/664, OJ L223 14.8.68 p30; Council Directive (EEC) 82/712, OJ L297 23.10.82 p31. For methods of analysis, see Council Directive (EEC) 81/712, OJ L257 10.9.81 p1, at Annexes I, II.
4.   Article 8(1)(a).
5.   Article 8.
6.   There are various exceptions with respect to disclosures involving mixtures; ibid., at Article 8(1)(d). No quantitative disclosures are required, but the percentage disclosure rules are more stringent than the general requirements in the 1978 labelling directive, as amended. Above at Chapter 3, para 3.3.1.
7.   Article 8(2), as amended.
8.   Article 9.
9.   Article 10(2). For the issue of export products, see below at Chapter 9, para 9.3.5.
10.   Article 10(1).
11.   Council Directive (EEC) 78/143, OJ L44 5.2.78 p18; Council Directive (EEC) 81/962, OJ L354 9.12.81 p22; Council Directive (EEC) 87/55, OJ L24 27.1.87 p1.

In 1987, the Scientific Committee for Foods re-evaluated the long-term safety implications of anti-oxidants[1]. Its report was stimulated in part by questions about the effects of butylated hydroxytoluene (BHT), but the committee also made a comprehensive reassessment of all anti-oxidants. The committee did not substantially alter its previous conclusions regarding the safety of anti-oxidants, but recommended further study of butylated hydroxyanisole (BHA)[2]. The committee did not find a basis for new concerns, but neither did it eliminate all of the existing safety questions.

With the assistance of the committee's report, the Commission prepared a draft Council directive in 1990 to revise the Community's rules for anti-oxidants, as well as its rules for preservatives and miscellaneous other additives[3]. The draft directive would be one of the supplementary measures to the framework additives directive. It would create new positive lists, harmonise conditions of use and, in some cases, establish maximum levels of use. The discretion formerly given to Member States regarding propyl gallate and other substances would be replaced by Community rules. The 1970 directive would be repealed.

5.8   Modified starches

Starches are carbohydrates found in such familiar foods as corn, potatoes, rice and tapioca[4]. They are widely used without modification in compound foodstuffs, but may also be modified chemically to alter their physical characteristics. Modification may, for example, improve their solubility, stability or texture[5]. As modified, starches may be used as thickeners, binders or stabilisers for desserts, sauces, and other fabricated foods[6]. Despite their commercial usefulness, modified starches have not been important subjects of regulatory controls. Nonetheless, the Food Additives and Contaminants Committee in Britain recommended controls as early as 1980, including a positive list. In the Community, the Commission proposed a Council directive regarding modified starches in 1985, but the proposal was never adopted[7]. The 1985 proposal has now been withdrawn, and there are as yet no

---

1.   *Reports of the Scientific Committee for Food*, Twenty-second Series, EUR 12535 EN (1990). The report was adopted in late 1987, but not published until early 1990.

2.   For a toxicological evaluation of BHA, see Proceedings of the 33rd Meeting of the Joint FAO/WHO Expert Committee on Food Additives, *Toxicological Evaluation of Certain Food Additives and Contaminants* p3 (1989). It has been denied that there is any scientific basis for banning BHA, BHT or propyl gallate. Daniel, "Phenolic Antioxidents", in R. Walker & E. Quattrucci, eds., *Nutritional and Toxicological Aspects of Food Processing* pp15, 20 (1988). In contrast, another commentator has termed their use "chemical roulette". E. Millstone, *Food Additives* p120 (1986).

3.   Above at para 5.4.

4.   R. Igoe, *Dictionary of Food Ingredients* p131 (2nd ed. 1989).

5.   Ibid., at p90. See also B. Fox & A. Cameron, *Food Science, Nutrition and Health* pp107-108 (5th ed. 1989); C. Catsberg & G. Kempen-van Dommelen, *Food Handbook* p60 (1990).

6.   R. Igoe, *Dictionary of Food Ingredients* p131 (2nd ed. 1989).

7.   COM(84) 726 final, OJ C31 1.2.85 p6.

Community rules directly applicable to modified starches[1]. Nonetheless, the 1985 proposal warrants description as an indication of one phase of the Commission's approach to such products.

The 1985 proposal defined such starches as products obtained by chemical treatments of edible starches, after those starches may have undergone physical or enzymatic treatment[2]. The measure provided a positive list of permissible modified starches, together with purity criteria[3]. The criteria included maximum content levels for arsenic, lead, cadmium, mercury, sulphur dioxide, and moisture. Member States would generally have been required to permit the marketing of products on the positive list, and to forbid all other modified starches[4]. Two products on the positive list would have been forbidden for use in foodstuffs intended specifically for infants and young children[5]. Seven others would have been limited to a level of 5 percent in such foods. The substances which would have been entirely prohibited in such foods were hydroxpropyl starch and hydroxpropyl distarch phosphate[6].

For a maximum period of three years, Member States would have been allowed to permit the use within their domestic markets of starches not included in the positive list[7]. Uses of those products would have been monitored by national authorities, and the products would have been required to carry a special labelling notice of their temporary status. Conversely, Member States could have temporarily suspended trade in products on the positive list, but only based upon evidence that the products could constitute a hazard to human health[8]. Any national suspensions would have been subject to review by the Community, which could have either overridden them or made corresponding changes in the Community's own rules.

Modified starches included on the positive list would also have been subject to special labelling rules[9]. Their labels would have been required to state "modified starch" and an EEC reference number, or the name of the particular starch[10]. They would also have included the words "for human consumption", or a more specific indication of their intended use. Labels would have disclosed net quantity, the date of manufacture or a lot number, and the name and address of the manufacturer, or of

---

1. For the withdrawal, see the Economist Intelligence Unit, European Trends, No. 2 (1990) at p20. For the Codex rules, see sec. 5.1, Codex Alimentarius (2nd ed. 1991).
2. COM(84) 726 final, OJ C31 2.1.85 p6, at Article 1.
3. Annex I contains the positive list. It includes such products as oxidised and bleached starch, acetylated starch, and monostarch phosphate. The purity criteria are in Annex II.
4. Articles 2(1), 2(2).
5. Article 3.
6. Annex 1.
7. Article 5(1).
8. Article 6.
9. Article 7.
10. Article 7(1)(a).

a seller established within the Community[1]. Some of this information could have been provided in accompanying commercial documents[2]. Rules for sampling and methods of analysis were to have been adopted through a committee procedure involving the Standing Committee for Foodstuffs[3].

In lieu of the 1985 proposal, the Commission has now proposed a new directive regarding many categories of additives, including some starches[4]. Modified starches are defined in the new proposal as they were in 1985, with the additional provision that they may be acid-thinned or bleached after modification[5]. Various starches would be included in the positive lists both of generally approved additives and of carriers[6]. At the same time, many starch products, including starches treated by acid, enzymes or physical processes, would not be treated as food additives[7].

5.9   Extraction solvents and other processing aids

Food processing techniques often require chemical products or other substances as adjuncts to the manufacturing process. They may facilitate extraction, dissolution or other steps in the manufacture or preparation of foodstuffs. They are not themselves food ingredients, but are instead designed to perform a technical function and thereafter to be eliminated from the final foodstuff[8]. Although residues are often left, they are intended to be minimal in quantity and significance. Accordingly, these substances are commonly described as "processing aids", rather than additives. Where residues are left, the distinction is one of degree. Where residues are excessive, they are usually described as contaminants.

The number and variety of processing aids have greatly increased as food processors have developed new products and new methods for the manufacture of existing products. Nonetheless, since processing aids are largely eliminated by good manufacturing practices from the products actually sold to consumers, they have received little attention from the Community's regulatory authorities. Hygienic and purity standards, together with manufacturing controls, have usually been thought sufficient to prevent substantial residues[9]. There were no Community rules

---

1.   Article 7(1)(b)-(e).
2.   Article 7(2).
3.   Articles 8, 9.
4.   For a more complete description of the draft proposal, see above at para 5.4.
5.   COM(92) 255 final (17 June 1992) at Article 1(2).
6.   Annexes I, V.
7.   Article 1(4)(d).
8.   The functions performed by processing aids are described by, for example, B. Fox & A. Cameron, *Food Science, Nutrition and Health* pp379-380 (5th ed. 1989). For an inventory of processing aids, see sec. 5.7, Codex Alimentarius (2nd ed. 1991).
9.   The Community demands adherence to good manufacturing practices, but does not define precisely what practices it endorses. For the definition used for extraction solvents, see below.

regarding processing aids until 1988, when the Council adopted a directive to harmonise national laws with respect to extraction solvents[1]. There are, however, many substances approved as additives but also used, partly or alternatively, as processing aids[2].

The 1989 directive is applicable to all extraction solvents intended for use in the production of human foodstuffs or food ingredients[3]. Extraction solvents are defined simply as substances used in an extraction procedure in food processing and intended to be removed, even if they result in unintentional or technically unavoidable residues[4]. The directive does not apply to solvents used in the production of vitamins or nutritional additives, except insofar as the additives are listed in an annex to the directive. The annex lists such products as defatted flours and cereal germs[5]. With respect to these products, the Member States must ensure that the additives cannot transfer dangerous levels of solvent residues to the foods in which they are used[6]. The directive was approved only after substantial debate, and one consequence was the creation of several national derogations[7]. In particular, the directive does not affect national laws relating to the use of methanol, propan-1-ol, propan-2-ol, and tricholoroethylene as extraction solvents[8]. The status of these substances is, however, to be reviewed by the Commission and the Scientific Committee for Food. For the first three substances, review is to occur in or after 1992. For the fourth, it is scheduled after 1996[9]. As described below, the Council has recently adopted an amendment to the 1988 directive which resolves some of these issues.

The directive's annex includes a positive list of permissible extraction solvents. There are also conditions of use and, in some instances, maximum residue limits. The first part of the annex includes propane, butane, butyl acetate, ethyl acetate, thanol, carbon dioxide, acetone, and nitrous oxide. They are approved for all uses, provided that good manufacturing practices are followed. A "good manufacturing practice" is one which results in the presence of residues only "in technically

---

For the rules in the United States, see 51 Fed. Reg. 22458 (1986). For an industry perspective, see, e.g., P.J. Fellows, *Food Processing Technology : Principles and Practice* (1988).

1. Council Directive (EEC) 88/344, OJ L157 24.6.88 p28. Britain previously had adopted rules regarding extraction solvents. See Solvents in Food Regulations 1967, SI 1967/1582; Solvents in Food (Amendment) Regulations 1980, SI 1980/1832. See also Food Additives and Contaminants Committee, *Report on the Review of Solvents in Foods* (1978). Solvents may be used in food processing for purposes other than extraction.
2. B. Fox & A. Cameron, *Food Science, Nutrition and Health* p379 (5th ed. 1989).
3. Council Directive (EEC) 88/344, above at Article 1(1).
4. Article 1(3)(b). A similar definition is provided by section 11(2)(1) of the 1974 German statute on foodstuffs and other products; *Gesetz ber den Verkehr mit Lebensmitteln* [1974] I BGBI. 1945.
5. Annex, Part II. Other examples are protein products and defatted soya products.
6. Article 1(1).
7. See, e.g., EIS, Europe Environment, No. 380 at IV-6 (4 Feb 1992).
8. Article 1(2).
9. Article 2(b).

unavoidable quantities presenting no danger to human health"[1]. The definition suggests, without expressly requiring, that "good" practices conform to the best existing technical standards, so as to reduce residues to the lowest possible levels. Those levels may alter as manufacturing techniques improve.

Part II of the annex places limitations upon the use of four solvents. Hexane, methyl acetate, ethylmethylketone, and dichloromethane are authorised only for designated purposes, and only subject to maximum residue limits[2]. For example, methyl acetate may be used to produce sugar from molasses, but only if there is a residue no greater than one mg/kg in the sugar. Part III of the annex allows the use of other solvents, provided they do not result in residues beyond specified maximum limits. It includes such solvents as diethyl ether and cyclohexane. Their maximum residue levels are generally one mg/kg, but may range from 0.1 to 2 mg/kg[3]. Eleven solvents included in the annex were designated for reconsideration within two years after the directive's adoption[4]. They include, for example, hexane, isobutane, and diethyl ether. The review was to be completed by mid-1990. Its results are reflected in the Council's new measure regarding solvents.

Member States are prohibited from restricting the marketing of foodstuffs whose processing has been in compliance with the directive[5]. Member States are, however, permitted temporarily to suspend trade in products if they have "detailed grounds" to believe human health might be endangered[6]. Here, as in other similar directives, no further description is offered of the necessary evidence. Conversely, Member States are prohibited from authorising any solvents not included in the positive lists[7]. Nor may they extend the permissible conditions of use[8]. Nonetheless, Member States may permit the use in their domestic markets of other substances to dilute or dissolve flavourings, or for the extraction of flavourings[9]. This derogation is subject to future Community rules regarding such substances. Member States may also continue to permit the use of ethanol, water to which substances regulating alkalinity or acidity have been added, and food substances which possess solvent properties[10]. Member States are required to take "all measures" to ensure that solvents satisfy various purity criteria. In particular, solvents may not contain a toxicologically dangerous amount of any substance, or

1.   Part I of the Annex, note 1.
2.   Annex, Part II. All of these are designated for reconsideration. Article 2(5).
3.   Annex, Part III.
4.   Article 2(5).
5.   Article 2(1).
6.   Article 5.
7.   Article 2(2).
8.   This does not, however, override the derogations for methanol and the other three solvents listed in Article 1(2).
9.   Article 2(3).
10.   Article 2(4). The article does not expressly describe the use of such substances as a national option, and they may in essence be intended as additions to the positive list.

more than one mg/kg of arsenic or lead[1]. Other purity criteria may be adopted by the Community through a committee procedure[2].

The 1988 directive also imposes labelling and disclosure requirements. Member States must ensure that solvents are not marketed unless their packagings or labels indicate their commercial name, which must be one of those included in the directive's annex[3]. Their labels must also indicate that the products are suitable in quality for the extraction of foods or food ingredients[4]. There must be a reference to the product's lot or batch; the name and address of the manufacturer or packer, or of a seller established within the Community; the net quantity expressed in units of volume; and any special storage conditions or conditions of use. The last four items may appear in trade documents supplied with or prior to the product's delivery[5]. With this exception, the required information generally must be provided in labelling in a language "easily understood by purchasers". Nonetheless, the information may be omitted from labels if other measures have been taken to inform purchasers[6]. Any labelling disclosures must be easily visible, clearly legible, and indelible. No more specific format requirements are provided[7].

The directive is applicable to solvents used for the processing of foods within the Community for consumption there. It also applies to solvents used in the production of foodstuffs or ingredients imported into the Community[8]. Presumably the directive encompasses imported products wherever the solvents were actually used. The directive is not, however, applicable to foodstuffs or solvents intended for export outside the Community[9]. Export products may, in other words, be produced using solvents which are forbidden by the Community, or may contain residues in excess of the Community's maximum limits.

As described above, certain of the directive's provisions are subject to revision based upon proposals from the Commission after consultations with the Scientific Committee for Food[10]. The questions to be reviewed include the continued authorisation of eleven specified solvents. They include all of the solvents listed in Parts II and III of the Annex, plus methyl-propane-2-01. In addition, the Commission and Scientific Committee are to consider whether the limitations upon solvent residues should apply to flavourings, rather than to foodstuffs which

1.   Article 3.
2.   Article 3(c). The procedure involves the Standing Committee for Foodstuffs; Article 6.
3.   Article 7(1).
4.   The reference to quality seems curious, unless it is intended to have the effect of a warranty. The word "quality" may mean technically suitable for the purpose.
5.   Article 7(2).
6.   Article 7(4). This same undefined option appears in other measures.
7.   Article 7(1).
8.   Article 8(1). No enforcement or inspection mechanism is prescribed with respect to imported products. For Community products, the general rules relating to official controls are applicable. For those, see below at Chapter 8, para 8.6.
9.   Article 8(2).
10.   Article 2(5).

include flavourings. Finally, they are to determine whether the national derogations for methanol and the other three solvents listed in Article 1(2) should continue. As described above, the reviews for three substances are to occur three years after the directive's adoption, and the fourth after seven years[1]. These issues were thought too sensitive to permit a committee procedure, and any amendments to the directive regarding them must be made through Article 100a of the Treaty. This requires the Council to act in co-operation with the Parliament[2].

In 1991, the Commission proposed new rules to resolve some of the questions left unanswered in 1988[3]. The proposal was largely an implementation of judgments reached by the Scientific Committee. Based upon the Scientific Committee's recommendations, the Commission proposed, for example, to withdraw its approval for decaffeination and to permit propan-2-ol only for designated uses. It would alter some residue limits and conditions of use. Further use of dioxane and 2-nitropropane would be disapproved. Apart from the temporary approval of other substances, the remaining issues regarding solvents would be deferred. In June 1992, the Council adopted most of the Commission's proposed changes.

1.   Article 2(6).
2.   Ibid. For a description of the process under Article 100a, see T. Hartley, *The Foundations of European Community Law* pp30-37 (2nd ed. 1988).
3.   COM(91) 502 final (9 Dec 1991).

CHAPTER 6 : MATERIALS AND ARTICLES INTENDED TO COME IN CONTACT WITH FOODSTUFFS

A major priority in the Community's food regulatory programme since 1985 has been the adoption of revised rules regarding materials and articles intended to come into contact with foodstuffs. Plastic films, bottles, tins and paperboard packaging are familiar examples of materials used to wrap, contain or transport foodstuffs. Metal machinery, plastic tubing and other equipment may also be used to process or manufacture foods. As many as 10,000 different substances may come in contact with foods during their processing, storage, transport or sale[1]. The principal concern arising from such materials is that their constituents, which generally are not approved for use as food additives, may be transferred to the foods with which they are in contact[2]. In some instances, hazards to human health could result[3]. Paper products may, for example, be impregnated with formaldehyde compounds. Plastic products may include toxic compounds used as antioxidants, catalysts or stabilisers to protect them from discoloration, or to increase their flexibility. Some of these substances are potentially harmful. The first prohibitions of packaging materials began as early as 1912, and materials intended to come into contact with foodstuffs have been the subject of Community legislation since 1976[4]. As described below, the Community's early directives were inadequate and incomplete. More comprehensive rules are now in progress, but much important work remains uncompleted.

In December 1988, the Council adopted a new framework directive for contact materials[5]. Early in 1990 it added an ancillary directive regarding most plastic materials[6]. The latter includes temporary and permanent positive lists of approved plastic materials. The lists are, however, still incomplete and the materials which are temporarily approved must all be reviewed before permanent authorisations can be granted. The Commission has since adopted amendments to

---

1. Many may be found in the air to which foods are exposed at every stage prior to consumption. For a review of FDA's efforts to control contamination, see P. Hutt & R. Merrill, *Food and Drug Law, Cases and Materials* pp295-297 (2nd ed. 1991). Related efforts have been the subject of criticism by the General Accounting Office. *Further Federal Action Needed to Detect and Control Environmental Contamination of Food*, CED-81-19 (1980).
2. On the other hand, the Codex Commission has concluded that packaging migration does not warrant a high priority by the Joint Expert Committee on Food Additives; *Report of the Nineteenth Session of the Codex Alimentarius Commission* p14 (1991).
3. B. Fox & A. Cameron, *Food Science, Nutrition and Health* pp375-376 (5th ed. 1989); Lox & Pascat, "Echanges entre le produit alimentaire et son emballage: migration," in G. Bureau & J-L Multon, eds., *L'Emballage des Denrées Alimentaires de Grande Consommation* pp57-75 (1989).
4. J. Botrel, *L'Emballage : Environment socio-economique et juridique* p61 (1991).
5. Below at para 6.1.
6. Below at para 6.2.

the 1990 directive. In 1992, Commission adopted revised rules for regenerated cellulose film[1]. The 1988 framework directive contemplates other ancillary directives regarding other contact materials, but they have not yet formally appeared. All other contact materials and articles are now regulated at the Community level, if at all, only by directives adopted prior to 1985.

In the view of some commentators, the situation is no better in the United States. FDA has been unable to provide clear rules regarding packaging and other contact materials, and its failure to do so has caused considerable confusion[2]. FDA's "inscrutable" attitudes have produced uncertainty and delays[3]. Whatever the deficiencies of the Community's rules, they are at least a systematic effort to provide greater clarity than any FDA has been able to offer. Indeed, the Community may sometimes go too far in its pursuit of certainty. For example, the preparation of the new plastics positive lists, and particularly the process of deciding which substances on the temporary list should be permanently authorised, has caused lengthy regulatory delays and threatens to create impediments to innovation[4]. Other new positive lists regarding other categories of contact materials could have similar results.

In a separate area, American and Canadian rules may offer important advantages. FDA's approvals of packaging materials must take into account whether those materials may result in adverse environmental consequences. Each new material must be the subject of an environmental impact analysis[5]. An environmental assessment must also form part of the reviews of proposed new food additives. Similar arrangements exist in Canada[6]. These rules do not eliminate the environmental problems created by food packaging, but they at least compel examinations of the relevant issues. If nothing more, they are reminders of regulatory goals. The Community is now beginning to address the problems of

---

1. Below at para 6.3.
2. For a sceptical review of FDA's rules, see Heckman, "Fathoming Food Packaging Regulation : A Guide to Independent Industry Action", 42 Food D.C.L.J. 38 (1987).
3. Ibid., at p38. See also Heckman, "Closing in on Zero", 45 Food D.C.L.J. 599 (1990). For a judicial decision that constituents migrating from pottery foodware must be regulated under US law as additives, see *United States v Articles of Food Consisting of Pottery* p370 F. Supp. 371 (E. D. Mich. 1974). For an analysis of the applicability of the additive rules to acrylonitrile copolymer used to manufacture plastic beverage bottles, see *Monsanto Co. v Kennedy* 613 F.2d 947 (D.C. Cir. 1979). For FDA's approval process, see Heckman, "To File or Not to File: Coming to Terms with the Indirect Additive Petition Process", 46 Food D.C. L.J. 441 (1991).
4. Below at para 6.2. US producers have complained that the framework directive itself may prove discriminatory and unduly restrictive. USITC, *The Effects of Greater Economic Integration within the European Community on the United States* pp6-64 (1989). It is said that the rules may have a "major impact" upon US producers; USITC, Second Report 4-57 (1990).
5. Hoffmann & Nowell, "The FDA's Environmental Impact Analysis Requirements: Food Packaging and Solid Waste Management", 45 Food D.C.L.J. 615 (1990).
6. In Canada, all major changes in policy must be preceded by a "socioeconomic impact statement", which is available for public scrutiny and comment; Health Protection Branch, *Health Protection and Food Laws* p11 (4th ed. 1985).

packaging waste, but it has not yet required environmental factors to be included in its appraisals of new packaging materials and additives[1]. Its failure to do so does not inevitably produce results less sensitive to environmental considerations, but it increases the risk that environmental interests may be discounted or ignored.

6.1   The framework directives

The Community's framework directive for food contact materials is its second effort to address the health and safety issues which may arise from such articles. The first effort was made in 1976, when the Council adopted a directive to approximate national laws regarding contact materials[2]. The purpose of the 1976 directive was to ensure that contact materials and articles do not transfer constituents to foodstuffs in quantities which could endanger human health[3]. The directive did not itself provide all of the necessary rules and standards, but instead established a framework of general principles to guide the preparation of more detailed requirements. Those requirements were to be embodied in more specific directives relating to particular categories of contact materials. The 1976 directive imposed labelling and disclosure obligations, but they were subject to supplementation by the ancillary directives[4]. In addition, all contact materials were required to be manufactured in conformity with good manufacturing practice[5]. With these exceptions, most regulatory standards were deferred. The ancillary directives were expected to provide compositional standards, migration limits and other requirements[6]. They were, "if possible and if necessary", to include positive lists, purity standards, and special conditions of use[7].

The Council subsequently adopted several more specific directives regarding particular products and issues. One measure adopted a mandatory symbol to identify food contact materials[8]. Others regulated the use of vinyl chloride, monomer[9], ceramic articles[10], migration limits for plastic materials and articles[11]

---

1.   Snodin, "Sweeteners: Statutory Aspects", in S. Marie & J. Piggott, eds., *Handbook of Sweeteners* p281 (1991).
2.   Council Directive (EEC) 76/893, OJ L340 9.12.76 p19. The directive was repealed by Council Directive (EEC) 89/109, OJ L40 11.2.89 p38 at Article 10(1).
3.   Council Directive (EEC) 76/893, above at Article 2.
4.   Article 7.
5.   Article 2.
6.   Article 3.
7.   Article 2.
8.   Commission Directive (EEC) 80/590, OJ L151 196.80 p21.
9.   Council Directive (EEC) 78/142, OJ L44 15.2 78 p15. The directive limited the level of vinyl chloride in contact materials to one mg/kg (Annex I), forbade its migration to foodstuffs in any detectable level (Article 2), provided for the creation of methods of analysis (Article 3), and contemplated further steps after additional scientific information was received (Article 4). For Codex guideline levels, see *Codex Alimentarius* sec. 6.3 (2d ed. 1991).
10.   Council Directive (EEC) 84/500, OJ L277 20.10.84 p12. The directive provided migration limits for lead and cadmium for cooking ware and other ceramic articles (Article 2), contemplated (but did not establish) other measures regarding articles with which the mouth is intended to

regenerated cellulose film[1], and simulants for testing the migration of constituents of plastic materials[2]. The Commission later adopted rules regarding methods of analysis to ensure compliance with these directives[3]. Even in combination, these measures did not provide comprehensive rules for all food contact materials. They did, however, represent a substantial effort to address the principal issues.

They were supplemented by other measures regarding the manufacture, composition, or use of food contact materials. Many relate to food packaging[4]. For example, the Council has sought to reduce the energy and raw materials consumed by the manufacture of packaging materials. In 1975, it adopted a directive regarding waste recycling, and in 1985 added rules specifically for the recycling of containers of liquids for human consumption[5]. Several Member States have adopted their own recycling rules, some of which are quite stringent. The Commission is now considering new measures in this area, including repeal of the 1985 directive and its replacement by broad new restrictions upon the disposal of packaging waste. These questions are described below[6].

The 1976 contact materials directive became the subject of increasing dissatisfaction. Nonetheless, the Council argued in 1988 that the directive still represented an appropriate method of approach, and that only consolidation and greater clarity were needed[7]. Some of the difficulties arose from the number and

come into contact (Article 4), and provided "basic rules" for determining lead and cadmium migration (Annex I).

11. Council Directive (EEC) 82/711, OJ L297 23.10.82 p26. The directive applied to most materials and articles consisting exclusively of plastic (Article 1) and provided basic rules for measuring migration (Annex), but authorised the domestic use of other testing methods where Member States found the basic rules to be unsuitable (Article 3). For new rules regarding plastics, see Commission Directive (EEC) 90/128, OJ L75 21.3.90 p19; OJ L349 13.12.90 p26.

1. Council Directive (EEC) 83/229, OJ L123 11.5.83 p31. The directive created a positive list of permissible uses for most regenerated cellulose films and established maximum migration limits. It also prohibited contact between foods and the printed surfaces of such films (Article 3), and permitted Member States to forbid the use of certain substances in contact with foodstuffs containing fat (Article 4). See also Council Directive (EEC) 86/388, OJ L228 14.8.86 p32 (regarding a proposed German ban on the use of a film softener). The Commission has since adopted other revisions; below at Chapter 6, para 6.3.

2. Council Directive (EEC) 85/572, OJ L372 31.12.85 p14. The directive provided a positive list of simulants (Article 1 and the Annex), but permitted variations where "appropriate" (Article 2).

3. See, e.g., Commission Directive (EEC) 80/766, OJ L213 16.8.80 p42; Commission Directive (EEC) 81/432, OJ L167 24.6.81 p6. Both relate to methods of analyses for the official control of vinyl chloride.

4. These same issues have become important elsewhere in the world. In the United States, they are addressed by FDA partly under the National Environmental Protection Act, P.L. No. 91-190, 83 Stat. 852 (1970), codified at 42 U.S.C. sec. 4321-4361 (1982). See Hoffmann & Nowell, "The Food and Drug Administration's Environmental Impact Analysis Requirements : Food Packaging and Solid Waste Management", 45 Food D.C.L.J. 615 (1990).

5. Council Directive (EEC) 85/339, OJ L176 6.7.85 p18. It was designed to help implement Council Directive (EEC) 75/442, OJ L194 25.7.75 p39, regarding the prevention, recycling and processing of all types of waste. The 1975 directive was in turn an implementation of Community action programmes for the environment, which began as early as 1973; OJ C112 20.12.73 p1.

6. Below at Chapter 7, para 7.2.

7. See Council Directive (EEC) 89/109, OJ L40 11.2.89 p38; OJ L347 p37 (No. 28, 1989), at the first and fourth recital of the preamble.

variety of contact materials. Other problems were caused by the rapidity with which the packaging industry developed new or modified products[1]. Technical changes in packaging have generally outpaced the regulations intended to control them[2]. A more important source of dissatisfaction was the increasing scientific evidence that migrations of the constituents of some contact materials may create hazards for human health. Much of the new evidence related to plastic containers and films. The likelihood of migration did not surprise scientists, but it had not been fully appreciated by regulators and consumer groups[3]. These problems did not invalidate the 1976 directive, but together they confirmed that the Community's food contact measures warranted reconsideration.

Nonetheless, it was not until December 1988 that the Council succeeded in adopting a new framework directive[4]. The 1988 directive applies to most materials and articles which are intended to be, or actually are, brought into contact with foodstuffs intended for human consumption[5]. There are, however, significant exceptions. Covering or coating substances which may be consumed with foodstuffs are excluded. Antiques are also excluded[6]. "Antiques" are not defined, and this could conceivably prove an important basis for avoiding the directive's limitations. Items intended for export outside the Community are also excluded[7]. The directive generally applies to materials and articles placed in contact with water intended for human consumption, but not to fixed water supply equipment[8].

The 1988 directive does not establish specific migration limits for contact materials. Instead, it creates a series of principles to guide the formulation of migration limits. In particular, contact materials are permissible only if they do not, under "normal or foreseeable conditions of use", transfer their constituents to foodstuffs in undesirable quantities. Those quantities are not given any precise definition. They are described simply as migration levels which could endanger

---

1. The packaging industry has been one of the most rapidly changing and innovative of all the industrial sectors relating to foods. See, e.g., Rees, "Introduction," in J. Rees & J. Bettison, eds., *Processing and Packaging of Heat Preserved Foods* pp1,5 (1991); Griffin, "Retortable Plastic Packaging", in F. Paine, ed., *Modern Processing, Packing and Distribution Systems for Food* pp1-19 (1987); Flory, "Packaging for Consumer Convenience", ibid. at pp146-160.
2. See, e.g., Willhoft, "Packaging for Preservation of Snack Food", in R. Gordon Booth, ed., *Snack Food* pp349, 365 (1990); de Leiris, "Les films plastiques," in G. Bureau & J-L Multon, eds., *L'Emballage des Denrées Alimentaires de Grande Consommation* p274 (1989).
3. An American judge has observed, citing C.P. Snow, that the inevitability of migration from contact materials is an example of those many facts known to virtually all scientists and unfamiliar to virtually all laymen; *Monsanto Co. v Kennedy*, 613 F.2d 947 (D.C. Cir. 1979).
4. Council Directive (EEC) 89/109, above. For Britain, see Materials and Articles in Contact with Food Regulations 1987, SI 1987/1523. For Spain, see Crown Decree 397/1990, B.O.E. No. 29 p112 (16 March 1990).
5. Council Directive (EEC) 89/109, at Article 1(1).
6. Article 1(3).
7. Article 12. For the issues created by the inapplicability of safety standards to export products, see below at Chapter 9, para 9.3.5.
8. Article 1(2). The directive does not make clear whether "fixed" equipment includes such ancillary items as gaskets and valves. But see Commission Directive (EEC) 90/128, OJ L75 21.3.90 p19 at Article 2. The equipment may be public or private in ownership.

human health or cause either an "unacceptable" change in a food's composition or a deterioration of its organoleptic characteristics[1]. Consistent with the 1976 directive, contact materials must be produced in accordance with good manufacturing practices. Those practices are not, however, described or specified. Whatever their practical implications these broad and undefined principles are intended simply as statements of regulatory policy. Their role is to guide the formulation of more specific standards embodied in subsequent directives relating to particular contact materials. They were also expected to quiet public and parliamentary concerns regarding contact materials.

The 1988 directive contemplates ancillary measures addressed to several categories of contact materials[2]. The Community has already adopted rules relating to many plastic materials[3] and regenerated cellulose film[4]. The 1988 directive is also to be supplemented by measures relating to textiles, paper, waxes, glass, and rubber[5]. These materials may be used in various combinations, and at least some of the combinations may also be the subject of new rules[6]. The ancillary directives are to include positive lists, purity standards, conditions of use, and other requirements[7].

Member States may supplement these measures with temporary national authorisations of additional contact materials[8]. The temporary approvals may be valid for as long as two years, but only if the materials are controlled by special regulatory requirements under national law. Their packages must be distinctively marked, and they must be subject to regular inspections by national authorities[9]. A notice of each national authorisation must be given to the Commission, and all the authorisations must be reviewed by the Scientific Committee for Food. In addition, Member States may temporarily suspend authorisations to use particular substances based upon information which has emerged after the substance's approval by the Community. Notice must be given to the Community, and the issues may be referred to the Scientific Committee for evaluation.

The directive imposes labelling requirements for materials marketed before they are actually in contact with foodstuffs. They must, however, ultimately be

---

1.   Article 2. No quantitative limits are offered to define "unacceptable" changes in food composition.
2.   Those ancillary directives are evidently not intended to be completed until well after 1992. Fuster, "The Implementation of the EC Commission's White Paper of 1985," 1 World Food Reg. Rev. 10 (Oct 1991).
3.   Below at para 6.2.
4.   Below at para 6.3.
5.   Council Directive (EEC) 89/109, above at Article 3(1) and Annex I. A committee procedure involving the Standing Committee for Foodstuffs is to be used. Articles 3(2), 8, 9.
6.   Article 3(1).
7.   Article 3(3).
8.   Articles 4, 5.
9.   Article 4.

intended to have contact with foods[1]. For example, the directive's requirements are applicable to plastic films or containers sold to consumers, distributors or processors for later use in wrapping or transporting foods. The labels of these products must include the words "for food use", or some symbol or indication of their intended uses[2]. They must also disclose any special conditions of use. Finally, they must disclose the name or trade name and address, the registered office, or the registered trade mark of the manufacturer or processor, or of a seller established in the Community. This offers more options for identifying a product's supplier than are permitted, for example, under the 1978 labelling directive. There is, however, an exception to these requirements. The requirement that labels must state "for food use" does not apply to materials which "by their nature" are intended to come into contact with foodstuffs[3].

These disclosures must be stated conspicuously, legibly and indelibly on the product's package. Consistent with the Community's practice, there are no specific instructions regarding the size, format or placement of the mandatory disclosures[4]. The requisite information must be provided in a language easily understood by purchasers, unless the purchaser has been adequately informed by other means[5]. At retail, the information must be provided on the materials, their packages or labels. Alternatively, they may be made through a notice posted in the "immediate vicinity" of the materials. A notice may, however, only be used if packaging disclosures are not technically feasible[6]. The directive offers no further guidance regarding the nature or positioning of the notice. Presumably it must be posted near the shelving location of the product, or perhaps where the article would be paid for. Finally, the directive provides that, at any marketing stage prior to retail, the information may be provided in accompanying documents, rather than on labelling or packaging.

6.2   Plastic materials and articles

The most controversial of the issues surrounding contact materials have involved plastics. In part, the issues arise from the increasing commercial significance of plastic films and containers. Many of the foodstuffs on grocery shelves are now wrapped in plastic film or contained in plastic bags, boxes or bottles. Many products sold by mass caterers are packaged in similar materials. Consumers now frequently store foodstuffs in their homes in plastic films or containers. Many foodstuffs are placed in contact with plastic materials prior to their consumption, and the

---

1.   Article 6.
2.   Article 6(1).
3.   Article 6(3).
4.   Article 6(2).
5.   Article 6(6). This undefined exception is found in several other directives.
6.   Article 6(2).

exposure may have persisted over periods of weeks or even months. The polymers used for packaging materials are generally not toxic, but more hazardous substances may be added to alter their properties[1]. Other substances may, for example, be included in plastic films to prevent discoloration or increase flexibility. Few, if any, of those additional substances are approved as food additives.

Much of the controversy about plastic products arose in the early 1980's. Researchers in the United States reported that high dosages of a substance used in the production of plastic films caused carcinogenic effects in rats[2]. Similar fears were soon expressed about other substances used for the production of films. The significance and reliability of these findings were widely debated. In Britain, a review by a scientific advisory committee concluded that any hazard is remote[3]. Nonetheless, there was general agreement that the question warranted continuing scientific scrutiny and at least rudimentary precautions. In Canada, for example, rules were adopted limiting the kinds and levels of stabilisers used to manufacture polyvinyl chloride films for food[4]. In Britain, a special advisory committee has conducted two reviews of the potential hazards[5]. It sought to calculate the probable intake of plastic constituents in an "average" diet, and recommended precautionary measures to minimise the risks to human safety[6]. The committee's recommendations included labelling to alert consumers to the possible risks, as well as a prohibition against the use of such films to wrap foods with a high fat content[7]. Cheeses are a common example. In addition, the committee recommended that any substance proposed for use in food packaging which might result in any appreciable human intake should not be permitted until appropriate testing and evaluations have been conducted[8]. The views of the British committee were generally supported by two reports of the Community's Scientific Committee for Food[9].

1. For a general discussion of the properties and problems of plastic materials, see B. Fox & A. Cameron, *Food Science, Nutrition and Health* pp375-376 (5th ed. 1989); P.J. Fellows, *Food Processing Technology: Principles and Practice* pp421-428 (1988).
2. *Plasticisers: Continuing Surveillance*, Report of the Steering Group on Food Surveillance, Subgroup on Plasticisers of the Working Party on Chemical Contaminants, Food Surveillance Paper No. 30 (1990) at p3.
3. The issues were reviewed by Britain's Committee on Toxicity of Chemicals in Food, Consumer Products and the Environment ("COT").
4. Health Protection Branch, *Health Protection and Food Laws* p80 (4th ed. 1985).
5. The first report was in 1987, and the second in 1990; *Plasticisers: Continuing Surveillance* (1990) at 1.
6. In 1990, the British advisory committee found that reformulations of some plastic films had led to significant reductions in the maximum intakes of some constituents, based upon an average presumed diet; *Plasticisers: Continuing Surveillance* (1990) at p22.
7. Ibid., at p2. These recommendations were endorsed by COT and the Food Advisory Committee; ibid., at pp32-33. Some labelling already exists in Britain for DEHA films based upon an industry agreement, but the committee urged its extension to all plastic films. The Food Advisory Committee also urged clear instructions for the use of such films.
8. Ibid., at p2.
9. *Reports of the Scientific Committee for Food*, Nineteenth Series, EUR 11322 (1988); Twentieth Series, EUR 11558 (1989).

It became apparent that the Community's rules for the regulation of plastic contact materials, most of which antedated these events, warranted reconsideration. Early in 1990, the Commission adopted a new directive to harmonise national laws regarding plastic materials intended to come into contact with foodstuffs[1]. The directive is the first of the ancillary measures contemplated by the framework directive for food contact materials[2]. It does not expressly override the Community's earlier measures regarding vinyl chloride monomer, migration limits for plastic materials, regenerated cellulose film, and simulants for testing the migration of plastic constituents. To the contrary, the 1990 directive relies upon provisions of the 1982 directive regarding migration limits[3]. The Commission emphasised that the directive was based upon an agreement with the Scientific Committee[4].

The 1990 directive is applicable to most plastic materials and mixtures of plastics intended to come into contact with foodstuffs[5]. This includes plastic packaging, kitchen and eating utensils, and production equipment. There are, however, significant exceptions. The directive does not apply to materials or articles composed of two or more layers, one or more of which is not exclusively plastic. This is true even if the layer which actually comes into contact with food is plastic[6]. This is subject to further action by the Commission, on the basis that composite materials require special rules[7]. The 1990 directive also does not apply to plastics used to manufacture coatings, epoxy resins, adhesives and inks[8]. Although the directive does not expressly provide for their adoption, such materials will evidently be the subject of special rules.

The directive prescribes an overall migration limit for the plastic materials to which it is applicable. In most instances, this is 10mg per square decimetre of surface area. In other cases, it may reach 60 mg/kg[9]. The directive also includes

---

1. Commission Directive (EEC) 90/128, OJ L75 21.3.90 p19. For corrigenda, see OJ L249 13.12.90 p26. "Plastics" are generally defined as organic macromolecular compounds obtained by various processes. They include silicones and other similar macromolecular compounds. Article 1(3).
2. Article 1(1). As such, it was adopted by the Commission through use of a simplified committee procedure.
3. See, e.g., Commission Directive (EEC) 90/128, above at Articles 2(2), 3(2)(c), 5. The 1982 directive is described above.
4. Commission Directive (EEC) 90/128, above at the twelfth recital of the preamble.
5. Article 1(2). The directive does not reiterate all of the various exclusions found in the framework directive for contact materials. Presumably the omitted provisions were thought inapplicable to plastics.
6. Article 1(4). This same exception was found in Council Directive (EEC) 82/711, above at Article 1(4).
7. Commission Directive (EEC) 90/128, above at Article 1(4).
8. Article 3(5). Such materials are not forbidden by the directive, although they are not included in its two positive lists.
9. Article 2. Special migration rules also exist for containers, caps, gaskets and stoppers.

rules for verification of compliance with the limits[1]. In addition to migration limits, the directive includes a positive list of monomers authorised for the manufacture of food contact plastics[2]. The list is divided between monomers permanently authorised for use, and those authorised only provisionally. The latter list includes monomers for which the available migration and toxicity data are insufficient to permit the Scientific Committee to confirm their safety[3]. The Commission's initial goal was to complete the review of the substances on the temporary list by early 1993. Those approved will be added to the list of permanent authorisations.

Under the present rules, any monomer not included on the permanent list by January 1993 will thereafter be banned for commercial use[4]. This leaves open the question of a new product not developed, or at least not authorised, by 1993. The directive would evidently require such a product to be authorised, if at all, only by a new directive. This would involve all the delays which attend the Community's legislative process, as well as subsequent transpositions into twelve sets of national laws. The situation is complicated by the fact that no specific arrangements have been made for additions to the provisional list[5]. It is unlikely that the Commission supposed that packaging technology would remain static, but its silence regarding new products leaves the situation in an unfortunate state of uncertainty. Although decisions regarding transfers to the permanent list from the temporary list must currently be made by January 1993, the Commission permitted itself a measure of flexibility. Until January 1992, it could elect to extend the 1993 deadline[6]. Late in 1991, the Commission drafted amendments to the 1990 directive to resolve some of the issues[7]. The proposal revised the provisional list in Annex II of the 1990 directive to delete some substances, add others, move others to the permanent list, and amend the restrictions on still others. It postponed the 1993 deadline for transfers until 1997, but again permitted further delays in "justified" cases. In May 1992, the Commission adopted the proposal as its own directive[8].

---

1.   Article 5. Verification is to occur in accordance with Council Directive (EEC) 82/711, above, and Council Directive (EEC) 85/572, above. Provisions for confirming compliance are also included in Annex I of the plastics directive itself.
2.   Article 3(1).
3.   Annex II, Sections A, B.
4.   Article 3(4).
5.   No limitation on the list's content is expressly stated in the directive, but neither is there an express method for supplementing it, except insofar as this may be implicit in the fact that the directive states that both lists omit certain categories of products; Article 3(5). There is, however, a general reference to the provision for "adaptations" under Article 4 of Council Directive (EEC) 82/711, above. Article 4 of the 1982 directive recites simply that adaptations are to be made in light of progress in scientific and technical knowledge. It is, in other words, a promise and not a procedure.
6.   Article 3(4).
7.   Various versions of the draft proposal were prepared. The version described here is III/3274/91-Rev.1.
8.   Commission Directive (EEC) 92/39, OJ L168 23.6.92 p21.

The 1990 directive's labelling and disclosure requirements are essentially those imposed by the framework directive for contact materials[1]. For sales at retail, the required disclosures must be made either in labelling or on the product's packaging[2]. If this is not feasible, a suitable notice may suffice. At all marketing stages other than at retail, the disclosures may again be made in labelling or on packaging, but they may alternatively be set forth in a written declaration which accompanies the product. In both situations, the product must be labelled to declare its intended use with foodstuffs, unless its "nature" already makes this plain.

When the 1990 directive was adopted, the Commission acknowledged that more than one-half of all the plastic materials now authorised by national laws had still not been approved by the Community[3]. A Commission spokesman complained that the information regarding those materials was insufficient to permit their approval, and urged the prompt submission of more adequate toxicological data[4]. The problem was by no means new. As early as 1986, the Scientific Committee informed the Commission that additional data were needed regarding many plastic substances[5]. Whatever the reasons for this continuing problem, it will certainly prolong the approval process for many plastic materials. The difficulties will increase as new or modified plastic materials are developed[6].

6.3   Regenerated cellulose film

As described above, the Community adopted rules in 1983 for regenerated cellulose film intended to come into contact with foodstuffs[7]. In early 1992, the Commission amended the rules to conform them to the 1989 framework for contact materials and take account of recent scientific research[8]. Among other changes, the new directive establishes maximum permissible levels for the use of phthalic esters and authorises additional substances for the manufacture of cellulose films.

---

1.   Article 6(1).
2.   For a description of the labelling and disclosure requirements of the framework directive for contact materials, see above at para 6.1.
3.   *Financial Times* p4 (27 Feb 1990).
4.   Nonetheless, the Commission averred that the plastics directive was the result of "close consultation with industrial and consumer organisations"; ibid.
5.   *Reports of the Scientific Committee for Food*, Nineteenth Series, EUR 11558 (1987) at p3. The advice was provided to the Commission in 1986, but not published until the following year.
6.   DG III has drafted guidelines for applicants seeking approval for use of a substance in plastic contact materials. III/1025/91 (1 Aug 1991).
7.   Council Directive (EEC) 83/229, OJ L123 11.5.83 p31.
8.   Commission Directive (EEC) 92/15, OJ L102 16.4.92 p44.

CHAPTER 7 : THE VERTICAL DIRECTIVES

Despite the Community's change in regulatory direction in 1985, important areas of its food policies are still governed by vertical rules[1]. Agricultural commodities and unprocessed foods are, for example, regulated principally through a vertical approach. In addition, many compositional and other vertical rules adopted prior to 1985 are still in force. They include directives relating to cocoa and chocolate products, certain sugars, honey, fruit juices, dehydrated or preserved milk, erucic acid in oils and fats, coffee and chicory extracts, mineral waters, and fruit jams and jellies. With the exception of the erucic acid directive, which was the result of suspected hazards to human health, these are quite literally recipe laws. They control every important aspect of the names, composition, manufacture, labelling, and even package sizes of the products. Rather than standards, they prescribe formulae[2].

The Community generally abandoned the development of compositional standards in 1985, but important exceptions continue to appear. Yellow fats and minced meats are among the disparate products for which vertical rules have been adopted or proposed since 1985. In addition, none of the vertical directives listed above has been designated by the Commission for rescission or replacement[3]. In a categorisation of the Community's rules in 1991, the Commission grouped the recipe laws with several other directives, some of them sectorial in nature[4]. Apart from the sectorial directives, the Commission's list included measures relating to caseins and caseinates, spirit drinks, and aromatised wines. The rules relating to alcoholic beverages are particularly voluminous and complex, but the principal rules are identified below. The Commission also included quick-frozen and irradiated foods in the same category, although the former are subject to a relatively recent measure

---

1.   For the distinctions between vertical and other forms of rulemaking, see above at Chapter 2, para 2.4.

2.   There are many similar national rules. In Britain, for example, there are compositional standards for more than 20 product categories, including bread, cheese, cream, curry powder, ice cream and margarine. S. Fallows, *Food Legislative System of the UK* pp20-21 (1988). Some have now been abandoned. The US analogues are food standards of identity, of which FDA has adopted some hundreds pursuant to 21 USC. sec. 341 (1982). For them, see 21 C.F.R. part 130 (1991). The approach was generally abandoned by FDA in the 1970's. US rules for non-standardised products are set forth in 21 C.F.R. part 102 (1991). The latter were approved in principle, without a ruling as to their actual effectiveness, in *Federation of Homemakers v Schmidt*, 385 F. Supp. 362, 366 (D.D.C. 1974). Canada also has compositional or identity standards for some 300 products; Health Protection Branch, *Health Protection and Food Laws* p25 (4th ed. 1985).

3.   EC Commission, Background Report on European Community Food Legislation p4 (6 Feb 1991).

4.   The Commission has stated simply that these directives will "remain in force until replaced", without any deadline. EC Commission, Background Report on European Community Food Legislation p4 (6 Feb 1991).

and the latter have still not been authorised on a Community basis. Both are sectorial issues, and as such are described in an earlier chapter[1].

Apart from the legislation described above, the Community has adopted or proposed numerous measures which, although usually not classified with its food regulations, are essentially vertical foodstuff rules. Many are designed to regulate the Community's markets for raw or semi-processed agricultural products[2]. For example, the Council has adopted extensive rules for the common organisation of the Community's market in oils and fats[3]. They include an array of subsidies and controls intended to benefit the Community's farmers. As part of those rules, the Community has established compositional and processing standards for oils and fats, including different kinds of olive oil. The rules for olive oil define the organoleptic properties of "extra virgin" and other forms of oil, prepared with assistance from the International Olive Oil Council[4]. There are similar rules for many other agricultural products. It would be impractical to describe them all, but an illustrative account is provided below of the Community's principal rules regarding meats and meat preparations.

7.1   Cocoa and chocolate products

The earliest of the Community's recipe laws was adopted in 1973, and relates to cocoa and chocolate products intended for human consumption[5]. The chocolate directive includes all the elements which have become characteristic of the Community's vertical measures. It begins by defining various product names, and by establishing compositional and product specifications which must be satisfied if a producer is to use those names[6]. For example, "cocoa powder" is defined as a powder obtained by mechanical processes from cocoa press cake. The latter is itself separately defined. Cocoa powder must contain at least 20 per cent cocoa butter and not more than nine per cent of water[7]. There are similar specifications for such products as chocolate, plain chocolate, white chocolate, milk chocolate, and gianduja.

---

1.   Above at Chapter 4, paras 4.2, 4.3.
2.   Above at Chapter 2, para 2,2.2.
3.   Council Regulation (EEC) 136/66, OJ 172 p3025 (30 Sept 1966).   The regulation has been repeatedly amended.
4.   Council Regulation (EEC) 356/92, OJ L39 15.2.92 p1. See also Commission Regulation (EEC) 3472/85, OJ L333 10.12.85 p5; Commission Regulation (EEC) 2677/85, OJ L254 25.9.85 25.9.85 p5; Commission Regulation (EEC) 2568/91, OJ L248 5.9.91 p1; Commission Regulation (EEC) 1008/92, OJ L106 24.4.92 p12; Commission Regulation (EEC) 1996/92, OJ L199 18.7.92 p18. For their interpretation, see Cases C-161/90, 162/90 *Petruzzi v AIPO* (Transcript) 10 October 1991, upon referral from the Pretura di Lecce.
5.   Council Directive (EEC) 73/241, OJ L228 16.8.73 p23.
6.   Article 3 and Annex I(1).
7.   Annex I, para 1.8.

Only products which satisfy the directive's specifications may be sold under its prescribed names, and the labels of all products which satisfy them must bear those names. Member States were originally permitted to authorise various other names, but most of those exceptions have now expired[1]. The exceptions are now applicable only in Italy, Ireland and the United Kingdom[2]. Nonetheless, the directive continues to permit the supplemental use of local customary names if they cannot be confused with the names specified in the directive[3]. Brand and trade names are not forbidden, but they must be used in conjunction with the names demanded by the directive. They cannot be used as substitutes.

These rules are supplemented by other product specifications. For example, the directive requires the use of sound and wholesome cocoa beans, and forbids the use of shells or residual products[4]. It contemplates the adoption of purity criteria and a positive list of permissible solvents, but does not itself provide such rules[5]. No expressly applicable rules have subsequently appeared. Until they do, the only solvents which may be used in the manufacture of cocoa and chocolate products are Essence B (which is petroleum spirit 60/75) and any authorised by Member States for products marketed within their own territories[6].

One compositional issue has been left unresolved by the directive. At the time of its adoption, the directive allowed Britain, Ireland and Denmark to permit the sale within their own territories of chocolate products containing vegetable fats. Those products could not, however, be sold in other Member States under the name "chocolate". The Commission sought to authorise the use of vegetable fats throughout the Community in 1986, but its proposal failed. The situation remains an impasse, under which products containing vegetable fats must be sold under different trade descriptions in different Member States. As a practical matter, the market for chocolate products is still partly regionalised[7].

The recipe laws characteristically include restrictions upon packaging sizes and weights, and the 1973 directive is no exception. It imposes detailed limits upon the weights in which various chocolate products and cocoa powder may be sold[8]. For example, milk chocolate may be sold in bars or tablets only in various specified

---

1.   Article 9.
2.   Article 3(1).
3.   Article 3(2). See also Articles 8, 9.
4.   Article 4.
5.   Purity criteria and a positive list of solvents were to have been adopted by the Council, acting upon a proposal from the Commission; Article 5 (1).
6.   Article 5 (1).
7.   The controversy's history is recounted in du Bois, "An industry's point of view", in H. Deelstra, et al., eds., *Food Policy Trends in Europe* pp33, 35-36 (1991).
8.   Article 6.

weights between 85 and 500 grammes[1]. Weights of less than 85 or more than 500 grammes are also permitted, but between those limits only the specified weights may be used. Similarly, cocoa powder in packaged units weighing between 50 grammes and one kilogramme may be sold only in specified sizes[2]. Units smaller than 50 grammes or larger than one kilogramme are also permitted.

The vertical measures also generally include special labelling obligations, and again the 1973 directive is no exception[3]. It requires the labels of chocolate and cocoa products to include the name established for the product by the directive's annex. Other disclosures are also designated for each product category[4]. For example, the labels of some products must disclose the minimum percentage of dry cocoa solids[5], while others must disclose the types of chocolate used in the product's manufacture[6]. Similarly, some labels must disclose any use of dextrose, flavourings, lecithins or other substances[7]. Except for small packages containing less than 50 grammes, all labels must reveal the product's net weight[8]. The name and address of the manufacturer or packer, or of a seller established within the Community, must also be provided[9]. In addition, Member States are permitted to retain national rules requiring the disclosure of the factory in which domestic products have been produced[10]. National rules may also require the labels of products made outside the Community to reveal the product's country of origin. Products manufactured in other Member States may not be subjected to such an obligation[11].

The directive does not provide detailed rules regarding the manner in which these disclosures must be made. It states simply that the mandatory disclosures must be made conspicuously, legibly and indelibly[12]. They must be made in the product's label or upon its packaging, except for packages weighing at least 10 kilogrammes sold at wholesale. In such cases, the requisite disclosures may be made in documents which accompany the product[13]. There are also separate rules for special claims of quality. The labels of chocolate and milk chocolate products may claim that the products are "fine", or are otherwise of special quality, only if they contain prescribed minimum levels of dry cocoa solids and cocoa butter[14]. "Fine" milk

---

1.   Article 6(1).
2.   Article 6(2).
3.   Article 7.
4.   In some cases, an indication of the filling product is needed. Article 7(1) (a).
5.   The disclosure must be stated as "cocoa solids ___% minimum"; Article 7(1) (b).
6.   This is required only for some products; Article 7(1) (c).
7.   These disclosures are required only for some products, and there are various limitations. Annex 1 (4) to (7).
8.   Article 7(1) (e).
9.   Article 7(1) (f).
10.   Article 7(2).
11.   Declarations of origin present sensitive issues in the Community. Above at Chapter 3, paras 3.3.1, 3.8. See also Painter, "The Original of Food Products", 4/91 Eur. Food L. Rev. 282.
12.   Article 7(1)
13.   Article 7(2) (a).
14.   Article 8.

chocolate products must also contain prescribed levels of sucrose, milk solids and butter fats. The directive's labelling obligations must now be read in light of the more detailed requirements established by the 1978 labelling directive, as amended[1].

The 1973 directive has been amended on four occasions. Some of the amendments simply altered the deadlines for the implementation of various rules. Others imposed minor changes in the rules with respect to specific products[2].

7.2   Certain natural sugars

The Community's second vertical directive was adopted late in 1973. It was designed to harmonise national laws relating to various natural sugar products intended for human consumption[3]. In terms which have become talismanic, the Council observed that differences in national laws regarding sugars had impeded the free movement of those goods and could result in unfair competition[4]. The directive includes detailed product specifications for a lengthy series of natural sugar products. It does not apply to artificial sweeteners, which are the subject of a proposed new Community measure[5]. The products to which the 1973 directive applies include semi-white sugar, white and extra white sugar, sugar and invert sugar solutions, glucose and dried glucose syrups, dextrose monohydrate, and dextrose anhydrous[6]. These products are required to satisfy detailed specifications, and only products which satisfy the specifications may be sold under those names. Customary names may continue to be used as supplements, but only if they may not be confused with the prescribed names[7].

The product specifications relate to such matters as minimum dry matter by weight, minimum dextrose equivalence, maximum sulphur dioxide content, maximum

---

1.   Above at Chapter 3, para 3.3.
2.   Council Directive (EEC) 76/628, OJ L223 16.8.76 p1 (nominal values for prepackaged cocoa powder); Council Directive (EEC) 78/609 OJ L197 22.7.78 p10 (gianduja); Council Directive (EEC) 80/608, OJ L170 3.7.80 p33 (ammonium salts of phosphatidic acids as an emulsifier); Council Directive (EEC) 89/344, OJ L142 25.5.89 p19 (chocolate a la taza). For the last, see P. Deboyser, *Le droit communautaire relatif aux denrées alimentaires* p396-397 (1989).
3.   Council Directive (EEC) 73/437, OJ L356 27.12.73 p71. As of December 31, 1989, the directive had been adopted by all Member States except Portugal. Portugal has since done so. OJ C338 31.12.91 p1 at p119. For the UK rules, see Specified Sugar Products Regulations 1976 , SI 1976/509, as amended. For the Dutch rules, see *Voedingsraad* at p890. For the Italian rules, see Alimenti e Bevande at pp1094-1102. For the Spanish rules, see, e.g., Codigo Alimentario at chap. 23, sec. 1; Real Decreto 1261/1987, B.O.E. 246 (14 Oct 1987). Sugar is also the subject of a series of Community regulations organising the internal market in such products. See, e.g., Council Regulation (EEC) 1785/81, OJ L177 30.3.81 p4.
4.   Council Directive (EEC) 73/437, above, at the second recital of the preamble. The Council assumes that any substantial lack of harmonisation may lead to trade barriers, potential deception, and unfair trade advantages with respect to products imported from other Member States. Similar recitals appear in virtually all of the foodstuffs directives. They are in essence jurisdictional.
5.   Above at Chapter 5, para 5.3.
6.   Article 1.
7.   Article 3(2).

sulphated ash content, loss on drying, and colour[1]. The name "sugar" may not be substituted for the directive's prescribed names when a product is sold separately, but it may be used as a shorthand description in ingredient lists for natural sugar products contained in compound foodstuffs[2]. In other words, a glucose syrup sold separately cannot be described as "sugar", but it could appear simply as "sugar" in the ingredient list of a confectionery. The descriptive word "white" may be added only if a natural sugar product satisfies requirements relating to ash content and colour[3].

There are also processing requirements. Manufacturers are forbidden to use blueing processes, but colorants may be added if authorised by the Community's rules for colouring materials[4]. There are restrictions on residual sulphur dioxide content, as well as limits on the weights in which sugar products may be sold[5]. Only packages of specified weights between 100 grammes and 5 kilogrammes are permitted, although packages either less then 100 grammes or more than 5 kilogrammes may also be sold[6].

There are special labelling obligations for sugar products. Their labels must include one of the names designated in the directive[7]. If they include colorants, this must be disclosed[8]. The descriptive words "monohydrate" and "anhydrous" are generally optional. The product's net weight must be stated, unless it is less than 50 grammes[9]. Labels must disclose the true dry matter content and the content of invert sugar[10]. The term "crystallised" must be included whenever appropriate[11]. Glucose syrups must generally disclose the products for which they are intended, and their maximum sulphur dioxide content must be indicated in accompanying documents[12]. Any other product descriptions may not be misleading[13]. In any case, only product descriptions in "current" use in the Member States in 1973 are not precluded. Except for sugars originating within the Community, national laws may require the

---

1.   Article 2.
2.   Article 3(3).
3.   Article 3(1).
4.   Article 7.
5.   Article 4, 5, 6 and 8.
6.   Article 8.
7.   Article 9.
8.   Article 9(1) (a).
9.   Article 9(1) (b). This does not apply to multi-packs, which in total exceed 50 grammes. The net weight in such cases must be given on the outer package; ibid. The labels for products sold in pieces or small sachets may use a minimum net weight, rather than an actual or nominal net weight.
10.   Article 9(1) (d). The latter requirement applies to sugar solutions and invert sugar solutions and syrups.
11.   Article 9(1) (e). This applies to invert sugar syrups containing crystals.
12.   Article 9(1) (f). This is applicable if the sulphur dioxide content exceeds prescribed levels.
13.   Article 9(3). As a matter of Community law, each Member State is therefore obliged to prohibit, and thereafter to prevent, the use of "misleading" descriptions.

disclosure of a product's country of origin[1]. National law may also require a disclosure of the producing factory if sugar has been domestically produced[2].

Consistent with Article 36 of the Treaty of Rome, Member States are forbidden to limit trade in products which conform with the directive's requirements unless to protect public health, prevent fraud, protect property rights, or prevent unfair competition[3]. In 1979, the Commission adopted a supplemental directive prescribing methods of analysis to test sugars to determine whether they comply with the 1973 directive[4]. The directive provides methods to verify composition, calculate losses of mass on drying, measure dry matter, and determine other physical characteristics[5].

7.3 Honey

The Community adopted its third vertical directive in 1974 to harmonise national laws relating to honey[6]. The directive states that differences in national laws hindered the free movement of honey products and could result in unfair competition[7]. It provides definitionsof the principal types of honey, and forbids trade in honey which does not conform to the directive's rules regarding the relevant type[8]. Use of the name "honey", as well as the names of the various defined types of honey, is restricted to products which satisfy the directive's definitions and specifications[9]. The directive provides detailed compositional standards regarding such matters as moisture and sucrose content, ash, acidity, and content of water-insoluble solids[10]. It also forbids foreign matter and foreign tastes

---

1. Article 9(5). Such national provisions may be "retained". Logically, any rules adopted after 1973 would be forbidden.
2. Such provisions could again be "retained" by the Member States. Any post-1973 national rules would presumably be prohibited.
3. Article 10. These same exceptions are generally found in the recipe laws. They are a rough summary of the provisions of Article 36 of the Treaty of Rome.
4. First Commission Directive (EEC) 79/786, OJ L239 22.8.79 p24. Previously, the Commission adopted a regulation establishing methods for determining the quality of sugar. Commission Regulation (EEC) 1265/69, OJ L163 4.7.69 p1.
5. First Commission Directive 79/786, above at Article 1 and Annexes I and II. There is some room for discretion. For example, the directive generally requires the Luff-Schoorl method for determining reducing sugars, but permits Member States to authorise the domestic use of alternative methods. Article 1(2).
6. Council Directive (EEC) 74/409, OJ L221 12.8.74 p1. As of December 31, 1990, the directive had been adopted by all Member States except Spain. Eighth Annual Report to the European Parliament on Commission Monitoring of the Application of Community Law, OJ C338 31.12.91 p1 at p117. For the UK rules, see Honey Regulations 1976, SI 1976/1832. For the Italian rules, see Alimenti e Bevande at 700-708. For the unharmonised Spanish rules, see, e.g., Codigo Alimentario at chap. 23, sec. 2. For the Spanish rules of analysis, see Order of June 12, 1986, B.O.E. 145 (18 June 1986).
7. Council Directive (EEC) 74/409, above at the second recital of the preamble.
8. Articles 1(2), 2 and the Annex. The directive defines honeys in terms of origin (blossom and honeydew honey) and in terms of presentation (comb, chunk, drained, extracted, and pressed honeys).
9. Article 3.
10. Article 6 and the Annex. Moisture content generally may not exceed 23 per cent, depending on the type of honey, but national laws may permit exceptions up to 25 per cent. Article 6(1).

or odours[1]. Honey may not be sold if it has begun to ferment or effervesce, and may not be given an artificial level of acidity. There are also processing limitations. For example, honey may not be heated to a level which destroys natural enzymes, or makes them inactive[2]. These rules are similar to, but generally more strict than, standards recommended by the Codex Alimentarius Commission[3].

Labels must conspicuously, legibly and indelibly display the name "honey" or one of the more specific names defined in Article 1(2)[4]. "Comb" and "chunk" honey must be described as such. So too must "baker's honey" and industrial honey. Each product's net weight must be expressed in grammes or kilogrammes. The name and address of its producer or packer, or of a seller established in the Community, must be stated. The name "honey" may be supplemented by a reference to the plant or blossom of origin. It may also be supplemented by a regional or territorial name if the product originated entirely in that region or territory[5]. For domestic products, Member States may require the name "honeydew honey", but only if the products predominantly originate from honeydew sources, and only if their labels do not claim any more specific origin[6]. For packages of 10 kilogrammes or larger, the mandatory information may be provided in accompanying documents rather than by labelling[7]. National format rules are forbidden, although Member States may demand that a product's name be given on one side of its container in the national language[8]. These provisions must now be read in light of the 1978 labelling directive, as amended[9].

Except for honey originating within the Community, Member States may require the disclosure of a honey's country of origin[10]. The directive forbids Member States to limit trade in honey which conforms to the directive's requirements, unless to protect public health, prevent fraud, protect property rights, or prevent unfair competition[11]. The directive authorises methods of sampling and analysis, but no expressly applicable methods have yet been adopted[12].

1.   Article 6(2).
2.   Article 6(2) (b) (iii).
3.   Written Question 1938/91, OJ C66 16.3.92 p30.
4.   Article 7(1).
5.   Article 7(4).
6.   Article 7(2).
7.   Article 7(5).
8.   Article 7(6).
9.   Above at Chapter 3, para 3.3.
10.   Article 7(3). For more recent developments regarding indications of geographical origin, see above at Chapter 3, para 3.8.
11.   Article 8.
12.   Article 9. These issues are to be decided by proposals submitted by the Commission to the Standing Committee on Foodstuffs. If the Standing Committee fails to approve them, the proposals may be adopted by a qualified majority of the Council, as defined by Article 148 of the Treaty of Rome. Article 10.

The directive has not eliminated continuing complaints in the European Parliament regarding the economic difficulties of the Community's beekeepers[1]. The Community provides various indirect subsidies and supports to its honey producers, but the fundamental difficulty is that their costs of production greatly exceed those in many other areas of the world. Despite the directive's stringent standards, some 60 per cent of the Community's honey is imported. The European Parliament urged additional support for beekeepers in 1985, and some Member States also provide economic assistance[2].

7.4   Fruit juices

The Council adopted a directive to harmonise national requirements for fruit juices and similar products in 1975[3]. The directive has been amended on five occasions, including minor changes made by the Acts of Accession for Greece, Spain and Portugal[4]. As amended, the directive provides product specifications for fruit puree, concentrated fruit puree, fruit juice, concentrated fruit juice, fruit nectar, and dried fruit juice[5]. Those trade descriptions may be used only if applicable specifications are satisfied. In some cases, the directive permits the alternative use of other descriptive terms in several national languages, such as "succo e polpa" and "vruchtendrank"[6]. If a product is derived from a single fruit, its name must be substituted for the generic word "fruit" in the product's name[7].

The directive provides recipes for fruit juices, concentrated fruit juices and fruit nectars[8]. For example, fruit juices may be manufactured from one or more juices or purees treated with specified substances. Only the "usual" physical processes and treatments may be used. These include heating, centrifuging and filtering[9]. The substances used for processing or treatment may include, for example, L-Ascorbic acid, nitrogen, carbon dioxide, tannins and charcoal[10]. The permissible quantity of sugar is specified[11]. The addition of both sugars and acid to the same juice is

---

1.   Written Question 1938/91, OJ C66 16.3.92 p29.
2.   OJ C343 12.12.85 p1.
3.   Council Directive (EEC) 75/726, OJ L311 1.12.75 p40. As of December 31, 1989, the directive had been adopted by all Member States except Portugal. It has since done so; OJ C338 31.12.91 p1 at p119. For the UK rules, see Fruit Juices and Fruit Nectars Regulations 1977, SI 1977/927; Fruit Juices and Fruit Nectars (Amendment) Regulations, SI 1982/1311. For Spanish rules, see, e.g., Codigo Alimentario at chap. 22, sec. 2; Real Decreto 667/1983, B.O.E. 77 (31.3.83); B.O.E. 168 (15.7.83). For comparable US rules, see, e.g., 21 C.F.R. part 146 (1991).
4.   Most recently, see Council Directive (EEC) 89/394, OJ L186 30.6.89 p14. The various Acts of Accession generally modify the voting requirements set forth in directives, but may also contain provisions relating to local products or pre-existing national rules.
5.   Council Directive (EEC) 75/726, above at Article 1.
6.   Article 3(2).
7.   Article 3(3).
8.   Articles 4, 7, 8.
9.   Article 4 (1).
10.   Special rules are provided for grape and pineapple juices. Articles 4 (2) (b), (c).
11.   Article 4 (2). The limits range from 15 to 200 grammes per litre, depending on the product.

prohibited[1]. Maximum acid and sulphur dioxide contents are prescribed[2]. The kinds of sugars used in processing are restricted[3]. Similar restrictions are imposed upon concentrated fruit juices and fruit nectars[4]. Dried fruit juice may be processed by "almost total dehydration", using any physical treatment other than direct flame[5]. The restoration or recovery of essential volatiles is, however, required. None of these treatments may result in any substance in the final product dangerous to human health[6].

Fruit juices and similar products are subject to the 1978 labelling directive, as amended, but special labelling requirements are also imposed[7]. The names under which they are sold must be those reserved for them by the directive. They must, for example, describe themselves as "fruit puree" or "fruit nectar" in accordance with the directive's requirements[8]. Nonetheless, the description "fruit nectar" may be made optional by Member States if one of the local names reserved by Article 3(2) is used. Similarly, the adjective "dried" may be replaced by "powdered" or the particular process which has been used[9]. The specific fruits or purees used in processing must be identified in the label[10].

Products containing added sugar must be described as "sweetened", and the product's label must disclose the maximum quantity of added sugars in terms of grammes per litre[11]. Ingredients must generally be listed, although various exceptions are permitted[12]. For example, substances used to restore flavour or the original state of concentrates and dried products need not be listed. Where appropriate, the phrases "carbonated" or "contains ____ made from concentrate" must be included. These disclosures must be "in bold lettering"[13]. The quantity of any water needed to restore concentrated and dried juices must be specified. For fruit nectars, the actual minimum content of juices or purees by percentage must be shown. Apart from the single requirement for bold lettering, there are no format requirements. There are, however, minimal field of vision requirements similar to the provisions of the 1978

1. Article 4 (3).
2. Articles 4 (2), 4 (4), 6. The basic sulphur dioxide limit is 10 mg per litre, but 20 mg per litre is permitted in orange juice. Article 6.
3. Article 1(4). One list of permissible natural sugars is given for fruit juices, and another for fruit concentrates and nectars.
4. Articles 7, 8. There are, for example, limits on water, sugar and acid in nectars. Article 7(2). See also the Annex.
5. Article 9.
6. Article 10.
7. Article 11(1).
8. Articles 11(2), (3).
9. Article 11(2) (a) (ii).
10. Article 11(b) (i).
11. Article 11(b) (ii).
12. Article 11(3). The exceptions include, for example, substances used to restore flavour or the original state of concentrates and dried products.
13. Article 11(4).

labelling directive[1]. There are also various limitations on labelling. For example, the addition of L-Ascorbic acid does not permit a reference to Vitamin C[2]. In addition, Member States are free to establish special labelling requirements regarding products not delivered as such to the ultimate consumer[3]. This provision applies to wholesale transactions and juices sold for further processing or mixing.

Identity and purity criteria may be established through a committee procedure involving the Standing Committee for Foodstuffs[4]. This may be done "where necessary", but no special criteria have in fact been adopted. The directive does not apply to products for export or to dietary products[5]. The usual exceptions are permitted for the application of non-harmonised national laws justified on grounds of public health, prevention of fraud, protection of property, or prevention of unfair competition[6]. The directive also does not invalidate national rules regarding several issues. These include vitaminisation, various diffusion processes, the use of dimethylpolysiloxane in pineapple juice, the use of lactic and citric acids in some fruit nectars, and various uses of malic acid[7].

The directive's preservation of national rules regarding vitaminisation does not, however, necessarily assure the effectiveness of those rules. The Treaty of Rome may still invalidate them. Dutch rules, for example, forbid the marketing of foodstuffs with added vitamins without prior national approval. The Dutch rules were sustained by the European Court under Articles 30 and 36 of the Treaty, but only upon condition that the Netherlands grants the requisite approvals whenever the safety of the foodstuffs is shown[8]. The European Court forbade any use of competitive or marketing considerations as a basis for rejection. All applications must be considered carefully and with a presumption in favour of approval. The Court held that without those constraints the Dutch rules could not have been saved by Article 36 of the Treaty.

---

1.   Article 11(5). "Field of vision" is not defined, but presumably demands that the information must be placed together in a manner which permits them to be seen at the same time. This is in essence its meaning under Britain's food labelling rules; above at Chapter 3, para 3.3.
2.   Article 11(6).
3.   Article 11a.
4.   Article 13.
5.   Article 17.
6.   Article 12(2).
7.   Article 16(1). Many of these derogations are expressly subject to any contrary Community rules. Article 16(2). Lactic acid is produced by the fermentation of milk sugar, and is used in confectionery, soft drinks and other products; A. Bender, *Dictionary of Nutrition and Food Technology* p158 (6th ed. 1990).
8.   Case 174/82 *Officier van Justitie v Sandoz BV* [1983] ECR 2445, [1984] 3 CMLR 43, decided by the European Court in 1983.

7.5   Dehydrated preserved milk

In December 1975, the Council adopted a directive to harmonise national rules regarding partly or wholly dehydrated preserved milk intended for human consumption[1]. It does not apply to fresh milk. The Community has extensive rules for the production and marketing of fresh milk, and now is considering new rules regarding health issues, as well as labelling of different levels of butterfat content[2].

The 1975 directive has been amended four times, including special provisions included in the Acts of Accession for Greece, Spain and Portugal[3]. It has also been supplemented by a directive prescribing methods of analysis for use in the inspection of such products[4]. As amended, the directive establishes compositional and other specifications for various preserved milk products[5]. It reserves designated trade names for products which satisfy those specifications[6]. The permissible methods of preservation include heat treatments, dehydration, or the addition of sucrose[7]. In all cases, there must be a heat treatment at least equivalent to pasteurisation[8]. There are also restrictions on the preservatives and other additives which may be used[9]. The directive provides for, but does not itself include, criteria for establishing the purity, wholesomeness and quality of dehydrated milk products[10].

---

1. Council Directive (EEC) 76/18, OJ L24 30.1.76 p49. For the UK rules, see Condensed Milk and Dried Milk (Amendment) Regulations 1986, SI 1986/2299. For the Italian rules, see Alimenti e Bevande at 655-659. For the Spanish rules, see, e.g., Codigo Alimentario at chap. 15, sec. 2; Real Decreto 503/1986, B.O.E. 63 (14 Mar 1986).
2. Milk in Britain has 4 per cent butterfat, while elsewhere the usual level is 3.5 per cent. The Commission's draft proposal would permit these to be described as "natural" and "adjusted" fat content, respectively. EIS, Europe Environment, No. 377 at IV-2 (10 Dec 1991). The proposal has evidently now been accepted by the Council. EIS, Europe Environment, No. 388 at IV-5 (2 June 1992). See also Council Directive (EEC) 92/46 (16 June 1992), establishing health rules for milk and milk-based products. For the rules regarding the common organisation of the Community's market for milk, see Council Regulation (EEC) 804/68, OJ L148 28.6.68 p13. For amendments, see, e.g., Regulation (EEC) 773/87, OJ L78 20.3.87 p1.
3. See, e.g., Council Directive (EEC) 78/630, OJ L206 29.7.78 p12; Council Directive (EEC) 83/635, OJ L357 21.12.83 p37. Acts of Accession may include special transitional or other provisions designed to take account of particular national rules or products, but more often simply compel changes in the voting and approval provisions for supplementing or amending directives.
4. First Commission Directive (EEC) 79/1067, OJ L327 24.12.79 p29.
5. Council Directive (EEC) 76/18, above at Article 1(2). "Wholly" dehydrated milk must have a moisture content which does not exceed five per cent by weight. Member States were permitted to retain any pre-existing rules forbidding the use of wholly dehydrated milk to produce partly dehydrated products.
6. Article 3(2).
7. Article 1(3).
8. Article 4.
9. Article 5. The permissible substances include sodium and potassium bicarbonates and calcium chloride. Limits are placed on the total quantity by weight of these substances in the final products. Member States are permitted to allow the addition of vitamins. Article 5 (7). They may also permit the use of additives in dehydrated milk sold from vending machines. Article 5 (6).
10. Article 11.

The 1975 directive also imposes special labelling obligations[1]. Labels must include one of the trade names defined in the directive. If a product is dried, its label generally must include the word "instant", together with an acknowledgement of any use of lecithins[2]. Labels must also include the product's net quantity in terms of units of mass or volume[3]. They must disclose the product's percentage of milk fat expressed in weight, and recommended methods of dilution or reconstitution[4]. If a product is to be used without alteration, the latter may be replaced by information regarding its proper use[5]. The words "ultra heat treated" or the letters "UHT" must be included if that process has been used[6]. If a product is imported from a third country, the country of origin must be disclosed[7]. The date of manufacture must be shown, or some marking must be provided from which the batch can be identified[8]. All this information must be displayed visibly, legibly and indelibly. Some of the disclosures must appear within the same field of vision[9]. The disclosures must be made in a language easily understood by the purchaser, unless the requisite information is provided by other means[10]. Member States may also require the disclosure of information regarding the nature and extent of any added vitamins[11].

Member States are forbidden to hinder trade in products which comply with the directive, unless to protect health, prevent fraud, protect property rights, or prevent unfair competition[12]. Products destined for retail sale must be packaged by the manufacturer or packer in sealed containers to protect the product from "harmful influence." The containers must be delivered intact to the consumer[13]. The directive does not apply to dietetic products, products specifically prepared for babies or young children, or products intended for export outside the Community[14]. Any national rules regarding indications of special quality for products manufactured in a Member State's own territory are unaffected[15].

---

1.   Article 7.
2.   Lecithins are fatty substances often used as emulsifiers or anti-spattering agents. A. Bender, *Dictionary of Nutrition and Food Technology* pp161-162 (6th ed. 1990).
3.   Articles 7(3), 7a (1) (b).
4.   Article 7(4).
5.   Article 7(4) (a), (b).
6.   Article 7(4) (d).
7.   Article 7a (1) (d).
8.   Article 7a (1) (e).
9.   Articles 7(5), 7a (1).
10.   Article 7a (2). Permission for the alternative use of other means of providing information is included in other directives, but always without further explanation. Such authorisations usually depend on the impracticality of labelling disclosures. Presumably other means might include signs at the point of sale, leaflets or other materials furnished separately from the actual product label.
11.   Article 7(5).
12.   Article 9.
13.   Article 8.
14.   Article 15. For more recent developments regarding foods for particular nutritional uses, including infant formulae, see above at Chapter 4, para 4.5.
15.   Article 14.

7.6   Erucic acid in oils and fats

In July 1976, the Council adopted a directive to harmonise national rules fixing the maximum levels of erucic acid in oils and fats[1]. Erucic acid is a fatty acid found in rape and mustard seed, and often used in the manufacture of margarine[2]. The directive stated that evidence from animal testing had suggested that erucic acid might produce adverse health effects in humans. It found that further study and research were necessary to evaluate any possible risks, and that in the interim it was desirable to restrict the ingestion of erucic acid[3]. Although the directive did not expressly identify the possible health issue, animal testing has suggested an association between erucic acid and fatty infiltrations of heart muscle[4].

The directive is applicable to all oils, fats and mixtures of oils and fats intended for human consumption. It also applies to compound foodstuffs to which oils or fats have been added, but only if the overall fat content of the compound product is greater than five per cent[5]. None of these products may contain more than five per cent of erucic acid, calculated as a percentage of the total fatty acids in the product's fat component[6]. This maximum level may be temporarily reduced by Member States if they have "detailed grounds" to believe that it may endanger human health, but reductions are subject to review and confirmation by the Commission and the Standing Committee for Foodstuffs[7]. The phrase "detailed grounds" is left undefined, but certainly demands more than a mere suspicion or apprehension. A reasonable scientific basis may be the essence of the requirement, although this is not expressly stated. A committee procedure was created to establish methods of analysis, and the Commission adopted a directive providing such methods in 1980[8].

---

1.   Council Directive (EEC) 76/621, OJ L202 28.7.76 p35. For the UK rules, see Erucic Acid in Food Regulations 1977, SI 1977/691. For the Italian rules, see *Alimenti e Bevande* at 680.
2.   See, e.g., A. Bender, *Dictionary of Nutrition and Food Technology* p100 (6th ed. 1990).
3.   Council Directive (EEC) 76/621, above at the first four recitals of the preamble.
4.   S. Fallows, *Food Legislative System of the UK* p41 (1988); A. Bender, *Dictionary of Nutrition and Food Technology* p100 (6th ed. 1990).
5.   Council Directive (EEC) 76/621, above at Article 1(a). Member States are, however, permitted the option of applying the directive to products with an overall fat content of less than five per cent. Article 1(b).
6.   Article 2(1). A temporary level of ten per cent was originally permitted. Article 2(2). In Sweden, the maximum level is evidently two per cent. A. Bender, *Dictionary of Nutrition and Food Technology* p100 (6th ed. 1990).
7.   Articles 4, 5. As noted above, Member States may also elect to apply the directive to products containing less than five per cent of overall fat content.
8.   Article 3. See Commission Directive (EEC) 80/891, OJ L254 27.8.80 p35. The directive followed approval by the Standing Committee on Foodstuffs; ibid., at the eighth recital of the preamble.

7.7   Coffee and chicory extracts

The Council adopted a directive for the harmonisation of national rules regarding coffee and chicory extracts in 1977[1]. It provides definitions of the various products, and establishes specifications for each product category[2]. Coffee extracts are generally defined as extracts from roasted coffee using only water and without hydrolysis, and containing the soluble and aromatic constituents of coffee. Insoluble oils and "traces" of other insoluble substances are permitted[3]. Only sound, genuine and merchantable raw materials may be used[4]. The Council is to adopt a positive list of permissible solvents and limits for the content of insoluble substances[5]. In addition, the directive limits the weights in which such products may be sold[6]. Larger or smaller packages are still permitted, but only designated weights are permissible for solid or paste products sold in individual packages with net weights between 25 grammes and 10 kilogrammes. The directive also contemplated the establishment of sampling and analytical methods[7]. Those methods were provided by another directive adopted in 1979[8].

Member States may not impede trade in products which comply with the 1977 directive's terms except to protect public health, prevent fraud, protect industrial and commercial property, and prevent unfair competition[9].

Labels must include one of the directive's prescribed names[10]. Where applicable, they must add the words "concentrated", "roasted with sugar", "preserved with sugar", or "with added sugar". They must also indicate the minimum coffee-based or chicory-based dry matter content. If a product is not intended for sale to the ultimate consumer, it is enough if its package or label, or an accompanying document, reveals the name specified under the directive, the product's nominal net quantity, a batch or lot identification, and the name of the manufacturer or of a

---

1.   Council Directive (EEC) 77/436, OJ L172 12.7.77 p20. For the UK rules, see Coffee and Coffee Products Regulations 1978 , SI 1978/1420; Coffee and Coffee Products (Amendment) Regulations 1987, SI 1987/1986. For the Spanish rules, see, e.g., Codigo Alimentario at chap. 25; Real Decreto 2362/1985, B.O.E. 42 (18 Feb 1985). For the Italian rules, see *Alimenti e Bevande* at 349-355.
2.   Council Directive (EEC) 77/436, above at Article 1(2). The ingredients of any blends must also satisfy the definitions. Article 2(2).
3.   Chicory extracts are similarly defined; ibid. See also the directive's Annex, where products are defined in terms, for example, of their percentage of content of coffee-based dry matter, as well as the quantity of raw coffee used in their manufacture.
4.   Article 3(1).
5.   Article 3(2). No separate requirements have appeared, but coffee is among the products included in the Community's legislation for extraction solvents. Above at Chapter 5, para 5.9.
6.   Article 4, as amended.
7.   Article 8.
8.   First Commission Directive (EEC) 79/1066, OJ L327 24.12.79 p17.
9.   Those provisions roughly correspond to the terms of Article 36 of the Treaty. Council Directive (EEC) 77/436, above at Article 7.
10.   Article 6.

seller established within the Community[1]. The word "decaffeinated" may be used in labelling, but only if a product's anhydrous caffeine content does not exceed 0.3 per cent by dry weight. The directive's labelling provisions must also be read in light of the 1978 labelling directive, as amended[2].

The directive was amended by the Council in 1985[3]. The amendment extends the 1977 directive to include concentrated chicory extract products[4]. It also supplements certain of the directive's labelling requirements[5]. The changes require a means of identifying the product's batch, and also alter the conditions under which some of the other disclosures must be made. In addition, the amendment abolishes the 1977 directive's minimum requirements regarding the quantities of raw coffee used for the production of some products[6]. It also eliminates the directive's maximum limits for insoluble substances in coffee extract[7], reduces the dry matter minimum content for extract[8], alters the definitions and descriptions, and makes other technical changes[9]. For example, the original annex required that at least 2.3 kilogrammes of raw coffee must be used for the manufacture of one kilogramme of finished soluble coffee, with a coffee-based dry matter content in the final product of 96 per cent. The amended annex omits the reference to the quantity of raw coffee and reduces the percentage of coffee-based dry matter to 95 per cent.

7.8   Fruit jams and jellies

The Council adopted a directive to harmonise national rules regarding fruit jams and jellies, marmalades and chestnut purees in 1979[10]. The directive was amended in 1988 to make clarifying and technical changes[11]. As amended, the directive applies to jam, extra jam, jelly, extra jelly, marmalade, and sweetened chestnut puree[12]. These products are defined in an annex to the directive[13], and only products which conform to the rules provided in the annex may be marketed under those

---

1.   Article 6(2).
2.   Above at Chapter 3, para 3.3.
3.   Council Directive (EEC) 85/573, OJ L372 31.12.85 p22. Articles 4 and 6 of the 1977 directive were amended, together with the definitions provided in the Annex. As of 31 December 1989, the directive had been adopted by all Member States except France. France has since done so. OJ C338 31.12.91 p1 at p132.
4.   Council Directive (EEC) 85/573, above at the second recital of the preamble.
5.   Article 1(3).
6.   Annex, paragraph 1.
7.   Article 1(1).
8.   Annex, paragraphs 1(a), 2(a).
9.   Annex, paragraph 2(c).
10.   Council Directive (EEC) 79/693, OJ L205 13.8.79 p5. For the UK rules, see Jam and Similar Products Regulations 1981, SI 1981/1063. For the Dutch rules, see *Voedingsraad* at p604. For the Italian rules, see *Alimenti e Bevande* at pp686-690. For comparable US rules, see, e.g., 21 C.F.R. part 150 (1991).
11.   Council Directive (EEC) 88/593, OJ L318 25.11.89 p44. Seven Member States had adopted it as of 31 October 1991. EC Commission, National Implementation Measures p138 (1992).
12.   Council Directive (EEC) 79/693, above at Article 1.
13.   Annex I.

names[1]. More generally, only products with a soluble dry matter content of at least 60 per cent may be marketed. Nonetheless, Member States may, with some exceptions, permit domestic sales of products with a lower dry matter content[2]. Only the raw materials described in another annex may be used, and only prescribed additives and treatment processes are permitted[3]. The maximum content of sulphur dioxide is limited[4]. No substance may be included in quantities which will endanger human health[5].

Member States are permitted to suspend trade in products which include substances dangerous to human health, but their decisions are subject to review by the Commission and the Standing Committee for Foodstuffs[6]. If necessary, a committee procedure may be used to adopt purity criteria[7]. No such criteria have yet been adopted. Subject to contrary Community legislation, national rules may continue to regulate the uses of malic acid[8], preservatives, colorants, and replacement sugars[9]. The directive does not apply to export products. Nor does it apply to products used for the manufacture of fine bakers' wares, pastries and biscuits[10]. Finally, the directive does not affect national rules regarding dietary products[11].

Various labelling rules are provided[12]. Labels must use one of the prescribed product names, supplemented by the names of the fruits used in the product's manufacture. If any of the ingredients listed in an annex to the directive has been included, this fact must be disclosed[13]. For example, any use of red beetroot juice for colouring must be revealed, and sulphur dioxide must be listed as an ingredient if its residual content exceeds 30 mg/kg[14]. There are also special rules for products made from apricots and products including three or more fruits. Labels must bear the words "prepared with ___ grammes of fruit per 100 grammes," and the words "total sugar content ___ grammes per 100 grammes," including the applicable insertions. The

---

1.   Article 2.
2.   Article 3. The Council was to fix names for non-conforming products "before 1 January 1991." It has not yet done so.
3.   Annex II. It provides listings of the permissible parts of various fruits and specified sugars which are permitted, as well as authorised treatments.
4.   Article 6(2) and Annex IV. The maximum sulphur dioxide content is 10 mg/kg for some products and 50 mg/kg for others, but Member States were permitted for five years to authorise maximum levels as high as 100 mg/kg.
5.   Article 6(1).
6.   Article 10.
7.   Article 11.
8.   Malic acid is an organic acid found particularly in apples, tomatoes and plums. A. Bender, *Dictionary of Nutrition and Food Technology* p173 (6th ed. 1990).
9.   Article 15 (1).
10.   Article 16.
11.   Article 16(a). As to such products, the national rules must now be read in light of the framework directive for foods intended for particular nutritional uses; above at Chapter 4, para 4.5.
12.   Article 7. These rules must be read in light of the 1978 labelling directive, as amended; above at Chapter 3, para 3.3.
13.   Article 7(1).
14.   Article 7(2).

words "keep in a cool place" must be added if the product has a soluble dry matter content of less than 63 per cent[1]. For marmalade, there must be an indication either of the absence of peel or of the peel's style of cut[2]. The inclusion of L-Ascorbic acid does not permit a labelling reference to Vitamin C[3]. Subject to contrary Community legislation, Member States may set different rules for products not intended for supply as such to the ultimate consumer[4].

7.9   Mineral waters

The Community is a major producer of mineral waters, which are the subject of detailed national rules in several Member States[5]. In 1980, the Council adopted a directive to harmonise national laws regarding the exploitation and marketing of natural mineral waters[6].

National laws had adopted differing definitions of natural mineral waters, and disparate rules for their exploitation and sale[7]. Those inconsistencies had hindered the free movement of the products throughout the Community. The directive defines products which may be sold as "natural mineral waters"[8], and imposes standards and criteria for satisfying the definition[9]. In contrast, "spring" water is not controlled by specific Community legislation, and is governed simply by general legislation relating to all drinking water other than natural mineral waters[10]. There are, however, national rules relating to spring waters[11].

Natural mineral waters are defined as microbiologically pure waters, originating in an underground deposit and emerging from a spring through natural or bore exits. They are distinguished either by their nature, which is characterised by mineral

---

1.   Article 7(3).
2.   Article 7(3). There are various limitations, as well as field of vision requirements.
3.   Article 7(5).
4.   Article 8.
5.   A list of recognised mineral waters produced within the Community is published periodically by the Commission. See, e.g., Commission Communication, Consolidated List of the Natural Mineral Waters Recognised by the Member States, OJ C186 27.7.90 p6; OJ C271 27.10.90 p29; OJ C307 7.12.90 p11. For the current UK rules, see Natural Mineral Waters Regulations 1985 , SI 1985/71. For the Italian rules, see *Alimenti e Bevande* at 195-208, and esp. 201-203. For the Spanish rules, see, e.g., Codigo Alimentario at chap. 27, sec. 2. For comparable US rules, see, e.g., 21 C.F.R. part 129 (1991).
6.   Council Directive (EEC) 80/777, OJ L229 30.8.80 p1. As of December 31, 1989, the directive had been adopted by all Member States except Portugal. Seventh Monitoring Report, OJ C388 31.12.91 p1 at p120.
7.   Council Directive (EEC) 80/777, above at the first and second recitals of the preamble.
8.   Article 1 and Annex I.
9.   Annex I, part II. Part III contains supplemental rules for effervescent waters.
10.   Written Question 2206/91, OJ C78 30..3.92 p40. For drinking water generally, see Council Directive (EEC) 80/778, OJ L229 30.8.80 p11.
11.   For Belgium, for example, see Moniteur Belge (26 Nov 1985). Few distinctions are drawn by the Belgian decree between "spring" and "mineral" waters.

content or trace elements, or by their "effects"[1]. They are also characterised by the natural state in which they continue to be found. Their sources must have been preserved intact and free from pollution[2]. Products may be marketed as "natural mineral waters" only if they have first been subjected to physical and chemical surveys and analyses. Clinical and pharmacological studies may also be required[3].

The directive limits the treatment processes and additives which may be used[4]. Permissible treatments include filtration or decanting, oxygenation, physical removal of free carbon dioxide, and the introduction or reintroduction of carbon dioxide. Disinfection is forbidden[5]. The directive authorises sampling and analytical methods[6]. It also imposes requirements for containers and closures[7]. Closures must prevent any possibility of adulteration or contamination. There are also extensive purity rules, including limits on the total colony count[8]. In addition, the waters must be free from parasites and pathogenic micro-organisms, and may not have any organoleptic defects.

The directive also creates special labelling and advertising requirements[9]. A product's sales description must include one of the following phrases: "natural mineral water", "naturally carbonated natural mineral water", "natural mineral water fortified with gas from the spring", or "carbonated natural mineral water"[10]. The sales descriptions of any waters fully or partly de-carbonated must reveal that fact. Labels must also disclose the existence or results of a chemical analysis, as well as the name and location of the spring[11]. Labels must either give the water's analytical composition or state that the water's composition is in accordance with the results of an officially recognised analysis, with the date on which it occurred. It is, for example, common in Italy and Spain for the labels of mineral waters to state the place and detailed results of a chemical analysis, generally with the

---

1.　　　The requisite "effects" are not defined. The provision appears to invite medicinal claims.
2.　　　Council Directive (EEC) 80/777, above at Annex I, part I, paragraph 1. "Pollution" is not defined or described.
3.　　　Article 5 and Annex I, part II.
4.　　　Article 4 (1).
5.　　　Article 4 (2).
6.　　　Article 11.
7.　　　Article 6.
8.　　　Article 5.
9.　　　Article 7. These rules must now be read in light of the 1978 labelling directive, as amended. Above at Chapter 3, para 3.3. Under the 1978 directive, the required disclosures must be made in a language easily understood by purchasers. The European Court has interpreted this to mean that Belgium may not compel a mineral water sold in its Flemish-speaking areas to be labelled in Flemish rather than other languages, such as German or French, which are widely understood in those areas. See Case C-369/89 *Piageme v BVBA Peeters* (Transcript) 18 June 1991.
10.　　　Article 7(1). Some room for puffery is preserved, or at least assumed. The English mineral water Hildon, for example, describes its product as "gently" carbonated.
11.　　　Article 7(2).

name of a supervising university faculty or professor, sometimes in conjunction with a claim that the water is "bacteriologically pure" ("batteriologicamente pura")[1].

Member States may require the country of the water's origin to be disclosed, unless it comes from a spring located within the Community[2]. The name of a locality may be included in a water's sales description, provided that its inclusion is not misleading[3]. This might, for example, permit the sale of "Welsh" or "Auvergne" mineral water. Such designations would presumably be misleading only if the water in fact has a different place of origin. Water from the same spring cannot be sold under more than one trade description[4]. The key question is whether the spring (or bore hole) is the same, and not whether the same underground deposit has been tapped. Water from the same deposit obtained through adjacent bore holes may therefore be sold under different trade descriptions. In addition, labelling may not suggest a characteristic the water does not possess, nor create a basis for likely confusion with other products[5]. Labels cannot suggest some false characteristic in terms of the water's origin, the period of the spring's exploitation, or the results of any scientific analysis[6].

Waters which do not satisfy the directive's definition of "natural mineral water" cannot be labelled or presented in a fashion which permits their confusion with waters which do[7]. Nor may a label claim medicinal qualities[8]. Certain qualities (for example, "low mineral content" or "may be diuretic") may, however, be claimed if the water satisfies criteria set forth in Annex III to the directive. Proof of compliance with the criteria must be provided by physical or chemical analyses, supported where necessary by clinical evidence[9]. For domestic sales, national rules may authorise the use in labelling of such phrases as "stimulates digestion"[10]. For example, the Spanish water Bezoya claimed in its Spanish label in 1991 to be "diuretic and digestive, ideal for the kidneys". Similarly, the Italian mineral water San Pellegrino included in 1991 on its labelling in Italy (although not, for example, in Belgium or the United Kingdom) the following passage in three languages:

---

1. Such claims were, for example, found in the labels of the waters "Lora di Recoaro," produced in Vicenza, as sold in Italy in April 1991, and Solande Cabras, produced in Cuenca, as sold in Spain in April 1991.
2. Article 7(3).
3. Article 8 (1).
4. Article 8 (2).
5. Article 9.
6. Article 9(1).
7. Article 9(1) (a).
8. Article 9(2).
9. Article 9(2) (b).
10. Article 9(2) (c). See, e.g., Article 2 of the Italian Decreto Ministeriale (1 Feb 1983), which transposed the 1980 directive.

"[It]... may have diuretic actions and it may contribute to the urinary elimination of uric acid. It stimulates the digestion and it may help the hepatobiliary functions."

7.10   Caseins and caseinates

In 1983, the Council adopted a directive to harmonise national rules regarding certain lactoproteins intended for human consumption[1]. The relevant lactoproteins are caseins and caseinates, which are milk proteins obtained from skimmed milk. They are used for the fortification of bread and cereals, and in fabricated cheeses[2]. They may also be used to clarify wines[3]. Before the directive's adoption, some Member States had adopted rules for the composition and manufacture of casein products[4]. This created barriers to the free movement of such products within the Community[5]. The directive defines caseins and caseinates, and prohibits trade in those products unless they conform to the directive's requirements, or unless they are labelled so as not to mislead buyers regarding their nature, quality or use[6]. Caseins are generally defined as the principal protein components of milk, which have been washed and dried. They are insoluble in water and obtained by a precipitation process using acid, rennet or other methods[7]. Caseinates are obtained by drying caseins treated with neutralising agents[8].

The directive includes specific labelling requirements for such products[9]. The label must use one of the names defined in the directive's annexes. If the product is a mixture, its label must indicate its contents. Labels must also provide the product's net weight, disclose any third-country place of origin, and provide a method of identifying the product's lot or batch[10]. The directive also forbids Member States to create any barrier to trade in the products[11]. The only circumstances in which Member States may limit trade are to protect public health, prevent fraud, protect property rights, or prevent unfair competition[12]. The directive also permits Member States to adopt temporary protective measures where there are threats to public health[13]. The directive created the basis for, but did not itself impose, purity

---

1.   Council Directive (EEC) 83/417, OJ L237 26.8.83 p25. For the UK rules, see Caseins and
       Caseinates Regulations 1985 , SI 1985/2026; Caseins and Caseinates (Amendment) Regulations
       1989, SI 1989/2321. For the Italian rules, see *Alimenti e Bevande* at 580-587.
2.   R. Igoe, *Dictionary of Food Ingredients* p32 (2nd ed. 1989).
3.   T. Parratt, *Name Your Poison: A Guide to Additives in Drinks* p173 (1990).
4.   Council Directive (EEC) 83/417, above at the first recital of the preamble.
5.   The second recital of the preamble.
6.   Article 1(2) and Annexes.
7.   Rennet is an extract from calf stomachs, and contains an enzyme used to clot milk. A. Bender,
       Dictionary of Nutrition and Food Technology p243 (6th ed. 1990).
8.   Council Directive (EEC) 83/417, above at Article 1(2).   See also Article 2.
9.   Article 4.
10.   These requirements are without prejudice to the 1978 labelling directive, as amended.
11.   Article 6.
12.   Article 6(2).
13.   Article 7.

criteria and methods of analysis to enforce those criteria[1]. These are to be adopted by the Council "where necessary". The Standing Committee for Foodstuffs was given responsibility for reviewing the proposed methods, as well as other issues[2]. Rules for methods of analysis were adopted in 1985, and rules for sampling in 1986[3].

7.11   Alcoholic beverages

The regulation of alcoholic beverages stimulates complex political and economic issues within the Community. It is a major producer of such beverages, and many of the world's dominant brands are manufactured in its Member States[4]. Beer, wine and other alcoholic beverages have traditionally been the subject of elaborate regulations in most Member States to ensure quality and control competition[5]. Subsidies and other state aids have often accompanied the regulatory process. Some of the earliest examples of foodstuff regulation involved alcoholic beverages, and from the beginning national regulations have sought to shield local producers against distant competitors[6]. Competition is now international rather than local or national, and several Member States have important economic interests in encouraging the commercial success of their wines, beers and other beverages in other Community markets.

In these circumstances, it is hardly surprising that alcoholic beverages have been important subjects of both litigation and legislation in the Community[7]. The issues range from labelling and ingredient requirements to restrictions on the cultivation of hops and vines[8]. The Community has accumulated lakes of wine as well as mountains of grain and butter, and one problem has been to give equitable protection to the various national producing groups while also discouraging excess production. The appearance of new worldwide competitors in the production of wines, beers and other products has greatly complicated the Community's regulatory difficulties[9].

---

1.   Article 8.
2.   Article 10.
3.   For methods of analysis, see First Commission Directive (EEC) 85/503, OJ L308 20.11.85 p12; for methods of sampling, see First Commission Directive (EEC) 86/424, OJ L243 28.8.86 p29.
4.   Council Regulation (EEC) 1576/89, OJ L160 12.6.89 p1 at the second recital of the preamble.
5.   An account of the early history of brewing and beer regulation, particularly in England, is provided by J. Patton, *Additives, Adulterants and Contaminants in Beer* p4-42 (1989).
6.   There are many early examples, but two illustrations are the Assize of Beer and Bread in England and the Reinheitsgebot in Germany.
7.   For an extensive treatment of the issues, see P. Deboyser, *Le droit communautaire relatif aux denrées alimentaires* pp335-379 (1989).
8.   See, e.g., Council Regulation (EEC) 1170/77, OJ L137 17.5.77 p7; Council Regulation (EEC) 2776/78, OJ L133 23.11.78 p1. For interpretations of these or related provisions, see, e.g., *Liselotte Haner v Land Rhineland-Pfalz* [1979] ECR 3727; *EC Commission v Germany* [1983] ECR 1173.
9.   France's surplus in wine trading has, for example, gradually slipped in the face of non-European competition. See, e.g., *Eurofood* 10 (Dec. 1991).

Much of the litigation relating to alcoholic beverages has involved national programmes of financial or other assistance under the Treaty's restrictions upon state aids[1]. In essence, the issues are how much assistance, and in what forms, Member States may rightly grant domestic producers. There have, however, also been disputes regarding advertising, labelling designations, bottling and ingredient restrictions[2]. For example, the European Court has held that alcohol-free beverages cannot be presented as "wine"[3], and that wine bottled by others under contract cannot be described as "bottled by the producer"[4]. It has also held that Catalonia may prohibit the advertising of beverages containing more than 23 per cent alcohol[5].

A widely publicised example is the European Court's decision that various aspects of the German rules for beer purity are forbidden by Article 30 of the Treaty of Rome[6]. The Court held that the Reinheitsgebot, which evolved from early local and regional rules, including a Bavarian decree issued in 1516, placed undue restrictions upon the designation "bier" and was unnecessarily rigid in prohibiting the sale of beers containing additives[7]. German law forbade all additives, without regard to labelling disclosures or proof that any particular additive might be harmless. The European Court found that Germany offered no effective mechanism by which an importer or brewer could seek to justify an additive[8]. It held that the German legislation violated Article 30 of the Treaty and was not protected by

---

1. For illustrative cases involving state aids relating to alcoholic beverages, see, e.g., *EC Commission v Italy* [1984] ECR 1603; *France v EC Commission*, [1979] ECR 321; *Luxembourg v EC Commission*, [1984] ECR 2931. State aids are a major topic of Community disputes, and there are cases involving most important industrial sectors.

2. See, e.g., *Anton Adriaan Fietje* [1980] ECR 3839 (Dutch requirements for "likeur"); *Firma Joh. Eggers Sohn & Co. v Bremen*, [1979] 1 CMLR 562 (holding invalid German quality designations for wine applicable only to products processed largely in Germany). More recently, the European Court has overturned a Spanish rule requiring rioja wine to be bottled locally if it is to receive a certificate of origin. Europe, No. 5749 (n.s.) 14 (13 June 1992).

3. Case C-75-90 *Procureur de la Republique v Guitard* (Transcript) 15 July 1991. The case was returned to the French courts for a decision as to whether "alcohol-free wine" would be permissible under national law. The issue is the subject of differing national rules. See, e.g., 1 World Food Reg. Rev. 11 (Sept. 1991).

4. *Erzcugeergemainschaft Goldenes Rheinhessen v Land Rheinland Pfalz* [1990] 3 ECR 27.

5. Cases C-1/90, C-176/90 *Aragonesa de Publicidad Exterior v. Departamento de Sanidad y Seguridad Social* (Transcript) 25 July 1991. A trade association of beverage producers has subsequently expressed concern regarding such advertising prohibitions, and urged harmonised rules. See EIS, Europe Environment, No. 382 p.IV-4 (3 March 1992).

6. *EC Commission v Federal Republic of Germany* [1987] ECR 1213, 1262, [1988] 1 CMLR 780. For a discussion of the decision and related issues, see Clark, "The Free Movement of Goods and Regulation for Public Health and Consumer Protection in the EEC: *The West German 'Beer Purity' Case*", 28 Va. J. Int'l Law 753 (1988). For the Commission's assessment of the decision, see XXIst General Report on the Activities of the European Communities 1987, at p358 (1988) For a similar decision, see *Re Beer Purity Standards, E.C. Commission v. Greece*, [1988] 1 CMLR 813.

7. The Reinheitsgebot and related rules generally forbid additives and restrict use of the word "bier" to products containing only a short specified list of traditional ingredients. Some derogations are permitted under the *Biersteuergesetz*. [1988] 1 CMLR at 801.

8. [1988] 1 CMLR at 801-803. Ironically, it may also be said of the Community's additive rules that the possible mechanisms for obtaining the approval of new additives are likely to prove slow and difficult, to the point that they may be non-tariff trade barriers.

Article 36 because it offended the principle of proportionality[1]. Labelling was held to be a sufficient alternative. Germany has since attempted to modify the result by demanding exceptions to the proposed directives for the use of sweeteners and other additives in low-alcohol beers. The effort has thus far been rebuffed by the European Parliament[2].

A similar example is offered by a decision of the European Court regarding Dutch rules for the minimum alcohol content of gin[3]. The Dutch rules required a minimum alcohol content of 35 per cent and prohibited the sale of gins with lower alcohol levels. Belgian rules required a minimum alcohol content of 30 per cent, and Dutch authorities sought to prevent the sale of Belgian gins with alcohol contents below 35 per cent[4]. Upon reference from a Dutch court, the European Court held that the Dutch rules violated Article 30 of the Treaty unless consumers might be confused by the difference between the Dutch and Belgian products. The Belgian product was labelled to show its actual alcohol content, and the Dutch court had already held that there was no substantial risk of confusion[5]. On the other hand, the higher alcoholic content of the Dutch products meant that they were subject to higher taxes, and hence carried higher retail prices. In the absence of Community rules regarding minimum alcoholic content, the Dutch rules were forbidden by Article 30 of the Treaty[6]. The Dutch could continue to require higher alcohol content for their own products, but the rules could not be applied to properly labelled imported products.

A third example relates to Dutch rules which limited the acidity of beer and prohibited statements in labelling of the strength of the beer's original wort[7]. The rules were used to prohibit the sale of German beer which was more acid than the Dutch standard and whose label declared the strength of its original wort. The European Court held that the rules were intended to protect the traditional taste of local beer, and that under Article 30 of the Treaty they could not be used to prevent the sale of beers imported from other Member States[8].

---

1. In fact, most beers imported into Germany have elected to comply with the purity laws. *Eurofood* 10 (April 1992). For the principle of proportionality, see above at Chapter 3, para 3.1.
2. Above at Chapter 5, para 5.3.
3. *Miro BV* [1986] 3 CMLR 545, decided by the European Court in 1985 upon reference from the Gerechtshof of Arnhem.
4. Ibid., at p555.
5. Ibid., at p556.
6. Ibid., at pp560-561. Harmonised rules for spirit drinks, including gin, had been proposed at the time of the Court's decision, but had not then been adopted. They are described below.
7. The wort ("wert") is a mixture of crushed malt and water to which hops, yeast and sometimes sugar are added. See, e.g., T. Parratt, *Name Your Poison: A Guide to Additives in Drinks* p70 (1990).
8. *De Kikvorsch Groothandel-Import-Export BV* [1984] 2 CMLR 323, decided by the European Court in 1983 upon reference from the District Court in Arnhem. For a similar decision of the European Court overturning an Italian rule limiting the sulphur dioxide content of beer, while permitting higher levels in Italian wines, see *Europe* No. 5749 (n.s.) 13 (13 June 1992).

The Community's legislation regarding alcoholic beverages has been equally extensive, and has involved even more diverse issues. They range from vine cultivation to labelling, and from composition to pricing. Illustrations will show the breadth of the Community's rules. As early as 1972, for example, the Community began classifying vine varieties and examining the suitability of different varieties for cultivation in various regions of the Community[1]. It also adopted or proposed rules for classifying and describing "quality" wines, sparkling wines, and wine and grape musts[2]. In some instances, these rules limit the regions from which grapes could be used for various wines[3]. In 1990, the Commission issued a regulation which provides elaborate rules for the analysis of wines[4]. The regulation establishes methods of analysis regarding such questions as alcoholic strength by volume, reducing sugars, ash content, sulphates, total acidity and fluorides. The Community has also adopted rules governing the common organisation of the market in wines. They establish pricing systems, price interventions and supports, and other devices intended to "improve market conditions"[5]. As part of these efforts, the Commission publishes representative prices for table wines in locations ranging from the Rheinpfalz to Bari to Heraklion[6]. The programme offers economic protection to growers and producers by maintaining relatively stable prices throughout the Community.

Other measures warrant more detailed descriptions. As described below, the Community has adopted or proposed labelling and packaging requirements for most alcoholic beverages. It has also adopted recipe laws for many spirit drinks and aromatised wines. Some include protective measures for traditional products. All of these steps correspond to measures adopted or proposed for foodstuffs generally[7]. Together with the legislation described in earlier chapters, the Community's measures regarding alcoholic beverages illustrate its continued taste both for product formulae and for protective and promotional measures for well-established products.

---

1. The first step involved methods for determining the suitability of various varieties for cultivation. Commission Regulation (EEC) 2314, OJ L248 1.11.72 p53; Regulation (EEC) 3296/80, OJ L344 19.12.80 p13. For classifications of varieties, see Commission Regulation (EEC) 3800/81, OJ L381 31.12.81 p1. The most recent amendment is Commission Regulation (EEC) 3774/91, OJ L356 24.12.91 p36. See also Council Regulation (EEC) 2389/89, OJ L232 9.8.89 p1, as amended by Regulation (EEC) 3577/90, OJ L353 17.12.90 p23 .
2. See, e.g., Regulation (EEC) 817/70, OJ L99 5.5.90 p1; Regulation (EEC) 823/87, OJ L84 27.3.87 p1; Regulation (EEC) 2043/89, OJ L202 14.7.89 p1. For proposed amendments, see COM(90) 554. For similar Italian rules, see G. Andreis, et al., eds., *Codice di Diretto Alimentare Annotato* (1990), vol. 3 p.2202.
3. See 1 World Food Reg. Rev. 4 (Nov. 1991).
4. Commission Regulation (EEC) 2676/90, OJ L272 3.10.90 p1.
5. See Council Regulation (EEC) 822/87, OJ L84 27.3.87 p1, at Article 1(1) and Title III.
6. For examples of such price listings, see OJ C140 30.5.91 p2; OJ C289 7.11.91 p2.
7. For proposed measures for the protection and promotion of selected products, see above at Chapter 3, para 3.8.

7.11.1 Labelling and packaging rules

The Community's rules for the labelling and packaging of alcoholic beverages are not codified in any single measure. Like most of the Community's requirements, they have appeared incrementally in a series of separate measures. No more than illustrations can be given here. For example, as described above, it has adopted rules for the characterisation and presentation of "quality" wines[1]. In addition, the Commission adopted a directive in 1987 governing the display and placement on labels of statements of alcoholic content[2]. The directive is applicable to all alcoholic beverages containing more than 1.2 per cent of alcohol by volume[3]. It requires that alcoholic strength be measured at a particular temperature[4], describes how it must be indicated on the beverage's label[5], and specifies various tolerances for its disclosure with respect to particular beverages[6]. In 1990, the Commission prepared a working draft of a proposal to require ingredient labelling of alcoholic beverages[7]. The proposal would amend the 1978 labelling directive to compel ingredient labelling of beverages with an alcohol content greater than 1.2 per cent by volume[8]. The idea has a lengthy history. The 1978 labelling directive stated that by 1982 the Council would impose rules for both indications of alcohol content and ingredient labelling[9]. The promises proved, as others have, unduly optimistic. Rules for the disclosure of alcohol content were not adopted until 1987, and framework rules for ingredient labelling are still only a proposal[10].

By the mid-1980's, the Commission may have thought that suggestions of ingredient labelling had been abandoned. If so, the idea was "reactivated" when the European Court overturned portions of the German beer purity law[11]. Rather opaquely, the Commission has described ingredient labelling as necessary to "draw the consequences" of the Court's decision. The Commission presumably means that, rather than prohibitions against additives, labelling should ensure that consumers may if they wish choose among beers on the basis of "purity". The 1990 draft

---

1.   Regulation (EEC) 823/87, OJ L84 27.3.87 p1; Regulation (EEC) 2043/89, OJ L202 14.7.89 p1.
2.   Commission Directive (EEC) 87/250, OJ L113 30.4.87 p57 See also Commission Directive (EEC) 86/197, OJ L144 29.5.86. The substance of the proposal had been advanced five years before. See OJ C124 9.6.83 p23.
3.   Commission Directive (EEC) 87/250, above at Article 1. The Economic and Social Committee had unsuccessfully recommended that the rules should be applicable to all beverages with an alcohol content of at least 0.5 per cent. See OJ C124 9.5.83 p23.
4.   Article 2(1). The appropriate temperature is 20 degrees centigrade.
5.   Article 2(2).
6.   Article 3. Before the directive's adoption, the Economic and Social Committee noted that disclosing the alcohol content by volume might cause difficulties in countries where other forms of disclosure were traditional. See OJ C124 9.6.83 p23, above at 2.1.2. The European Parliament urged the adoption of reasonable tolerances, at least for beer. OJ 104 16.4.84 p139, at para 4.
7.   Working Document III/9081/90 - Rev. 1 (1990).
8.   At pages 4-5.
9.   Council Directive (EEC) 79/112, OJ L33 8.2.79 p1, at Article 6(3).
10. For declarations of alcohol content, see above at Chapter 3, para 3.3.1.
11. Working Document III/9081/90-Rev.1, above at 5. "Reactivate" is the expression used by the Commission.

proposal would amend Article 6 of the 1978 labelling directive to require ingredient labelling of alcoholic beverages. It would not, however, actually establish the rules for labelling, but instead would create a committee procedure which would later devise those rules. Somewhat different rules would be established for each product category[1].

The Community's rules also impose restrictions upon the containers in which alcoholic beverages are sold. In 1988, for example, the Council adopted a directive regarding the making-up by volume of certain prepackaged liquids[2] The directive imposes uniform container sizes for certain alcoholic beverages. Some sizes are "definitively" allowed, while others are permitted only on a temporary basis[3]. The temporary authorisations all expire by 1992[4]. The approved sizes differ in some instances from existing international sizes, and this may, in the view of the US Commerce Department, hamper importations of third-country products into the Community[5]. As described below, the Community also has imposed restrictions upon the shapes of wine bottles and other beverage containers[6]. The rules are intended to prevent confusion, but they also protect products traditionally bottled in containers of a certain shape. More recently, the Commission has proposed to eliminate leaded capsules for wine bottles by the end of 1993[7].

7.11.2 Spirit drinks

In 1989, the Council adopted a regulation designed to harmonise national laws regarding the definition, description and presentation of "spirit drinks"[8]. It defines such drinks in essence as those with an alcohol content greater than 15 per cent by volume[9]. They must be intended for human consumption, have particular organoleptic qualities, and have been produced either directly by distillation or by

---

1.   Ibid. The Economic and Social Committee has urgued that it is desirable and "necessary" to introduce rules for all beverages at the same time to avoid discrimination; OJ C104 16.4.84 p139 at para. 2.   For proposed revisions of the 1978 labelling directive regarding alcoholic beverages, see COM(91) 536 final, OJ C122 14.5.92 p12; above at Chapter 3, para 3.3.
2..   Council Directive (EEC) 88/316, OJ L142 10.6.88 p26. "Making-up" refers to permissible tolerances for the fill levels of containers.
3.   Annex III.
4.   Articles 5 (2), 5 (3) (c).
5.   US Dept. of Commerce, *EC 1992: A Commerce Department Analysis of European Community Directives*, vol. 1, pages 50-51.
6.   Council Regulation (EEC) 822/87, OJ L84 27.3.87 p1; Commission Regulation (EEC) 3201/90, OJ L309 8.11.90 p1; Commission Regulation (EEC) 153/92, OJ L17 24.6.92 p20. Below at Chapter 8, para 8.1.
7.   COM(92) 55 final, OJ C69 18.3.92 p12. See also, e.g., Reports of the Scientific Committee for Food, Twenty-sixth Series (1992); 1 World Food Reg. Rev. 9 (Jan 1992); *Wine Spectator* p8 (31 Oct 1991). The proposal has been endorsed by the Economic and Social Committee; OJ C169 6.7.92 p1.
8.   Council Regulation (EEC) 1576/89, above. For modifications and additions, see also Regulation (EEC) 3773/89, OJ L365 15.12.89 p48; Regulation (EEC) 1014/90, OJ L105 25.4.90 p9; Regulation (EEC) 1759/90, OJ L162 28.6.90 p23; Regulation (EEC) 3207/90, OJ L307 17.11.90 p11. For the UK rules, see Spirit Drinks Regulations, SI 1990/1179.
9.   Article 1(2).

a mixture of distilled and other products. Egg liqueur and advokat are exceptionally permitted an alcohol content of 14 per cent. The regulation acknowledges the importance of such drinks for the Community's farmers, many of whose products are used by the distilling industry. It sought to ensure the quality of the Community's spirit drink products by defining their permissible compositions and methods of production[1]. Concerns regarding international competition were undoubtedly a major factor in the regulation's adoption. Although adopted after the Community's switch to horizontal rulemaking in 1985, the regulation is in substance a series of recipe laws for particular spirit drinks.

Whisky, vodka, brandy, fruit liqueurs, and numerous other beverages are all defined in terms of their taste, strength and preparation[2]. Products which do not conform to the definitions are forbidden to use the names given to each product category[3]. Each category is assigned a minimum alcohol content by percentage of volume, although Member States may set higher minimums if they wish[4]. Additives are governed by the 1988 additives directive and flavourings by the 1988 flavourings directive[5]. Processing aids will be separately regulated, using a committee procedure involving the Implementation Committee for Spirit Drinks[6]. Colourings are governed by the 1962 colourings directive, as amended[7]. Except for some liqueurs, which may use nature-identical flavourings and preparations, only natural flavouring substances and preparations may be used[8]. As the name suggests, "nature-identical" flavourings are synthetic additives, but identical to those found in nature[9]. Any added water must conform to the Community's directives regarding water quality and purity[10].

Labelling must comply with the 1978 labelling directive, as amended, as well as additional rules imposed by the regulation itself[11]. The regulation requires labels to include one of the names for which it provides definitions. They must also include a listing of the agricultural alcohols used in the product. No quantitative disclosures are required, but the alcohols must be listed in descending order of

1.   The second recital of the preamble.
2.   Article 1(4). The article provides specifications for rum, whisky, grain spirit, wine spirit, brandy, grape marc spirit, fruit marc spirit, raisin spirit, fruit spirits, cider spirit, gentian spirit, fruit spirit drinks, juniper-flavoured spirit drinks, caraway and aniseed-flavoured spirit drinks, bitter, vodka, liqueur, and egg liqueur or advokat.
3.   Article 2.
4.   Article 3. Except for egg liqueur and advokat, which are assigned 14 per cent, the percentages range from 15 per cent for aniseed-flavoured drinks to 40 per cent for whisky. Article 3(1). For the use of labelling to eliminate trade barriers resulting from higher national minimums of alcohol content, see *Miro BV* [1986] 3 CMLR 545.
5.   Article 4.
6.   Articles 13(1) and 4(3). The committee consists of representatives of the Member States, chaired by a representative of the Commission.
7.   Article 4(4).
8.   Article 4(5).
9.   A. Bender, *Dictionary of Nutrition and Food Technology* p193 (6th ed. 1990).
10.   Article 4(6).
11.   Article 7.

quantity. In certain situations, the regulation permits labelling to use the word "blend". If a product's aging has been appropriately supervised, a maturation period may be indicated. A recent amendment prohibits the use of generic terms in compound names (for example, "cherry brandy") unless all of a product's alcohol comes exclusively from that source[1]. It also limits the compound names which may be used, and provides field of vision and other format requirements for the labelling of products which bear those names[2].

7.11.3 Aromatised wine products

In June 1991, the Council adopted a regulation establishing Community rules regarding aromatised wines and similar products[3]. The regulation divides such products into three categories. The first is aromatised wines. They include such products as vermouths, bitters, and such egg-based aromatised wines as cremovo zabaione[4]. The second category is aromatised wine-based drinks. They include such products as sangria, clarea, and mai wein[5]. These are drinks made from flavoured wines, sometimes sweetened, to which no alcohol has been added, and with an actual alcoholic strength greater than seven and less than 14.5 per cent by volume. The third category is aromatised wine-product cocktails. They include both wine-based products and semi-sparkling grape-based products[6]. These are drinks made from wine or grape must, flavoured, sweetened and sometimes coloured, to which no alcohol has been added. They have an actual alcoholic strength of seven per cent by volume. Wine coolers are to be the subject of a separate proposal from the Commission[7].

The regulation defines each of the categories and establishes requirements regarding their composition and manufacture[8]. The requirements include such matters as alcoholic strength[9], colouring[10], sweetening[11], flavouring[12], and other

---

1.   Commission Regulation (EEC) 1781/91, OJ L160 25.6.91 p5 at Article 7(1).
2.   Articles 7b(2), 7b(3). The Commission has also proposed a prohibition of lead-based capsules for closures, to be effective 1 January 1993, but with a right to use existing stocks. COM(92) 55 final, OJ C69 18.3.92 p12. The Economic and Social Committee has endorsed the proposal. OJ C169 6.7.92 p1.
3.   Council Regulation (EEC) 1601/91, OJ L149 14.6.91 p1. For the views of the Parliament and Economic and Social Committee, see OJ C124 9.5.83 p16; OJ C127 14.5.84 p185; OJ C129 20.5.91 p1. The Commission had proposed the regulation nearly five years before its adoption. OJ C269 25.10.86 p15.
4.   Council Regulation (EEC) 1601/91, above at Article 2(1) (a).
5.   Article 2(1) (b).
6.   Article 2(1) (c).
7.   Article 7(3). This was to have been proposed during 1991, but has not yet appeared publicly.
8.   Processing and raw material requirements may also be adopted through a committee procedure. Article 5 (2).
9.   Article 2. The regulation also defines "actual", "potential", "natural" and "total" alcoholic strengths. Articles 3(e)-(h).
10. Article 3(c). These must comply with the colourings directive, above at Chapter 5, para 5.5, and the proposed new colourings rules.
11. Article 3(a). All of the approved sweeteners are natural.

additives[1]. The regulation restricts both the types of alcohol and the quality of waters which may be used in the products[2]. Only the labels of drinks which satisfy the regulation's compositional and other requirements may use the sales descriptions defined by the regulation. Drinks which do not satisfy those requirements cannot be marketed with those descriptions, even if their names include such words as "type", "like" or "style"[3]. To prevent counterfeits, the regulation authorises national systems of supervision and protection. These may include requirements for mandatory authentication documents[4]. Verified commercial documents are required. Member States are to monitor compliance by designating one or more national regulatory agencies.

The products' labels must comply with the 1978 labelling directive as amended, but specific labelling and presentational requirements are also established[5]. Each product's sales description must be one of those defined by the regulation, although it may be supplemented by a reference to the "main" flavouring which has been used[6]. "Main" flavourings are not defined, but are presumably either the largest in volume or the predominant in organoleptic results. If the alcohol has come from only one raw material, it may be indicated on the label[7]. If the alcohol has come from multiple sources, no special indication may be included[8]. Ethyl alcohol used to dilute or dissolve additives is disregarded for this purpose. There are also definitions of "extra-dry", "dry", "semi-dry", "semi-sweet", and "sweet", each in terms of grammes of invert sugar per litre[9].

A committee procedure involving yet another implementation committee is to approve special labelling or presentational language relating to a product's particular properties, such as its history or method of production[10]. This appears to contemplate pre-marketing clearance, although perhaps on the basis of product categories rather than individual brands. In the original regulation, there was no express provision regarding pre-existing national rules. As described below, transitional rules have since been added[11]. The same committee procedure will

---

12.   Article 3(b). The flavourings must comply with the 1988 flavourings directive. Above at Chapter 5, para 5.2.

1.   Article 4(1). The additives must comply with the provisions of the 1989 framework additives directive. Above at Chapter 5, para 5.1.

2.   Articles 3(d), 4 (2), 4 (3). The permissible characteristics of ethyl alcohol in terms of strength and residues are set forth in Annex I.

3.   Articles 7(1), (2).

4.   Articles 9(1),(2).

5.   Article 8 (1).

6.   Articles 8 (2), (3).

7.   Article 8 (4).

8.   Ibid. The word "several" is used, and presumably means simply more than one.

9.   Article 2(5). The definitions of "extra-dry" and "dry" appear to have been reversed. Articles 2(5)(a), (b).

10.   Article 8 (9) (a). The new implementation committee is not named, but consists of representatives of the Member States, voting in accordance with Article 148 (2) of the Treaty, and chaired by a representative of the Commission. Article 12.

11.   Commission Regulation (EEC) 3664/91, OJ L348 17.12.91 p53.

create labelling rules for products before they are placed in containers intended for the final consumer[1]. For products sold in containers intended for the final consumer, the labelling disclosures must be given in one or more of the Community's official languages. This must be done in a fashion which permits consumers readily to understand them[2]. Alternatively, purchasers may be given the information by leaflets or other means.

The labels of products imported from outside the Community may include the requisite information in the official language of the product's country of origin, provided it is also given in one of the Community's official languages[3]. No provision is made for the use of alternative means of notification. This suggests, for example, that a Greek product sold in France with a label in Greek might satisfy the labelling requirements with a notice or leaflet in French, while a Turkish product with a label in Turkish would require a special French label. Products intended for export outside the Community must comply with the regulation's requirements, except insofar as separate rules are established through the committee procedure[4]. This is designed "to defend the reputation of Community aromatised drinks on the world market[5]." The provision may conceivably mark a more general change in the Community's attitudes regarding export products, which often have been permitted more lenient standards.

One of the regulation's goals is protective. It is designed to reserve the use of geographical descriptions to products which acquire their distinctive properties in those locations[6]. If the reputation of a product category is "closely linked to a traditional origin", consumers must be informed of a product's actual provenance[7]. Accordingly, manufacturers are required to disclose the true origins of products which do not come from a drink's traditional region of production. For example, labels for sangria must disclose the product's place of actual production unless it is Spain or Portugal[8]. In addition, three designations are reserved for aromatised drinks actually produced in specified regions. The reservation is, however, available only if the consumer is not misled as to the raw materials which have actually been used[9].

---

1.   Article 8 (9) (b).
2.   Article 8 (6).
3.   Article 8 (7).
4.   Article 11.
5.   The eleventh recital of the preamble.
6.   The fourth and sixth recitals of the preamble.
7.   The sixth recital of the preamble.
8.   Article 2(3) (a). This is also true of "clarea". Article 2(3) (b). The provisions are somewhat opaque, in that they state that (a) "sangria" must be accompanied by the words "produced in (the location of production)", unless it is Spain or Portugal; and that (b) "sangria" may replace the descriptive phrase "aromatized wine-based drink" only if the drink is produced in Spain or Portugal. Article 2(3) (a).
9.   Article 6(2) (b). The three designations are for Nurnberger Gluhwein, Vermouth de Chambery and Vermouth di Torino. Annex II. The standard set by Article 6(2) (b) is curious and perhaps

The regulation provoked substantial concern among producers and some Member States. There were widespread fears that the change from national to Community rules might prove confusing and disruptive. As a result, the Commission adopted transitional rules in December 1991[1]. Under the rules, products prepared or imported before December 17, 1991 may continue to be labelled and presented in accordance with any national rules previously applicable[2]. This derogation expires on December 16, 1992. The same derogation is permitted for products whose preparation began before December 17, 1991, and was completed by June 17, 1992. This includes all steps through bottling and labelling for the final consumer. Moreover, Member States may continue to apply their 1991 national rules until rules of application are adopted for the regulation. This is scheduled to occur in 1992[3]. Since additional transitional measures may be necessary when the rules are adopted, the regulation may not take full effect until 1993.

7.12   Meats and meat preparations

A principal topic of Community regulation since 1964 has been the production and marketing of fresh meats and meat preparations. Many of the measures are aspects of the Community's agricultural policies, and only indirectly relevant to its food regulatory programme. Some are, however, addressed to labelling, health and sanitation issues. A full description of the rules would be impractical here, but illustrations will suggest the scope and direction of the Community's policies. A more complete description has been included of the controversial problems surrounding minced meat.

The Council adopted rules regarding health problems affecting intra-Community trade in fresh meat as early as 1964[4]. It subsequently adopted similar measures relating specifically to poultry and other meats[5]. Those measures are designed to establish minimum sanitary standards for the slaughter of animals and poultry,

---

contradictory. The geographical designations are reserved for drinks the production of which took place in a geographical area where they acquired their "character and definitive qualities"; ibid. This is imprecise, but might be understood to suggest that the place of production, and not the place from which the raw materials came, should be decisive. At the same time, the consumer must not be "misled" as to the raw materials. If grapes from Sicily are used for vermouth made in Turin, is the consumer misled? If he or she may be deceived, why did the Council not say simply that the origin of the raw materials must be disclosed if it is not the place of production? Perhaps because it was prepared to ignore some (but not all) instances where raw materials have different origins.

1.   Commission Regulation (EEC) 3664/91, OJ L348 17.12.911 p53.
2.   Article 1.
3.   Article 2.
4.   Council Directive (EEC) 64/433, OJ 121 29.7.64 p2012. There have been many amendments, including Directive (EEC) 88/657, OJ L382 31.12.88 p3.
5.   See, e.g., Council Directive (EEC) 71/118, OJ L55 8.3.71 p23; Directive (EEC) 90/654, OJ L353 17.12. 90 p48; Commission Regulation (EEC) 1906/90, OJ L173 6.7.90 p1; Commission Regulation (EEC) 1980/92 OJ L198 17.7.92 p31.

and for their packaging, transport, and storage prior to sale[1]. They are in essence hygiene rules addressed to the particular problems of fresh meat. More recently, the Council has adopted a series of new measures which replace the earlier rules with respect to a wide variety of meat and other products. They include new rules for meat hygiene[2], live bivalve molluscs[3], fishery products[4], poultrymeat[5], rabbit, and farmed game meat[6]. Additional rules for poultry are in preparation. These measures are in essence all vertical hygiene rules. Nonetheless, they also regulate methods of processing and preparation, provide for the licensing of processing facilities, and establish standards for storage and transport[7]. In some cases, they incorporate packaging and labelling obligations[8]. There are also rules for supervision of slaughter and processing activities[9]. In many instances, they impose special requirements upon products imported from third countries[10]. Importers must provide health certifications and permit Community or national authorities to conduct inspections of their processing facilities, including those located outside the Community.

An example will indicate the content of the Community's measures. The best illustration is minced meats. Minced meat products present sensitive problems of consumer protection because of the readiness with which they may be adulterated[11]. Moreover, decisions of the European Court have partly eroded the effectiveness of national guarantees of product quality in this area. The Court has, for example, held that Member States may not prohibit the sale of "prepared meat products" imported from within the Community because they exceed local limitations on the content of water and non-fat organic matters[12]. In response, the Community has established standards for the production and marketing of minced meats and compound foodstuffs which contain minced meats[13]. More recently, the Commission has proposed to replace those rules with revised requirements[14].

1. For health markings, see, e.g., Directive (EEC) 80/879, OJ L251 24.9.80 p10; Commission Decision (EEC) 92/189, OJ L87 p25 (2 April 1992).
2. Council Directive (EEC) 91/497, OJ L268 24.9.91 p69; Council Directive (EEC) 91/498, OJ L268 24.9.91 p105. For broader new rules, see Council Directive (EEC) 92/5, OJ L57 2.3.92 p1; Consumer Law Bull. No. 66 p 5 (March 1992).
3. Council Directive (EEC) 91/492, OJ L268 24.9.91 p1.
4. Council Directive (EEC) 91/493, OJ L268 24.9.91 p15.
5. Council Directive (EEC) 91/494, OJ L268 24.9.91 p35.
6. Council Directive (EEC) 91/495, OJ L268 24.9.91 p41.
7. See, e.g., Annex to Council Directive (EEC) 91/492, above.
8. See, e.g., Annex to Council Directive (EEC) 91/492, above; Annex to Council Directive (EEC) 91/493, above.
9. Consumer L. Bull. No 66 p5 (March 1992).
10. See, e.g., Council Directive (EEC) 91/494, above at Chapter 3.
11. Council Directive (EEC) 88/657, OJ L382 31.12.88 p3, at the sixth recital of the preamble.
12. Case C-269/89 *Criminal Proceedings against Bonfait BV* [1990] ECR I-4169. The Court has also invalidated a Belgian prohibition against the importation of prepared meats containing more than a specified quantity of edible gelatin. *EC Commission v Belgium* [1990] 8 ECR 87.
13. Council Directive (EEC) 88/657, above.
14. COM(89) 671 final, OJ C84 2.4.90 p120.

The existing rules encompass all meat products which are either minced or cut into pieces of less than 100 grammes each[1]. Member States may permit the export of such products to other Member States only if they satisfy specific standards. They must be made from fresh meat, and the meat must have been processed in compliance with the Community's rules[2]. The products must have been prepared in processing facilities which satisfy detailed hygienic and methodological rules. The facilities must have been approved by national authorities, and they must have been identified in advance to the Commission[3]. Special inspection, packaging and storage requirements are applicable[4]. There are also labelling and transport rules[5]. Health marks must be displayed on labels or packaging, together with a disclosure of the species from which the meat came, the date of preparation, a list of any seasonings or other ingredients, the words "percentage of fat under ___", and the words "collagen: meat protein ratio under ___"[6]. A special health certificate must accompany export shipments to other Member States[7]. If the products are chilled or frozen, there are special temperature and processing requirements[8]. The rules for chilled minced meats are among the few requirements in the Community's food laws relating specifically to chilled products. Irradiation is forbidden[9]. So too are ultra-violet treatments. There are also limitations on the quantities of seasonings which may be included. Seasonings may not exceed three per cent of the finished product if added in a dry state, or ten per cent if added in another form[10].

In 1989, only a few months after the directive's adoption, the Commission began drafting new rules. In April 1990, it proposed that the 1988 directive's rules should be revised and extended, and that it should be replaced by a Council regulation[11]. Few legislative measures can have been designated for repeal so quickly after their adoption. The Commission's proposal would impose more stringent requirements regarding the processing and handling of minced meat products, and also create a

---

1. Council Directive (EEC) 88/657, above at Article 2(2). There are also definitions of meat preparations, seasonings, and other terms.
2. Article 3(1) (a).
3. Article 3(1) (b). Annex I to the directive contains conditions for the approval of processing facilities, conditions for the production of various meat products and preparations, inspection requirements, and other provisions.
4. Article 3(1) (c), (d). The rules, including compositional and microbiological standards, are set forth in annexes.
5. Article 3(1) (e), (f). The rules are set forth in Annex I to the directive.
6. Chapter VII of Annex I.
7. Article 3(1) (g). A designated form is provided.
8. Article 3(2) (c). They must be cooled to an internal temperature of less than 2°C. in a period of one hour or less. There are rules for both frozen and deep-frozen products.
9. Article 3(2) (d).
10. Article 3(2) (e).
11. COM(89) 671 final, OJ C84 2.4.90 p120. The fact that a regulation has been proposed suggests concern that regulatory action should be taken more uniformly and with greater urgency than has occurred through the 1988 directive. For amendments to the proposal see COM(91) 374 final, OJ C288 6.11.91 p3.

mechanism for continuing revisions through a committee procedure involving the Standing Veterinary Committee[1].

The proposal would distinguish between products intended for direct and indirect use, and require labelling or notices which would advise consumers of proper methods of preparation[2]. Labels might, for example, be required to warn consumers that the meat should be thoroughly cooked before consumption[3]. The proposal would also require meats to be processed within specified periods after slaughter, and impose additional chilling and packaging obligations[4]. The proposal has, however, provoked debate in both industry and the European Parliament, and extensive revisions may be made before any measures is adopted[5].

One of the Commission's proposed additions to the 1988 directive warrants special attention. The proposal would permit veterinary experts from the Commission to conduct inspections to ensure that its rules are uniformly and rigorously enforced[6]. The Commission's inspectors would visit processing facilities and make on-the-spot evaluations of equipment and procedures. The proposal has not yet been adopted, but merely the inclusion of such a device marks an important new stage in the Commission's approach to the issues of official controls for foodstuffs[7]. Although a small veterinary staff already existed in DG VI, the Commission has only recently acceded to proposals for a Community food inspectorate[8]. Even if the minced meat proposal does not signal a general change in the Commission's policies, it will be compelled to find some distinction between minced meats and such controversial issues as additives. It will be difficult to explain why a more lenient attitude should be taken regarding the latter, or why Community inspections are practical and necessary only regarding the former.

---

1.   Articles 8, 9. The Standing Veterinary Committee was created by Council Decision (EEC) 68/361, OJ L255 18.10 68 p23. It includes representatives of each of the Member States.
2.   See, e.g., Written Question 1030/91, OJ C315 5.12.91 p25.
3.   The European Parliament has proposed such warnings, as well as a special campaign to educate consumers about the hygiene risks of animal products.
4.   The principal debates regarding the proposal centre on the rapidity of the meat's use after slaughter and of cooling after its preparation. For a review of the controversy, see Fogden, "European Community Minced Meat Legislation", 2-3/91 Eur. Food L. Rev. 150 (1991).
5.   Ibid. For Parliament, see OJ C183 15.7.91 p57.
6.   COM(89) 671 final, at Article 6.
7.   For the Commission's other policies in the area of official controls, see below at Chapter 8, para 8.6.
8.   With prompting from the European Parliament, it has agreed to a "small" group of Commission officials who would assist national inspectors and encourage cooperative national efforts. Below at Chapter 8, para 8.6.3.

7.13   Yellow fat products

As described above, the Community has adopted rules for the common organisation of the markets both for milk products and for oils and fats[1]. They are aspects of the Common Agricultural Policy, and provide various marketing and production controls and incentives. An important purpose is to stabilise agricultural production and protect the Community's farmers against external competition. Although they and other measures have stimulated relatively high butter consumption in the Community, there are continuing complaints that the market for butter is threatened by margarine and other fat-based products[2]. In response, the Commission proposed a new regulation in 1991 to control the trade descriptions and labelling of butter, margarine and similar products[3]. The proposal states that fat-based products have caused a general reduction in butter consumption, and that new rules are needed to ensure market "stability" and protect a "fair standard of living for the agricultural population"[4].

The proposal would establish trade descriptions for various products with fat contents between 20 and 95 per cent by weight[5]. Different names would be assigned to 22 categories of products based upon their percentages of fat and whether the fats are milk, non-milk, or blends of plant or animal products[6]. Products with fat contents above 95 per cent or below 20 per cent would be excluded from the proposal, and would continue to be governed by any applicable national laws[7]. In addition, blended products with a milk-fat content greater than 80 per cent or less than 15 per cent of the total fat content are not unequivocally included[8]. Similarly, non-milk fat products with milk fats which exceed 3 per cent of the total fat content also appear to be omitted[9]. Nor would the proposal apply to products which do not remain solid at ambient temperatures and are not suitable for use as spreads[10]. These omissions are not explained, and may reflect either inadvertence or implicit derogations for selected product categories.

---

1. See, e.g., Council Regulation (EEC) 804/68, OJ L148 28.6.68 p13; Regulation (EEC) 1630/91, OJ L150 15.6.91 p19; Council Regulation (EEC) 136/66, OJ 172 30.9.66 p3025; Regulation (EEC) 1720/91, OJ L162 26.6.91 p27.
2. For butter consumption and the Common Agricultural Policy, see above at Chapter 2, para 2.2.2.
3. COM(91) 462 final, OJ C36 14.2.92 p12.
4. The fifth recital of the preamble.
5. Article 1.
6. Annex II. The trade descriptions include butter, dairy spread, margarine, low-fat spread, blended spread, and blended low-fat spread.
7. The thirteenth recital of the preamble.
8. Annex II at C. Such blended products are defined as containing a milk-fat content of between 15 and 80 per cent of the total fat content. A product with, for example, a milk-fat content of 90 per cent of a total fat content of 20 per cent appears to be outside all of the proposed definitions.
9. Annex II at B.
10. Article 1(2).

The proposal would amend the 1978 labelling directive to impose special disclosure obligations[1]. Labels would be required to use the appropriate trade descriptions defined in the proposal's annex; state the total percentage of fat content by weight; provide an "indication" of anhydrous milk fat, butter fat or concentrated butter; and state that the product is "salted" if its salt content exceeds 0.1 per cent by weight[2]. The information would have to be readily understandable, easily recognisable, indelible, clearly visible, and legible. For sales not made to consumers or mass caterers, it would be enough if the label revealed the trade description, net quantity, a lot or batch identification, and the name and address of the manufacturer or distributor, or of a vendor established in the Community[3]. Member States could adopt rules for quality levels, based upon organoleptic characteristics and physical and microbiological stability[4]. Imported products would be required to satisfy the proposal's rules, but the Council could permit derogations in "peculiar" situations[5]. More detailed rules would later be adopted for the application of the proposal, for sampling, and for statistical compilations regarding the relevant markets[6]. Penalties for violations of the proposal would be established by Member States[7].

The proposal is chiefly intended as an additional source of protective devices for the Community's dairy farmers. Nonetheless, its unaccountable limits and distinctions suggest that the Commission also seeks to shield selected producers or product categories from Community regulation. The number and subtlety of its distinctions are more likely to confuse than to inform consumers. The Community's legislative process is, however, only beginning, and substantial revisions in the proposed regulation may yet be made. In the interim, the proposal does nothing to enhance the Commission's reputation for regulatory neutrality[8].

---

1.   Article 4 (1).
2.   Weights are measured as of the time of use. There are various limits.
3.   Article 5 (1).
4.   Article 6.
5.   Article 7. No explanation is offered of the "peculiar" circumstances which might justify exceptions for some third countries.
6.   Article 9. The statistical compilations would presumably be intended in part to facilitate any additional protective steps which might be thought appropriate.
7.   Article 11.
8.   The Commission has separately instructed Denmark to postpone proposed rules for labelling the fat content of emulsified fats, other than margarine and halvarine. Commission Decision (EEC) 92/238, OJ L121 6.5.92 p48.

CHAPTER 8 : MECHANISMS FOR OFFICIAL CONTROL AND MISCELLANEOUS ISSUES

In addition to the substantive regulations described above, the Community has adopted numerous ancillary rules which relate, exclusively or in part, to foodstuffs. Some of those measures, such as those regarding official controls and inspections, have major importance for the effectiveness of the Community's harmonisation programme. They were priorities in the 1985 programme for the completion of the internal market[1]. Other measures were outside the immediate boundaries of the 1985 programme. For example, the Community has had rules regarding the permissible fill levels of pre-packaged products since the 1970's[2]. Those rules are designed to prevent deception by establishing maximum tolerances for the actual contents of jars, bottles and other containers. Among other products, the rules govern the fill levels of foodstuff containers. Still other measures were within the 1985 harmonisation programme, but also form part of the Community's agricultural policies. For example, the Community has had rules since 1976 regarding the maximum levels of pesticide and other chemical residues in or on foodstuffs[3]. Those rules have become increasingly controversial as consumer groups and the European Parliament have demanded more stringent limitations upon the use of agricultural chemicals.

There are many other ancillary measures. For example, the Community adopted unit pricing policies in 1979 with respect to many consumer products, including foodstuffs. Those policies were revised in 1988, but their requirements are still subject to numerous exceptions. Indeed, the rule remains the exception[4]. Similarly, the Community is preparing framework standards for the handling of packaging waste. Its proposed rules are likely to include stringent obligations for recycling and limitations upon the use of landfills[5]. They may have an important impact upon the food industry, which is a major source of packaging waste. The Council has also adopted a directive establishing Community rules for product liability. It is applicable to virtually all products, including foodstuffs, and creates substantial liabilities if defective products result in damage or injury[6]. The Commission has recently adopted a general safety directive, which again reaches foodstuffs and virtually all other products[7]. It demands a high standard of product safety, and

---

1.   1985 Foodstuffs White Paper, COM(85) 603, above at 13-14.
2.   Below at Chapter 8, para 8.1.
3.   Below at Chapter 8, para8.3.1.
4.   Below at Chapter 8, para 8.4.
5.   Below at Chapter 8, para8.2.
6.   Below at Chapter 8, para 8.7.1.
7.   Below at Chapter 8, para 8.7.1.

authorises recalls and other regulatory sanctions when products fail to satisfy that standard. Both measures could have significant implications for the food industry.

The most important of these ancillary areas is the creation of an effective system of official inspections and controls. No issue of food regulation is more urgent than the "terrible" problem of ensuring uniform monitoring and control of food labelling and safety[1]. As the trade in foodstuffs becomes increasingly international, the enforcement of food law grows more urgent and complex[2]. Surprisingly, the Community is only now beginning serious efforts to address the problem. Although direct Community inspections are authorised in special situations, the Community has generally relied upon national authorities to interpret and enforce its harmonised food rules. Until recently, there were no Community guidelines for the exercise of those powers. It was not until 1989 that the Council adopted a framework directive which imposed general standards regarding official foodstuff controls[3]. The Commission has proposed supplemental measures to implement the 1989 directive, as well as measures regarding food hygiene and the prevention of contamination[4].

In all, the Community's record of progress regarding these disparate issues remains uneven and unsatisfactory. Its pesticide residue rules are still incomplete. Unit pricing remains largely a theory. The issues of packaging waste have not yet been effectively addressed. Although adopted in 1985, the product liability directive has still not been transposed into national law by two Member States[5]. Serious questions may be asked about the policies of the general safety directive. Unpackaged products are still not the subject of systematic rules. Many of these deficiencies are relatively minor. The inadequacies of the Community's rules regarding pesticide residues are more serious, and its failure to ensure effective food controls and inspections is a major omission from its regulatory efforts.

---

1. One member of the European Parliament prominent in the discussion of food issues has rightly observed that "the problem of enforcement is a terrible one for the European Community at the moment." She added that the Parliament knows "perfectly well that a number of Member States actually take no notice [of Community measures] at all." Interview with Dr. Caroline Jackson, MEP, 1 World Food Reg. Rev. 22, 23 (July 1991).
2. See, e.g., Gray, "Whither Food Regulation?", 1 World Food Reg. Rev. 33,35 (July 1991).
3. Below at Chapter 8,para 8.6.3.
4. Below at Chapter 8, paras 8.6.1- 8.6.3.
5. At the time of writing, the delinquents were France and Spain. Ireland and Belgium did not adopt the directive until 1991, although the official deadline for doing so was in 1988.

8.1   Prepackaging standards

Beginning early in its history, the Community has sought to ensure the accuracy and fairness of the quantities of products sold in a pre-packaged form[1]. The issue has been a recurrent source of legislation[2]. While the prepackaging rules are applicable to a wide range of consumer products, they have special relevance to the food industry, where processed foods have made prepackagings common and important[3]. Consumers understandably expect similar containers to provide similar weights or volumes of products. Within minimal tolerances, they expect a litre bottle to contain a litre of product. A reasonable standardisation of the sizes, fill and labelling of different containers may facilitate intra-Community trade and permit consumers to make more rational choices among brands and products. The Community's prepackaging rules are addressed to all of these issues. In addition, there are emerging Community and national rules imposing limitations upon the shapes of some packaging.

A threshold problem is to ensure the accuracy with which the necessary measurements are made. In 1971, the Community adopted a directive intended to harmonise national laws regarding measuring instruments and methods of metrological control[4]. In 1974, it adopted another directive relating to bottles used as measuring containers[5]. At the same time, the Council began addressing the problems of slack fill[6]. It adopted another directive relating to the "making-up" by volume of pre-packaged liquids[7]. The directive is applicable to such products as

---

1.   Prepackaging is essentially that form of packaging which is provided before the time of purchase and not at the purchaser's direction. See, e.g., Council Directive (EEC) 75/106, OJ L42 15.2.75 p1.

2.   There is also extensive national legislation. For France, for example, see J. Botrel, *L'Emballage: Environment socio-economique et juridique* pp71-89 (1991); Souverain, "Réglementation des emballages", in G. Bureau & J-L Multon, eds., *L'Emballage des Dénrees Alimentaires de Grande Consommation* pp101-11 (1989); Castan, "Normalisation des emballages", ibid. at pp128-139.

3.   For a review of similar legislation in the United States, see Hutt, "Development of Federal Law Regulation of the Slack Fill and Deceptive Packaging of Food, Drugs, and Cosmetics", 42 Food D.C. L.J. 1 (1987).

4.   Council Directive (EEC) 71/316, OJ L202 6.9.71 p1. The directive created approval standards for measuring instruments, verification procedures, rules for the control of instruments while they are in service, and procedures for updating the directive's rules.

5.   Council Directive (EEC) 75/107, OJ L42 15.2.75 p14. The directive applies to bottles with a capacity between 0.5 and five litres intended for the storage, transportation or delivery of liquids; ibid. at Article 1. They must be specially marked and satisfy various tolerance levels for error. Annex I. As of 31 December 1989, the directive had been adopted in all of the Member States except Portugal. Seventh Annual Report to the Council regarding the Application of Community Law, COM(90) 288 final, at p115.

6.   "Slack fill" is used to describe less than complete fill of a container. Incomplete fill may be deceptive, in the sense of providing less than appears to have been promised, but it may also result from technical packaging limitations. A bottle not filled to the top may be deceptive, or it may be an honest consequence of the packaging process. The difference will depend on the candour of the packaging and labelling.

7.   Council Directive (EEC) 75/106, OJ L42 15.2.75 p1. The term "making-up" is used to denote the appropriate fill level, within prescribed tolerance levels, of various containers. Together with other requirements, the 1975 directive requires prepackages to include an indication of a nominal volume, and limits the permissible nominal volumes which may be selected. Article 4. As of 31 December 1990, the directive had been adopted by all Member States except

beer, wine, milk and fruit juices[1]. In 1976, the Council adopted another directive regarding the making-up by weight or volume of other pre-packaged products[2]. It is principally applicable to non-liquid products. Both directives were intended to ensure candour and reasonable accuracy in the packaging of foodstuffs, although other consumer products were also included. To assist these efforts, the Council created an advisory committee in 1971 with the formidable title of the Committee on the Adaption to Technical Progress of Directives Designed to Eliminate Technical Barriers to Trade in the Measuring Instruments Sector[3].

In 1978, the Commission revised the requirements of the 1975 and 1976 directives with respect to both liquid and non-liquid products[4]. Several amendments have subsequently followed[5]. In 1980, the Council supplemented the 1976 directive by adopting another measure relating to the nominal quantities and volumes of other pre-packaged products[6]. The 1980 directive applies to such products as butter, cheeses, salt, certain sugars, cereal products, rice, pasta, coffee, and various frozen products[7]. It requires the products' labels to include disclosures of nominal weights and volumes. It also limits the permissible weights and volumes in which the products may be marketed[8]. This too has subsequently been amended[9].

The rules established by these directives are too numerous and complex for complete description. They are, however, all premised upon a belief that packaging standardisation may both increase market transparency and encourage cross-border sales. The directives recognise that Member States had established elaborate national requirements regarding packaging fill and sizes[10]. They also recognise that variations in those national requirements can create barriers to the circulation

---

Portugal. Eighth Annual Report to the European Parliament on Commission Monitoring of the Application of Community Law, OJ C338 31.12.91 p1 at p118.

1.　Among other products, the directive also applies to cider, spirits, vinegar, edible oils, and bottled waters; Annex III.

2.　Council Directive (EEC) 76/211, OJ L46 21.2.76 p1. The directive applies to foodstuffs and other products, provided they are not encompassed by Directive (EEC) 75/106, above. It requires the disclosure of nominal weights and volumes, Article 4, and provides extensive rules for the fill of prepackagings. Annexes I, II. As of 31 December 31, 1989, the directive had been adopted in all Member States except Portugal. Seventh Annual Report to the Council regarding the Application of Community Law, COM(90) 288 final, at 116.

3.　Council Directive (EEC) 71/316, above at Article 18.

4.　Commission Directive (EEC) 78/891, OJ L311 4.11.78 p21 (revising certain of the Annexes to Directives 75/106 and 76/211, above. As of 31 December 1989, the directive had not yet been adopted by Spain or Portugal. It has since been adopted by them. COM(90) 288 final, at p119.

5.　Council Directive (EEC) 85/10, OJ L4 5.1.85 p20; Council Directive (EEC) 88/316, OJ L143 10.6.88 p26; Council Directive (EEC) 89/676, OJ L398 30.12.89 p18. All these amend Council Directive (EEC) 75/106, above.

6.　Council Directive (EEC) 80/232, OJ L51 24.2.80 p1.

7.　Annex I.

8.　Article 3. As of December 31, 1989, the directive had been adopted by all Member States except Spain and Portugal. COM(90) 288 final, at 120. Spain has since adopted it.

9.　Council Directive (EEC) 86/96, OJ L80 25.3.86 p55 (revising certain of the product designations). As of 31 December 1989, the directive had not yet been adopted by Spain or Portugal. Seventh Annual Report to the Council regarding the Application of Community Law, COM(90) 288 final, at 129.

10.　See, e.g., Council Directive (EEC) 75/106, above, at the first recital of the preamble; Council Directive (EEC) 76/211, above, at the first recital of the preamble.

of goods throughout the Community. A producer distributing a foodstuff packaged in a size permissible in Italy may, for example, find that another size is required in Germany or France. A third size may be needed in Britain or Spain. Special sizes for each Member State result in higher packaging costs and discourage intra-Community trade. Similar problems may arise from inconsistent national rules regarding fill levels and tolerances. Moreover, consumers may be misled if apparently comparable containers from different Member States in fact contain different volumes or weights[1].

To avoid such problems, the Community has sought to harmonise national requirements regarding the size, labelling and markings of prepackages[2]. In particular, it has limited the permissible sizes and maximum allowable tolerances for prepackagings used for many product categories[3]. For example, such products as butter and pasta may be sold to consumers throughout Community only in specified package sizes. Within narrow tolerance limits, those packages must contain specified weights or volumes. Their labels must accurately disclose that weight or volume. Unfortunately, the prepackaging directives are not yet comprehensive, and there are still products as to which national requirements may differ[4]. This is not an area of urgent regulatory priority for the Community. It is, however, one of the many areas in which incomplete harmonisation may permit consumer deception or the preservation of trade barriers.

Even harmonised prepackaging rules do not, however, always resolve the potential problems. In 1985, for example, a Dutch producer wished to affirm to his German buyer that boxes of chicken conformed to the weight and measurement requirements of the 1976 directive[5]. For reasons left unclear, the Dutch authorities failed to affix a designation of compliance with the directive's rules[6]. Upon reference from a

---

1. See, e.g., Council Directive (EEC) 80/232, above, at the third recital of the preamble, reciting the need for "greater market transparency."
2. For example, Council Directive (EEC) 75/106, above, defines "nominal volume" and requires an indication of that volume on prepackages. Article 4 and Annex I, paragraph 2.1. It also fixes a tolerable negative error. Annex I, paragraph 2.4. There are separate requirements for the inspection and verification of packaging sizes and weights or volumes. See, e.g., Council Directive (EEC) 78/891, above at Annexes I and II.
3. As noted above, the product categories include wines, vermouths, cider, sparkling wines, malt beers, spirits, vinegar, edible oils, milk, waters, lemonades and fruit juices. Council Directive (EEC) 75/106, above, at Annex III. Since 1980, they also include butter, fresh cheeses, table salt, sugars, cereal products, pasta, rice, dried fruits and vegetables, coffee, frozen products, ice creams, and products sold in aerosols. Council Directive (EEC) 80/232, above at Annexes I, III. Many of the early recipe laws also included requirements as to permissible packaging sizes; above at Chapter 7. For alcoholic beverages, see Council Directive (EEC) 88/316, above.
4. For example, Council Directive (EEC) 80/232, above, provides permissible sizes for some products (e.g., truffles and tomatoes) but not many others. Annex II, para 1 (2). Nonetheless, Council Directive (EEC) 88/316, above, recognises that "total" harmonisation is desirable "whenever possible". The second recital of the preamble.
5. Case 96/84 *Vereniging Slachtpluimvee-Export eV v REWE-Zentraal AG* [1986] 3 CMLR 467, decided by the European Court in 1985 upon reference from the Amtsgericht in Cologne.
6. Under Council Directive (EEC) 76/211, above, a sign is used to designate containers which comply with its requirements.

German court in Cologne, the European Court held that producers are entitled to add the designation themselves if they measure or sample the containers in accordance with procedures established by national authorities. If national authorities do not establish procedures, producers may rely upon the directive itself to justify any procedures reasonably calculated to ensure that a container's stated contents correspond to its actual contents[1]. The decision sensibly resolves a minor issue of application. It is, however, a useful reminder that harmonised rules are not self-executing, and that some supervision of national implementational measures is important.

Separate problems may arise from rules regarding packaging shapes. Two forms of issues may be presented. First, some packaging shapes are potentially deceptive. This is particularly likely when souvenir or other special containers are used. The Community has generally refused to impose restrictions upon the form or content of such packagings, although the 1978 labelling directive may be sufficiently broad to prohibit any which are actually deceptive[2]. In another area, however, the Community has adopted special rules defining and limiting the use of certain wine bottles[3]. One of their purposes was to prevent consumer confusion regarding the types and origins of wines contained in the bottles.

Related issues arise from national rules which limit the permissible packaging shapes for particular foods or beverages[4]. Such rules are not generally forbidden by Community legislation unless they create barriers to intra-Community trade prohibited by Article 30 of the Treaty of Rome. For example, the European Court has held that a Member State may not reserve bottles of a particular shape for designated domestic wines, while forbidding their use by imported wines[5]. The Court reasoned that such rules may give a competitive advantage to domestic products, and thus represent a non-tariff trade barrier. Similarly, national rules which required margarine to be sold in a particular shape to distinguish it from butter were held invalid because they hindered the sale of imported margarine[6]. The Court's principal concern in these cases was the existence of impediments to intra-Community trade, and not whether the packagings may be deceptive.

---

1.   [1986] 3 CMLR at 474-475.
2.   For the rules imposed by the 1978 labelling directive, see above at Chapter 3, para 3.1.
3.   Council Regulation (EEC) 822/87, OJ L84 27.5.87 p1; Commission Regulation (EEC) 3201/90, OJ L309 8.11.90 p1; Commission Regulation (EEC) 153/92, OJ L17 24.1.92 p20.
4.   France, for example, established rules for the shapes of wine bottles in 1930 and for the shapes of margarine products in 1931. J. Botrel, *L'Emballage: Environment socio-economique et juridique* p262 (1991).
5.   See *Criminal Proceedings against Karl Prantl* [1984] ECR 1299, [1985] 2 CMLR 238, decided by the European Court in 1984 upon reference from the Landsgericht in Munich. The Court held that no property right to a particular bottle shape is protected by Article 36 of the Treaty.
6.   See Case 261/81 *Walter Rau Lebensmittelwerke v De Smedt* [1982] ECR 3961, [1983] 2 CMLR 496, decided by the European Court in 1982 upon reference from the Landsgericht in Hamburg. See also Case 341/82 & 189/83 *Re the Packaging of Margarine, EC Commission v Belgium* [1985] 1 CMLR 120, which terminated without a judgment.

Nonetheless, Member States are entitled to defend their national rules under Article 36 of the Treaty on the basis that they prevent deception. In such cases, the national rules are valid only if proportional to their asserted goals. In other words, national rules are permissible only if there is no alternative device which, by imposing fewer restrictions, could still prevent consumer deception. Labelling requirements will often represent such an alternative.

8.2   Packaging waste

The Community and several Member States have begun giving increasing attention to the reduction, recovery and recycling of packaging waste. The problems of packaging waste are not restricted to the food industry. Nor are those problems new. Soldered cans, for example, date from 1810, and three-piece cans from 1888[1]. Plastics have been in widespread use for several decades.

Nonetheless, take-away restaurants and the growing use of processed foodstuffs have made food packaging an obvious subject of regulation. Indeed, food and beverage packagings reportedly constitute 40 percent of all packagings in the United States, and perhaps 12 percent of all solid waste[2]. Some estimates are higher, and it has been suggested that food and beverage packaging may represent 60 percent of all packaging[3]. In Britain alone, some 7.5 million cans of foods are consumed annually[4]. Other forms of food packaging are equally important, and the relative volumes are certainly comparable in other Member States. On the other hand, Europe with a larger population consumes less packaging than the United States[5]. The debate in Europe over food packaging waste may, as one commentator has argued, be characterised by "emotion" and an absence of "real understanding", but the public concerns are nonetheless genuine and influential[6]. Substantial controls upon packaging waste are likely, and those controls may involve important obligations for the food and packaging industries.

1.   Griffin, "Retortable Plastic Packaging", in F. Paine, ed., *Modern Processing, Packaging and Distribution Systems for Food* p1 (1987).
2.   Hoffmann & Nowell, "The FDA's Environmental Impact Analysis Requirements: Food Packaging and Solid Waste Management," 45 Food D.C.L.J. 615, 617 (1990).
3.   Ibid. For an account of the problems, see Graff, "The Looming Crisis in Plastic Waste Disposal", 4 Issues in Science & Tech. 105 (1988).
4.   Rees, "Introduction," in J. Rees & J. Bettison, *Processing and Packaging of Heat Preserved Food* p1 (1991). The figure includes jars and plastic containers of heat preserved foods.
5.   Karjalainen, "Packaging of Carbonated Beverages," in F. Paine, *Modern Processing, Packaging and Distribution Systems for Food* pp110, 126 (1987).
6.   See Proffit, "Packing of Heat Preserved Foods in Plastic Containers," in J. Rees & J. Bettison, *Processing and Packaging of Heat Preserved Food* p186 (1991).

241

Much of the impetus for controlling packaging waste has come from the Member States[1]. Germany has adopted an ordinance which imposes stringent restrictions on packaging, requires deposits, and sets high goals for recycling[2]. Producers elsewhere in the Community fear that the results may be impediments to intra-Community trade, and have challenged the German rules both before the Commission and at the German Cartel Office[3]. In the Netherlands, a voluntary agreement between industry and government has established recycling and other goals[4]. France has adopted its own measure and Ireland is preparing legislation. Other Member States have adopted or are considering measures[5]. A group of associations of consumer goods firms has proposed its own principles[6]. The issues have become a major source of public and governmental controversy to which the Community is only belatedly responding.

Faced with a changing situation over which it has exercised little control, the Commission has prepared several versions of a new Community measure. All of the versions recognise that the Community's earlier efforts in this area produced little progress. A 1985 directive requiring the recycling of some liquid containers has had "disappointing" results[7]. The Council has also adopted a resolution regarding waste policy and a strategy for waste management, but there have been few practical consequences[8]. Less than 20 percent of all packaging waste in the Community is now recycled, and only ten percent of domestic waste[9]. These are overall levels, and there are higher averages in Germany, for example, and lower averages elsewhere[10]. In Britain, only 5 percent of all solid waste is said to be recycled[11].

---

1.   International pressures have also had a role. The Organisation for Economic Co-operation and Development endorsed the principle that the "polluter pays" as early as 1972.
2.   The German Verpackungs-verordung was issued in June 1991. For it, Sse, e.g., "Survey of the Food Industry," *Financial Times* (10 May 1991); *Eurofood* 7 (May 1991); Explanatory memorandum accompanying Working Document XI/369/91 (21 Feb 1992) at para 3.2.
3.   *Financial Times* p10 (14 Aug 1991); Explanatory memorandum accompanying Working Document XI/369/91 (21 Feb 1992) at para 4.2.
4.   Covenant Verpakkingen (16 May 1991); *Eurofood* 1, 3 (April 1991).
5.   See, e.g., 2/9 Mealey's European Environment L. Rep. 6 (Dec. 11, 1991); *Eurofood* 4 (Dec. 1991); Explanatory memorandum accompanying Working Document XI/369/91 (21 Feb 1992) at para 3.2. The French rules are in Law 75-633, as amended by Law 92-646 in July 1992.
6.   Europe, No. 5469 at 14 (11 April 1991); *Eurofood* 6 (May 1991).
7.   See the Explanatory memorandum accompanying Working Document XI/369/91 (21 Feb 1992) at para 1.5. Several versions of the new proposal have been prepared. The earlier directive was Council Directive (EEC) 85/339, OJ L176 6.7.85 p18.
8.   Community Strategy for Waste Management, SEC (89) 934 final; Council Resolution, OJ C122 18.5.90 p2.
9.   The overall Community percentage for the recovery of packaging waste is more than 43 per cent for industrial waste, but only 10 per cent for domestic waste. For other estimates, see *The Times* p2 (7 Oct 1991).
10.   For example, some 72 percent of all drinks packaging is evidently now recycled in Germany; *Financial Times* p10 (14 Aug 1991).
11.   *The Times* p2 (7 Oct 1991).

The Commission's proposed directive would establish a framework of goals and criteria to guide national rulemaking[1]. Those goals and criteria have, however, changed from one to another of the Commission's drafts. Early versions emphasised the importance of collecting additional information regarding packaging waste. An elaborate database would have been created. It would have been used to establish benchmark levels of waste, and Member States would have been required to restrict future waste levels to the benchmarks. The final proposals still include databases, but place greater emphasis on the creation of waste management criteria and goals[2]. Recycling would be greatly increased, and the use of waste for energy conversion reduced. Landfill would become a last resort[3]. Within 10 years, the Commission hopes that 90 percent of packaging will be recovered, and 60 percent recycled[4].

These goals would extend to all levels of the distribution chain, including waste left in the hands of consumers. A system of Community symbols or markings would be used to inform producers and consumers about packaging recovery and recycling[5]. Taxes, deposits and fees could be used to encourage recoverable packaging[6]. National implementational measures would be notified to the Commission for review by it and other Member States[7]. A new technical committee would be established[8]. Extensive national databases would be established[9].

Fundamental alterations may be made before any directive is adopted. At this stage, it may only be said that the Commission's proposal includes ambitious goals and difficult obligations. Many issues would be left for national resolution, and the proposal might do little more than establish minimum standards. Little harmonisation might result. Surprisingly, the proposed rules do not include obligations for the Commission or national authorities to consider environmental and waste issues in their approvals of new packaging and food contact materials.

Moreover, it must be remembered that packaging offers advantages as well as costs. Packaging reduces contamination and spoilage, maintains quality, inhibits tampering, and provides surfaces for labelling disclosures[10]. Some changes in

---

1.   Explanatory memorandum accompanying Working Document XI/369/91 (21 Feb 1992) at para 5.1. For the final proposal, see COM(92) 278 final, OJ C263 12.10.92 p1.
2.   Ibid., at Articles 7 (essential requirements), 8 (information systems), and Annex II (essential requirements).
3.   Article 4.
4.   Ibid.; EC Food Law 10 (July 1992).
5.   Article 6.
6.   Article 11.
7.   Article 13.
8.   Article 17.
9   Article 8.
10.   Report of the Committee on the Microbiological Safety of Food, Part I, para 7.10 (1990); Hoffmann & Nowell, "The FDA's Environmental Impact Analysis Requirements: Food

packagings could result in increased risks of microbiological contamination[1]. Not all changes would create such risks, and there is undoubtedly room for improvement in the quantities and forms of packagings, but the changes must be selected with care. In addition, new restrictions upon the forms and compositions of prepackagings could prove a source of trade barriers. The new German rules have already been challenged upon this basis. Other illustrations may readily be found in existing national and local legislation. For example, some Italian municipalities have prohibited the use of plastic bottles for the packaging of mineral water[2]. Plastic bottles create disposal problems not presented by reusable glass bottles, and in general are environmentally less desirable. On the other hand, glass bottles are more costly and difficult to transport[3]. As a result, a requirement for glass containers offers a competitive advantage to regional or local producers against their more distant international rivals. Italy's municipal rules may have been adopted entirely for environmental reasons, but their consequences include the protection of local markets and the creation of trade barriers.

Similarly, producers of German mineral water designed a plastic container suitable for compliance with Germany's recycling obligations[4]. The container was made available only to German producers. As a result, foreign producers were less able to satisfy the stringent German requirements, and were placed at a competitive disadvantage. Even if foreign producers were permitted to use the German container, the obligation to use a special container for Germany would itself tend to discourage imports. The German container is simultaneously a contribution to environmental improvement and an impediment to foreign competition.

A third example is provided by a decision of the European Court in 1988[5]. To reduce packaging waste, Danish law required all beer and soft drinks to be sold in reusable containers approved by national authorities. Foreign producers were permitted limited exceptions to test the Danish market or make sales in small quantities. The Court acknowledged the problems of packaging waste and the logic of reusable containers, but held that Denmark's rules nonetheless violated Article 30 of the Treaty. It found that the obligation to use only approved containers was a barrier to

---

Packaging and Solid Waste Management," 45 Food D.C.L.J. 615, 617 (1990); J. Botrel, *L'Emballage: Environment socio-economique et juridique* pp305-313 (1991); Dimitrova, "Physical Distribution Today", in F. Paine, ed., *Modern Processing, Packaging and Distribution Systems for Food* pp132, 136 (1987).

1. Report of the Committee on the Microbiological Safety of Food, Part I, para 7.10 (1990).
2. The Italian rules were evaluated on behalf of the Commission by Group MAC as part of its studies of non-tariff trade barriers. See The "Cost of Non-Europe" in the Foodstuffs Industry, volume 12, part B of Research on the "Cost of Non-Europe", at pp395-427.
3. Karjalainen, "Packaging of Carbonated Beverages," in F. Paine, ed., *Modern Processing, Packaging and Distribution Systems for Food* pp110, 129 (1987).
4. The 'Cost of Non-Europe' in the Foodstuffs Industry, volume 12, part B, at pp371-394.
5. Case 302/86 *Re Disposable Beer Cans, EC Commission v Denmark* [1989] 1 CMLR 619, decided by the European Court in 1988. See also Explanatory memorandum accompanying XI/369/92 (21 Feb 1992) at para 1.6.

foreign products, and that the quantitative exceptions permitted by the Danish rules were inadequate to remedy the defect.

The examples show the readiness with which packaging rules may, deliberately or not, become impediments to foreign competition. National rules are particularly susceptible to such abuse, but requirements adopted by the Community could also permit either barriers to international competition or distortions of intra-Community trade. The Community should encourage reductions in packaging waste and more vigorous competition in packaging efficiency, but care will be needed to ensure that environmental measures do not impair product safety or create new trade barriers. The pace of rulemaking for packaging waste was not set by the Community, and it has still shown little leadership, but it may nonetheless eventually regret the haste with which complex and important issues are being addressed.

8.3   Pesticide and other chemical residues

For centuries, the most urgent issues of food regulation were purity, price, and availability. Foods were often adulterated, costly, and scarce. The regulatory focus has now changed. Scarcity has become plenty, real prices have declined, and choices have multiplied. The public's fears about adulteration have become anxieties about additives, chemical contaminants and environmental quality. Consumers are now separated from farmers by complex networks of processors and distributors[1]. Many foods have become manufacturing products, and many diets consist largely of processed or fabricated foods. There is growing disagreement about the seriousness, and even the reality, of widely publicised hazards. Consumers may imagine one set of risks, while scientists and regulators perceive quite different hazards[2]. The results are sometimes uncertainty and mistrust.

Many of the most controversial issues arise from the public's fears about agricultural chemicals. Pesticides are a particular subject of dispute. The question links doubts about food safety with demands for environmental protection[3]. For example, a committee of the European Parliament found that agricultural

---

1.   For the changes, see, e.g., Hermus, "The Consequences of 100 years' evolution of dietary habits in Europe with regard to nutrition", in H. Deelstra, et al., eds., *Food Policy Trends in Europe* pp67-73 (1991); R. Tannahill, *Food in History* pp332-371 (rev. ed. 1988).

2.   Scientists and consumers often have different perceptions of risk regarding such issues as pesticides and additives. See, e.g., Slovic, "Perception of Risk", 236 Science 280 (17 April 1987). For other observations of the differences, see, e.g, Foster, "Perennial Issues in Food Safety", in D. Cliver, ed., *Foodborne Diseases* pp372-374 (1990); P. Hutt & R. Merrill, *Food and Drug Law, Cases and Materials* pp176-177 (2nd ed. 1991); Scheuplein, "Do Pesticides Cause Cancer?", Consumers' Research p30 (Dec. 1991).

3.   For the interrelationships among food safety, processing, agriculture and the environment, see above at Chapter 2, para 2.2.2.

chemicals create "enormous risks" for both the environment and human health[1]. It urged the Commission to ban all chemicals "alien to the ecosystem", and to do so "forthwith". In the same spirit, a commentator claimed that Britain's regulation of pesticides represents a public "crisis"[2]. He argued that most pesticides should be prohibited because there are no harmless levels of residues[3]. There are many who disagree with these views, but the pressures they impose upon the Community's food policies are genuine and important[4].

Those pressures are not restricted to the Community. Controversies relating to pesticides and other agricultural chemicals have been particularly strident in the United States, but they are a worldwide phenomenon[5]. Virtually all of the major international food and health organisations have demanded regulatory measures. There have, for example, been studies by the United Nations Environmental Program and the Council of Europe, and regulatory proposals by the Codex Alimentarius Commission[6]. The United Nations Food and Agricultural Organization has prepared an International Code of Conduct on the Distribution and Use of Pesticides. The Organisation for Economic Cooperation and Development has urged adoption of the FAO's code by all nations[7]. The World Health Organization has proposed principles for evaluating the safety consequences of pesticide residues[8]. These and similar efforts have made pesticides

1. Report of the Committee on Agriculture, Fisheries and Rural Development, Document A3-0311/90 (19 Nov 1990) at 36.
2. C. Robbins, *Poisoned Harvest* p169 (1991). Since his complaints, some additional steps have been taken. One is the National Pesticides Retrieval Scheme, sponsored by industry but endorsed by government, to retrieve illegal or unwanted pesticides. MAFF Food Safety Directorate Information Bulletin 8 (Aug 1991). The programme is reportedly successful; *Daily Telegraph* p2 (1 Jan 1992).
3. C. Robbins, *Poisoned Harvest* pp113, 119-124 (1991). The absence of a threshold safety level is disputed. See, e.g., Taylor, "Chemical Intoxications", in D. Cliver, ed., *Foodborne Diseases* p174 (1990); National Research Council, *Regulating Pesticides in Food: The Delaney Paradox* pp13-14 (1987).
4. For other fears about the health issues, see, e.g., Bartle, "Quiet Sufferers of the Silent Spring", *New Scientist* pp30-35 (18 May 1991); P. Hurst, A. Hay & N. Dudley, *The Pesticide Handbook* (1991); A. Watterson, *Pesticides and Your Food* (1991).
5. For the principal US measure, see Pesticide Chemicals Act, P.L. No. 83-518, 68 Stat. 511 (codified as 21 U.S.C. 346a). For reviews of the issues in the United States, see, e.g., National Research Council, *Regulating Pesticides in Food: The Delaney Paradox* (1987); Merrill, "Regulating Carcinogens in Food: A Legislator's Guide to the Food Safety Provisions of the Federal Food, Drug, and Cosmetic Act", 77 Mich. L. Rev. 171 (1978); Ely, "Regulation of Pesticide Residues in Food: Addressing the Critical Issues", 40 Food D.C.L.J. 494 (1985); Middlekauff, "Pesticide Residues in Food: Legal and Scientific Issues", 42 Food D.C.L.J. 251 (1987); Poliner, "The Regulation of Carcinogenic Pesticide Residues in Food: The Need to Reevaluate the Delaney Clause", 7 Va. J. Nat. Res. Law 111 (1987).
6. Mestres, "L'analyse des résidues toxiques; son interêt et ses limites; exemple des résidues de pesticides", in R. Derache, ed., *Toxicologie et Sécurité des Aliments* pp105-127 (1986); P. Hurst, A. Hay & N. Dudley, *The Pesticide Handbook* p227 (1991). There are, however, wide differences in the various rules and standards which have been adopted. Although the United States, for example, has approved more than one-half of the Codex proposals, the remaining differences are still substantial. 1 World Food Reg. Rev. 13 (Nov 1991).
7. P. Hurst, A. Hay & N. Dudley, *The Pesticide Handbook* pp226, 231 (1991).
8. See World Health Organisation, *Principles for the Toxicological Assessment of Pesticide Residues in Food* (1990).

an important subject of international debate. They are rightly said to "arouse strong emotions" and to present questions about which few are neutral[1].

One source of the controversy is the number and diversity of pesticide products. There are some 1500 pesticides, and they represent a heterogeneous mixture of features and risks[2]. Another source of concern is the perception that pesticides are poorly regulated. In Britain, for example, pesticides are said to be both over-used and misused, and subject only to incomplete controls[3]. Britain's enforcement programme has been termed a "mockery"[4]. No prosecutions have reportedly ever been instituted for violations of its residue limits[5].

Very different views are, however, held by others. Many scientists see little evidence of substantial risks to human health from most pesticide residues[6]. They perceive far greater risks from naturally-occurring pesticides found in virtually all foods[7]. By one estimate, the average human intake of natural pesticides exceeds that of synthetic chemicals by ten thousand times[8]. These scientists discount the importance of pesticides and deride the assumption that nature is benign[9]. They urge some balance between "chemophobia" and the "sensible management" of industrial chemicals[10]. They argue that absolute safety is unattainable, and that it should be sufficient if any risks are negligible[11]. They also agree with Canada's Health Protection Branch that pesticides should be credited with major increases in agricultural productivity[12].

1.   P. Hurst, A. Hay & N. Dudley, *The Pesticide Handbook* p1 (1991).
2.   Periquet, "Toxicité des résidus de pesticides", in R. Derache, ed., *Toxicologie et Sécurité des Aliments* pp326-327 (1986).
3.   London Food Commission, *Food Adulteration and How to Beat It* pp79-109 (1988).
4.   Ibid., at 104.
5.   Ibid. See also C. Robbins, *Poisoned Harvest* p113 (1991).
6.   See, e.g., Foster, "Perennial Issues in Food Safety", in D. Cliver, ed., *Foodborne Diseases* p378 (1990); Taylor, "Chemical Intoxications", ibid., at p174. An expert panel of the National Research Council in the United States found that significant risks are limited to a relatively few foods and pesticide products. Some 80 per cent of the risks were said to be confined to 10 compounds found in 15 food products. National Research Council, *Regulating Pesticides in Food: The Delaney Paradox* p14 (1987).
7.   Pariza, "Diet and Cancer", in D. Cliver, e.d., *Foodborne Diseases* p310 (1990); Scheuplein, "Do Pesticides Cause Cancer?", Consumers' Research p30 (Dec. 1991).
8.   Ames, et al., "Ranking Possible Carcinogenic Hazards", 236 Science pp271, 272 (17 April 1987)
9.   Ibid., at p277. See also Mitjavila, "Substances naturelles nocives des aliments", in R. Derache, ed., *Toxocologie et Sécurité des Aliments* p129 (1986).
10.   Ames, et al., "Ranking Possible Carcinogenic Hazards", 236 Science 1256, 1261 (23 Sept 1983).
11.   For the impossibility of absolute safety, see, e.g., Cliver "Organising a Safe Food Supply System", in D. Cliver, ed., *Foodborne Diseases* pp353, 354 (1990); Rico, "Medicaments vétérinaires et hygiène publique", in R. Derache, ed., *Toxicologie et Sécurité des Aliments* pp383, 401 (1986); Gray, "Whither Food Regulation?", 1 World Food Reg. Rev. pp33, 34 (1991). The issue of zero risk versus negligible risk has been vigorously debated in the United States, where an expert panel of the National Research Council urged the latter standard. *Regulating Pesticides in Food: The Delaney Paradox* p13 (1987). The appropriateness of a negligible risk standard is disputed by, e.g., C. Robbins, *Poisoned Harvest* pp113, 119-124 (1991).
12.   Health Protection Branch, *Health Protection and Food Laws* p83 (4th ed. 1985).

The Community's response to these conflicting claims is characteristically equivocal. It has proceeded cautiously, neither prohibiting most agricultural chemicals nor permitting their unrestricted use. Its assumptions are unarticulated and its rules incomplete. Although the Community adopted limitations for pesticide residues in fruits and vegetables as early as 1976, the 1976 directive does not include many foodstuffs[1]. Moreover, it has not eliminated important differences in national laws even with respect to the fruits and vegetables to which it is applicable[2]. The Council has more recently adopted four measures which supplement the 1976 rules. Two provide more rigorous rules for many foodstuffs, but another is only a framework for future rulemaking. The fourth measure, adopted in 1991, establishes a registration system and positive list for pesticide products. It also authorises provisional residue limits. Nonetheless, the Community must still agree upon the residue levels which should be permitted with respect to many pesticides and foodstuffs. The rules relating to other agricultural chemicals are equally incomplete[3]. The Community has adopted measures regarding many phytosanitary and veterinary issues, including growth hormones, harmful substances in animal feedingstuffs, and plant protection chemicals. Other important issues must still be resolved.

Nor have the Community's measures quieted the public's fears[4]. Despite repeated complaints from the European Parliament and consumer groups, the Community has done little to encourage alternative methods for controlling pests and plant disease[5]. Its principal interest has remained the elimination of trade barriers. Human health has naturally been an important consideration, but the Community's level of concern about agricultural chemicals is still far short of that demanded by some consumer groups and members of the European Parliament. It is perhaps unfair to claim, as one parliamentary committee has done, that the Commission displays the "greatest possible sympathy for the interests of the chemical industry", but the Commission's measures have certainly been guided by consensus and compromise[6].

---

1. Council Directive (EEC) 76/895, OJ L340 19.12.76 p26. The Community's efforts have been in part encouraged by the Council of Europe. See, e.g., Mestres "L'analyse des résidues toxiques; son interêt et ses limites; exemple des résidues de pesticides", in R. Derache, ed., *Toxocologie et Sécurité des Aliments* pp105-127 (1986). There are of course also many national rules. For those in Italy, for example, see G. Andreis, et al., eds., *Codice di Diretto Alimentare Annotato* (1990) vol.1, p519.
2. Above at para 8.3.1.
3. Above at para 8.3.2.
4. Illustrations of the public concerns may be found, for example, in a report of the House of Lords Select Committee on the European Communities. See *1992: Health Controls and the Internal Market*, Session 1988-89, 9th Report (1989).
5. The Community's principal effort is a measure relating to the labelling and production of organic foodstuffs. Above at Chapter 3, para 3.7. There is also a proposed Council regulation to encourage agricultural methods which will better protect the environment; COM(90) 360 final (30 Jan 1991). The proposal would offer incentives to farmers to reduce their use of pesticides and other chemicals. See, e.g., EC AgVet Briefing (Feb. 1992).
6. Report of the Committee on Agriculture, Fisheries and Rural Development, Document A3-0311/90 (19 Nov 1990) at p37.

8.3.1   Pesticide residues

The Community began addressing the classification, packaging and labelling of dangerous substances as early as 1967[1]. Rules specifically for pesticides were adopted in 1978[2]. The Community began regulating pesticide residues two years earlier, when the Council adopted a directive establishing maximum residues for fruits and vegetables[3]. The 1976 directive relates to food products derived from fruits and vegetables and intended for human consumption[4]. The specific fruit and vegetables to which the directive applies are listed in two annexes, and include the most commonly used varieties. The directive imposes residue limits both for pesticides and for toxic breakdown or metabolised products which result from pesticides[5]. It establishes maximum permissible levels for some 55 residues, and prevents Member States from prohibiting trade in foodstuffs with residues which do not exceed those limits[6]. Annex II to the directive contains a list of pesticides and the permissible levels for their residues in and on various fruits and vegetables. It has been amended on five occasions, generally to revise the permissible levels[7]. The prescribed levels range from nil to 15 ppm, but vary by pesticide and foodstuff[8]. The limits for lindane, for example, range from 0.1 ppm for carrots to 2.0 ppm for leafy vegetables.

Member States may temporarily reduce a maximum level fixed by the 1976 directive for products consumed within their own territories, but only if the prescribed level might endanger human health[9]. Such decisions are reviewed by the Community to determine whether the directive's annex should be amended, or whether instead the national action should be overridden. The Commission refers the issues to a committee of national representatives known as the Standing Committee on Plant Health[10]. A more important derogation permits Member States to make upward changes in the prescribed limits. Member States may permit sales within their own territories of products with residues in excess of the maximum limits established by the directive[11]. In 1979, the Commission adopted a

1.   Council Directive (EEC) 67/548, OJ 196 16.8.67 p1, as last amended by Directive (EEC) 90/517, OJ L287 19.10.90 p37.
2.   Council Directive (EEC) 78/631, OJ L206 29.7.78 p13, as last amended by Directive (EEC) 84/291, OJ L144 30.5.84 p1.
3.   Council Directive (EEC) 76/895, OJ L340 19.12.76 p26. For a description of the role and calculation of maximum residue levels ("MRLs"), as well as no observable effect levels ("NOELs") and acceptable daily intakes ("ADIs"), see, e.g., A. Watterson, *Pesticides and Your Food* 11-12 (1991).
4.   Council Directive (EEC) 76/895, above at Article 1.
5.   Article 2(1).
6.   Article 3(1).
7.   Commission Directive (EEC) 80/428, OJ L102 19.4.80 p26; Council Directive (EEC) 81/36, OJ L46 19.2.81 p33; Council Directive (EEC) 82/528, OJ L234 9.8.82 p1; Council Directive (EEC) 88/298, OJ L126 20.5.88 p53; Council Directive (EEC) 89/186, OJ L66 10.3.89 p36.
8.   Council Directive (EEC) 76/895, above at Annex II.
9.   Article 4(1).
10.   Ibid. See also Council Decision (EEC) 76/894, OJ L340 9.12.76 p25. There is also a Scientific Committee on Pesticides.
11.   Article 3(2).

supplemental directive establishing methods of sampling for use in measuring pesticide residues[1].

The 1976 directive soon became a subject of increasing dissatisfaction. In large measure, this resulted from the provision allowing Member States to authorise higher residue levels with respect to products sold within their own territories[2]. This led to a patchwork of differing national levels, and compromised the harmonisation which the 1976 directive was intended to achieve[3]. It is likely that products containing higher residue levels permitted in one country have been sold or consumed in other Member States. This may have occurred even where the importing nation had not elected to permit higher levels[4]. Other complaints arose from the failure of the 1976 directive to establish maximum residue levels for many pesticides, and fears that the uncontrolled residues could threaten human health[5]. Those concerns were somewhat reduced by a decision of the European Court that neither the 1976 directive nor the Treaty of Rome prevents Member States from forbidding the sale of imported products treated with pesticides not covered by the directive[6]. Nonetheless, the Council adopted a new directive in 1990 to establish revised maximum levels for pesticide residues in and on many products of plant origin[7].

The 1990 directive is applicable to tea, hops, oil seeds, pulses, fungi, fruits and vegetables[8]. It is not applicable if they are used for the manufacture of products other than foodstuffs[9]. Nor does it apply if they are used for sowing or planting[10]. More important, the 1990 directive is only a regulatory framework. It authorises, but does not itself provide, new maximum levels of pesticide residues[11]. A committee procedure involving the Standing Committee for Plant Health is to establish the new limits[12]. Residues now controlled by the 1976 directive will

1. Commission Directive (EEC) 79/700, OJ L207 15.8.79 p26.
2. Council Directive (EEC) 90/642, OJ L350 14.12.90 p71, at the eighth recital of the preamble.
3. The ninth recital of the preamble.
4. It has been argued that Britain, for example, maintains inadequate controls over pesticide residues in and on imported food products. See, e.g., C. Robbins, *Poisoned Harvest* pp126-127 (1991); P. Hurst, A. Hay & N. Dudley, *The Pesticide Handbook* pp248, 250-254 (1991).
5. In Britain, only 64 of some 400 approved products have been assigned maximum residue levels. C. Robbins, *Poisoned Harvest* p103 (1991). As described above, an American report concluded that 80 percent of all pesticide risks relate to 10 products found in 15 foods. National Research Council, *Regulating Pesticides in Food: The Delaney Paradox* p14 (1987).
6. Case 54/85 *Ministere Public v Mirepoix* [1986] ECR 1067, [1987] 2 CMLR 44, decided by the European Court in 1986 upon reference from the Tribunal de Police of Dijon.
7. Council Directive (EEC) 90/462 above. USITC describes the debate which preceded the 1990 directive's approval as "protracted". USITC, *The Effects of Greater Economic Integration within the European Community on the United States, Third Report*, 4-25 (1990).
8. Council Directive (EEC) 90/462, above at the Annex.
9. Article 1(4) (a).
10. Article 1(4) (b). The scope of these exceptions was evidently once a matter of concern to US industry, but it is reportedly now satisfied. USITC, *The Effects of Greater Economic Integration within the European Community on the United States, Third Report*, p4-25 (1990).
11. Council Directive (EEC) 90/462, above at Article 1(1).
12. Article 10.

gradually be moved to control under the 1990 directive as new limits are established[1]. Until the process is complete, both directives will remain in effect[2]. Once new limits are established, Member States will be required to sample relevant food products to ensure those limits are not exceeded. If they are not, Member States cannot impede trade in the products[3]. Unlike the 1976 directive, Member States may not authorise higher levels of residues in foodstuffs intended for consumption within their own territories. As a result, a much greater degree of agreement must be reached among the Member States regarding permissible residue levels. As the absence of specific levels in the 1990 directive suggests, the process of reaching agreement may be prolonged.

An important area of dispute in the preparation of the 1990 directive related to labelling. The Commission originally proposed that the labelling of products with residues resulting from post-harvest preservation treatments should be required to disclose those treatments[4]. A notation would have been required stating "treated with", followed by the product's common name or, if none, its chemical name. For wholesale, this information would have appeared on invoices and one external side of the packaging. For retail, there would have been "some visible indication giving the consumer clear information". Alternatively, other steps could have been used to give consumers notice of the treatment. A similar proposal was made in Britain by the Food Advisory Committee[5]. The proposed disclosure rules proved to be controversial, and were omitted from the final directive. The proposed notices were a major concern to American producers, on the basis that they might alarm consumers[6].

The 1990 directive applies special rules to products intended for export. They will generally be subject to the new residue limits, but exceptions will be permitted where the receiving country wishes a product to receive an additional treatment[7]. The importing country might prefer this, for example, to protect the product during transport or against local hazards. In such cases, it is permissible to exceed the Community's maximum limits. The directive does not, however, indicate clearly how and by whom such treatments must be requested. For example, what would occur if a private buyer requested an additional treatment, but the buyer's

---

1.   The fourteenth recital of the preamble and Article 1(1).
2.   The fifteenth recital of the preamble.
3.   Article 5.
4.   COM(88) 798 final, OJ C46 25.2.89 p5, at Article 6.
5.   The Food Advisory Committee proposed the requirement of a labelling notice of a post-harvest treatment where it is applied to a food, and not merely to a food ingredient. Food Advisory Committee Report on Food Labelling and Advertising 1990 (1991) at para 184. It also suggested consumer educational campaigns, and a requirement to provide proper handling instructions. At paras 165-186. The latter might include, for example, instructions to peel or wash food before use; at para 286.
6.   USITC, *The Effects of Greater Economic Integration within the European Community on the United States*, Third Report, 4-25 (1990).
7.   Council Directive (EEC) 90/462, above at Article 1(3).

government neither approved nor disapproved its use? Would the sale be required to await governmental approval? And must the approval be specific to the sale? The directive offers no answers. One indication is offered by the International Code of Practice adopted by the United Nations Food and Agricultural Organisation, which provides that the importing nation must grant "prior informed consent" to any pesticide treatment[1]. It is likely that the directive is intended to create a similar rule[2].

Member States may reduce the maximum residue limits for products sold within their territories, but only if human or animal health is endangered and "swift action" is required[3]. This is, in other words, designed to permit emergency responses to unanticipated health risks, and not to provide another invitation to separate national rules. There is no repetition of the arrangement in the 1976 directive which permitted national derogations from Community residue limitations. National actions are reviewed by the Standing Committee on Plant Health to determine whether they should be overridden, or whether instead the directive's limits should be altered[4].

Some of the sampling methods used to enforce the 1990 directive will be derived from the 1979 sampling directive[5]. Others will be established through a committee procedure involving the Standing Committee on Plant Health[6]. The same procedure will be used to establish analytical methods to determine residue levels. Significantly, any amendments to the forthcoming annex, which will establish the actual limits upon pesticide residues, must be adopted by the Council based upon proposals from the Commission. The full legislative process under the Treaty will be required, rather than a simplified committee procedure. Member States were hesitant to allow changes in permissible residue levels without full legislative review.

In 1986, ten years after its original directive regarding residues on fruits and vegetables, the Council adopted two directives to broaden the range of foodstuffs to which residue limitations are applicable[7]. The 1986 directives established a pattern of rules subsequently followed in the 1990 directive. The first of the 1986 directives was intended to harmonise national laws regarding pesticide residues in

1.   P. Hurst, A. Hay & N. Dudley, *The Pesticide Handbook* p227 (1991).
2.   On the other hand, the Commission has rejected the idea of prior informed consent by nations importing the Community's pharmaceutical products, describing it as an "unmanageable bureaucratic system". Written Questions 2420/91 and 2470/91, OJ C141 3.6.92 p18.
3.   Council Directive (EEC) 90/462, above at Article 8(1).
4.   Article 8(2).
5.   Commission Directive (EEC) 79/700, OJ L207 15.8.79 p26.
6.   Council Directive 90/462, above at Article 6(1).
7.   Council Directive (EEC) 86/362, OJ L221 7.8.86 p37; Council Directive (EEC) 86/363, OJ L221 7.8.86 p43.

and on cereals[1]. It applies rules similar to those in the 1976 directive to wheat, rye, barley, oats, maize, paddy rice, buckwheat, millet, grain sorghum and other cereals[2]. Unlike the 1976 directive, however, the cereals directive generally does not permit Member States to authorise residue levels for domestic sales higher than those prescribed by the directive's annex[3.] Nonetheless, Member States may permit higher levels if the product is not intended for immediate consumption and a control system will ensure that it cannot reach consumers until the residues no longer exceed the directive's maximum levels[4]. On the other hand, Member States may impose temporary lower residue levels if they believe that human or animal health may be endangered by the directive's prescribed level, and that swift protective action is required[5]. Such national actions may be overriden through a committee procedure involving the Standing Committee on Plant Health[6]. The 1986 directive's list of maximum permissible residue levels for various pesticides and cereals was updated in 1988[7].

The second 1986 directive was issued simultaneously with the cereals directive. It was intended to harmonise national laws for pesticide residues in and on foodstuffs of animal origin[8]. The directive applies to the most commonly used animal foodstuffs, including meats, eggs, cheeses, milk and cream[9]. Its rules are similar to those established by the 1986 cereals directive.

In 1991, the Council supplemented these measures with a registration system and positive list for plant protection chemicals[10]. Such rules were initially proposed in 1976, abandoned in 1983, and finally revived in 1989[11]. The directive provides that products marketed before 1993 may, at the election of the Member States, remain on the market until 2003[12]. In the interim, they are to be evaluated by the Commission and Member States. A future regulation will prescribe standards and methods for the evaluative process. Products introduced after 1993 may be approved only if, after the submission of an extensive application and technical dossier, they are found to satisfy safety and environmental standards[13]. Initial approvals are to be for no longer than ten years[14]. These approvals are to be given by Member States,

1. Council Directive (EEC) 86/362, above.
2. Article 1 and Annex I. The directive applies the provisions of Council Directive (EEC) 74/63, OJ L38 11.2.74 p31, as amended, regarding undesirable substances in feedingstuffs.
3. Article 4(1).
4. Article 6.
5. Article 9(1).
6. Articles 9(2), 13.
7. Council Directive (EEC) 88/298, OJ L126 20.5.88 p53.
8. Council Directive (EEC) 86/363, above.
9. Article 1 and Annex I.
10. Council Directive (EEC) 91/414, OJ L230 19.8.91 p1.
11. ECAg/Vet Briefing 3 (Jan 1992). For Council Directive (EEC) 79/117, OJ L33 8.2.79 p35, and other plant production measures, see below at subsection 2.
12. Council Directive (EEC) 91/414, above at Article 8(2).
13. Article 4.
14. Article 5.

but only after coordination with the Commission and other Member States[1]. Duplicative testing is to be avoided by mutual recognition of national authorisations[2]. Member States will assign maximum residue limits to the approved products, which will be provisionally effective pending the establishment of limits under the 1986 and 1990 pesticide directives[3]. Member States have discretion to refuse mutual recognition to approvals if their climatic and other conditions are not comparable to those in an approving state[4]. The directive leaves substantial room for national variations, and it is not yet clear whether it will result in any significant degree of harmonisation[5]. It may also signal that residue limits will not quickly be established under the 1990 pesticides directive.

8.3.2   Other agricultural chemicals

Pesticides represent only a few of the thousands of agricultural chemicals which may, directly or indirectly, affect the safety of human foodstuffs. The Community has adopted measures regarding such issues as animal feedingstuffs, animal growth hormones, and veterinary medicines. It has also adopted rules relating to harmful plant organisms, animal diseases, slaughtering and hygienic meat practices, and general health issues which may arise from the consumption of meat[6]. All of these measures cannot be fully described here, but the scope and goals of the Community's activities should at least be suggested by illustrations.

The Council adopted a directive in 1974 establishing maximum permissible levels of various undesirable substances in animal feedingstuffs[7]. The directive includes such substances as arsenic, lead, fluorine, mercury, nitrites, hydrocyanic acid, and volatile mustard oil[8]. It sets maximum levels for these and other substances, and designates the Standing Committee on Feedingstuffs to monitor the issues[9]. The

---

1.   Article 6.
2.   Article 10.
3.   Article 4(1) (f).
4.   Article 10 (1).
5.   Before the directive, the European Court held that Member States are entitled to require prior approval of plant protection products used within their territories, although they may not demand testing or analyses which simply duplicate work conducted in other Member States. The decision was based on Article 36 of the Treaty; *Frans-Nederlandse Mij voor Biologische Producten BV* [1982] 2 CMLR 35, decided in 1981 on reference from the Gerechtshof in The Hague.
6.   Rules relating to health issues arising from fresh meat are generally described above. Above at Chapter 7, para 7.12.
7.   Council Directive (EEC) 74/63, OJ L38 11.2.74 p31. For additives in feedingstuffs, see Council Directive (EEC) 70/524, OJ L270 14.12.70 p1; Council Directive (EEC) 82/471, OJ L213 21.7.82 p8. There are many amendments. Similar issues involving feedingstuffs and veterinary drugs have been addressed in the United States. For a sampling of the rules and issues, see Generic Animal Drug and Patent Term Restoration Act, P.L. No. 100-670, 102 Stat. 3971 (1988); Geyer, "Ensuring Food Safety with Generic Animal Drug Use", 45 Food D.C.L.J. p517 (1990).
8.   Council Directive (EEC) 74/63, above at the Annex.
9.   Annex and Article 9(1).

directive has been updated on several occasions[1]. Similarly, the Council issued a regulation in 1990 creating a procedure for establishing maximum residue limits for veterinary medicinal products in foodstuffs of animal origin[2]. The regulation does not itself impose limits, but creates a mechanism by which they may later be fixed.

The Community entered the area of phytosanitary controls as early as 1976, when the Council adopted a directive establishing protective measures against the introduction of organisms harmful to plants or plant products[3]. The directive recognised that some organisms may be harmful in some regions and not others, and provides lists of forbidden organisms tailored to different parts of the Community[4]. The directive provides for phytosanitary certificates, and establishes lists of restricted organisms[5]. They include organisms and plant products whose introduction is prohibited throughout the Community, others prohibited in certain Member States, and still others prohibited in association with particular plants or plant products[6]. The directive has been revised on numerous occasions[7]. The Standing Committee on Plant Health is responsible for the directive's revision[8].

In December 1978, the Council adopted a directive prohibiting the marketing and use of plant protection products containing various active substances[9]. The directive forbids the use of designated chemical products to protect crops and plants against blights and other hazards. The prohibited substances include compounds of mercury and persistent organo-chlorine compounds, such as DDT and aldrin[10]. In some

1. See Commission Directive (EEC) 76/934, OJ L364 31.12.76 p20; Council Directive (EEC) 80/502, OJ L124 20.5.80 p17; Third Commission Directive (EEC) 83/381, OJ L222 13.8.83 p31; Fourth Commission Directive (EEC) 86/299, OJ L189 11.7.86 p40; Council Directive (EEC) 86/354, OJ L212 2.8.86 p27; Commission Directive (EEC) 87/238, OJ L110 25.4.87 p25; Council Directive (EEC) 87/519, OJ L304 27.10.87 p38. For rules regarding the marketing of compound animal feedingstuffs, see Council Directive (EEC) 79/393, OJ L86 6.4.79 p30. Among the amendments, see most recently Council Directive (EEC) 90/44, OJ L27 31.1.90 p35. See also COM(91) 90 final, OJ C103 19.4.91 p18.
2. Council Regulation (EEC) 2377/90, OJ L244 18.8.90 p1. For amendments, see Commission Regulation (EEC) 762/92, OJ L83 28..3.92 p14.
3. Council Directive (EEC) 77/93, OJ L26 31.1.77 p20. For a challenge based upon its transposition into German law, see Case 87/83 *Rewezentrale AG v Direktor der Landwirtschaftskammer Rheinland* [1984] ECR 1229, [1985] 2 CMLR 586, decided by the European Court in 1984 on reference from the Administrative Court in Cologne. For amendments, see Commission Directive (EEC) 92/10, OJ L70 17.3.92 p27.
4. Council Directive (EEC) 77/93, above at the eleventh recital of the preamble.
5. Article 7 and Annex VIII, Part A. The certificates will be replaced by "plant passports" which may be required even for transport regionally within the same nation. See House of Lords Select Committee on the European Communities, 1992: *Health Controls and the Internal Market* p27 (1989).
6. Council Directive (EEC) 77/93, above at Annexes I - V.
7. For a recent example of more than two dozen revisions, see Council Directive (EEC) 90/168, OJ L92 7.4.90 p49.
8. Council Directive (EEC) 77/93, above, at Articles 16, 17.
9. Council Directive (EEC) 79/117, OJ L33 8.2.879 p35. There have been six revisions, including most recently Commission Directive (EEC) 91/188, OJ L92 13.4.91 p42.
10. Council Directive 79/117, above. It has been argued that compulsory changes to new plant protection chemicals, such as those caused by the prohibition of DDT, have invariably meant the adoption of less desirable alternatives. See Foster, "Perennial Issues in Food Safety", in D. Cliver, ed., *Foodborne Diseases* p378 (1990).

instances, plant protection substances are permitted only for specified uses. For example, heptachlor is prohibited except to treat beet seeds. The directive permits the Commission, after consultations with the Scientific Committee on Pesticides, to revise the prohibited list[1]. Negligible impurities which do not threaten human or animal health or the environment are not forbidden[2]. The Scientific Committee on Pesticides and the Standing Committee on Plant Health are responsible for monitoring the scientific evidence and revising the directive's rules[3]. The directive has been revised on several occasions[4]. A five-year limitation on the effectiveness of the original list of prohibited products, which first became effective in 1981, was eliminated in 1986[5]. The list, as amended, is now effective indefinitely.

The Council has adopted other measures regarding animal diseases and health issues arising from animal products[6]. They include, for example, a directive regarding the sale and importation of animals and meat products derived from animals raised with growth hormones[7], other measures regarding health problems involving fresh poultry meat[8], and still others regarding health problems involving other fresh meats[9]. Most of these measures have been revised on several occasions. They are supplemented by measures regarding veterinary inspections, slaughtering practices, and hygiene rules. These are essentially vertical measures, addressed to safety and wholesomeness questions regarding specific product categories[10].

---

1. Ibid., at Article 6(3). For an example of the revisions, see Commission Directive (EEC) 91/188, above, deleting the last of various temporary derogations. Some changes may be made by the Commission without Council approval, but after consultations with the Scientific Committee on Pesticides. Council Directive (EEC) 79/117, above at Article 6(1). See also Article 8 for a committee procedure involving the Standing Committee on Plant Health.
2. Council Directive (EEC) 77/93, above at Article 3.
3. Ibid., at Articles 6, 8. See also Council Decision (EEC) 78/436, OJ L124 12.5.78 p16.
4. See Commission Directive (EEC) 83/131, OJ L91 9.4.83 p35; Commission Directive (EEC) 85/298, OJ L154 13.6.85 p48; Council Directive (EEC) 86/214, OJ L152 6.6.86 p45; Council Directive (EEC) 86/355, OJ L212 2.8.86 p33; Council Directive (EEC) 87/181, OJ L71 14.3.87 p33; Commission Directive (EEC) 87/477, OJ L293 26.9.87 p40; Council Directive (EEC) 89/365, OJ L159 10.6.88 p58; Commission Directive (EEC) 91/188, above.
5. Council Directive (EEC) 86/214, above, at Article 1.
6. The Commission has also initiated a computerised network linking veterinary authorities, called ANIMO, to assist in border clearances and other issues. Commission Decision (EEC) 91/398, OJ L221 p30 (9 Aug. 1991). For a general review of animal health measures as of June 1992, see MAFF Animal Health and Intra-Community Trade Newsletter No. 6 (30 June 1992).
7. Council Directive (EEC) 85/649, OJ L382 31.12.85 p228. For an account of a trade dispute which arose from the directive, see Halpern, "The US - EC Hormone Beef Controversy and the Standards Code: Implications for the Application of Health Regulations to Agricultural Trade", 14 N.C.J. Int'l L. & Com. Reg. 135 (1989).
8. Council Directive (EEC) 71/118, OJ L55 8.3.77 p1. It has been frequently amended. See e.g., Council Directive (EEC) 85/326, OJ L168 286.85 p1.
9. Council Directive (EEC) 64/433, OJ L121 29.7.64. Among many amendments, see, e.g., Council Directive (EEC) 89/136, OJ L49 21.2.89 . See also Council Directive (EEC) 72/471, OJ L302 31.12.72; Council Directive (EEC) 87/64, OJ L34 5.2.87; Council Directive (EEC) 87/489, OJ L280 3.10.87.
10. The principal measures are described above in connection with the Community's rules for meat products; see above at para 8.12.

8.4   The pricing of foodstuffs

Just as the Community has sought to ensure the accuracy of the weights and volumes of foodstuffs offered to consumers, so too it has sought to ensure the clarity of the prices quoted to consumers[1] In 1979, the Council adopted a directive regarding consumer protection in the indication of foodstuff prices[2]. Despite the breadth of the directive's title, its purpose is essentially to create a system for the unit pricing of foodstuffs. Unit pricing demands a disclosure of the price for a quantity of one kilogramme or litre of a foodstuff, regardless of the quantity actually contained in a particular package[3]. Among other advantages, the Council observed that unit pricing increases "market transparency"[4]. In other words, it helps consumers to judge more easily and accurately the fairness of prices demanded for packages of differing sizes and shapes. It provides a common denominator to facilitate comparative shopping.

The 1979 directive was only a declaration of regulatory policy. It provided for unit pricing, but postponed the requirement's actual effectiveness. Except insofar as national laws otherwise provide, unit pricing would become effective only after the Council decided the conditions for its application and the foodstuffs for which it would be required[5]. Pending these decisions, Member States remained free to impose unit pricing as and when they deemed appropriate[6]. The Council undertook to reach its decisions by the end of 1983, "at the latest"[7]. In fact, the Council did not adopt another unit pricing directive until 1988.

The 1979 directive also permitted important exemptions from the unit pricing policy. The policy did not apply to foodstuffs consumed in restaurants, canteens and other mass catering establishments[8]. Nor did it apply to foodstuffs purchased by a "consumer" for professional or commercial reasons[9]. In addition, Member States could exempt foodstuffs sold on a farm, and those sold in especially small or large quantities[10]. With respect to small or large quantities, the upper and lower limits were five grammes or millilitres and 10 kilogrammes or litres, respectively. The directive also excluded foodstuffs sold by "certain" shops and "handed directly" to

---

1.   For prepackaging, weights and volumes, see above at para 8.1.
2.   Council Directive (EEC) 79/581, OJ L158 26.6.79 p19. For various earlier Spanish rules, see, e.g., Decreto 2807/1972, B.O.E. 247 (14 Oct.1972).
3.   Council Directive (EEC) 79/581, above at Article 2(f).
4.   The second recital of the preamble.
5.   Article 8.
6.   Article 8(2).
7.   Article 8(1).
8.   Article 1(2).
9.   The reference to "consumers" rendered the provision confusing, and probably meaningless. It was eliminated in 1988.
10.   Article 7(4).

purchasers, but only if unit prices would be impracticable or an excessive burden[1]. In addition, the directive exempted foods for which unit prices would be "meaningless"[2]. These included goods sold by the piece, those sold from vending machines, prepared dishes, and products in "fancy" packagings[3]. Finally, the directive excluded highly perishable foodstuffs sold at reduced prices because of a danger of deterioration[4]. The directive offered no justification for this last exception. The risk of deterioration may explain urgency in marketing, and perhaps reduced prices, but it is difficult to see any necessary basis for waiving unit pricing. Perhaps there is an expectation that distress prices may be continually reduced, which would require repeated recalculations of the unit price. As and when unit prices were actually contemplated, they were to be calculated in terms of a litre or kilogramme. Member States were, however, also permitted to authorise them in terms of various smaller weights and volumes[5].

The 1979 directive was amended in 1988[6]. The 1988 directive is more demanding than its predecessor, but numerous exceptions are still permitted. As amended, the directive generally applies to all prepackaged foodstuffs[7]. This includes all foods not packaged in the purchaser's presence, whether or not the packaging encloses the foodstuff completely[8]. Foods consumed on the premises of hotels, restaurants, cafes, hospitals and similar establishments are still excluded[9]. So too are foodstuffs purchased for purposes of a trade or commercial activity, and those supplied in the course of providing a service[10]. The latter includes caterers. In addition, Member States may exclude foodstuffs sold on a farm or in "private" sales. "Private" sales are not defined, but presumably include those conducted outside shops. It is not clear whether the exception includes public markets.

Member States may continue to waive the requirement wherever unit prices would be "meaningless". This includes foodstuffs sold by the piece, those sold from an automatic dispenser, prepared dishes, multi-packs, and "fancy" packagings[11]. The listed situations are only illustrative of those which may be exempted. "Fancy" products are not defined, but the Community elsewhere uses the term for figurines, models and other souvenir packages. There is no explanation as to why unit pricing is "meaningless" for multi-packs or fancy packaging. It might have been supposed

---

1.   Article 1(3). The directive offers no other guidance as to the shops which might be intended. The effect is to permit an exemption wherever Member States find the requirement burdensome or difficult.
2.   Article 7(1).
3.   Article 7(2).
4.   Article 7(3).
5.   Article 6(2). This provision was not altered in 1988.
6.   Council Directive (EEC) 88/315, OJ L142 9.6.88 p23.
7.   Article 1.
8.   Article 1(2) (b).
9.   Article 1(1).
10.   Ibid. The reference to "consumers" in the 1979 directive was eliminated.
11.   Article 1(5).

that such packaging may often be misleading, and thus particularly in need of unit prices. In addition, the requirement does not apply to prepackaged sales of products already subject to Community rules regarding weights and packaging. Most such rules are provided by the recipe laws, which commonly contain weight and packaging restrictions. The exempted products include cocoa and chocolate, sugars, coffee and chicory, and various liquids[1]. Finally, the Member States were granted a seven-year transitional period in which to apply the requirement to milk, beers, and other products listed in an annex to the directive[2].

Insofar as they are required, unit prices must be unambiguous, easily identifiable and clearly legible[3]. The requirement for their disclosure is not limited to grocery shelves, but also includes any advertisement or catalogue which mentions the selling price of a foodstuff to which the requirement is applicable. No other format or display obligations are imposed. Unlike the 1978 labelling directive, which forbids national format rules, the 1988 unit pricing directive permits Member States to adopt more specific rules regarding the forms, means and locations in which unit prices must be indicated[4].

In sum, the unit pricing requirement created by the 1979 directive, even as amended in 1988, is subject to numerous and important exceptions. Those exceptions still essentially constitute the rule. Nonetheless, efforts are in progress to broaden the requirement's application. Simultaneously with its adoption of the 1988 directive, the Council requested the Commission in consultation with the Member States to propose methods to extend the requirement to additional products, and to revise the rules for its application[5].

8.5   Unpackaged foods

Most of the measures described in earlier chapters relate to foodstuffs sold in prepackagings. In large measure, this reasonably approximates the ways in which most foods are sold in the Community. To an increasing degree, foodstuffs are marketed in the Community in pre-measured, pre-labelled containers. In Britain, it has been estimated that 75 percent of the average diet consists of processed foods.

---

1.   Article 1(6).
2.   Article 1(7) and the Annex. The annex refers to earlier directives relating to such products as wines, beers, vinegar, oils, water, fruit juices, butter, cheeses, pasta, rice, cereal flakes, dried fruits and vegetables, frozen foods, ice cream, and pet foods. For Brtain's rules, see Price Marking Order 1991, SI 1991/1382. For France, see *Lamy-Dehove* at p2-551.
3.   Council Directive (EEC) 88/315, above at Article 1(4).
4.   For the Italian rules, for example, see G Andreis, et al., eds., *Codice di Diretto Alimentare Annotato* (1990), vol. 1, p743.
5.   Council Resolution, OJ C153 11.6.88 p1.

Most of those have been sold in prepackagings[1]. Even fresh meats, fruit and vegetables are often sold in prepackaged wrappings.

Moreover, prepackaged foodstuffs are more likely to involve issues which the Community's rules are designed to address. They are more likely to have been processed, to have required processing aids, to contain additives, and to have come into contact with substances from which constituent migration may have occurred. They are the source of a substantial part of the packaging waste whose disposal is beginning to trouble the Community. In these circumstances, the Community's legislation understandably emphasises prepackaged foods.

Nonetheless, many products continue to be sold without prepackaging. Meats, fish, cheeses, fruit and vegetables are common examples. Other products may be sold without prepackaging in specialty shops. Indeed, some observers report a shift toward unpackaged foods because they are perceived by some consumers to be healthier and environmentally preferable[2]. In fact, however, unpackaged foods displayed without proper protection inside or outside shops may be exposed to contamination and spoilage[3]. Unpackaged goods have not been a frequent subject of legislation, but the Community has adopted several measures addressed to their problems. Many unpackaged foods are unprocessed agricultural products which are the subject of measures providing for the "common organisation" of the Community's marketplace. Those measures are principally aspects of the Community's agricultural policies, rather than applications of its food regulatory policies. Nonetheless, some of those measures establish quality standards and labelling obligations. These ancillary requirements may properly be regarded as parts of the Community's food regulations.

An example will indicate their significance. The Council issued a regulation in 1972 establishing a common organisation for the Community's market in fruits and vegetables[4]. Previous regulations had existed, but the 1972 regulation was designed to codify the earlier rules[5]. It has since been frequently amended[6].

---

1. See, e.g., London Food Commission, *Food Adulteration and How to Beat It* p43 (1988).
2. See, e.g., Flory, "Packaging for Consumer Convenience", in F. Paine, ed., *Modern Processing, Packaging and Distribution Systems for Foods* p146 (1987). He also notes the effects of packaging errors and malfunctions. One study has, however, found fresh foods, and not processed ones, to be the principal sources of foodborne illnesses. See Roberts, "Sources of Infection: Food", in *The Lancet*, ed., *Foodborne Illness* p31 (1991).
3. Outside displays of foodstuffs without proper protection provoked a proposed resolution in the European Parliament in December 1991 calling for Community legislation. The proposed resolution's sponsors were all from the United Kingdom.
4. Council Regulation (EEC) 1035/72, OJ L118 20.5.72 p1.
5. The first recital of the preamble. A list of the previous measures is provided in an annex to the regulation.
6. Regulation (EEC) 1193/90, OJ L119 11.3.90 p43; Regulation (EEC) 1156/92, OJ L122 7.5.92 p3. There are similar rules for products processed from foods and vegetables. See, e.g., Council

The 1972 regulation was intended to achieve a balance between supply and demand, and to ensure "fair" prices to the producer[1]. The 1972 regulation and similar measures define fairness exclusively in terms of the producer's interests. The regulation seeks to encourage consumption and exports through subsidies and refunds[2]. It grants support to producers' organisations, and provides for withdrawal prices, buying-in prices, and other assistance to farmers[3]. A management committee was created to conduct the programme[4]. The committee consists of representatives of the Member States, assigned weighted voting rights roughly in accordance with population. The committee is chaired by a representative of the Commission[5].

The 1972 regulation provides quality standards for the most widely produced fruits and vegetables[6]. The standards are applicable to products delivered fresh to the consumer, but the regulation also authorises standards for products intended for industrial processing[7]. Products which do not satisfy the quality standards may not be sold, delivered or marketed within the Community[8]. Exceptions are granted for industrial consignments and sales at farms made directly to consumers for their personal use[9]. If demand temporarily exceeds the supply of particular products, downward adjustments of the minimum standards are permitted[10]. These may remain in effect for an undefined "limited period"[11]. In particular, minimum size requirements may be waived[12].

The 1972 regulation also establishes special labelling and disclosure rules. Similar but separate rules are provided for packaged and unpackaged foods. For those sold without prepackaging, the retailer must display a "show card" which clearly discloses the product's origin, variety, and quality class[13]. Similar rules are applicable to products imported from outside the Community[14]. A distinction is drawn for some purposes between third countries generally and "European third countries and the non-European countries of the Mediterranean area". Rules for the

Regulation (EEC) 426/86, OJ L49 27.2.86 p1; Commission Regulation (EEC) 2405/89, OJ L227 4.8.89 p34; Regulation (EEC) 1943/91, OJ L175 4.7.91 p1.

1. Council Regulation (EEC) 1035/72, above at the third recital of the preamble.
2. The twenty-third recital of the preamble.
3. Title III.
4. Article 32.
5. Article 32 (2).
6. Title I. There are many implementing measures. For example, the Council has established sizing and quality requirements for strawberries, cherries, and kiwi. See, e.g., Council Regulation (EEC) 1435/91, OJ L137 31.5.91; Commission Regulation (EEC) 305/92, OJ L32 8.2.92 p15. For tomatoes, see Commission Regulation (EEC) 778/83, OJ L86 31.3.83 p14; Commission Regulation (EEC) 1657/92, OJ L172 27.6.92 p53.
7. Council Regulation (EEC) 1035/72, above at Article 2(1).
8. Article 3(1).
9. Articles 3(2)-(3).
10. Article 5.
11. Article 5(1).
12. Article 5(2).
13. Article 7. There is no specific requirement as to the languages which must be used. As to location, the regulation provides only that the card must be displayed "with" the products.
14. Article 9.

latter are very similar to those applied to the Community's own products. With respect to prepackaged products, the various labelling requirements are parts of the quality standards[1]. Disclosures are to be made legibly and indelibly on one side of the package. Unlike the 1978 labelling directive, there is no express requirement that they must be made "conspicuously". The regulation's obligations differ in other respects from the provisions of the 1978 labelling directive, as amended, but those differences are now being reconciled[2].

The 1972 regulation and similar measures are extensions of the Community's agricultural policies. They are only incidentally measures for the regulation of foodstuffs, and it should not be surprising that their principal beneficiaries are farmers and agricultural distributors. Indeed, a central purpose of the 1972 regulation is to shield the Community's producers against low prices from imported products[3]. There is no apparent concern that the protection given to farmers results in higher retail prices for consumers. Nor is it clear that the measures reflect any substantial attention to consumer interests with respect to the labelling, presentation and hygiene of unpackaged products[4].

An important goal of the Community's food regulatory policies should be to provide its rules in a uniform, accessible and coherent form. The Commission itself has declared that greater "transparency" of the Community's rules would facilitate enforcement and encourage compliance[5]. For this purpose, it has begun to consolidate and codify some internal market rules. One area in which codification could prove helpful is the marketing and sale of unpackaged foods. The existing rules are widely scattered and poorly understood. Their reconciliation into a single measure would draw greater attention to their special problems. One result might be greater rigour and consistency in presentational and hygiene rules, including the disclosures made to consumers.

8.6   Official controls and inspections

The Community has belatedly recognised that harmonised regulations are only the first step toward an integrated marketplace for foodstuffs. Largely in response to demands from the European Parliament, the Commission has acknowledged that regulatory standards mean little unless they are enforced by uniform control and

---

1. Article 6(1).
2. For example, there is no express net weight requirement in the 1972 regulation, as there is under the 1978 labelling directive; above at Chapter 3, para 3.3.1. For the Commission's proposal to reconcile the measures, see COM(90) 428 final (21 Sept 1990).
3. Council Regulation (EEC) 1035/72, above at the twentieth recital of the preamble.
4. The European Parliament has demanded additional labelling requirements for perishable and unpackaged foodstuffs. Resolution No. A3-0060/92 (11 March 1992).
5. See, e.g., Europe, No. 5643 (n.s.) at 13-14 (10 Jan 1992).

inspection procedures[1]. Indeed, this is said to be an area to which the Commission has given regulatory priority since 1985[2]. Until 1989, there was little evidence either of the priority or of any appreciable progress. There is, however, no doubt that such a priority is appropriate, and that improvements in national food controls now warrant a substantial commitment of the Community's resources. Consumers in Britain or Germany, for example, are ultimately dependent on food inspectorates in Greece and Italy, and there are rising incidences of foodborne illnesses under even the most rigorous national systems[3].

Reliable estimates of the incidences and costs of foodborne diseases do not exist. Many national reporting systems are inadequate. Only the most serious cases are registered, and diagnoses are not always accurate[4]. The most complete data probably relate to England and Wales, where food poisonings are at a high and rising level[5]. An expert advisory committee concluded that there is an "overall upward trend" in the incidences of food poisoning, gastrointestinal pathogens, and listeriosis in England and Wales[6]. Twice as many cases of food poisoning were reported in Britain in 1984 than in 1968, and the number has grown still higher since 1984[7]. Other studies have found increases in incidences of listeriosis and salmonellosis[8]. In all, foodborne illnesses have become a major health concern, resulting in "immense" costs[9]. Similar problems have been identified throughout the Community and in Sweden, the United States and Canada[10]. In the United States, for example, the costs are said to be $10 billion annually. One food service

1.   The European Parliament has been particularly influential in the area of official controls. See interview with Dr. Caroline Jackson, MEP, 1 World Food Reg. Rev. 22 (July 1991).

2.   The Commission has said that one of its two principal areas of focus in the foodstuffs sector since 1985 has been the "enforcement of existing Community legislation"; XXIInd General Report on the Activities of the European Communities 1988, at p120 (1989). In this case, the promise exceeds the product.

3.   Interview with Dr. Caroline Jackson, MEP, 1 World Food Reg. Rev. pp22-23 (July 1991).

4.   Waites & Arbuthnott, "Foodborne Illness: An Overview", in *The Lancet*, ed., *Foodborne Illness* p1-8 (1991).

5.   Ibid. at p2. The authors judge Britain's reporting system to be the "most comprehensive in Europe", and describe the systems in North America as "patchy". Ibid. Even in the United Kingdom, the data are said to reflect only trends and not true incidences. Cook, "Epidemiology of Foodborne Illness: UK", ibid. at 16-17. See also B. Hobbs & D. Roberts, *Food Poisoning and Food Hygiene* p9 (5th ed. 1987).

6.   Report of the Committee on the Microbiological Safety of Food, Part I, at p103 (1990).

7.   B. Hobbs & D. Roberts, *Food Poisoning and Food Hygiene* p9 (5th ed. 1987). Cases in Britain are said to be substantially higher in the first months of 1992 than in the corresponding period of 1991; *The Observer* p24 (July 19, 1992).

8.   Doyle & Oliver, "Salmonella", in D. Cliver, ed., *Foodborne Diseases* pp185-204 (1990); Bahk & Marth, "Listeriosis and Listeria monocytogenes", ibid., at pp247-257.

9.   Waites & Arbuthnott, "Foodborne Illness: An Overview", in The Lancet, ed., *Foodborne Illness* p1 (1991).

10. See, e.g., A. Tuffs, "Germany: Food Matters", p337 *The Lancet* 1336 (June 1, 1991); Bahk & Marth, "Listeriosis and Listeria monocytogenes", in D. Cliver, ed., *Foodborne Diseases* pp247-257 (1990); E. Todd, "Epidemiology of Foodborne Illness: North America", in *The Lancet*, ed., *Foodborne Illness* pp9-15 (1991). For French estimates, see, e.g., Goulet, et al., "Recensement des Listeriosis humaines en France á partir d'un échantillon de laboratoires", in H. Beerens, ed., "Microorganismes pathogènes dans l'alimentation humaine", Sciences des Aliments, vol. 9, series X, pp65-68 (1987).

meal in every 9,000 in the United States produces illness[1]. The World Health Organisation has reported increases in foodborne diseases in both developed and developing countries[2]. Indeed, food poisoning has been described as the second largest cause of human illness[3]. Many illnesses result from faulty storage and preparatory methods in the home. Others are caused by unsanitary practices in restaurants and other mass catering establishments[4]. Product tampering may sometimes be a problem[5]. Nonetheless, there are enough cases of food contamination involving processors and distributors to make the adequacy of official inspections an important regulatory issue[6].

Serious attention is at last being given to the issue. The Commission itself has acknowledged that "public and government concern with food safety and nutrition has been increasing in recent years"[7]. This has caused several Member States to strengthen their national systems, and provoked considerable concern in the European Parliament. In 1991, Parliament adopted a resolution demanding a comprehensive directive regarding food hygiene, in which rigorous standards would be imposed[8]. The increased scale of many food production facilities, together with the free circulation of goods throughout the Community, means that the ill-effects of even occasional errors may be serious and widespread[9]. Those hazards can be controlled only if national inspection rules are applied as rigorously to products

1. Guzewich, "Practical Procedures for Using the Hazard Analysis Critical Control Point (HACCP) Appraisal in Food Service Establishments by Industry and Regulatory Agencies," in C. Felix, ed., *Food Protection Technology* p91 (1987).

2. 1 World Food Reg. Rev. p11 (July 1991). In the United States alone, estimates suggest a median of 2 million cases of salmonellosis annually, with many more cases of other illnesses and several thousand deaths. E. Todd, "Epidemiology of Foodborne Illness: North America", in *The Lancet*, ed., *Foodborne Illness* pp10-11 (1991). By another estimate, there are 5 to 10 million cases of gastroenteritis annually in the United States. N. Marriott, *Principles of Food Sanitation* p26 (2nd 1989).

3. Elton, "Allocation of Priorities - Where Do the Real Risks Lie?", in G. Gibson & R. Walker, eds., *Food Toxicology - Real or Imaginary Problems?* p4 (1985).

4. By one estimate, "many" of the contamination and temperature abuses which lead to illness are "perpetuated by consumers". Many processing problems are beyond a manufacturer's reasonable control. See Cliver, "Organising a Safe Food Supply System", in D. Cliver, ed., *Foodborne Diseases* pp357-361 (1990). The impossibility of preventing all processing errors despite a processor's best efforts has been recognised by Britain's Food Safety Act 1990, c.16 (1990) at Section 21. See also Bradgate & Howells, "Food Law in the United Kingdom," 46 Food D.C.L.J. 447 (1991).

5. 1 World Food Reg. Rev. 27 (March 1992).

6. Food contamination is "increasing" and a "growing threat in Western Europe". Interview with Dr. Caroline Jackson, MEP, 1 World Food Reg. Rev. 23 (July 1991). A dramatic example was provided by the cases of toxic oil syndrome in Spain in the late 1970's and early 1980's, when contaminated cooking oil resulted in some 450 deaths. The oil contained crude rape oil, but was sold as olive oil. See, e.g., A. Bender, *Dictionary of Nutrition and Food Technology* p263 (6th ed. 1990). For a rejection of claims that pesticides were involved, see Written Question 1591/91, OJ C112 30.4.92 p8. More recently, poor sanitary practices with respect to cheeses reportedly caused 29 deaths in France from Listeria; *The Sunday Times* pp1-9 (19 July 1992).

7. See paras 9, 10 of the Explanatory Memorandum which accompanied COM(91) 16 final, OJ C108 23.4.91 p7.

8. Resolution of the European Parliament on Food Hygiene, OJ C183 15.7.91 p52.

9. The consequences of error or abuse can easily be international. One American incident, for example, reportedly resulted in the death of a Community resident. P. Hutt & R. Merrill, *Food and Drug Law, Cases and Materials* pp278-279, 283 (2nd ed. 1991). See also Report of the Committee on the Microbiological Safety of Food, Part I, paras 7.13, 7.14 (1990).

intended for export to other Member States as they are to products intended for domestic consumption[1]. In the view of an enforcement officer, however, Community institutions continue to give too little attention to the problems of effective enforcement[2].

Many of the Community's foodstuffs measures include provisions designed to facilitate effective monitoring procedures. They are, however, generally limited to purity standards, sampling rules, and methods of analysis. Moreover, they provide rules for particular product categories, and not for foodstuffs generally. The Council adopted a directive in 1985 for uniform sampling and analytical measures, but it merely provides a framework for such measures[3]. The measures themselves are to be adopted through a committee procedure involving the Standing Committee for Foodstuffs[4]. The goal of the 1985 directive was to introduce some standardisation into the sampling and analytical methods used in the Community. The desirability of that modest goal has, however, more recently been questioned by the Commission, which reported a "consensus" that standardisation might prove inflexible[5]. Apart from rules regarding sampling and analytical methods, the Community has begun to develop various other monitoring and inspection mechanisms. Many are still in formative stages, and some may never be adopted, but together they offer a prospect of more adequate control systems.

8.6.1   Hygiene and sanitation rules

There is still no general Community legislation regarding food hygiene and sanitation. There are, however, vertical hygiene directives regarding some foodstuffs and the Commission, after lengthy pressures from Parliament and Britain's cooperative movement, has proposed both additional vertical rules and a more general directive[6]. The proposed general directive would create little more than a frameworth for future rulemaking. It would establish a general requirement that food processing and handling must be conducted hygienically, and provide broad standards for buildings, equipment, waste, water supply, personnel, and

---

1. Similar arguments suggest that the same health and safety standards should generally also apply to goods intended for export outside the Community. Below at IX(C)(5).
2. Roberts, "European Enforcement," 1/92 Eur. Food L. Rev. 1,8 (1992). He reports that the Commission gives "little shrift" to the views of enforcement officers; ibid., at p7.
3. Council Directive (EEC) 85/591, OJ L372 31.12.85 p50 (Dec. 31, 1985). By 31 October 1991, all Member States had adopted the directive. EC Commission, *National Implementing Measures* p132 (1992).
4. Council Directive (EEC) 85/591, above at Articles 1(1), 4.
5. Below at para 8.6.3.
6. COM(91) 525 final, OJ C24 31.1.92 p11. Numerous proposals for its revision have been made. See also Written Question 2772/90, OJ C187 18.7.91 p9. The European Parliament has pressed for such a measure since at least 1988. See Resolution on Food Hygiene, OJ C183 15.7.91 p52. The Commission has also proposed new vertical rules for several products, including minced meat, above at VII(L), and the Council has recently adopted rules for milk and milk-based products; Council Directive (EEC) 92/46.

training. The standards are based upon the Recommended Code of Practice issued by the Codex Alimentarius Commission[1]. They would be implemented in accordance with the "HACCP" system (hazard analysis of critical control points)[2].

One of the proposal's goals would be to encourage voluntary industry codes of hygiene practice. Member States would ask industry representatives to prepare the codes, based upon Codex's Recommended Code of Practice[3]. The voluntary codes would be submitted to the Commission for review and approval. Member States would be required to ensure compliance with the general hygiene obligation and any applicable codes of practice[4]. They could require market recalls or product destructions, and even compel the closure of manufacturers[5]. There is, however, no provision for the registration of food processors[6]. The proposal would authorise the establishment of microbiological criteria for at least some foods[7]. The Scientific Committee would be consulted regarding the criteria, which would be adopted through a committee procedure involving the Standing Committee for Foodstuffs.

A proposal which recapitulates Codex principles and encourages private rulemaking cannot be described as a substantial achievement. Significant questions must still be resolved regarding the proposal's relationship with the vertical directives, the role of private codes, and the value of static versus active hygiene controls. In these and other areas, the Commission's proposal represents only an initial step toward systematic rules. There are, however, partial explanations for the Commission's difficulties. All foods do not present the same kinds or degrees of risk, and the variations demand important differences in the proper methods of handling and transport[8]. The problems are increased by the diverse processes used

1.   A revised version of the Codex's Recommended Code of Practice and General Principles of Food Hygiene was adopted in 1985. See Codex Alimentarius sec.7 (2nd ed. 1991). The Codex has also adopted detailed sanitation rules for low-acid and acidified low-acid canned foods; ibid. at sec.7.1.
2.   HACCP is an American system developed as part of the space programme and first adopted by FDA for use with foods in 1973. It has also been endorsed by the World Health Organisation. For descriptions of the system's history and content, see, e.g., D. Shapton & N. Shapton, *Principles and Practices for the Safe Processing of Foods* pp21-35 (1991); N. Marriott, *Principles of Food Sanitation* 9-10 (2nd ed. 1989).
3.   COM(91) 525 final, at Article 5. Many such codes already exist. For standards adopted by British industry regarding frozen and chilled foods, for example, see M. Boast, *Refrigeration Pocket Book* pp394-410 (1991). For experience with private codes, see, e.g., Kupfer, "Development of Standards and Regulations by a Third Party Consensus Process," in C. Felix, ed., *Food Protection Technology* p235 (1987).
4.   Article 7. The applicable standards are assigned priorities, with European standards at the top, national standards next, and industry codes in the lowest level. Article 5(2).
5.   Article 8(1). Closures are to be for an "appropriate" period. Rights of appeal must be granted. Article 8(2).
6.   Registration rules have, however, been adopted in Britain. Food Safety Act 1990, at section 19 (1)(a); Food Premises (Registration) Regulations 1991. There is also a new register in Spain. *Eurofood* p5 (April 1992).
7.   COM(91) 525 final, at Article 4.
8.   For the variations, see, e.g., P. Gaman & K. Sherrington, *The Science of Food* pp215-228 (3rd ed. 1990). See also Report of the Committee on the Microbiological Safety of Food, Part I, para 7.4 (1990).

by firms of varying sizes and levels of sophistication to perform similar tasks[1]. A job performed by hand in one firm may be done by machine in another, and by a different machine in a third firm. Firms may employ different processing aids and additives to manufacture similar products, and they may organise their work in different manners. Work environments may present varied risks of contamination. In combination, these variations greatly complicate the preparation of effective hygiene rules. At the same time, the industry's growing size and concentration means that hygiene violations may have widespread consequences[2]. The simplicities of the Commission's proposal may result from haste, and perhaps an unwillingness to address the complexities implicit in any genuine measure. One disadvantage of the 1992 deadline for the internal market programme is an encouragement of superficiality. Not surprisingly, there are substantial demands in the European Parliament for a more rigourous measure.

The ultimate answer may be to categorise foods according to the nature and degree of their microbiological risks. The National Advisory Committee on Microbiological Criteria has proposed such a system in the United States, and the Richmond Committee made a similar proposal in Britain[3]. It should be supplemented by a system for microbiological surveillance, which takes account of the different risk categories into which the foods have been placed[4]. The risk categories could be used to formulate hygiene rules for the handling, processing and storage of different categories of foodstuffs. They could also facilitate the design of safer facilities for food manufacture and distribution[5]. The Commission may see its proposed directive as one step toward such systems, and the microbiological criteria authorised by the proposal might be intended to provide the basis for risk categorisations. If so, the Commission has described its intentions with unusual reticence.

Simultaneously with its consideration of a framework hygiene directive, the Community is also continuing to adopt health rules for specific product categories. In June 1992, for example, the Council adopted detailed hygiene rules for the

---

1.   Para 7.2.
2.   Canada's Health Protection Branch has, for example, observed that the "food industry has become more and more concentrated, with foods from one source now reaching a much wider area". It notes that a single incident may put "thousands of people at risk". It recounts an incident involving one improper procedure in one dairy which made hundreds of people ill throughout Canada; Health Protection Branch, *Health Protection and Food Laws* p52 (4th ed. 1985).
3.   Report of the Committee on the Microbiological Safety of Food, Part I, paras 7.5, 7.6 (1990). For applications, see, e.g., W. Harrigan & R. Park, *Making Safe Food: A Management Guide for Microbiological Quality* (1991).
4.   Report of the Committee on the Microbiological Safety of Food, Part I, chapter 5 (1990).
5.   At paras 7.15 - 7.40. See also Vanderzant, "Microbiological Criteria for Foods and Food Ingredients: A Review of the Report of the National Research Council," in C. Felix, ed., *Food Protection Technology* pp101-111 (1987).

production of raw milk, heat-treated milk, and milk-based products[1]. The Council's directive establishes health requirements for the production, packaging, labelling, storage and transport of milk products. There are microbiological criteria for cheeses, ice cream, powdered milk and other products[2]. Health marks and an identification of the consigning country are required[3]. Packaging and sealing must occur promptly, and must be adequate to ensure the continued purity and safety of the products[4].

8.6.2 Food contamination

There are no general Community rules regarding food contamination. A few measures have, however, been adopted with respect to specific issues, and the Commission has proposed a framework directive[5]. Following an outbreak of toxic oil syndrome in Spain, when hundreds of deaths and illnesses resulted from contaminated cooking oil, the Community established an emergency network for exchanging information regarding safety hazards[6]. The system has since handled many cases, but will now be strengthened to take account of the added burdens of a more integrated marketplace[7]. There is also a demonstration project for the exchange of information regarding accidents[8].

In addition, the Community has adopted special measures regarding particular health or safety hazards. Following the Chernobyl disaster, the Community imposed monitoring and control rules regarding the radioactive contamination of foods and animal feedingstuffs[9]. The rules include maximum permissible radioactivity levels for baby foods, dairy products, and other foodstuffs. The European Parliament has, however, challenged the Council's legal basis for adoption of the rules[10]. Similarly, the Community has occasionally prohibited the import or sale of particular foodstuffs which present safety hazards. In 1992, for example, it banned the importation of scallops from Japan because some contained a

---

1. Council Directive (EEC) 92/46 (June 16, 1992).
2. Annex C, chapter II.
3. Annex C, chapter IV.
4. Annex C, chapter III.
5. COM(91) 523 final, OJ C57 4.3.92 p11. See also Fuster, "The Implementation of the E.C. Commission's White Paper of 1985", 1 World Food Reg. Rev. 10, 11 (Oct 1991).
6. Twentieth General Report on the Activities of the European Communities 1985 at 108, 232 (1987); Gray, "EEC Food Law", Address to Annual Conference of European Association of Lawyers (June 1991). For the Spanish toxic syndrome cases, see, e.g., A. Bender, *Dictionary of Nutrition and Food Technology* p263 (6th ed. 1990).
7. COM(91) 16 final, OJ C108 23.3.91 p7.
8. Council Decision (EEC) 90/534, OJ L296 27.10.90 p64.
9. Council Regulation (Euratom) 3954/87, OJ L371 p11 (Dec. 30, 1987); Council Regulation (Euratom) 2218/89, OJ L211 22.7.89 p11. For Codex rules, see Codex Alimentarius sec. 6.1 (2nd ed. 1991).
10. Case 70/88 *Re Radioactive Food: European Parliament v EC Council* [1992] 1 CMLR 91, decided by the European Court in 1990. The Court found that the Parliament has a "common law" right to seek annulment.

paralytic toxin[1]. There are also restrictions on the use of lead-foil capsules for wine and other beverage bottles[2]. The Community's rules for residues of pesticides and agricultural chemicals are other examples of measures against food contaminants[3].

Many other issues have not been addressed at the Community level. For example, there are no rules regarding the blending of contaminated and uncontaminated foodstuffs[4]. Nor are there rules for the reconditioning of foods[5]. In addition, many individual contaminants are not yet subject to Community restrictions[6]. Dioxins, for example, have been widely found in milk, eggs, fish and other foodstuffs[7]. Some are environmental, and others may migrate from cartons and other paper products in contact with foods. Legal limitations have been imposed in Britain and the Netherlands, and Britain has instituted a surveillance programme, but Community rules have not yet been adopted[8]. Increasing concerns for public health may stimulate additional national rules for dioxins and other contaminants, which may in turn encourage harmonised Community standards[9]. The Commission's proposed framework directive would merely create procedures for the establishment of such standards[10]. It defines contaminants as any substances added unintentionally to foods in connection with their production, packing, transport or storage, or because of environmental contamination. The directive generally forbids the sale of any foodstuff containing a contaminant in an amount which is "toxicologically unacceptable"[11]. All contaminants should be kept to the lowest levels "reasonably achievable"[12]. Maximum levels for specific contaminants may later be established through a committee procedure. In the interim, Member States are to notify the Commission of their contamination rules[13].

1.   Council Decision (EEC) 92/91, OJ L32 8.2.92 p37. For an amendment, see Commission Decision (EEC) 92/293, OJ L155 6.6.92 p39. See also Imported Food (Safeguards Against Paralytic Toxin) (Pectinidae from Japan) Regulations 1992, SI 1992/1122.

2.   *Reports of the Scientific Committee for Food*, Twenty-sixth Series (1992); *Wine Spectator* p8 (31 Oct 1991); 1 World Food Reg. Rev. (9 Jan 1992). Lead-foil capsules are to be phased out in both the Community and the United States, although more rapidly in the latter.

3.   Above at para 8.3.1.

4.   For the rules in the United States, see 21 C.F.R. sec. 110.99(d) (1991); P. Hutt & R. Merrill, *Food and Drug Law Cases and Materials* pp254-259 (2nd ed. 1991).

5.   For US rules, see ibid. at p249.

6.   There are of course national rules. See, e.g., Britain's Tin in Food Regulations 1992, SI 1992/496.

7.   Steering Group on Chemical Aspects of Food Surveillance, *Dioxins in Food* pp38-39 (1992).

8.   Ibid., at pp12-14.

9.   Microbial contamination is judged by many observers to be the most serious hazard presented by foodstuffs. See, e.g., Foster, "Perennial Issues in Food Safety", in D. Cliver, ed., *Foodborne Diseases* pp369, 374 (1990); Marth, "Mycotoxins", ibid. at pp138-157; Taylor, "Chemical Intoxications", ibid. at pp171-182. For estimates of the problems of contamination by lead and other substances, see Written Question 320/91, OJ C66 16.3.92 p3. There are Codex guideline levels for methylmercury in fish. Codex Alimentarius sec.6.2 (2nd ed. 1991).

10.   COM(91) 523 final, OJ C57 4.3.92 p11.

11.   Article 3(1).

12.   Article 3(2).

13.   Article 4. Once notified, they may be evaluated in accordance with the 1983 directive for the review of national technical standards. Above at Chapter 2, para 2.4.

8.6.3   Foodstuff inspections and controls

The measures described above represent important elements of the Community's programmes for food safety and harmonisation, but none directly addresses the problem of ensuring the uniform enforcement of the harmonised rules for foodstuffs. For this purpose, the key measures are those which either enhance the expertise of national authorities or provide mechanisms for verifying national controls. National inspection agencies must in some cases be strengthened, and devices must be found to ensure the adequacy and uniformity of national controls. Until recently, the Community had taken only isolated steps in this area. Actual enforcement has been left almost exclusively to the Member States. Some Community inspections are authorised for fresh meats, fish, fruits and vegetables, and wines, but they are vertical measures intended to deal with particular issues[1].

The Council adopted a framework directive in 1989 requiring the harmonisation of national inspection and control procedures[2]. An indication of the delays in the Community's legislative process is offered by the fact that "preparatory studies" for the directive were in progress in 1985[3]. The 1989 directive recognises that inconsistencies in national control programmes may threaten human health and impede free movement of goods[4]. This recital is stated hypothetically, but it is nonetheless one of the few instances in which the Community has even implied the possibility of differences in the rigour of national inspection systems[5].

The 1989 directive establishes the Community's basic requirements for the control of food processing and manufacturing[6]. As a general matter, control is still exercised through inspections performed by national authorities. The inspections are to include facilities, foodstuffs, additives, and materials and articles which come into contact with foodstuffs[7]. The inspections must ensure that food products comply with all applicable rules and do not constitute a hazard to human health. They must also ensure that products are labelled and presented in a manner which is consistent with commercial fairness, does not threaten consumer interests, and provides appropriate consumer information. Despite the flourish of general standards, the basic issue is whether foodstuffs satisfy the 1978 directive and other

---

1.   See Commission Decision (EEC) 85/446, OJ L260 2.10.85 p19 (fresh meat); Council Regulation (EEC) 1319/85, OJ L137 27.5.85 p39 (fruit and vegetables); Council Regulation (EEC) 2241/87, OJ L207 29.7.87 p1 (fish); Council Regulation (EEC) 2048/89, OJ L202 14.7.89 p32 (wine).
2.   Council Directive (EEC) 89/397, OJ L186 30.6.89 p23. As of 31 October 1991, the directive had been adopted in five Member States. See EC Commission, *National Implementing Measures* pp130-131 (1992).
3.   1985 Foodstuffs White Paper, COM(85) 603, at p14.
4.   Council Directive (EEC) 89/397, above at the first, second and third recitals of the preamble.
5.   See also COM(91) 408 final, OJ C299 20.11.91 p25, at the first recital of the preamble.
6.   As described above, the Commission has proposed a framework directive to address the problems of food hygiene. See also Written Question 2772/90, OJ C187 18.7.91 p9. For another description of the Commission's work in this area, see *Eurofood* p5 (July 1991).
7.   Council Directive (EEC) 89/397, above at Article 1(2).

labelling legislation. The 1989 directive's rules are without prejudice to any more specific Community requirements which may later be adopted for these purposes[1].

The directive's requirements are applicable to all foodstuffs. This includes food products for domestic consumption, those for export to other Member States, and those for export outside the Community. Products intended for export to other Member States must be inspected with the same care as products intended for domestic consumption. In contrast, products intended for export to third countries are not expressly subject to this requirement[2]. Any distinction is only implicit, but the directive's language suggests a possible difference in the required rigour of controls between products destined for third countries and those intended for other Member States. Such a difference would be consistent with the distinction frequently drawn in Community's food legislation between domestic and export products[3].

Inspections must be conducted both routinely and whenever non-compliance is suspected[4]. They may encompass every stage of the production and marketing processes[5]. Inspections must, however, be "proportionate" to their purposes[6]. This is intended to prevent harassment, or inspections conducted with unreasonable fastidiousness. As a general rule, inspections are conducted without prior warning[7]. They may include direct inspections of finished or unfinished products; sampling and analyses; inspections of staff hygiene; reviews of written materials and records; examinations of control systems; and reviews of the results of control systems[8]. They may include production and transport facilities, raw materials, tools and equipment, cleaning materials and pesticides, manufacturing and processing practices, labelling, and preservation methods[9]. They may involve interviews of employees. Inspections may use measuring instruments either installed by the undertaking or provided by the inspecting authority[10]. Copies may be taken of the producer's records[11]. "Note" may also be taken of the records[12]. This authorises the preparation of written summaries by the inspectors, who may require the inspected firm to verify their accuracy.

---

1.   Article 1(3).
2.   Articles 2, 3. As to export products, Article 3 provides simply that a product shall not be excluded from appropriate national controls because it is intended for export outside the Community.
3.   Below at Chapter 9, para 9.3.5.
4.   Article 4(1).
5.   Article 4(3).
6.   Article 4(2).
7.   Article 4(4).
8.   Article 5.
9.   Article 6(1).
10.   Article 6(2).
11.   Article 9(2).
12.   Article 9(1).

Any physical or chemical analyses performed in connection with the inspections must be conducted either by official governmental laboratories or by private laboratories designated for that purpose by national authorities[1]. The national inspectors are bound by an obligation of "professional secrecy"[2]. The obligation prevents inspectors from revealing information to competitors, the press, and others not part of the regulatory process. In essence, it is a confidentiality requirement[3]. Member States are required to compel processors to submit to inspections. Those inspected must cooperate with inspectors in the accomplishment of their tasks[4]. Member States must also grant rights of appeal to persons "concerned" with an inspection, but there are no Community standards regarding the nature, scope or promptness of those rights[5].

The 1989 directive instructed the Commission to report to the European Parliament and Council during 1990 regarding several control issues. The Commission was asked to provide views regarding the desirability of training programmes for national food inspectors, quality standards for national testing laboratories, and a Community foodstuff inspection service[6]. These requests were made under prompting from the European Parliament[7]. In addition, Member States must submit annual reports regarding their inspection programmes, and the number and types of infringements they discover[8]. In response, the Commission makes annual recommendations to the Member States for coordinated programmes of inspections during the following year[9]. Finally, each Member State must provide the Commission with the names of the inspecting authorities and laboratories which perform the obligations imposed by the directive[10].

---

1.   Article 7(2). Samples may be taken for purposes of such analyses. Article 7(1).
2.   Article 12 (2).
3.   For the implications of a similar rule in the competition area, see Lister, "Dawn Raids and Other Nightmares: The European Commission's Investigatory Powers in Competition Law Matters", 24 Geo. Wash. J. Int'l L. & Econ. 45 (1991).
4.   Inspectors must be given a "right" to conduct the inspection operations, Article 11 (1), and those inspected must "assist" the inspectors; Article 11 (2).
5.   Article 12 (1). Most of the persons "concerned" with an inspection will be those whose facilities are inspected, but the provision is arguably broad enough to include, for example, competitors and consumer groups. The European Court has, however, narrowly construed standing under Article 173 of the Treaty to limit the persons "concerned" with a decision to those whose legal position is affected by it because of facts which differentiate them from the general public in the same way as the person to whom the decision is addressed. See, e.g, Case 253/86 *Sociedad de Agro-Pecuaria Vicente Nobre Lda. v EC Council* [1988] ECR 2725, [1990] 1 CMLR 105, decided by the European Court in 1988.
6.   Council Directive (EEC) 89/397, above at Article 13.
7.   Commission Communication regarding the Official Control of Foodstuffs, COM(90)392 final (13 Sept 1990).
8.   Council Directive (EEC) 89/397, above at Article 14.
9.   Article 14 (3).
10.   Article 15.

In September 1990, the Commission submitted comments to the Council and Parliament regarding the requests made in the 1989 directive[1]. The Commission agreed that it would be useful to define areas of appropriate training for national food inspection officials[2]. Some national officials are not now academically qualified[3]. The Commission undertook to propose standards and other measures for their training, and an annex to the Commission's comments provided a catalogue of relevant subject areas[4]. The Commission also agreed to prepare quality standards for laboratories which conduct food analyses on behalf of national authorities[5]. The Commission acknowledged that it would be possible to standardise analytical methods, but reported a "consensus" that standardisation might prove inflexible. It concluded that standardisation should be sought only in "exceptional circumstances"[6]. With respect to a Community inspection service, the Commission agreed that a "small group" of Commission officials could usefully audit national food controls. They could also mediate between Member States regarding regulatory disputes[7]. The Commission acknowledged that it is already empowered to conduct foodstuff inspections regarding special issues, and agreed to submit a proposal for a general food inspectorate during 1991[8]. No public proposal was made in 1991, and it was subsequently suggested that the Commission had abandoned any plans for a Community food inspectorate. The justification was said to be a "pretext" that Community citizens have "widely differing tastes in food"[9].

In fact, the Commission has since proposed measures which in essence would create a Community food inspectorate. In February 1992, it published a proposed Council directive which would oblige Member States to ensure the expertise of their food inspectorates and laboratories[10]. Laboratories would be subject to random quality audits conducted by national officials[11]. Proficiency testing would be required, and national laboratories would be obliged whenever possible to employ Community

1.   Commission Communication regarding the Official Control of Foodstuffs, COM(90)392 final (13 Sept 1990).
2.   Para 5.
3.   Para 2.
4.   Ibid. The Commission has initiated exchange and coordinational programmes for national regulatory officials. For a proposed Council decision, see COM(91) 408 final, OJ C299 20.11.91 p25.
5.   COM(90) 392 final, above at paras 8-10.
6.   Ibid., para 11. The Commission did not indicate who formed this "consensus". It added that a European Association of Food Analysts is planned, which would carry out the technical work of standardisation. Ibid. at para 12. The fact that two Member States use different methods of analysis to enforce the same substantive standard does not, in the absence of other factors, violate Article 30 of the Treaty; Case 202/82 *Re Pasta Analysis: EC Commission v France* [1984] ECR 933, [1985] 2 CMLR 185, decided by the European Court in 1984.
7.   COM(90) 392 final, above at para 13.
8.   Ibid., para 13 and Annex II.
9.   Written Question 1009/91, OJ C210 12.8.91 p36.
10.   COM(91) 526 final, OJ C51 26.2.92 p10. For revisions, see COM(92) 128 final, OJ C107 28 4.92 p15).
11.   Article 4.

methods of sampling and analysis[1]. Member States would be required to cooperate with one another in administrative and legal questions[2].

In addition, the Commission would designate certain of its employees to cooperate with Member States in the control of foodstuffs[3]. The Commission officials could conduct inspections under the 1989 directive, and Member States would be obliged to provide any assistance needed for the inspections. The results of the Community's inspections would be confidential, but could be employed by the Commission or Member States in the same way as the results of national inspections[4]. Annual reports would be given to the Council and European Parliament[5]. It is unclear how many inspectors would be designated, how extensive would be their activities, or how they would cooperate with national officials. Conceivably the Commission contemplates only a gesture. It need not be merely that, however, and the Commission's proposal could mark a significant step toward implementation of the 1989 directive.

8.7 The product liability and general safety directives

The product liability and general safety directives are important sources of obligations for the producers of food and other consumer products[6]. They authorise regulatory and monetary penalties whenever products are found defective or unsafe. The penalties may include monetary damages, product recalls, exclusions from the marketplace, or other regulatory steps. Both measures warrant careful study by consumer groups and industrial firms, including firms engaged in the processing and distribution of foodstuffs.

8.7.1 The product liability directive

In 1985, the Council adopted a directive to harmonise national rules regarding liability for injuries or damage caused by defective products[7]. The directive has

---

1.   Articles 4(2), 5. The Community rules would be those provided under Council Directive (EEC) 85/591, above.
2.   COM(91) 526 final, at Article 7.
3.   Article 6.
4.   Article 9.
5.   Article 10.
6.   The product liability directive is Council Directive (EEC) 85/374, OJ L210 7.8.85 p29. The Commission's first proposal for a general product safety directive is COM(89) 162 (26 April 1989). As described below, the proposal was subsequently amended. The directive was adopted in June 1992, in the last hours of the Portugese presidency of the Council, but was unpublished at the time of writing.
7.   Council Directive (EEC) 85/374, above. For a detailed review of the directive and related issues, see, e.g., Reich, "Product Safety and Product Liability - An Analysis of the EEC Council Directive of 25 July 1985 on the Approximation of the Laws, Regulations, and Administrative Provisions of the Member States concerning Liability for Defective Products", 9 J. Consumer Policy p133 (1986).

still not been transposed into national law by two Member States, although the deadline for doing so was July 1988. Two other Member States did not adopt the directive until 1991[1]. Except for injuries resulting from nuclear accidents governed by international conventions, the directive applies to any damage or injury caused by any "movable" except unprocessed agricultural products. The term "movable" is not defined, but it evidently denotes all goods except fixtures and real property. Member States may elect to include even agricultural products[2].

The directive provides that the manufacturer of a product is liable for any damage caused by any defect in the product[3]. A product is "defective" whenever it does not provide the degree of safety which a person is entitled to expect, taking into account all of the relevant circumstances[4]. The relevant circumstances include such matters as the product's presentation, its anticipated uses, and the time it was put into circulation. It is no evidence of a defect that a better product was subsequently offered for sale[5]. There are several exceptions, some of which may be eliminated by the Member States. For example, a producer is not liable if he proves that a defect "probably" did not exist when the product was placed in circulation[6]. Nor is he liable if the defect was the result of compliance with mandatory regulations issued by public authorities. In other words, if a defect occurred because the manufacturer complied with standards prescribed by government regulators, no liability will follow[7]. Liability is also excluded if existing scientific and technical knowledge did not permit the discovery of a defect when the product was placed in circulation. This has become known as the "state of the art" defence. Finally, there is no liability if the defendant has provided only a component of a larger product which was itself defectively designed. In the foodstuffs area, for example, the supplier of an ingredient or additive would not be liable if a defect arose from other aspects of a compound food.

---

1. By June 1992, the 1985 directive had still not been implemented by France and Spain. Belgium and Ireland adopted the directive in 1991. For Britain's adoption of the directive, see Consumer Protection Act of 1987, Chap. 43 Eliz. II; for Germany, see Gesetz über die Haftung für fehlerhafte Produkte (15 Dec 1989); for Belgium, see Law 91-737 (25 Feb 1991), Moniteur Belge 5884 (22 March 1991). The Commission has evidently questioned the British and Italian transpositions.
2. Council Directive (EEC) 85/374, above at Article 2.
3. Article 1.
4. Article 6.
5. Article 6(1).
6. Article 7.
7. The word "mandatory" might be taken to suggest that the producer must have been complying with governmental instructions, rather than meeting a governmental standard or accepting an option offered by legislation. This is not, however, the implication of Britain's transposition of the directive. See Consumer Protection Act of 1987, above at sec. 4(1)(a). If indeed the governmental direction must be "mandatory", this would, for example, suggest that a producer's use of an additive included in a Community positive list would not, because its use was optional rather than mandatory, shield the producer from liability if the additive ultimately resulted in injury. As described below, this assumes that the Member State involved had elected to eliminate the state of the art defence.

Member States may eliminate the exemption for situations in which a defect was not discoverable when the product was first placed in circulation[1]. This has thus far been done only by Luxembourg[2]. On the other hand, Member States may also reduce or exclude a producer's liability when the injured person caused, or helped to cause, the defect[3]. In other words, if a purchaser abuses a product, or uses it in a fashion never intended by the manufacturer, Member States may exclude the manufacturer's liability. "Without prejudice" to any national contribution or recourse laws, the directive permits national laws to reduce a producer's liability if an injury was caused both by a defect and by a third party's act[4]. The directive authorises the recovery of damages for death, injury or property damage, and the Member States may also permit recoveries for non-material damage[5].

There are various ancillary rules. In particular, there is a three-year limitations period for damage claims. The period begins when the plaintiff knows or should have known of the damage, the defect, and the identity of the producer[6]. National rules for the suspension of limitations periods are not affected[7]. The directive also provides a ten-year period for the extinction of potential claims[8]. The period begins when the actual product is put into commercial circulation. An important rule is that a producer may not limit or exclude his liability for damages by a contractual provision[9]. The exculpatory provisions commonly included in sales agreements for consumer products are thus without effect. On the other hand, Member States may limit the monetary damages which may be recovered for death or injury. They may not, however, restrict those damages to an amount less than 70 million ECUs[10].

The directive raises significant issues of public policy. In essence, it imposes a standard of strict liability for damages caused within the Community by any product defects[11]. This represents a stringent obligation, and it may be made more onerous if Member States decline to reduce a producer's liability when the damage

---

1.   Article 15 (1) (b).
2.   Law of April 21, 1989. For the U.K. provision, see Consumer Protection Act of 1987, Chap. 43 Eliz. II, at sec. 4(1) (e).
3.   Council Directive (EEC) 85/374, above at Article 8(2).
4.   Article 8(1).
5.   Non-material damages may reach substantial sums in some Member States. For the rules in Italy, for example, see G. Alpa, *Il Danno Biologico* (1987); D. Pajardi, ed., *Danno Biologico e Danno Psicologico* (1990).
6.   Council Directive (EEC) 85/374, above at Article 10 (1).
7.   Article 10 (2).
8.   Article 11.
9.   Article 12. This prohibition applies to claims by an injured person. Contractual limitations conceivably would be might have relevance with respect to other claimants, although this is not addressed in the directive.
10.   Article 16 (1). Germany, Greece and Portugal have imposed limits.
11.   This is not necessarily a major change in previous national laws. For example, a law adopted shortly before Spain entered the Community imposes broad liabilities for product defects. The legislation has resulted in little litigation, but its potential obligations are comparable to those imposed by the directive. Law 26/1984, B.O.E. no. 176 (24 July 1984).

has been caused at least in part by a consumer's misuse of the product. In the foodstuffs area, this would suggest that a supplier might be liable even if an illness occurred because of faulty storage or preparation in the home. The directive's safety standard would be made even more severe if other Member States elected, as Luxembourg has done, to eliminate the exemption when a defect was not discoverable when the product was offered for sale[1].

It is premature to judge the directive's consequences for the marketing of foodstuffs. In particular, it will be important to see whether the directive results in the costly product liability litigation which occurs in the United States. Some protection against those results will be provided if national courts balance their natural sympathy for those who have suffered injury with reasonable concern for the realities of the modern marketplace. They may do so by adopting hospitable interpretations of those few limitations authorised by the directive. For example, courts should take into account the practical difficulties of proving that a defect did not exist when a particular product was placed in circulation, and give full weight to the product's compliance with government standards or requirements.

8.7.2   The general safety directive

In 1989, the Commission proposed a Council directive to harmonise national laws regulating general product safety[2]. The Commission's proposal provoked discussion[3], concern[4], suggestions for revision, and ultimately an amended proposal[5]. The proposal was ultimately adopted late in June 1992, but its final version was unpublished at the time of writing. It is clear, however, that the directive could have important implications for the regulation of food and other products. Food products may be made unsafe by contamination or adulteration, by the use of hazardous additives or processing aids, or by migration of the constituents of packagings or other products with which they are in contact. In all these circumstances, the general safety directive may require substantial regulatory steps, including product recalls and seizures.

---

1.   Council Directive (EEC) 85/374, above at Articles 5, 15 (1) (b). The state of the art defence allows manufacturers to avoid liability where the existing scientific or technical knowledge at the time of a product's introduction did not permit the discovery of a defect. To eliminate the exception, as the directive permits, makes manufacturers insurers of the adequacy of scientific and technical knowledge. Although only Luxembourg has thus far eliminated the defence, there is nothing which prevents other Member States from later doing so.
2.   See COM(89) 162 (26 April 1989).
3.   For the Parliament's initial discussions, see OJ C96 17.4.90 p284.
4.   For the views of Parliament's Committee on Legal Affairs and Citizens Rights, see Document A-3-56/ 90 SYN 192 (2 March 1990). See also the Report of the Committee on the Environment, Public Health and Consumer Protection; ibid.
5.   COM(90) 259 final, OJ C156 27.6.90 p8.

The directive's safety standards are applicable to all products, except insofar as other Community rules govern the safety of a particular product category[1]. Although this limitation was the subject of extensive discussion during the directive's consideration, the interrelationship between the proposed directive and other Community safety rules was left without an unequivocal resolution[2]. Whatever that interrelationship, the directive imposes its own stringent safety obligations. A product is deemed safe only if it either does not present "any" risk or presents an "acceptable" risk consistent with a high standard of protection for health and safety[3]. Only "safe" products may be marketed[4]. Suppliers are required to provide information which would permit consumers to identify and assess any risks[5]. In earlier versions of the proposal, a warning would not have nullified the general safety requirement or provided a defence if a product ultimately proved dangerous. Those rules would have created a significant dilemma for manufacturers. Warnings would have been obligatory, but would have offered no protection. Indeed, a warning might have been an admission that a product does not meet the general safety standard, or that it is "defective" for purposes of the product liability directive. The rule that a warning would offer no defence was, however, evidently eliminated from the version as adopted by the Council. Suppliers are also required to institute monitoring programmes to ensure the safety of their products[6]. Here again, producers may be confronted by overlapping risks. The monitoring may reveal dangers against which warnings would have to be issued, and may also establish "defects" justifying liability under the product liability directive. Under such a standard, many products might be prohibited, including skis, skateboards, motorcycles and perhaps even automobiles. Presumably it is meant that a product must be safe for its intended use, even if that use is itself dangerous.

The directive compels the Member States to establish agencies with broad powers to enforce the general safety requirement. The national agencies will monitor product safety, and impose suitable sanctions in instances of violations[7]. The nature of the sanctions is left to national discretion. The directive also creates a Committee on Product Safety Emergencies, consisting of representatives of the Member States. The committee will formulate Community measures for the

---

1.   Article 1(1). If the directive excludes products which are subject to other Community safety rules, it is in essence a residual regulatory regime for products not otherwise controlled.
2.   The need for some reconciliation of the proposed directive with existing safety rules was among the points made made by the Union of Industrial and Employers' Confederations of Europe (UNICE) in comments submitted to the Community in November 1990.
3.   Article 2.
4.   The second recital of the preamble. The recital is perhaps a reassurance rather than a standard.
5.   Article 3(1).
6.   Article 3(3).
7.   Article 5. Member States are required to provide "suitable sanctions" in the event of any violations of the directive's obligations. This may oblige them to order product recalls or other actions even where there had not been any preexisting notice of violation.

removal from the marketplace of products found to be unsafe[1]. Immediate seizures and product recalls are among the possible sanctions[2].

Producers are given rights of appeal, but nothing in the directive requires the appeals to be decided in a timely manner[3]. The directive is without prejudice to the product liability directive[4]. This presumably means that the latter governs private claims for damages, while the former creates general standards and powers to remove hazardous products from the marketplace. The directive also requires Member States to shield against liability any person who publicly calls into question the safety of a product. The only limitations are that the person's claims must be "intended" to be accurate, and must be made in good faith[5]. The standard may give protection to claims which later prove both false and injurious to a producer. It should be hoped that the requirement will at least be interpreted to exclude charges made without any serious effort to determine their truth. Honest errors should arguably be protected; recklessness amounting to an indifference to truth should not.

The directive raises important issues of industrial and consumer policy. Its breadth alone deserves notice. It encompasses virtually all suppliers, whether manufacturers, distributors or agents. It includes virtually all products, whether new or used. Suppliers are obliged to offer only "safe" products, and the safety of those products will be judged by a "high" standard of protection[6]. It is not obvious how these obligations will be applied to products whose use is inherently dangerous. Nor is it clear what will be required of products, such as foodstuffs, which may be made dangerous by consumer misuse[7]. The safety obligations are not restricted to the product's condition at the time of sale. They extend to the maintenance and disposal of products, and persist throughout the product's "foreseeable" period of use[8].

---

1.   Article 10.
2.   Article 6(j).
3.   Article 14 (4). The provision states simply that a judicial challenge to regulatory measures should be possible, without any requirement regarding the challenge's adequacy or promptness. For all the directive suggests, the appeal could occur months after a product had been withdrawn, and might be subject to the lengthy delays common in some national courts.
4.   Article 13.
5.   Article 14 (2).
6.   Article 2.
7.   For example, alcoholic beverages and many other foodstuffs may be dangerous if consumed in excess, or without proper preparation or storage, and those risks are foreseeable by producers.
8.   The key requirement is the period of "foreseeable" use, and not the period of use recommended by the producer. With respect to foodstuffs, this suggests that a processor might be liable for defects arising after a product's "use by" or "best before" date if its use after that date by some consumers was foreseeable. Durability dates already tend to be conservative, and such an obligation could stimulate even more cautious dating. For the problems of dating, see Hine, "Shelf-life Prediction", in F. Paine, ed., *Modern Processing, Packaging and Distribution Systems for Food* pp62-85 (1987).

CHAPTER 9 : THE ACHIEVEMENTS OF THE COMMUNITY'S FOOD POLICIES

The Community has been engaged in the regulation of foodstuffs for thirty years. It has adopted hundreds of measures regarding dozens of regulatory issues. Since 1985 it has sought to implement an ambitious programme for the harmonisation of national laws regarding all of the basic areas of food regulation. The target date for the completion of that programme is now at hand. The Community's efforts with respect to food regulation are paralleled by its efforts to control the marketing of agricultural and fishery products. They are supplemented by measures relating to advertising, environmental protection, product liability, and packaging. None of the Community's programmes is fixed or finished, and additional measures will certainly be adopted. It is not, however, too early to begin assessing the success with which the Community has addressed the complex problems of food regulation. The central question is not whether the Community will actually complete its 1985 agenda by any deadline. It is instead whether the Community's measures represent substantial progress toward a unified and well-regulated marketplace for foods.

9.1   Assessing the Community's achievements

Substantial steps have been taken toward the harmonisation of many aspects of national regulation. Labelling remains the best example. Since the 1989 amendments to the 1978 directive, labelling is an area of overall success for the Community[1]. Its rules are scattered and in some respects incomplete, but substantial progress has been made[2]. They appear to be observed with reasonable fidelity in most areas of the Community[3]. Similarly, additives are now subject to basic Community rules, including some conditions of use, and greater order has belatedly been given to those rules[4]. Much must be done before the additives rules have been revised, but the pace of achievement has increased significantly. There is also a revised framework directive for "parnuts" foods[5]. Articles and materials intended to come into contact with foodstuffs are subject to new framework requirements, and a plastics directive has been adopted[6]. In addition, there are rules regarding infant

---

1.   Above at Chapter 3, para 3.2.
2.   There are still areas in which additional labelling rules are now under consideration, and others in which new measures should be examined; above at Chapter 3, para 3.3.
3.   As explained below, however, there are apparently no audits of labelling practices.
4.   The progress is only belated given the relatively recent adoption of the central requirements. It was only in 1988 that the Council was able to adopt a new framework additives directive, and it remains a framework. There are still no updated rules for many specific categories of additives. Above at Chapter 5, para 5.1.
5.   Above at Chapter 4, para 4.5.
6.   Above at Chapter 4.

formulae and nutritional labelling, and new limits are in preparation for pesticide residues[1]. There is not yet a comprehensive hygiene directive, but steps have been taken toward strengthened systems of official inspections and controls[2]. These are essential parts of an effective regulatory programme, and it would be wrong to ignore either the efforts they have required or the progress they represent.

It would be equally wrong to ignore the problems which remain. Most of the measures referred to above are still incomplete. There is no Community measure regarding artificial sweeteners, nor any relating to processing aids other than extraction solvents[3]. The only new rules relating to specific contact materials are limited to plastics and regenerated films. The issues arising from novel food ingredients and processes remain unresolved[4]. Nor has any acceptable solution been found for the problems of irradiated foodstuffs[5]. There is a framework directive for foods intended for particular nutritional purposes, but the issues presented by specific "parnuts" products, apart from infant formulae, must still be addressed[6]. Most additives remain the subject of rules which require reconsideration[7]. The pesticide residue limits for many fruits and vegetables must be reevaluated and harmonised[8]. No comprehensive rules regarding food hygiene have been adopted[9]. Chilled and unpackaged foods are the subject of very incomplete rules[10]. Food contamination is the subject only of proposed rules, and those proposals represent only the first stages of regulation[11]. Community measures for auditing and verifying national enforcement systems are only now being developed[12]. The Community's direct enforcement efforts are still small and occasional. Even the Community's labelling rules warrant supplementation[13]. Genuine progress toward harmonisation has been made, but the road ahead is nearly as long, and conceivably more difficult, than the road behind.

One reason for the Community's failure to make greater progress is the belatedness of its start. The adoption of foodstuff measures began in 1962, but the first two

---

1.   New maximum residue limits will be established under the 1990 directive, as the 1976 directive is gradually replaced. Above at Chapter 8, para 8.3.1.
2.   Above at Chapter 8, para 8.6.
3.   Above at Chapter 5, para 5.1.
4.   Above at Chapter 4, para 4.4.
5.   Above at Chapter 4, para 4.3.
6.   Above at Chapter 4, para 5.5.
7.   Above at Chapter 5, para 5.1.
8.   Above at Chapter 8, para 8.3.1.
9.   Above at Chapter 8, para 8.6.1.
10.   For chilled foods, see above at Chapter 4, para 4.1; for unpackaged foods, see above at Chapter 8, para 8.5.
11.   Above at Chapter 8, para 8.6.2 .
12.   Above at Chapter 8, para 8, para 8.6.3.
13.   Format rules are one example, and compulsory nutritional labelling another; above at Chapter 3, para 3.3.2.

decades produced relatively little[1]. In particular, the sixteen-year period between the colourings directive in 1962 and the general labelling directive in 1978 was largely lost[2]. This may have reflected the absence of genuine urgency, but it also resulted from serious errors of regulatory approach. A few recipe laws were completed, but the choices were eccentric and the misallocation of resources extravagant[3]. The search for recipes for "Euro-chocolate" and "Euro-honey" was long and costly, and proved a lamentable diversion from the central issues of food regulation. The Community has laboured to harmonise national food laws for three decades, but only the years since 1985 have produced substantial progress.

9.2   Assessing compliance with the Community's rules

It is a fine thing to make rules, but it is finer still if they are obeyed. The Community is only now beginning to consider how best to ensure the uniform enforcement of its harmonised rules. Even the transposition of Community directives into national law has proved slower than might have been expected. Although some Member States have generally been prompt in adopting directives into national law, the failures are still numerous and significant[4]. Every Member State has been charged with failures to adopt or implement properly some directives, and some Member States have become notorious for their unwillingness or inability to do so[5]. Indeed, the food sector has presented the "most serious delays

---

1.   With respect to additives, for example, the Economic and Social Committee complained as late as 1986 about the absence of real progress during the previous twelve years. Above at Chapter 5, para 5.1.

2.   The period between 1962 and 1978 produced some 50 directives relating to foods, see, e.g., *Eurofood Monitor* X-1 (1990-91), but few related to central issues. Apart from the 1963 flavourings directive and the 1974 directive regarding emulsifiers, the Commission's principal attention was given to a handful of recipe laws. These were adopted on roughly an annual basis.

3.   The principal question arising from the recipe laws, apart from the unimaginativeness of the retail approach, is why those particular products were chosen. Why honey, for example, and not mustard or mayonnaise? There were long-standing British rules regarding both of the latter. See Food Standards (Mustard) (No. 2) Order 1944 (S.R.& O. 1944, No. 275); Salad Cream Regulations 1966, SI 1966/1051, SI 1966/1206. They were revoked by the Food (Miscellaneous Revocations) Regulations 1991, SI 1991/1231. Or why coffee but not tea or soft drinks? See, e.g., Soft Drinks Regulations 1964, SI 1964/760, and subsequent amendments. More important, why not food hygiene, conditions of use for additives, or control and inspection mechanisms?

4.   All of the Member States have failed to adopt some directives, but Denmark and Britain have long had good overall records for transpositions. France now has a good overall percentage, but many of its measures have been adopted behind schedule. Belgium has proved surprisingly slow, while Greece and Portugal have recently adopted many measures. Italy remains a fixture at the bottom of the table. For the transpositions as of early 1991, see The Eighth Annual Report to the European Parliament of Commission Monitoring of the Application of Community Law, OJ C338 31.12.91 p1. More recently, see EC Commission, *National Implementing Measures* (1992).

5.   As of 31 December 1990, for example, there was a long series of European Court decisions against Italy, some of them several years old, in which no action had been taken to correct a deficiency. Eighth Annual Report to the European Parliament on Commission Monitoring of the Application of Community Law, OJ C338 31.12.91 p1 at pp66-67. Some were second condemnations of the same failure, in which the first judgment of the European Court had not resulted in satisfactory action.

in transposal" of all the areas of harmonization[1]. Even when the Community succeeds in adopting the full 1985 programme for the completion of the internal market, many Member States will not for a substantial additional period actually transpose it into national law.

The transposition issue will be solved by time and persistence. The more difficult problem is how to ensure the uniform enforcement of Community measures once they eventually become parts of national law. If some Member States are tardy in adopting the Community's harmonisation directives, they are often no less dilatory in enforcing them[2]. In the absence of systematic monitoring, it is impossible to judge actual compliance with the harmonised rules in different parts of the Community[3]. Any assessment can be only impressionistic. Even a reliable evaluation of compliance with the labelling rules would require periodic reviews of grocery shelves, which does not now occur on a Community-wide basis[4]. Compliance with the rules for additives and contact materials would be far more difficult to verify. In the absence of compliance audits, it can only be said that the potential for abuse is substantial[5]. The Community's failure to institute systematic measures for verifying the enforcement of its harmonised rules is a major omission from its achievements.

9.3   The direction of the Community's policies

The 1985 White Paper marked a salutary change in the direction of the Community's food regulatory policies. The abandonment of recipe laws, at least for most purposes and in most areas, was welcome and overdue. The priorities

---

1.   Ninth Annual Report on Commission Monitoring of the Application of Community Law - 1991, COM(92) 136 final, OJ C250 28.9.92 p2.

2.   The need for more uniform enforcement has, for example, become a concern of the European Parliament. See Document A2-216/86, OJ C99 13.4.87 p68 at paras. E, F. As a general matter, the "enforcement of Community law continues to lag behind the transfer of competences to the Community level." CEPS, *The Annual Review of European Community Affairs 1990* p 47 (1991).

3.   In the United Kingdom, for example, an expert committee found an important need for more uniform regulatory enforcement. Report of the Committee on the Microbiological Safety of Food, Part I, 113 (1990). It expressed special concern about the "little control" exercised over the creation and operation of new food businesses; ibid. at p81.

4.   Just as the Community is now considering whether to enforce its rules by direct inspections of producers, so too it might undertake a monitoring of grocery shelves. Reports of its samples could be made publicly and to the Member States.

5.   For example, the British agricultural press has complained that other Member States lack the will and technology to detect forbidden growth hormones in beef cattle. *The Financial Times* p4 (2 April 1991). This is supported by claims of food poisonings in Spain because of the illegal use of clenbuterol to fatten cattle. 1 World Food Reg. Rev. 5 (March 1992). For reported concerns in Germany regarding chemical contamination of foods, see A. Tuffs, "Germany: Food Matters", 337 *The Lancet* p1336 (1 June 1991). Other evidence is available by analogy. The Community's Court of Auditors reviewed national programmes for the administration of refunds for exported agricultural products and allowances to farmers in less developed areas, and found wide differences in their methods and rigour; OJ C324 13.12.91 p1, at points 4.1.51, 9.2.5. In some instances, national monitoring programmes were based simply upon "trust"; ibid. It is unlikely that national food inspectorates are less diverse in their methods and effectiveness.

established in 1985 have permitted the Community to move forward more rapidly, to concentrate on matters of genuine significance, and to assign a higher priority to regulatory flexibility. They have relieved the Community's food policies from the threat of a "legislative straitjacket"[1]. Nonetheless, the 1985 programme is a blueprint for the Community's policies only through 1992, and the Commission has offered few intimations of its regulatory goals for subsequent years. The worst course would be to re-enter the regulatory thicket of the recipe laws. Such a venture would result in delay, inflexibility, and impediments to innovation[2]. The Community's achievements largely result from its change in regulatory approach in 1985, and any reversal would threaten the advances which have already been made. The issue is not, however, closed. The persistent pressures for better guarantees of product quality may well force a return to compositional standards and other vertical measures. Aside from that danger, other features of the Community's food measures should also be sources of concern. Those features raise important questions about the direction and content of the Community's regulatory policies.

9.3.1   The absence of substantive regulatory goals

The first feature which warrants concern is the Community's failure to identify values and goals by which it will guide its policymaking. For thirty years, the Community's overriding goal has been harmonisation. In the Community's special circumstances, harmonisation is genuinely important. Its achievement is one legitimate measurement of the Community's progress. In itself, however, harmonisation says nothing about the content or purpose of the harmonised rules. Success consists simply of some rough consistency in twelve national systems, without regard to the actual substance of the rules or the values they embody. It can be an invitation to the lowest common denominator. The Community has largely declined that invitation, but it has done so without articulating any systematic principles or approaches.

The growing demands for new guarantees of product quality create their own costs and hazards, but they still represent the Community's first hesitant steps toward regulatory goals beyond harmonisation[3]. With this exception, the Community has resolved food regulatory problems through a series of improvisational compromises. Those compromises have been drawn from different sources and based upon different goals. Some reflect the influence of the Codex Alimentarius

---

1.   Gray, "The Perspective to 1992", in H. Deelstra, et al., eds., *Food Policy Trends in Europe* pp11, 13 (1991).

2.   The disadvantages of compositional standards are described in, for example, National Academy of Sciences, Committee on Nutrition Components of Food Labeling, *Nutrition Labeling: Issues and Directions for the 1990's* pp320-342 (1990); Austern, "Food Standards: The Balance Between Certainty and Innovation", 24 Food D.C.L.J. 440 (1969).

3.   Below at Chapter 10, para 10.1.

Commission or Council of Europe, others give special weight to one national model or another, and still others are merely ad hoc political accommodations[1]. The results are, as the European Parliament has complained, incoherence and inconsistency[2]. As harmonisation is finally achieved, the absence of substantive goals will grow more obvious and troublesome[3].

9.3.2 The tendency toward rigidity

The second feature of the Community's policies which warrants concern is their tendency toward rigidity. The best examples are the recipe laws, with their tidy and confining formulae for every aspect of a product's composition, labelling and presentation. The Community has been more imaginative since 1985, but a continued inclination toward inflexibility may still be seen in many rules. The reasons are largely institutional. The Commission is only intermittently subject to public scrutiny, and it remains freer than most bureaucracies to indulge its tastes in rulemaking[4]. Because its rules are enforced by national authorities, the Commission naturally prefers standards which are relatively static and unequivocal. Wherever possible, it selects rules which are self-enforcing. This encourages rigidity and detail. Moreover, the Community's regulatory process is itself inflexible. Despite an increasing use of committee procedures, important measures must still be reviewed by the Parliament, examined by the Economic and Social Committee, and approved by the Council. Member States may compel even subsidiary issues to be resolved through the full legislative process[5]. The Commission is less subject to public and judicial secrutiny than comparable regulators in, for example, Britain or the United States, but it also enjoys less freedom to act quickly or independently. Delays are frequent in all regulatory schemes, but they are inherent in the Community's complex policymaking system.

Positive lists are an example. They promote safety by forbidding a substance until it has been proven to be without danger under proper conditions of use. Many categories of additive are appropriate for the imposition of positive lists. It does not follow, however, that all issues should be resolved on the basis that everything

---

1. See, e.g., Rees, "Introduction", in J. Rees & J. Bettison, eds., *Processing and Packaging of Heat Preserved Foods* pp1, 14 (1991).
2. Resolution of the European Parliament on food hygiene, OJ C183 15.7.91 p52.
3. The Commission is, however, considering a proposed directive which would establish uniform definitions and common principles of Community food law. The proposal is in early stages of preparation and currently provides only very general statements of principle, most of which reiterate the terms of earlier measures. It is more nearly a summary than a reevaluation or appraisal of regulatory goals.
4. One result is recurrent political disputes. For the Commission's difficulties in Britain regarding potato crisps, sausages and ice cream, see, e.g., *The Sunday Times* p8 (5 May 1991). For its demands for Euro-bottles for gin, see *The Times* p5 (1 April 1991). It even seems to demand straight and smooth-barked Euro-oaks. *The Independant* p1 (2 June 1991).
5. The approval of new pesticide residue limits for fruits and vegetables is an example; below at Chapter 7, para 7.3.1.

not expressly permitted is forbidden. To do so creates substantial barriers to innovation. Positive lists are difficult to compile and equally difficult to revise. A technical need for new products must be shown, and layers of Community and national approvals must be sought[1]. Lengthy delays are likely, and protectionist sympathies may inhibit changes. These disadvantages justify reticence in the use of positive lists. At a minimum, manufacturers must be assured timely and genuine opportunities to establish the safety and effectiveness of new products. Consistent with human and environmental safety, delays should be minimised. Once safety and effectiveness have been proved, approval should not be denied because existing substances can satisfy the same technical purposes[2].

9.3.3   The tendency toward ambiguity

Another characteristic of the Community's legislation is also rooted in its history and institutions. The Community's food measures generally take the form of directives rather than regulations. They are, in order words, instructions to Member States to alter their national rules rather than Community rules directly applicable to private conduct. Directives are often the results of lengthy negotiations and elaborate compromises, in which Member States haggle over special accommodations for local interests and needs. The preparatory process more nearly resembles that for treaties than that for administrative regulations. One consequence is often loose draftmanship[3]. Rigidity may be tempered by uncertainty. The Community's draftsmen understand themselves to be preparing general instructions, which will be applied in spirit rather than in their exact terms. They are sometimes correspondingly indifferent to the precision of those terms[4]. The ambiguities are increased by repeated translations and multiplied by national transpositions. National variations within some decent range of fidelity are tolerated. The final consequences are national measures which literally only approximate one another.

---

1.   For the Community's policy of demanding an unsatisfied technical need for new additives, see, e.g., Snodin, "Sweeteners: Statutory Aspects", in S. Marie & J. Piggott, eds., *Handbook of Sweeteners* pp266, 280-281 (1991).

2.   The Commission's view evidently remains that no additive should be approved without proof of a technical need, and that no need exists if other substances can perform the same function. See, e.g., Deboyser, "Le marché unique de produits alimentaires", 1-1991 Revue du marché unique européen pp63, 83 (1991).

3.   For the complaints of an enforcement official regarding the looseness of the Community's rules and the resulting problems, see Roberts, "European Enforcement", 1/92 Eur. Food L. Rev. 1 (1992).

4.   One example is offered by the unit pricing directive, which exempts shops identified only as "certain", where goods are "handed directly" to consumers; above at Chapter 2, para 2.6. Presumably the Council knew what it intended, but others can only speculate.

9.3.4 The tendency toward new trade barriers

Rigid rules, with the accompanying regulatory delays and impediments to innovation, are significant trade barriers. They shield existing producers against new competitors from both within and outside the Community[1]. In some instances, however, the new barriers go beyond the clumsiness of the regulatory process itself. For example, the Council's new certifications of geographical origin and product distinctiveness are more than labelling measures designed to reveal the actual sources of protected products[2]. They also represent promotional subsidies, conditioned upon adherence to unvarying local processing techniques. They are statements of a regulatory preference for traditional local products, and discourage alternative sources of similar products even from within the Community. The Commission's more general idea of quality certificates for products which satisfy Community standards might have similar results[3].

Similarly, the Commission's proposal to impose restrictions upon "novel" food products and processes threatens new barriers to innovation and competition[4]. The proposal would reach beyond biotechnological products and processes to impose limitations upon any product or technology new to the Community. Biotechnology is an appropriate subject of regulatory scrutiny; innovation demands more discriminating treatment. Novelty invites review, but the review should be no more burdensome than actually necessary to ensure safety. The Commission has sought to lessen the burdens of review, but it remains unclear whether its efforts will be successful. In the same way, the Commission's demand that new additives may be approved only if existing products cannot perform the same technical functions invites another potential trade barrier[5]. Community and national packaging waste requirements could be important sources of protectionist rules[6]. The Commission's reported willingness to authorise regional regulatory regimes might create trade barriers at regional or local levels[7]. Aside from the framework additives directive, none of these Community measures has yet been adopted. Nonetheless, the fact of their consideration suggests that the Community must constantly remind itself that its goal is to dismantle trade barriers, and not to erect them.

---

1. If American experience with pharmaceutical products is a guide, the burdens of rigid rules fall with particular severity on smaller firms. Large firms may even on balance profit from them because of the limits they impose on competition. Thomas, "Regulation and Firm Size: FDA Impacts on Innovation", 21 RAND J. of Econ. 497 (1990).
2. Above at Chapter 3, para 3.8.
3. Above at Chapter 3, para 3.8.3.
4. Above at Chapter 4, para 4.4.
5. Above at Chapter 5, para 5.1.
6. Above at Chapter 8, para 8.2.
7. Above at Chapter 3, para 3.8.

Nor should the Community create new barriers to competition from beyond its borders. There is evidence that, as many have feared and some have predicted, the Community sometimes uses the harmonisation process to impede international competition[1]. The Council's new regulations for certificates of origin and distinctiveness are again examples. The proposed novel food rules and the various positive lists provide others. "Fortress Europe" is not a reality, but there are many who would willingly join in its construction. The relative absence of protectionist measures thus far may owe as much to international monitoring as it does to the Community's self-restraint.

9.3.5   The tendency toward double standards

The Community frequently grants exemptions from its regulatory requirements for foodstuffs intended for export to third countries. It is certainly entitled to avoid prejudice to its export sales and to take account of the regulatory policies of the nations which purchase those exports. Comity cannot, however, fully explain the Community's export rules. Labelling and other informational questions must be decided by the nations in which the products will actually be consumed, but this is less obviously appropriate with respect to rules designed to ensure wholesomeness and human safety.

If an additive, processing aid, or food contact material is thought too dangerous for use within the Community, it is difficult to see why the Community should permit its use in export products. And if only prescribed levels of use are safe in the Community, why should higher levels be acceptable for products intended for consumption elsewhere? This is particularly true where the products are destined for nations which lack the Community's analytical and regulatory resources. Where the Community adopts rules designed to protect human health and safety, those rules should presumptively also apply to products intended for export[2]. The issue is not whether the Community should export its regulatory policies; it is instead whether it should export hazards against which it protects its own citizens[3].

---

1.   For the debate regarding the extent and reality of protectionist measures in the Community, see, e.g., I. Jenkins & A. Lorenz, "Assault on Fortress Europe", *The Sunday Times* pp4-7 (5 May 1991); I. Stelzer, "America Hits Back with Its Own Market"; ibid.

2.   The Community is not alone in exempting export products from its safety rules. Britain excluded exports from its food rules until the Food Safety (Exports) Regulations 1991, SI 1991/1476. The 1991 regulations still provide that it is a defence to violations if products satisfy local laws in importing countries; ibid. at Regulations 2, 3.

3.   One of the recitals to the Commission's rules regarding infant and follow-on formulae appeared to suggest that a proposal regarding export sales was in preparation. Commission Directive (EEC) 91/321, OJ L175 4.7.91 p35, at the thirteenth recital of the preamble. In fact, the proposal (and subsequent measure) was limited narrowly to infant and follow-on formulae; see above at Chapter 4, para 4.6; Written Question 906/91, OJ C311 2.12.91 p18.

9.3.6   The tendency toward uncoordinated policymaking

Coordinated decisionmaking is an unceasing problem in all regulatory organisations, and the Commission's difficulties may be no worse than those which face many national agencies. The familiarity of the problem does not, however, diminish its significance. Effective rulemaking for foodstuffs demands close coordination with the Community's policies concerning other issues. Agricultural policy is an important example, but competition and environmental policies are equally urgent. The Commission employs formal and informal methods to coordinate its activities, and its efforts are encouraged by the oversight of other Community institutions. Nonetheless, those efforts are still inadequate in many respects[1]. In particular, the relationships between the Community's food and agricultural policies are often strained. Moreover, only fitful attention appears to be given to the competitive consequences of foodstuff rules. As a result, some rules inhibit innovation and encourage the entrenchment of existing producers. These deficiencies erode the overall effectiveness of the Community's regulatory policies regarding foodstuffs.

9.3.7   The tendency toward non-public rulemaking

Another feature of the Community's policies is not restricted to the food sector. The Community's regulatory policies are formulated under conditions which largely exclude the open discussion and public debate common in democratic societies[2]. To an extraordinary degree, the Commission operates without public scrutiny. Indeed, it affects a distaste for "lobbying". By this, the Commission sometimes appears to mean any effort to bring to its attention the concerns of those whom it regulates. It regularly seeks the views of some industry and consumer groups, but the favoured groups are selected by the Commission itself and participate in the review of proposals only as and when the Commission finds appropriate[3]. The Commission's new proposal regarding novel foods, for example, was reviewed in its final stages only in an "informal" meeting with unidentified "interested parties"[4]. Nor do the groups selected by the Commission necessarily represent every relevant element of

---

1.   See, e.g., the resolution of the European Parliament on food hygiene, which complains about the "inconsistency and incoherence" of the Commission's food policies, OJ C183 15.7.92 p52.

2.   USITC, for example, notes the absence of an "open environment" in the Community's regulatory process. USITC, *The Effects of Greater Economic Integration within the European Community on the United States, First Report*, p6-75 (1990). Similarly, a former US ambassador to the United Nations has reported, with excessive drama, the Commission's increasing authority and lack of responsiveness. Kirkpatrick, "Is the European Community Finished?" *Washington Post* pA-ll (13 May 1990).

3.   It does not always consult even its selected advisors. The Commission reportedly did not, for example, consult industry before proposing its new certificates of geographical origin and product distinctiveness; above at Chapter 3, para 3.8. Moreover, Commissioner van Miert has conceded that the Commission sometimes neglects to consult its consumer agencies; *Eurofood* 2 (July 1991).

4.   Impact Assessment Form accompanying COM(92) 295 final (7 July 1992), at para. 6.

industry or the public[1]. The problem is not that better representatives may be available, but simply that no trade or consumer groups should be the Commission's dominant sources of opinion.

It is not enough that the Commission's proposals are published in the Official Journal. The delays are often significant, and publication may easily occur too late to permit effective participation in the decisionmaking process. Indeed, publication represents one of the later stages of rulemaking, and is a signal that at least the Commission has already made up its mind. In any event, there is no mechanism at the Community level for the submission of public comments regarding the Commission's proposals. So far as the Commission is concerned, publication is merely informational. In these circumstances, it is scarcely surprising that lobbying has begun to flourish in Brussels. The Commission has created an environment in which there is no meaningful alternative.

The Council is no better. Its sessions are closed and its proceedings not officially reported. When the Council reaches decisions, only the results are officially disclosed. Its goals and accommodations are hidden, and its reasoning literally inscrutable[2]. Only the European Parliament represents a partial gesture toward more democratic opportunities for public participation. Its role in the Community's governance has been strengthened, but it cannot yet provide the degree and consistency of legislative oversight common in Britain and most other Member States[3]. A closed government might have been tolerable in the Community's early years, when its role was small and occasional. With the increasing primacy of Community legislation and wider use of qualified Council majorities to approve that legislation, the existing arrangements are an anachronism.

Food regulation within the Member States is now largely shaped by Community legislation[4]. It is the Community which generally decides which additives will be permitted and what labels will be required. One example of the Community's impact upon national food policies is provided by Britain's efforts to require the

---

1. Smaller firms may be substantially affected by legislation tailored to the needs of their larger competitors, and yet be less influential in the trade groups upon which the Commission relies. Moreover, detailed rules tend to inhibit competition and hence may on balance benefit larger firms at the expense of smaller, newer rivals. One of principal industry groups is, because of its diversity, reportedly "not always able to come to a common view". Swinburn & Burns, "The EEC and the Food and Drink Industries", in A. Swinburn & J. Burns, eds., *The EEC and the Food Industries* pp155, 167 (1984). It would be surprising if any large and diverse group were always both unanimous and representative in its presentations of an industry's views.

2. See, e.g., Chambers, "Consolidation of Food-law Text - A Democratic Essential?", 1/91 Eur. Food L. Rev. 46 (1991); EC Food Law 4 (June 1992).

3. The continuing weaknesses of the Parliament's role are described above at Chapter 2, para 2.1.

4. Ryder, "UK Food Legislation", in *The Lancet, Foodborne Illness* 44, 51 (1991); S. Fallows, *Food Legislative System of the UK* p95 (1988). These judgments were expressed in terms of Britain, but they are equally valid about other parts of the Community.

fortification with vitamins A and D of fat spreads and margarines, which have replaced butter in many diets. The Commission forbade proposed British regulations which would have required fortification, on the basis that they could constitute a trade barrier[1]. A working group of Britain's Committee on Medical Aspects of Food Policy found the requirement's absence to be "unwise", especially for the elderly, children, and other vulnerable groups. Unless there is Community legislation permitting such requirements, the only option for Britain and other Member States is to justify them under Article 36 of the Treaty. The Commission is, however, now considering its own legislation regarding the fortification of yellow fat products[2]. A similar situation exists with respect to cheeses made from unpasteurised milk[3]. More widely publicised but nutritionally less significant disputes have involved additives in potato crisps and other snack foods.

The pressures for national conformity will be increased if, as now widely suggested, the Commission goes forward with an inventory of non-harmonised national laws and regulations. Under Article 100b of the Treaty of Rome, as amended by the Single European Act, the Commission is obliged to compile such an inventory during 1992. Once it is completed, the Council may decide which of the national rules are equivalent to those applied by other Member States[4]. The process would be lengthy and difficult, but its result could be a substantial reduction in the existing variations among national rules[5].

Food regulatory issues are not generally thought to be urgent matters of democratic concern, but many involve questions of human health and some provoke public debate. They affect the Community's residents more directly and concretely than most other regulatory questions. At a minimum, they illustrate the fundamental ways in which the Member States are being changed by the Community's rulings. Those changes will ultimately prove acceptable only if decided upon openly and by some semblance of a democratic process. A major challenge to the Community will be to devise new institutional arrangements for rulemaking which are both democratic and consistent with national jealousies.

---

1. Committee on Medical Aspects of Food Policy, Working Group on the Fortification of Yellow Fats, *The Fortification of Yellow Fats with Vitamins A and D*, ix, 2 (1991).
2. Ibid. In addition, the Commission has suggested new rules for butter and other fat products, which would establish trade descriptions and other requirements; above at Chapter 8, para 8.13.
3. Above at Chapter 2, para 5.
4. Under Article 100b(3), the Commission "shall" compile the inventory and submit proposals in time to permit the Council to act during 1992.
5. Article 100a(4) permits Member States a narrow power to opt-out of harmonisation measures based upon the factors listed in Article 36. Similar derogations are permitted under Article 100b(2). The scope of the two provisions is unclear, but, consistent with its reading of Article 36, the European Court is likely to interpret them narrowly.

CHAPTER 10 : THE FUTURE OF THE COMMUNITY'S FOOD POLICIES

For the immediate future, the Community's priority should remain the completion of the 1992 programme. There is little point in a job half-promised and half-done, and the 1985 programme remains fundamentally sensible. As the 1985 White Paper promised, the Community should give its highest priority to health and safety matters, labelling, additives, contact materials, and control mechanisms[1]. It should do so in a fashion hospitable to innovation and hostile to new trade barriers. The real problem is to determine what steps should follow the completion of the 1992 programme. Should the Community simply declare the single market a reality, retiring from the field except to take account of new developments? Or should it undertake a new agenda of institutional and substantive reforms?

Few outside Brussels, and none in southern Europe, believe that the 1985 programme will actually produce a single and unified market[2]. The differences in practices and attitudes between Catania and Copenhagen, or Athens and Amsterdam, are simply too great to permit the mere promulgation of rules, however elegant and detailed, to bring real harmonisation[3]. Only time and rigorous enforcement can give substance to the Community's rules and thus to the single market. Several steps are appropriate. First, the Community should begin considering the values and goals which will guide its future regulatory programme. An articulation of the Community's regulatory assumptions will promote consistency and help to identify issues which warrant new emphasis. Second, the Community should alter its institutional arrangements for regulatory decisionmaking. One important change would be to open its policymaking processes to meaningful public participation. Food regulation is too important to remain the protected preserve of the Commission and those outsiders whose views it elects to invite. Third, the Community should begin addressing a series of new or unresolved substantive problems. The problems differ in urgency, but taken together they offer the Community an important regulatory agenda.

---

1.   Above at Chapter 2, para 2.3.
2.   One indication of the continued fragmentation may be taken by analogy from another area of Community law. The director of the task force created to enforce the Community's Merger Regulation, Council Regulation (EEC) 4064/89, OJ L395 30.12.89 p1, was interviewed regarding his experience. He emphasised the importance of defining the relevant geographical market, and expressed surprise at the frequency with which the relevant market had proved to be only a small fraction of the Community; *International Herald Tribune* p7 (16 Sept 1991). By implication, his conclusion is that the Community continues to be fragmented into discrete markets. Foodstuffs are no exception.
3.   In the area of meat controls, for example, it has been observed that the rules are applied in "widely different" ways by local officials, creating "markedly unfair" trading conditions. Locke, "Meat and Meat Products", in A. Sminburn & J. Burns, eds., *The EEC and the Food Industries* pp131, 142 (1984).

10.1   Beyond harmonisation

The threshold issue is what values or goals should guide the Community's future regulatory programme. Food regulation cannot remain static, and mere harmonisation alone is no longer a sufficient answer. Many goals might be selected, and they could be variously balanced and described. At the most general level, a regulatory system may rightly be deemed successful if it embodies seven characteristics: clarity, simplicity, timeliness, accuracy, coherence, neutrality and enforceability. Without clarity and simplicity, firms cannot effectively regulate their own conduct and regulators may readily discriminate among products or producers[1]. Ambiguities create confusion and invite abuse. They promote continued national inconsistencies. Timeliness is the ability to respond promptly to new risks, products, or circumstances. It is possible only if both regulators and their rules have retained some reasonable measure of regulatory flexibility. Accuracy means conformity to reliable scientific and technical standards. Coherence denotes an integrated approach to the principal regulatory issues, as well as some reasonable consistency with related areas of policy. Neutrality requires evenhandedness in the treatment of products and producers, whether new or old, local or distant. Enforceability demands that rules be sufficiently clear in their terms and practical in their obligations to permit effective enforcement. The actual success of an enforcement programme must itself be judged by the other six characteristics; enforcement measures are successful if they are clear, simple, timely, accurate, systematic, and non-discriminatory.

At a different level, regulators must select intermediate values more directly related to the specific sector or issue they seek to address. They may not always make their selections consciously, and may not pursue their goals consistently, but without some framework regulation becomes haphazard and contradictory. With respect to foodstuffs, safety and healthfulness are undoubtedly fundamental goals. Nonetheless, absolute safety cannot be attained and should not be sought. The regulatory goal should instead be to reduce human and animal risks to negligible levels[2]. Consistency with other substantial policy goals, such as competition and environmental protection, is another important value. Few would doubt that regulators should also promote the quality of food products and the overall healthfulness of national diets, but the appropriate measures for the achievement of those goals are properly controversial[3]. Compositional standards may guarantee subjective conceptions of food quality, but they also discourage innovation and

---

1.   Gray argues that the "first guiding principle should be that of simplicity." Gray, "The Perspective to 1992", in H. Deelstra, et al., eds., *Food Policy Trends in Europe* pp11, 16 (1991).

2.   See, e.g., National Research Council, *Regulating Pesticides in Food: The Delaney Paradox* pp13-14 (1987); Rico, "Medicaments vétérinaires et hygiène publique", in R. Derache, ed., *Toxicologie et Sécurité des Aliments* pp383, 401 (1986).

3.   Food quality is in the mouth of the consumer, and for most of us reflects failing memories of childhood pleasures. For the controversial issues of dietary change, see, e.g., *The Health of the Nation* CM 1523 (1991); Senate Select Committee on Nutrition and Human Needs, *Dietary Goals for the United States: Second Edition*, 95th Cong., 1st Sess. (1977).

eventually constitute barriers to trade. Similarly, limitations upon new additives and ingredients present risks as well as advantages. They may prevent the introduction of products with low nutritional values, but also inhibit the development of foodstuffs offering nutritional improvements[1]. The best guide is regulatory modesty. Educated consumers are ultimately the only reliable guarantors of product quality, and regulators should hesitate to substitute their views for consumer preferences. Wherever possible, informed consumer choice should be the principal goal. In the absence of genuine safety risks, the provision of clear and meaningful information is a better response to regulatory issues than prohibitions or compositional limitations. The same judgment underlies most of the European Court's decisions regarding foodstuffs.

Any statement of regulatory values is quickly reduced to homilies. Those described above are no exception. Even homilies may, however, offer valuable reminders of what a regulatory system is designed to achieve. They may identify issues which a regulatory system has, consciously or unconsciously, discounted or omitted. They provide essential points of policy reference. As harmonisation is gradually achieved, the Community must agree upon points of reference to guide its future rulemaking. A modest device for stimulating discussions would be the appointment of an expert advisory committee. Advisory committees cannot establish regulatory policies, but they can identify alternatives and articulate assumptions. In this instance, an advisory committee should consist of regulators and outside experts from food technology, nutrition and law. Member States, as well as consumer groups and industry, should be represented. An advisory committee would necessarily assess the Community's existing policies, but its principal task should be to suggest values and goals to guide the formulation of future policies. Its report should be made public. The purpose would not be to constrain the Commission, but instead to furnish a basis for public discussions of the possible directions of Community policy.

10.2   Strengthening the institutions of food regulation

Most of the Community's institutional arrangements for the formulation of food policies are dictated by the Treaty of Rome. For example, processes for the preparation and approval of directives are governed by the Treaty, as amended by the Single European Act. There is little point in imagining alternative arrangements. Any revisions will be controlled by the Maastricht Treaty or other decisions regarding the Community's political and institutional future. There are, however, more modest changes which could improve the processes by which the

---

1.   See, e.g., McNamara, "Nutrition Regulation by the FDA in the Brave New World of Fabricated Foods", 32 Food D.C.L.J. 469 (1977); Johnson "Rationale for Constraints on Nutrient Additives", 34 Food D.C.L.J. 426 (1979); National Academy of Sciences, Committee on Nutrition Components of Food Labeling, *Nutrition Labeling: Issues and Directions for the 1990's* pp320-342 (1990).

Community formulates and implements its food regulations. None of the proposals described below would require any amendment of the Treaty, but in combination they could enhance the effectiveness of the Community's policies.

10.2.1   Codification of the Community's legislation

The first step should be the simplest. The Community's food rules now exist only in the form of scattered, poorly indexed separate pronouncements. Cross-referencing is incomplete and sometimes haphazard. The Community's Official Journal corresponds roughly in function to the national registers of new regulatory measures, but there is nothing comparable to the various codifications of national legislation[1]. In these circumstances, discovery of the relevant rules may require patience and good fortune[2]. There is presumably no Community code of food laws in part because directives are addressed to Member States, and it may once have been assumed that no one else could be interested. It is less easy to excuse the absence of a codification of Community regulations, which have direct and immediate application throughout the Community. In part, the omission may reflect the historical and political artifact that the Community must provide important documents in several languages. The task of providing a Community code in multiple languages would certainly be daunting. Whatever the causes, the absence of an official, coherent and timely source of Community law is an impediment to both compliance and enforcement. In many parts of the Community, food manufacturers and their counsel are poorly informed about the rules with which they must comply. Consumers are generally even less familiar with their rights. In addition, a codification of the Community's rules could stimulate improvements in the rules themselves. Codification could reveal gaps and omissions which might otherwise escape attention. It might also prompt the Community to standardise requirements which, although similar in substance, appear in different forms in different measures. Some have developed gradually over a period of three decades, and show changes in style and experience in their draftsmanship.

It is not enough that there are private services which provide compilations of the Community's rules. Valuable as they are, the private services often are not comprehensive and certainly are not official. They collect, but cannot codify. They accumulate, but cannot reconcile or rationalise. Each new measure adds to the

---

1.   Some help is provided by the lists offered by the *Directory of Community Legislation in Force and Other Acts of the Community Institutions*, which appears in periodic editions. The various computerised retrieval systems are another aid.

2.   The confusion is increased by other factors, including the delays which characteristically separate a Community action from its publication. The reports of the Scientific Committee for Food are, for example, frequently published more than a year after they are adopted. Another source of uncertainty is the Commission's practice of circulating working documents only to favoured outsiders. Working documents made available to trade groups, and circulated by the groups among their members, should also be available to any member of the public. Sunlight is the best disinfectant.

confusion, the need, and the difficulty. An important goal after 1992 should be the provision of a coherent, official and timely source of Community foodstuff legislation[1]. The Commission itself has described greater "transparency" of the Community's rules as an important policy goal[2]. Transparency would certainly be served by an appropriate codification.

10.2.2   A Community foodstuff inspectorate

The Commission was asked by the Council and Parliament in 1989 to formulate suggestions for a new corps of Community foodstuff inspectors to supplement and verify national inspections[3]. With apparent misgivings, it agreed to provide such suggestions. The Commission was careful to acknowledge the need only for a "small" group of inspectors, and to suggest mediation as one of their duties. Although the Commission once reportedly changed its mind about the idea, it has now proposed the essence of a Community inspection service[4]. The proposal should promptly be made a reality. Until the Commission can verify the adequacy of national inspections, the public is unlikely to be fully convinced of the effectiveness of the Community's harmonised rules.

The creation of a Community inspection service should not stimulate insuperable political barriers. The Commission has already proposed Community inspections of processing facilities for minced meat, and it has longstanding powers to inspect fresh meat and other products[5]. In a different regulatory area, it sends its inspectors throughout the Community to investigate possible violations of competition policies[6]. The inspectors may seize or copy documents, search offices, and interview employees. There is no reason why the public should tolerate such inspections, some of them in the controversial form of "dawn raids", and yet reject inspections to enforce rules relating to food hygiene, public health and human safety. Nor is there any reason why Community inspections should be appropriate for wine and minced meat, but inappropriate for additives or pesticide residues. One of the inspection service's functions might, as the Commission has suggested, be to mediate between national agencies. It would, however, be a mistake to reduce the Community's inspectors merely to intermediaries between feuding national

1. For a similar view, see Chambers, "Consolidation of Food-law Text - A Democratic Essential?", 1/91 Eur. Food L. Rev. 46 (1991).
2. *XXIst General Report on the Activities of the European Communities 1987* pp119-120 (1988).
3. Above at Chapter 8, para 8.6.3.
4. Written Question 1009/91, OJ C210 12.8.91 p36. Above at Chapter 8, para 8.6.3.
5. For the Commission's proposal to conduct inspections of processing facilities for minced meat, see above at Chapter 7, para 7.12. For its existing powers regarding other products, see above at Chapter 8, para 8.6.6. The Commission may also verify the organoleptic properties of foods stockpiled under the Common Agricultural Policy; Joined Cases 161-162/90 *Petruzzi v AIPO* (Transcript) 10 October 1990, decided by the European Court upon reference from the Italian Pretura di Lecce.
6. Lister, "Dawn Raids and Other Nightmares: The European Commission's Investigatory Powers in Competition Law Matters," 24 Geo. Wash. J. Int'l Law & Econ. 45 (1991)

authorities. Coordination among national agencies is important, but a mechanism for auditing national regulatory actions is more urgent. As the European Parliament evidently intended, the inspectors should perform an auditing and verification function.

10.2.3   A Community food regulatory agency

There have been recurrent suggestions for a Community food regulatory agency, which would be responsible for the preparation and revision of the Community's rules for foodstuffs. It might also have an enforcement role, although the two functions are not inevitably linked. At least until late 1990, such proposals were under active consideration in the Commission. It has now announced that the idea has been abandoned[1]. Nonetheless, there are disparate views within the Community regarding the desirability of an agency, and the idea can be expected to recur[2].

A new Community agency would undoubtedly stimulate significant political and administrative issues. The Community is still addressing the arrangements for its future governance, and those arrangements might well affect the desirability of a new Community agency. There are already complaints about the size and cost of the Community's bureaucracy, and a new agency would intensify those objections. Subsidiarity is more often a slogan than a programme, but it would not be advanced by a new Community agency. Moreover, some observers believe that a Community food agency is "impossible" because Community institutions lack rulemaking authority comparable to that given, for example, in the United States to FDA[3]. In addition, the creation of a Community food agency might distract the Commission's food specialists from the more immediate problems of completing the 1985 programme for the internal market. Finally, such an agency would duplicate personnel and services already provided by some national authorities[4]. These considerations offer a legitimate basis for the deferral of a new agency.

At the same time, troublesome questions arise from the Commission's announcement. As an alternative to a Community agency, the Commission proposes to strengthen the resources of the Scientific Committee for Food. Some method of alleviating the pressures on the Scientific Committee is essential because, as the Commission has

---

1.   Written Question 904/91, OJC311 2.12.91 p18; *Financial Times* (15 March 1991).
2.   Commissioner van Miert, for example, has reportedly suggested that an agency may well prove appropriate at some future moment; *Eurofood* 2 (July 1991). But see interview with Dr. Caroline Jackson, MEP, 1 World Food Reg. Rev. 22, 23 (July 1991) (urging better coordination and not an agency).
3.   USITC, *The Effects of Greater Economic Integration within the European Community on the United States* pp6-16 (1989).
4.   See, e.g., *Eurofood* 1 (April 1991).

conceded, the demands on the Committee are not "sustainable" by the present "administrative arrangements, resources and infrastructure"[1]. The Commission would reduce the burdens upon the Scientific Committee by allocating some of its work among national regulatory authorities[2]. To implement the programme, the Commission has proposed a new Council directive[3]. The proposed directive would require national regulatory authorities to enter into a cooperative programme. They would prepare risk assessment protocols, organise food intake surveys, investigate dietary components or food contaminants, collect data, and generally help conduct the Community's scientific work in the area of food control[4]. International organisations and third countries might be invited to participate[5]. This might encourage greater consistency between the Community's rules and those of its trading partners, as well as the proposals of the Codex Alimentarius Commission and other international groups[6]. The proposed programme could be used whenever a Council directive or regulation required an opinion from the Scientific Committee[7].

Such a reallocation could work effectively in some areas, and certainly the Scientific Committee should be both strengthened and relieved of some of its burdens. Nonetheless, an allocation might in practice multiply the regulatory delays. It is also unlikely to end the "chaotic and haphazard" arrangements which characterise the Community's food policymaking[8]. Moreover, the underlying issue is whether all twelve national authorities realistically can perform a wide range of regulatory evaluations. Perhaps they can, and perhaps a less centralised control system would therefore prove economical and efficient. Given the free circulation of foodstuffs, however, consumers are entitled to more than mere hopes that these advantages might be attainable. This is particularly true when those hopes appear to derive in part from political tactfulness[9]. The Commission should assure itself that national evaluations would in fact be

1.   COM(91) 16 final, OJ C108 23.4.91 p7, at para 3 of the Explanatory Memorandum.
2.   *Eurofood* at p2 (April 1991); *Financial Times* p4 (15 March, 1991). The idea is not new; it was mentioned to USITC early in 1990. USITC, *The Effects of Greater Economic Integration within the European Community on the United States, First Report* pp6-53 (1990).
3.   COM(91) 16 final, OJ C108 23.4.91 p7.
4.   Article 1 and the Annex.
5.   Article 4.
6.   The Commission has argued that greater international cooperation would be possible through its proposal than could be achieved through a European food agency. Written Question 1026/91, OJ C38 15.2.92 p15.
7.   The proposal would be applicable, inter alia, "in all cases where scientific appraisal of questions of public interest in the field of the free movement of foodstuffs proves necessary and particularly where there is a risk to public health"; Article 1(2).
8.   Rogers, "Europe: Parliament vs. Commission on Food," 339 *The Lancet* p799 (28 March 1992).
9.   Questions about the reliability and effectiveness of national implementation of the [...] for food safety are asked with increasing frequency. In 1987, for [...] adopted a resolution observing that there are "many doubts" about [...] ts, and complaining that the Community cannot "guarantee the safety [...] its consumers". See Document A2-216/86, OJ C99 13.4.87 p68 at paras

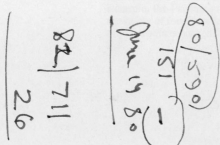

objective, non-discriminatory and reliable[1]. A partial answer is offered by the 1989 directive regarding the official control of foodstuffs[2]. The directive provides a catalogue of regulatory control mechanisms, and their implementation could produce substantial improvements in the overall level of regulatory controls. The mechanisms must, however, still be made a reality throughout the Community. By early 1992, most Member States had not even transposed the directive into national law[3]. They had certainly not begun its actual implementation. If the Commission does not wish a new Community food agency, it should at least implement vigorously the provisions of the 1989 directive for the coordination and improvement of national control mechanisms[4]. Additional help may be provided by strengthening the training of national regulators and exchanges of national officials engaged in enforcement efforts[5].

The Commission should also accept the advice of the European Parliament and greatly strengthen the resources of the Scientific Committee[6]. It now has no scientific staff assistance[7]. While some assistance may be obtained from the Member States, the Scientific Committee should also have its own secretariat, including an appropriate scientific support staff[8]. Such a staff could facilitate the committee's work and reduce the burdens placed upon its members. It might eventually provide the nucleus for a Community food agency[9]. Staff assistance is, however, appropriate even if it were thought that a separate Community agency will always be undesirable. The Community's responsibilities in the area of food

---

1. Much would depend upon how the Commission's proposal would operate in practice. The Commission's Explanatory Memorandum observes that the essence of much Community legislation has been to reduce national approvals to the level of temporary authorisations; COM(91) 16 final, above at para 4. The proposal would use national resources to conduct the Community's scientific assessments, "which will replace national assessments in food law"; ibid. The language is opaque, but leaves the impression that the Commission may be seeking simply to put Community labels on national assessments. Such a result would magnify any deficiencies in national regulatory programmes.
2. Above at Chapter 8, para 8.6.3.
3. EC Commission, *National Implementing Measures* pp130-131 (1992).
4. The Commission promised in 1990 that it would "make proposals for the introduction of Community machinery for the scientific evaluation of foodstuffs, in close collaboration with the competent institutes in the Member States". *The Commission's Programme for 1990*, Bull. E.C. Supp. 1/90 (1990). One such proposal was made in early 1992. Above at Chapter 8, para 8.6.3.
5. For the Commission's suggestions regarding training, see above at Chapter 8, para 8.6.3. The Commission has also proposed a Council decision to create an exchange programme for national enforcement officials, including those concerned with food. COM(91) 408 final, OJ C299 20.11.91 p25. The Commission has urged better training and greater expertise for national regulators, while insisting on the need for variations consistent with national differences in climate and eating habits. Written Questions 1175-81/91, OJ C38 15.2.92 p22.
6. See para 10 of the Explanatory Memorandum which accompanied the draft of COM(91) 16 final, OJ C108 23.4.91 p7.
7. Ibid., at para 9.
8. In contrast, Britain's Advisory Committee on Novel Foods and Processes, whose responsibilities are much narrower than the Community's Scientific Committee, has its own secretariat, including medical and scientific assistance provided by the relevant ministries; Annual Report, Annex IX (1990).
9. Commissioner van Miert has reportedly observed that strengthening the Scientific Committee would be "a welcome step along the way" toward a Community food agency. *Eurofood* 2 (July 1991).

safety should not be delegated to an unsupported group of unpaid independent experts. To do so is neither realistic nor fair to the Scientific Committee's overburdened members[1]. At the same time, its activities should be more open and public. Its reports and decisions should be published promptly[2].

A further answer would be to multiply the sources of advisory assistance. Separate advisory groups could be established to consider such issues as novel foods, contact materials, and additives and processing aids[3]. Those groups could be subordinate to the Scientific Committee, preparing evaluations for its consideration, or they could be established independently and assigned portions of the Scientific Committee's responsibilities. In either case, they could alleviate its regulatory burdens. A separate group could be established to review food labelling and advertising issues. This last group should include nutritionists and specialists in communications, as well as representatives of consumers and industry. The Scientific Committee has traditionally consisted chiefly of toxicologists, and an expansion of the Commission's advisory resources should include a wider range of relevant disciplines.

These and similar devices can help to satisfy the Community's needs for improved enforcement mechanisms. The more perplexing issue lies ahead. The logic of harmonisation leads directly to increased centralisation. The adoption of each Community rule strengthens the arguments for the creation of a centralised agency responsible for reviewing, adjusting, and ultimately overseeing the implementation of those rules[4]. This would now involve some duplication of the work of national authorities, but that would not everywhere be a disadvantage. Moreover, the long-run consequence of harmonisation is inevitably some diminution in the roles of national authorities. This is already occurring in competition policy, and it is increasingly true with respect to foodstuffs policies. These developments do not eliminate the need for national regulatory regimes. Absent major changes in the Community's political structure, important roles will remain for national foodstuff authorities throughout the foreseeable future. Indeed, it is precisely because of their continuing roles that attention should be given to strengthening national regulatory agencies. In the long-run, however, a Community food agency may prove unavoidable.

---

1. The Commission itself recognises that the burdens upon the Scientific Committee exceed its present capacities; COM(91) 16 final, OJ C108 23.4.91 p7 , at para 3.
2. Bull. Eco. & Soc. Comm., No. 10/1991 p19 (1991).
3. In Britain, for example, the Food Advisory Committee is supplemented by the Committee on Toxicity, the Advisory Committee on Novel Foods and Processes, the Committee on Medical Aspects of Food Policy, and others. See, e.g., S. Fallows, *Food Legislative System of the UK* pp71-73 (1988).
4. A US agency responsible for monitoring the programme has observed that an effective Community-wide control system is "necessary to provide consistency across the EC and to create a strong image of official approval of safety"; USITC, *The Effects of Greater Economic Integration within the European Community on the United States* pp6-16 (1989).

10.2.4   Opening the Commission's decisionmaking process

The Community's regulatory process is largely closed to public scrutiny and participation. Industry, consumer groups and the public have only the roles assigned to them by the Commission. Their interests are represented only by groups and individuals selected by the Commission. Many steps might be taken to ameliorate this situation, but only the most modest proposals are likely to be given serious attention. One of the most modest would be to establish mechanisms by which the public may be given opportunities to express their views during the Commission's decisionmaking processes. One possible mechanism is a public notice and comment procedure.

Under such an arrangement, the Commission could formulate its proposals precisely as it now does. It could draw upon outside advisors whenever it deemed helpful. Once the Commission had settled upon well-defined proposals, but prior to their submission to the Council, Parliament or Standing Committee, it would publish them in the Official Journal. The proposals would be accompanied by a summary of the considerations which underlie them. Preparation of the summaries would entail additional burdens, but also impose a salutary discipline upon the Commission's efforts. If health and safety issues were involved, a summary of the views of the Scientific Committee should be included. If the Commission were still examining other regulatory options, they should be described. The publication would invite interested persons to submit written comments within a prescribed reasonable period. The Commission would be free to accept or reject the submissions. It would, however, be required to republish the proposal's final text in the Official Journal, together with a summary of the submissions it received and an explanation for its acceptance or rejection of them. The republished version would constitute the Commission's proposal, and would form the basis for consideration by other Community institutions. To limit the burdens and delays, this would be done only once, even if significant changes in the Commission's proposals were subsequently made. The publication of possible options would permit public comments upon any variations which seemed particularly likely.

There would be many situations in which the submissions would result in few changes. There would undoubtedly be other situations in which substantial changes would be appropriate. At a minimum, the process would afford the Commission a better factual basis for its proposals. It would also provide an additional basis for the evaluation of those proposals by the Council and Parliament. Ambiguities and technical errors would be less likely. The relevant interests would all be assured an open and equitable opportunity to submit their views. Industry, consumer groups and the general public would all have a fair opportunity to be heard. As a result, the Commission could better insulate itself agains demands made separately and without public notice by special interests. If every group is entitled to a fair hearing, none can legitimately claim anything further or better. Indeed, a comment period could be accompanied by rules designed to ensure greater transparency of the Commission's private meetings with special groups, including public notice of the fact and subjects of such meetings. Such a system would not eliminate all the deficiencies of the Community's regulatory processes. Nor would it ensure effective public participation at all stages of the legislative process. It would, however, represent a substantial improvement in the real and perceived fairness of those processes.

The arrangements described above are similar to rules which have long been used in the United States. An alternative is offered by the Canadian rules for public comment. They involve four separate steps[1]. First, the Health Protection Branch, which is responsible for most issues of federal food policy, publishes an annual regulatory agenda. The agenda contains descriptions of the Branch's goals for the following year. It includes any changes in policy which the Branch expects to make and any initiatives it expects to take. The purpose is to alert the public and industry to proposals by which they may be affected. Each entry identifies a person from whom more information may be obtained. Second, the Branch publishes an information letter whenever it contemplates a major change in policy. The letter describes the proposal and invites public comments. Another information letter is published after the comments have been evaluated. The second letter summarises the comments, describes the Branch's final decisions, and explains the reasons. Finally, the Branch is required to prepare a socio-economic impact analysis of important new regulations if they may affect public health or safety, or fairness in the marketplace. A summary of the analysis must be published, and the public must be offered an opportunity to comment. The Branch must respond to the comments. All four steps are intended to encourage "increased public participation in the regulation-making process", and to provide notice of proposed new rules to "the widest possible audience"[2]. It would be an important step forward if the Community were to endorse the same goals.

10.3   A new regulatory agenda

After completion of the 1992 programme, the Community's principal regulatory goal should be to enhance the uniformity and effectiveness with which its food rules are enforced by national authorities. A Community inspection service and new training programmes for national regulatory officials would be lengthy steps in that direction. Enforcement measures cannot, however, be the Community's only

---

1.   The Canadian rules are summarised in *Health Protection and Food Laws* 10-11 (4th ed. 1985), issued by the Health Protection Branch under the authority of the Minister of National Health and Welfare.

2.   Ibid., at p11.

priority. Other areas of policy also warrant attention. Those areas have been described in earlier chapters, and it is necessary here only to recapitulate the central points. The areas differ in urgency, but together they offer an important new legislative agenda[1]. It should be supplemented by prompt and practical resolutions of the existing disputes regarding packaging waste and general product safety.

10.3.1 Labelling format requirements

The Community's rules for food labelling cannot be fully effective until they include specific requirements regarding the manner in which disclosures must be made. For most purposes, the rules now provide merely that disclosures must be made conspicuously and legibly. There are wide variations in the implementation of these requirements. The mandatory disclosures may be made in a manner which is confusing or obscure, and elderly or handicapped consumers may have particular difficulty reading them. The Community should adopt supplemental rules regarding the terms, relative size, relationship and placement of labelling disclosures. Those rules should demand the use of a standardised disclosure panel representing some minimum percentage of the product's labelling. Greater uniformity would avoid competitive unfairnesses and increase the value of labelling disclosures to consumers.

10.3.2 Nutritional labelling

The Community requires nutritional labelling only if nutritional claims have been made. Consumers are increasingly interested in the nutritional values of their foodstuffs, and those values are less predictable if foodstuffs have been processed or fabricated. Products about which no nutritional claims have been asserted may have minimal nutritional values, and consumers are entitled to be informed of that fact. The Community should compel the disclosure of basic nutritional facts concerning all foods, without regard to whether nutritional claims have been made.

10.3.3 Health, freshness and nutritional claims

Many promotional and marketing abuses involve misleading claims that a product is "fresh" or "natural", that it offers particular nutritional values, or that its use may result in health-related advantages. The Community has provided partial answers by its rules for nutritional labelling,[2] organic foodstuffs,[3] and the use of

---

1.   Several of the areas described below have also been demanded by the European Parliament. Resolution No. A3-0060/92 (11 March 1992).
2.   Above at Chapter 3, para 3.4.
3.   Above at Chapter 3, para 3.7.

such descriptive words as "natural"[1]. Until recently, the Commission was also preparing rules to restrict or prohibit other labelling and promotional claims[2]. It is now reconsidering its approach. The Community should adopt rules which impose specific preconditions to the assertion of each of the most common marketing claims. Penalties should be imposed whenever violations occur.

10.3.4 Other labelling matters

Britain's Food Advisory Committee has recommended a series of changes in other labelling obligations, including the Community's rules for customary names and descriptions of compound and generic ingredients[3]. These and other suggestions warrant prompt attention by the Commission. In addition, the Community should consider additional restrictions on national rules requiring declarations of product origins. Except where the absence of declarations of origin would be deceptive, or they are required by Community certification programmes, the Community should generally forbid labelling which encourages consumers to discriminate against products from other Member States.

10.3.5 Chilled foods

Chilled foods create complex and variable problems of proper storage and transport, and additional research is needed before all of those problems can be addressed effectively[4]. In the interim, the Community should adopt a framework measure which imposes basic storage and temperature requirements, and provides a mechanism for formulating ancillary measures addressed to particular food categories.

10.3.6 Unpackaged foods

Unpackaged foods have generally been left for regulation by the Member States, and one consequence is a growing disparity in the rigour of regulation for packaged and unpackaged foods. Nonetheless, some unpackaged foods are subject to Community rules adopted as parts of the common organisations of the markets for agricultural commodities. Others are subject to vertical health and safety rules. The result is an inconsistent mixture of rules scattered among a great variety of measures[5]. They should be codified in a single directive establishing the content and manner of disclosures made to consumers regarding unpackaged foodstuffs.

---

1. Above at Chapter 3, para 3.3.
2. Above at Chapter 3, para 3.5.2.
3. Above at Chapter 3, para 3.3.
4. Above at Chapter 4, para 4.1.
5. Above at Chapter 8, para 8.5.

10.3.7 Irradiated foods

Irradiated foods have provoked emotional and political disputes, as well as scientific and legal issues. There are no health or safety reasons why the Community should not permit the irradiation of selected products, provided always that careful controls are observed. At least for the moment, however, this appears to be politically impossible[1]. In the interim, the Community's legislation should recognise that seven Member States now permit food irradiation, and should impose harmonised rules for its conduct. Community legislation is also justified by of the possibility that irradiated foods may be sold in nations which forbid irradiation. A framework directive should be adopted which permits each Member State to decide independently whether to authorise the sale of irradiated products, but also establishes harmonised rules for the control of irradiation facilities and the labelling of irradiated foodstuffs.

10.3.8 Pesticide and other chemical residue limitations

The Community's rules permit significant variations in the maximum residue levels of pesticides in and on fruits and vegetables[2]. In addition, there are many pesticides and other agricultural chemicals for which no limitations have been established. New residue limitations should be promptly adopted under the 1990 pesticides directive. Residue limitations should be imposed upon all pesticides and agricultural chemicals which are now in widespread use within the Community.

10.3.9 Additives

Many categories of food additives are still subject to early and incomplete Community measures[3]. Artificial sweeteners and modified starches are not yet controlled by any Community requirements at all. New rules are now in preparation for many additives, and they should be promptly adopted. Additives which have long been in use without hazards to human health should be approved on a *quantum satis* basis. Where conditions of use are needed, they should be harmonised. So far as possible, negative lists should be preferred to positive lists. In particular, a negative list should be used for flavourings, and the Community should reconsider its determination to impose a positive list[4].

---

1.   Above at Chapter 4, para 4.3.
2.   Above at Chapter 8, para 8.3.1.
3.   Above at Chapter 5, para 5.1.
4.   Above at Chapter 5, para 5.2.

10.3.10 Food contact materials

The Commission should promptly complete its new rules for the control of materials and articles intended to come into contact with foodstuffs[1]. Negative lists should be used wherever possible. The Commission should assign particular importance to the implementation of the 1990 directive regarding plastic materials and articles. If the resources of the Scientific Committee are inadequate for expedited completion of the positive list for plastic materials, those resources should be supplemented.

10.3.11 Revision of the positive lists

Whenever positive lists are employed, well-defined mechanisms should be provided to modify or supplement them. Developers of proposed new products should be assured a prompt and meaningful opportunity to prove the products' safety and effectiveness. The Community should reconsider its intention to approve new additives only if there is a technical need which cannot be satisfied by any combination of existing products[2]. The Community's marketplace should not be closed to innovative products which offer cost or other advantages, even if the technical needs served by those products may also be satisfied by existing additives.

10.3.12 Foods for particular nutritional use

The framework directive for "parnuts" products should be supplemented by daughter directives addressed to each of the categories of products designated for special rules[3].

10.3.13 Nutritional supplements

Dietary integrators are not now subject to Community rules, and the Commission has taken the view that those products do not fall within the framework "parnuts" directive[4]. Nutritional supplements have increasing commercial and dietary significance, and are now controlled by diverse national requirements. They should be subject to harmonised Community rules regarding their composition, labelling and advertising.

---

1.   Above at Chapter 6, para 6.1.
2.   Above at Chapter 5, para 5.1.
3.   Above at Chapter 4, para 4.5.
4.   Above at Chapter 4, para 4.5.

10.3.14 Novel foods

The Community should adopt rules which recognise that novel foods represent a heterogeneous mixture of products and processes. The rules should classify the different levels of risk, and apply different controls carefully tailored to each level. So far as possible, they should be regulated in the same manner as other foodstuffs. The Commission's suggestion of a screening mechanism using independent experts should be replaced by a new advisory committee operating under the supervision of the Scientific Committee for Food[1].

10.3.15 Processing aids

The only processing aids now subject to Community rules are extraction solvents[2]. Framework legislation should be adopted to ensure the use of suitable manufacturing practices to restrict residues from other processing aids to the lowest practicable levels. A negative list of forbidden processing aids should be adopted.

10.3.16 Hygiene and contamination rules

A major priority should be a reduction of food-borne illnesses. Food contamination and spoilage remain significant problems, and the Community should adopt meaningful hygiene rules to reduce the hazards to human health. The Commission's current proposal should be regarded as a transitory and initial measure[3]. The Community's rules should ultimately include a classification of foodstuffs based upon their microbiological risks. Separate hygiene requirements should be addressed to each of the risk categories. A surveillance system should be instituted to monitor the actual hazards of food-borne illnesses throughout the Community. The results of the surveillance process should guide both the adoption of supplemental rules and the Community's enforcement activities.

10.3.17 Export products

The Community should adopt legislation generally addressed to food products intended for export outside the Community[4]. It should be presumed that the Community's health and safety requirements for products intended for consumption within the Community are also applicable to export products. Any exceptions should be based upon specific instructions from the importing nation that different rules should be applied.

---

1.   Above at Chapter 4, para 4.4.
2.   Above at Chapter 5, para 5.9.
3.   Above at Chapter 8, para 8.6.1.
4.   Above at Chapter 9, para 9.3.5.

10.3.18 International harmonisation

The Community should make prompt efforts to encourage the harmonisation of its foodstuff rules with those of its major trading partners[1]. The Codex Alimentarius Commission and other international organisations will continue to perform important roles in this area, but multilateral discussions among the world's principal traders in processed foods should also be initiated. The Community's harmonisation programme represents an important model which should be extended beyond the Community's borders. Its extension would help to ensure the safety and wholesomeness of imported foods consumed within the Community. It would also eliminate trade barriers which may otherwise hamper both competition and innovation in the world's marketplaces for foodstuffs.

10.4 The risks of the Community's future

The Community remains a political experiment. It is easily forgotten how brief has been its existence, how uncertain are its ultimate political arrangements, and how recently it began effective efforts to create a single marketplace. Few at the beginning would have predicted its present direction, or the extent of the changes it already has produced. Fewer still can anticipate what may occur over another generation. Much may depend upon the admission of new Member States. Each accession will bring additional problems and delays, as the new member seeks to harmonise its laws with Community rules and undoubtedly also seeks special derogations and limitations. There is an important danger that, by admitting any significant number of new members, the Community's reach might exceed its grasp. Much may also depend upon economic and political events. Unfavourable economic developments, or internal political pressures in one or more Member States, may stimulate new national protectionist measures[2]. In light of these uncertainties, it is possible to argue both that the pace of centralisation will accelerate and that it may diminish. The Community is still groping toward an appropriate political system, and the ultimate terms of that system will be important in determining its regulatory policies for foodstuffs.

The Community has been engaged in efforts to harmonise national rules for foodstuffs for thirty years. It has made significant progress in many areas, but remains mired in political or technical detail in others. Its move from retail to wholesale regulation in 1985 was indeed a switch in time, but it only ameliorated

---

1.   The Codex Alimentarius Commission has, for example, described such international harmonisation as "urgent", particularly to help increase exports from developing countries; *Report of the Nineteenth Session of the Codex Alimentarius Commission* p11 (1991).

2.   See, e.g., Wallace, "Negotiation, Conflict, and Compromise: The Elusive Pursuit of Common Policies", in H. Wallace & C. Webb, eds., *Policy Making in the European Community* p43, 53-54 (2nd ed. 1983).

the basic problems of uniform and effective regulation. The Community has a regulatory agenda for foodstuffs capable of completion soon after 1992, but that agenda is only the opening phase of its efforts to create an internal marketplace for foodstuffs which is genuinely free, unitary and open. Many difficult problems must still be resolved. The real questions are whether the Community actually wants such a marketplace and, if it does, whether it can overcome cultural and economic barriers more fundamental than any it has yet ventured to address. Its willingness and ability to surmount those barriers with respect to food products is an important test of its commitment to political and economic unification.

Appendix

LIST OF MAIN FOOD REGULATIONS

Council Directive (EEC) 79/112
OJ L33 8.2.79 p1
on the approximation of the laws of the member states relating to the labelling,
presentation and advertising of foodstuffs for sale to the ultimate customer

> article 1 amended by Directive 89/395
> article 2 amended by Directive 89/395
> article 3 amended by Directives 86/197, 89/395
> article 4 amended by Directive 89/395
> article 5 amended by Directive 89/395
> article 6 amended by Directives 86/197, 89/395, 91/72
> article 7 amended by Directive 89/395
> article 8 amended by Directive 89/395
> article 9 amended by Directive 89/395
> article 9a added by Directive 89/395
> article 10 amended by Directive 89/395
> article 10a added by Directive 86/197
> article 11 replaced by Directive 89/395
> article 12 amended by Directive 89/395
> article 17 replaced by Directive 89/395
> article 18 deleted by Directive 89/395
> article 23 deleted by Directive 89/395
> Annex III added by Directive 91/72

Council Directive (EEC) 89/107
OJ L40 11.2.89 p27
on the approximation of laws of the member states concerning food additives
authorised for use in foodstuffs intended for human consumption

Council Directive (EEC) 89/109
OJ L40 11.2.89 p38
on the approximation of the laws of the member states relating to materials and
articles intended to come into contact with foodstuffs

Council Directive (EEC) 89/397
OJ L186 30.6.89 p23
on the official control of foodstuffs

Council Directive (EEC) 89/398
OJ L186 30.6.89 p27
on the approximation of the laws of the member states relating to foodstuffs
intended for particular nutritional uses

Council Directive (EEC) 90/496
OJ L276 6.10.90 p40
on nutritional labelling